MW01492196

"Some of the most powerful people in New York City tried to convince the world that Eleanor Bumpurs's life did not matter. Brilliant historian LaShawn Harris has corrected the record with a beautiful and heartbreaking account of a beloved matriarch who fell victim to the unforgiving forces of poverty, housing insecurity, and police violence. An excellent study of the 1980s that captures the heart and soul of the social movements that foreshadowed calls to 'Say her name.' A timely and necessary book."

—MARCIA CHATELAIN, author of the Pulitzer Prize–winning
Franchise: The Golden Arches in Black America

"As state violence grows ever more unchecked, the story of Eleanor Bumpurs remains a stark reminder of the particular vulnerability of Black women. Beautifully written, deeply researched, and deeply felt, this powerful and groundbreaking narrative carefully traces Bumpurs's life, the aftermath of her killing, and the community response that helped ignite the early police abolition movement. A galvanizing history of resistance, reckoning, and our ongoing demand for justice. Harris's care shines through every page."

—BLAIR L. M. KELLEY, author of *Black Folk:*
The Roots of the Black Working Class

"The name Eleanor Bumpurs has come to symbolize intensifying police violence during the cruel 1980s. But LaShawn Harris's poignant account lifts the veil of symbolism to reveal a *life*—complex, intimate, and often tragic—and a history of bureaucratic, state-sanctioned, and interpersonal violence, to which she was subjected her entire life. If we wish to dismantle the structures of racism, sexism, ableism, and capitalism that killed Eleanor Bumpurs and continue to take Black lives, we need to read this book and tell her story."

—ROBIN D. G. KELLEY, author of *Freedom Dreams:*
The Black Radical Imagination

"*Tell Her Story: Eleanor Bumpurs & the Police Killing That Galvanized New York City* is a remarkable and captivating history of the intersection of policing, public policy, power, class, and more in 1980s New York City. Beyond the 1984 police killing of Eleanor Bumpurs, LaShawn Harris explores the conditions of America's largest city during an era that witnessed a national turn toward the economic neglect of cities, deindustrialization, and spiraling demands for public services that were met with increasingly austerity. This is a powerful and illuminating history that weaves rich commentary on policies related to treatment of the elderly and those with mental illness, as well as humanizing the central figure of this narrative."

—JEFFREY O. G. OGBAR, author of
*America's Black Capital: How African Americans
Remade Atlanta in the Shadow of the Confederacy*

"This is the book we have waited so long for. *Tell Her Story* narrates one of the most important yet underreported stories of the 1980s: the brutal murder of Eleanor Bumpurs by New York City police. Bumpurs's killing animated the political and cultural landscape of Black New York, emphasizing the ways that poverty and social marginalization could make all Black people vulnerable to the violence of police. *Tell Her Story* demonstrates powerful storytelling along with a gripping historical rendition of the tumultuous transition between the hope of the civil rights era to the misguided projections of a presumed post-racial Obama era. The book also sheds new light on and understanding about Reagan's regressive 1980s and its impact on Black women and their families. It is an absolute must-read."

—KEEANGA-YAMAHTTA TAYLOR, author of
*Race for Profit: How Banks and the Real Estate
Industry Undermined Black Homeownership*

"LaShawn Harris has given us a great gift. She has taken Eleanor Bumpurs from a poignant image on a poster and given us a rich sense of Bumpurs's life and family experiences, a crucial analysis of the 1980s economic and police violence that killed her, and a moving history of her family's and community's fight for justice. A must-read and an extraordinary piece of research."

—JEANNE THEOHARIS, author of *King of the North:
Martin Luther King Jr.'s Life of Struggle Outside the South*

"Harris's *Tell Her Story*, a powerful and poignant rescuing of the life and tragic murder of Eleanor Bumpurs, will both haunt and inspire. Told against the backdrop of the vicious 1980s, her searing narrative reminds us that this nation's too-regular and brutal police killings of Black women have always been met by extraordinary family and community mobilization, and the demand for justice. As it also makes clear, it is long past time for America to deliver on that demand."

—HEATHER ANN THOMPSON, author of the
Pulitzer Prize–winning *Blood in the Water:
The Attica Prison Uprising of 1971 and Its Legacy*

TELL HER STORY

ELEANOR BUMPURS
& THE POLICE KILLING
THAT GALVANIZED
NEW YORK CITY

LaShawn Harris

BEACON PRESS, BOSTON

BEACON PRESS
24 Farnsworth Street
Boston, Massachusetts
www.beacon.org

Beacon Press books
are published under the auspices of
the Unitarian Universalist Association of Congregations.

28 27 26 25   8 7 6 5 4 3 2 1

This book is printed on acid-free paper that meets the uncoated paper
ANSI/NISO specifications for permanence as revised in 1992.

Text design and composition by Kim Arney

*Library of Congress Cataloging-in-Publication
Data is available for this title.*
ISBN: 978-0-8070-1196-6; e-book: 978-0-8070-1249-9;
audiobook: 978-0-8070-2096-8

The authorized representative in the EU for product safety and compliance
is Easy Access System Europe 16879218, Mustamäe tee 50,
10621 Tallinn, Estonia: http://beacon.org/eu-contact

CONTENTS

INTRODUCTION

Tremendous socioeconomic and political and cultural challenges and developments characterized 1980s New York. Decay and disorder, crime and violence, extreme wealth and poverty, and the emergence of acquired immunodeficiency syndrome (AIDS) and crack cocaine, a highly potent and inexpensive drug, dogged the city. Equally important, a new musical genre and aesthetic took "The City That Never Sleeps" by storm. Emerging out of working-class South Bronx neighborhoods and vibrant block and houses parties, hip-hop culture enthralled the city and nation. Created by Clive "Kool Herc" Campbell, Cindy Campbell, and other racially and ethnically diverse teenagers and young adults, hip-hop birthed a wildly influential category of music, dance, fashion, and art. Delivering rhythmic speech and poetry over turntables, sound mixers, electronic instruments, and microphones, rap artists such as Sharon "MC Sha-Rock" Green and Grandmaster Flash and the Furious Five offered listeners engaging commentary on politics, poverty, and urban life in President Ronald Reagan's America. Emcees' bold verses and imaginative metaphors about city living also provided insight on a harmful and deathly epidemic affecting Black life: police violence. And throughout the 1980s, many lyricists rapped about one of New York City's most horrific acts of police abuse.

This incident happened on October 29, 1984, three weeks after my tenth birthday and a few days before Halloween.

In 1984, my childhood friends and I couldn't wait for Halloween. We spent a lot of time planning, selecting plastic costumes from the local Woolworth's store, and discussing which neighborhoods to visit, depending on who had the best candy. There were plenty of places to frequent around our Bronx neighborhood on 174th Street and University Avenue, also known as the Morris Heights community. With our parents monitoring us, we could stroll into the neighborhood bodegas and supermarkets or walk across University Avenue to New York City Housing Authority's (NYCHA) Sedgwick Houses, a residential development of seven fourteen-story red-brick high rises.

That year, our Halloween plans were interrupted. On Monday, October 29, 1984, a brutal tragedy struck my community. That morning, white New York Police Department (NYPD) officer Stephen Sullivan fatally shot sixty-six-year-old disabled grandmother and Sedgwick Houses tenant Eleanor Bumpurs during an eviction proceeding. A few days after Eleanor's killing, University Avenue erupted into chaos. City officials and police, investigating the shooting crowded the street and Sedgwick Houses. Local reporters and cameramen swarmed the area, hoping to interview anyone who heard the gunshots, knew Eleanor, or lived in or near Sedgwick Houses. Concerned about the large police and media presence in the neighborhood, some parents refused to allow their children to trick-or-treat on University Avenue. That year my friends and I trick-or-treated in our five-story apartment building, collecting Now and Later candies, Snickers bars, and other sugary treats from our neighbors. Although my friends and I achieved the goal of receiving candy, this wasn't the Halloween we'd planned for.

Primarily concerned about missing Halloween festivities, my ten-year-old self was clueless about what happened to Eleanor. I vaguely remember family and community members discussing her killing. Talking with my parents decades later about Eleanor's killing, they remembered neighborhood folks saying: "The lady across the street was murdered. The cops shot her down, right in her apartment. Why police evicting folks, now?"

The Bumpurs killing became an intense topic of conversation around the neighborhood. My neighbors were outraged. They were saddened. And they demanded answers to important questions including: How could police kill an elderly and disabled woman? And when police and NYCHA officials refused to answer those questions, my neighbors raised hell. They poured onto Bronx streets, staging candlelight vigils and protest rallies in front of Eleanor's apartment building and at the nearby police precinct. And they expressed their sorrow for Eleanor and her family in media interviews with popular New York journalists like *New York Daily News* columnist Jimmy Breslin. Humanizing Eleanor, some Sedgwick Houses tenants and other neighborhood residents described to reporters how they occasionally spotted her sitting on the park bench outside her apartment building and how she routinely sat at her living room windowsill, observing community happenings. Many described a quiet woman who kept to herself and minded her business. Others described a cantankerous woman who talked to herself and carried a butcher knife.

I didn't know Eleanor. Nor do I recall seeing the silver-haired grandmother walking through the neighborhood. As a teenager and young adult, I forgot about Eleanor and the upheaval that her killing ignited in the Morris Heights community.

While Eleanor faded from my mind, New Yorkers never forgot about the grandmother. Her death touched residents. Newspaper images of her and her grieving family inspired them. In the days, months, and even years after her death, city folks advocated for Eleanor. They demanded legal justice for her. They wanted police accountability. And as the city underwent massive socioeconomic and political changes throughout the early to mid-1980s, they kept the story of her death in the public's eye.

The Bumpurs killing became a cause célèbre, going viral 1980s style. Eleanor's name could be read in newspapers like the *New York Times* and *New York Amsterdam News* and heard on television, radio news broadcasts, and daytime TV shows, such as the Phil Donahue show. New Yorkers uttered her name during Sunday morning sermons, in university lecture halls, neighborhood beauty salons and barbershops, and while waiting for city buses and trains. They affixed her image and name to protest placards and apartment building structures. Some Black, Latinx, and white writers, singers, street artists, and filmmakers, including Audre Lorde and Spike Lee, dedicated poems, songs, graffiti art, and films to Eleanor. Eleanor's death inspired Lorde's moving 1986 poem "For the Record: In Memory of Eleanor Bumpers," which connects Eleanor's killing to the assassination of Indira Gandhi, the first and only female prime minister of India. Gandhi was murdered in her home several days after Eleanor on October 31, 1984. In 1986, Brooklyn filmmaker Spike Lee referenced Eleanor's death in his first feature film, *She's Gotta Have It*. A newspaper clipping on the Bumpurs case appears in main character Nola Darling's wall collage. Three years later, Lee dedicated his provocative Oscar-nominated film *Do the Right Thing*, centered on 1980s New York life and culture, to the Bumpurs families and other Black and Hispanic families that lost loved ones to police violence.[1] Eleanor's name is even mentioned in the film. After several NYPD officers in the movie fatally choked the character Radio Raheem, angry community members yelled: "They did it again. Just like Michael Stewart. Murder. Eleanor Bumpurs. Murder."[2] Likewise, 1980s and '90s hip-hop artists, such as Black Star, X-Clan, GhostFace Killah, Kool G. Rap, and Professor Griff, authored lyrics about Eleanor's killing.

Eleanor became a symbol for racially and ethnically diverse working-class New Yorkers. Her eviction and killing exposed long-standing urban issues, including housing inequities, police violence, and municipal disinvestment. And while Eleanor was the mother of five daughters and two sons, and grandmother to at least ten children, many New Yorkers, embracing the African diasporic belief in fictive kinship, viewed her as their mother and grandmother. This is similar to how many Americans, especially African American parents, interpreted the 2012 shooting victim and teenager Trayvon Martin. They viewed Martin as their own child. Public resonance with Eleanor sparked political action among New Yorkers.

Beyond the Big Apple, the tragic Bronx story attracted national and international media attention. Global citizens in California, Chicago, England, Australia, Jamaica, and South Africa were reading and talking about the police gun down of a New York grandmother. Popular newspapers and magazines—including *Jet*, the *Los Angeles Sentinel*, the *Detroit Free Press*, and Canada's the *Province* and *Vancouver Sun*—covered the killing. Captivating articles about the eviction and heartbreaking images of Eleanor's inconsolable family tugged at citizens' hearts, prompting many to think about their elderly family members' well-being and ponder the broader implications of police violence.

Everyday conversations about Eleanor's killing ignited a significant social justice campaign, one that many New Yorkers had not seen before. City dwellers witnessed, and many became politically active in, an early iteration of what legal scholar Kimberlé Crenshaw would call in 2014 the #SayHerName campaign, a movement dedicated to bringing visibility to police and state violence against Black women and girls. Mass political mobilization around Eleanor's killing represented one of New York's first anti-police-brutality campaigns centered on a Black woman. The political movement for Eleanor did not explicitly spotlight the gender dynamics of the police shooting or the NYPD's long history of brutality against Black women. This movement raised visibility about Eleanor's death and activists' demands for legal justice and municipal reforms. Having endured decades of city inequalities, activists called for the NYPD and other city agencies to implement new policies and revise existing ones to improve the quality of life for financially struggling residents and those living with mental health conditions.

I became gripped by Eleanor's death and the morbidly growing list of Black women and girls who were assaulted and killed by police in their homes throughout this and the previous century. Eleanor's killing and her varying encounters with state actors captivated me as a scholar of Black women's histories and as a New Yorker who lived in a neighborhood where the horrific killing occurred. I wanted to know more about Eleanor's life, the political protests launched in her name, and the aftershocks of police violence on the Bumpurs family. In between my teaching responsibilities at Michigan State University, I traveled to New York City, searching in library and courthouse archives for any trace of Eleanor, a working-class southern migrant who did not leave behind copious archival records documenting her life experiences. I collected oral testimonies and media photographs, hoping to uncover scenes from her life in others' memories and pictures. I visited Sedgwick Houses, spoke with some of Eleanor's apartment building neighbors, and took photos of her fourth-floor apartment door, the elevator, and narrow hallways she walked through. I listened to and viewed 1980s talk radio and local news broadcasts and New York City mayoral press conferences, attempting to gauge New

Yorkers' thoughts about her death. I even tried to read every social media post that mentioned her name, yearning to discover facts and details I had not uncovered in the archives, media reports, or interviews. I also hoped that social media would be a way for me to connect with Eleanor's family and friends, those individuals who loved and knew her best.

I strove to learn about Eleanor's full personhood. Who was Eleanor before the fatal encounter with the NYPD? What dreams and aspirations did she have for herself and her family? What disappointments and heartaches did her heart and mind harbor? Equally important, I wanted to know how New York City's socioeconomic and political landscape of the 1980s set into motion a chain of circumstances that adversely transformed Eleanor's life and how her killing became the catalyst for amending the city's mental health, public housing and welfare, and policing policies. What histories of New York City did Eleanor's killing expose, and what did this American crime story reveal about 1980s urban life and society?

Told through the story of one woman's life and death, this book presents new histories of police violence and community activism during the 1980s. It is about one of New York City's most well-known yet understudied incidents of police brutality. Eleanor's killing was the culmination of a multipronged system of urban inequities and state violence that adversely impacted the lives of New York's and the nation's most vulnerable citizens: the poor and working-class, minoritized communities, and persons living with mental health conditions. By "state violence," I mean life-threatening harms and byproducts of police brutality, municipal policies and bureaucracy, and judiciary and medical injustices. Historically, city officials and workers employed various forms of state violence, including social control and surveillance, disciplinary action, confinement, and inhumane treatment to maintain race, gender, and class order.[3] The city of New York's various public serving institutions and state actors were hostile entities in Eleanor's life.

Eleanor was a victim of expanding police presence and power, as well as municipal neglect. Before a NYPD militarized unit stormed into her one-bedroom apartment on the morning of October 29,

1984, government disinvestment and economic precarity had long been part of her life. A consequence of urban economic austerity and race, gender, and class exclusion, city abandonment made it difficult for Eleanor to survive in New York City, resulting in housing insecurities and inadequate social services, lack of empathy, and ultimately death. Her life was rendered disposable. City leaders, housing and social workers, and police were not interested in who Eleanor was, what she needed to live, or what she meant to her family or community. Akin to 1980s federal and state officials cutting millions of impoverished families from government assistance, New York City municipal workers were concerned with ridding their hands of someone they deemed to be a social and economic problem: a poor, elderly, and disabled woman.

Eleanor's killing laid bare the injustices that occur and the physical and mental carnage that awaits when multiple structures of oppression intersect and when social and economic safety nets are pulled from underneath vulnerable populations. Her apartment eviction and death illuminate the human cost of desertion, inequality, and a lack of empathy for vulnerable communities.

This book attaches the untold personal narrative to a shocking killing. It offers intimate portraits of an interior life, snapshots of family love and sorrow and city activism, and scenes from a legal justice battle. Moments from Eleanor's complicated life shine a spotlight on urban working-class and poor Black women, those struggling to navigate and survive in President Ronald Reagan's America. Her personal history serves as an entry point into the lives of American families grappling with the vestiges of economic austerity, carceral expansion, and city neglect. More broadly, Eleanor's life and subsequent police killing underscores the contradictions and flaws in the idea of American equality, exposing the cracks in the nation's fragile and failing mental health, public housing, and policing systems.

Excavating Eleanor's identity politics and complex stories about urban life, state violence, and political activism was no easy task. It required drawing from a wide range of primary documentation. This book is anchored in familiar archival sources, including newspapers, civil rights records, labor union documents, oral history collections, radio and television broadcasts, personal papers collections, photographs and cartoons, census and legal records, congressional reports, and the mayoral and gubernatorial papers of 1980s and 1990s New York politicians, including Edward Koch, David Dinkins, and Mario Cuomo. Archival evidence offers top-down and bottom-up perspectives on New York City's socioeconomic and political landscapes, as well as city dwellers' varying perceptions on police brutality. This project also draws on the fiction and nonfiction writings and intellectual critiques of some of New York's most influential Black writers, newspaper editors, journalists, and cultural producers of the late twentieth century. The political and cultural inscriptions, music, and films of Audre Lorde, June Jordan, Bronx high school filmmakers, and others capture Black New Yorkers' experiences with anti-Black rhetoric and violence, their participation in grassroots activism, and their thoughts about policing, race relations, and the Bumpurs killing.

This extensive research engendered opportunities to broadly explore 1980s New York. At the same time, legal and government records, newspaper editorials, and other documents are silent on Eleanor's interior life. When Eleanor does appear in archival documents, she is described in ways state actors and persons of privilege have historically treated working-class and poor Black women. She is objectified, debased, and muted.[4] The archival sources reinforce race, gender, and class stereotypes. They reproduce merciless violence and death and reveal pain, loss, and isolation. In these records, Eleanor's origin story begins with dispossession and death; joy, family, and community are absent from such records. Copious archival materials left me with incomplete and inaccurate biographical sketches, one-sided and biased accounts of Eleanor's life, and with unanswered questions about her childhood, her life in New York, and her thoughts about city living, motherhood, wage labor, and American equality.

Notwithstanding archival limitations, I searched for glimpses and snippets of Eleanor's public and private worlds in deliberate silences and causal omissions.[5] I read along and against the bias grain of archival documents. And in recounting some of Eleanor's and the Bumpurs family's life histories, I employed what scholar Sarah Haley identifies as speculative accountings—that is, "a historical musing upon emotions, ambivalences, and intimacies that might have marked [Eleanor's] experiences [and feelings] in the context of overwhelming violence," pain, and happiness.[6] A useful methodological tool for capturing Black women's intimate lives, speculative accounting granted the opportunity to explore aspects of Eleanor's interiority, as well as the Bumpurs family's feelings on maternal love and loss.

Oral history also became valuable to unearthing episodes from Eleanor's life. Between 2017 and 2023, I interviewed several former New York officials, journalists, political activists, cultural producers, Sedgwick Houses tenants, a former Bronx Supreme Court assistant prosecutor, and Eleanor's second-oldest daughter, Mary Bumpurs, the only Bumpurs family member interviewed for this book. Other family members were not interested in talking to me. They elected privacy over disseminating stories about Eleanor and themselves and their feelings about losing their kin to police violence. Conceivably, reliving and remembering painful moments of their lives would be difficult. They did not want their feelings and words documented or published in a book about police violence. Embracing an ethos of care toward Eleanor and her family, I respected the Bumpurs family's feelings and privacy, refusing to inundate them with interview requests and valuing the confidentiality often denied to historically targeted and surveilled populations.[7] Not having the opportunity to interview some of Eleanor's daughters, grandchildren, and other close relatives was disappointing. No doubt, their memories would have offered insight on Eleanor as a maternal figure, presented nuanced perspectives on how different Bumpurs family members coped with police violence and ongoing public and police attacks, and illustrated their thoughts about New Yorkers' struggle to secure legal justice for their mother.

Mary Bumpurs felt differently about sharing her family's histories with me. For the resilient Bronx activist and mother, it was important, even thirty years after her mother's killing, to keep her "spirit moving." And for Mary that meant sharing parts of Eleanor's life with a new generation of students, activists, politicians, scholars, and everyday folks. Mary was willing to risk her emotional well-being to recall the pain of losing her mother and share with me private scenes from her mother's life. This was not easy for her.

Mary was generous with her time, granting me numerous phone and in-person conversations. Her memories about family love and loss and her participation in citywide protests for her mother were critical to my research and writing process. Mary was the first family member to learn about her mother's killing; she became the media spokesperson for her family and led a social justice movement for her mother. Mary shared with me stories that did not figure into 1980s interviews with journalists and those narratives not housed in archival collections. Her memories about her family's history filled in many historical gaps, contextualized my archival materials, and provided a fuller yet curated picture of her mother. Mary understood the power of narrative. And she understood firsthand how public renderings of the victims of police brutality and their families were slanted and dehumanizing. Having experienced scathing public attacks from conservative media outlets like the *New York Post*, police unions like the Patrolmen's Benevolent Association, and ordinary New Yorkers, Mary was protective of her mother's narrative. During our conversations, she concealed many stories about her mother, demonstrating what historian Darlene Clark Hine calls a cult of secrecy.[8] Mary created the appearance of disclosure and openness, while remaining an enigma. Imposing a self-imposed invisibility, Mary did not answer many of my questions. She skillfully shifted conversations, selecting what stories she wanted to share with me. Some family stories were not for public consumption nor for this book.

Despite archival voids and historical figures' causal omissions and deliberate silences, I came to understand that I could not, as literary scholar Saidiya Hartman writes, "embody life in words."[9] Every aspect of Eleanor's life or family's lives could not be recounted. A complete account of their lives is unknowable. I had to be satisfied with knowing that I left no stone unturned.

In recounting Eleanor's life and the state and police violence that snatched her away from her family and community, this book is divided into three sections. Part I, titled "Eleanor," attaches a personal story to a highly publicized police violence case, tracing Eleanor's life from the end of World War I to 1984, the year she was killed. While it is important to understand the complex circumstances that led to

Eleanor's eviction and death, it is just as important to comprehend how she lived. Long before Eleanor was the face of state violence, she was a mother, a friend, and someone who desired happiness for herself and family. This section sheds light on Eleanor's lesser-known experiences as a southerner and northern migrant navigating racial segregation and violence and urban inequalities. From childhood to adulthood, Eleanor endured what novelist Toni Morrison described in her 1973 book *Sula* as "circles and circles of sorrow."[10] She experienced family tragedies, economic precarity, and debilitating illnesses. And while doing her best to cope with race and sex exclusion and personal traumas, she created and found joy where she could. Visibility of Eleanor's public and private worlds recognizes the fullness of her life.

The police killing of a Black grandmother was shocking, prompting diverse responses from New Yorkers. Part II, titled "Protest," surveys everyday urbanites, community activists, political leaders, and NYPD officers about Eleanor's killing. Expressed in local and national newspapers, radio and television broadcast interviews, and municipal reports, public commentary about the deadly eviction ignited citywide support for the NYPD and Eleanor. This section also explores the genealogy of the social justice campaign for Eleanor, paying close attention to anti–police brutality organizations and the political leaders and family activists who led that movement.

Part III, titled "Justice," surveys the legal journey toward holding police officer Stephen Sullivan accountabe for Eleanor's death. The legal case against Sullivan was a mix of judicial highs and lows, inspiring political protests and public conversations about how the legal system would treat the police killing of a Black woman.

This three-part book takes several approaches to discussing police violence. First, it elects a victim-centered perspective. It stresses the importance of resurrecting the under-studied life histories of victims and survivors of state violence, encouraging the public to go beyond individuals' brutal and deathly encounters with police. Much is lost when the public becomes preoccupied with narratives about harm. The erasure of personal narratives about individuals tragically struck down by police bullets, vicious beatings, and chokeholds marginalizes them and privileges stories centered on suffering and death. Not accounting for the totality of victims' lives reduces them, like how historian Kidada Williams describes the historical omission of lynching victims' personhood, to "disturbing and objectifying black bodies, without individuated subjectivity that is contingent on relations with others."[11] Erasure of victims' identity politics is an injustice to them and to those who loved and mourned them.

Second, this book chronicles the loss of a family, one whose lives were shattered by an unspeakable act. Police brutality victims are separated from their kin in the last moments of their lives. They are also isolated from their families in histories written about them.[12] Histories of state violence are incomplete without the narratives of those who lost loved ones to police violence. Stories about family loss need to be pulled from historical limbo and shared with the public.[13] This book takes seriously the human toll and cost of police brutality on the Bumpurs family. It grapples with the immediacy of a family's experience with a devastating loss, their courageous journey toward legal justice, and their struggles with ongoing public and police harassment. Police violence fractured the Bumpurs family. They suffered long after Eleanor's deathly encounter with police and long after media headlines, justice campaigns, and legal pursuits ceased. The Bumpurs family experienced what scholar Rob Nixon calls a "slow violence." This form of violence is gradual and veiled, delayed in destruction, and "an attritional violence that is typically not viewed as violence at all."[14] As victims of slow violence, the Bumpurs family experienced harms that unfolded across time, space, and place.

Finally, this book uses a 1984 police brutality case to reveal a broader story about how society treats underserved populations, those persons experiencing economic difficulties, living with disabilities, and facing various forms of exclusion. Many neoconservative and liberal policymakers, media personalities, and ordinary middle- and working-class Americans regard underprivileged citizens with contempt, refusing to recognize their value to American society. They view them as unproductive citizens and as socioeconomic drains and political threats to fluctuating local and national economies. This politics of indifference toward vulnerable communities is dangerous. Such positions engender the creation of and public support for government policies that place citizens at risk for police violence, housing insecurities, inadequate medical care, and everyday indignities and injustices.

But not all citizens embrace a culture of disregard toward marginalized populations. Those long committed to upending societal inequalities refuse to turn a blind eye from persons considered disposable. They see value in their fellow citizens. Believing in the interconnectedness of human beings, activists are invested in all citizens' wellbeing, and in their survival and futures. And they believe all individuals are vital to mobilizing against inequities and public policies and sentiments that strip individuals like Eleanor Bumpurs of their legal rights and dignity.

PART I
Eleanor

CHAPTER I

SOUTHERN GIRL

I n 1918, the United States witnessed vast socioeconomic and political changes and turmoil. That July, the City of Brotherly Love
endured several days of racial unrest, property damage, and white
violence. Philadelphia's racial conflict was part of a series of riots
happening across the country during the nadir of American race relations. In the closing months of 1918, Americans happily welcomed
the end of the Great War, which claimed the lives of over 110,000 US
servicemen. Just as one war was ending another one was already un-
derway. This war was short but lethal. This war was a public health
crisis fought in city hospitals and in the homes of millions of ordinary
Americans. Between 1918 and 1919, the influenza pandemic swept
the globe, infecting at least one-half of the world's population. At the
time considered to be the most severe pandemic in American history,
the highly contagious virus claimed the lives of over six hundred
thousand Americans and, for many citizens, generated fears of viral
contraction and death.

In that momentous year, North Carolina natives John Hilliard
Williams and his wife, Fannie Belle Egerton Williams, both in their
thirties, welcomed a summer baby. On Thursday, August 22, 1918,
Elna (Eleanor) Gray Williams took her first breath. African American
midwives and schoolteachers Sallie Perry and Estella Hill delivered
the pecan-colored baby in the Williams's rented wooden framed home
in Louisburg, North Carolina.[1]

As the county seat of Franklin County, Louisburg was a small
agricultural and industrial town during the early twentieth century,

consisting of an estimated 1,775 residents in 1910. Franklin County's population was just over 24,000 at the time. Marrying John in December 1901, Fannie Belle labored in the Williams home. John toiled as a farm laborer.[2] A hard worker, John earned less than thirty dollars per week, enough to sustain the household.[3] His menial wages covered rent, food, clothes, and other necessities. Given their limited economic circumstances, the couple did the best they could for themselves and their children. Committed to their family's economic survival, John and Fannie Belle miraculously sheltered, fed, and clothed seven children: Zollie (born 1905), Charlie (1912), James Edward (1914), Eleanor (1918), Raymond (1927), and two infant boys who died before the age of three.[4]

Like many Southern working-poor Black parents, the Williamses, born a few decades after the emancipation of enslaved people and having little-to-no formal education, desired a liberated future for Eleanor and her brothers. They envisioned radical possibilities for their children, hoping for a life for them that was better than theirs and better than the ones the children were born into. And for many Black parents of the Jim Crow segregation era, dreams of liberation entailed having bodily autonomy and access to formal education, equitable labor, and the ballot box. Black mothers and fathers interpreted having these citizenship rights as passports to individual happiness, racial progress, economic success, and community betterment.[5]

As the ladies of the house, Eleanor and her mother spent a significant amount of time together, and Eleanor assisted her mother with maintaining the Williams home. They cleaned the house, prepared meals, and cared for the younger Williams children. While keeping house, Fannie Belle conceivably instructed her daughter on household management and proper decorum for young ladies. Echoing lessons articulated in turn-of-the-twentieth century Black conduct books for girls such as Silas X. Floyd's 1905 *Floyd's Flowers* and rooted in generations of women and girls' kitchen table conversations about etiquette, Black mothers like Fannie Belle taught their daughters to respect their elders, speak politely, work hard, and impart values and traditions to their own families. Black parents emphasized proper conduct because they wanted well-behaved children. Concerned with their reputation, they also wanted their neighbors and members of their social and religious networks to know that their children were raised by parents of good moral character.[6]

Sadly, knowing that race segregation and a culture of white supremacy would govern Black children's lives, parents imparted to their sons and daughters lessons about race. Black households like that of the Williams home operated as critical institutional spaces for teaching children about race relations and racial violence. Desiring to keep their children safe from the realities of American apartheid, Black mothers socialized their children about the social mores and hierarchies of the American South, acquainting them with the humiliation and degradation felt by Southern Blacks and passing down stories about racial etiquette and performance and survival. Children learned a set of specific rules and scripts guiding interracial relations, underscoring to stay in their place around white folks.[7]

Understanding that Black girls would inherit the same exploitations of their female ancestors, mothers also schooled their daughters about the threat of sexual violence. Young girls learned that bodily attacks were omnipresent and that Black and white male predators saw Black girls' bodies as accessible and disposable. Girls were beaten and raped, and they endured sexist and racist insults on public streets and transportation, at work and school, and even in their homes.[8] Recalling white men's predatory behavior, Louisiana-born Black activist Audley "Queen Mother" Moore noted that Black girls "had no peace from white men. There was struggles all the time, white men trying to molest us all the time."[9] Acknowledging girls' sexual vulnerabilities and the limits of legal redress for Blacks, mothers educated their daughters about harm reduction strategies. They stressed behavioral modifications—encouraging girls to avoid strangers and to familiarize themselves with their surroundings. No method of defense against physical and sexual violence guaranteed complete safety. But lessons about self-protection made women and girls more conscious of their environments.

Outside the Williams home, Eleanor came directly into contact with North Carolina's system of de jure and de facto segregation laws, a set of rules designed to exclude Southern Blacks from public life and deny citizenship and legal protections. Black North Carolinians like the Williams family were subjected to segregated schooling and public accommodations, discriminatory labor practices, political disenfranchisement, and popular and cultural artifacts of white supremacy. Throughout the late 1910s, the Louisburg movie theater screened filmmaker D. W. Griffith's technologically advanced yet racist film *Birth of a Nation*. In 1923, Franklin County leaders and the United Daughters of the Confederacy "erected [one of the first] confederate flag monuments, a stone structure with carvings" in front of the Franklin County Courthouse. During the 1920s, caricatures of Black women appeared in the local white newspaper, the *Franklin Times*. The newspaper's classified section marketed Louisiana entrepreneur William Reily's racist Luzianne coffee ads. Black-and-white advertisements featured an image of an overweight, dark-skinned, and kerchief-wearing "Black Mammy," serving her well-dressed white employer a cup of hot coffee.[10]

Louisburg was also a site of anti-Black violence. With the 1920s national rebirth of the Ku Klux Klan (KKK), North Carolina had over eighty KKK chapters, including Louisburg's J. B. Clifton Klan. KKK membership in the state was close to fifty thousand.[11] Residing in Louisburg during the 1920s and 1930s, Rosanell Eaton, who was praised by former president Barack Obama for her fight against North Carolina's 2010s restrictive voting laws, recalled witnessing white townsfolk donning KKK paraphernalia and terrorizing Black residents. "More than once [the Eaton family] woke up to the sight of charred crosses on [our] tobacco and cotton farm," Eaton said.[12] Like Rosanell Eaton, Eleanor observed how white domestic terrorist groups threatened Black life. At an October 1985 political event in Harlem, Eleanor's second daughter, Mary Bumpurs, recounted her mother's shocking testimonies about Southern life and white terrorism. "My mother told me a story, when I was about 13 years of age, about the experience that she had with the Ku Klux Klan. She saw homes burnt down by these men in white sheets. She saw black people being taken in the woods and beaten to death. White people coming into your area and beating you up and killing you, and there was nothing done or nothing said about it."[13]

In Eleanor's home state, an estimated 168 African Americans were lynched between the end of the Civil War and 1941.[14] In Franklin County, several African American men were lynched between 1919 and 1935.[15] Both of these murders received national media coverage, capturing the attention of the Black press including the National Association for the Advancement of Colored People's (NAACP) magazine *The Crisis*. In December 1919, one year after Eleanor was born, a white mob murdered twenty-five-year-old Franklin County native Powell Green. He was accused of allegedly shooting a white man. The revenge-seeking whites tied a rope around the World War I veteran's neck, fastened him to a car, and dragged him for several miles. Before a crowd of hundreds of white townsmen, women, and children, Powell was then hung from a tree.[16] On July 30, 1935, one month before Eleanor's eighteenth birthday, a mob murdered twenty-five-year-old Franklin County resident and mentally ill person Govan "Sweat" Ward in Louisburg. Ward was accused of the brutal axe murder of sixty-seven-year-old white farmer Charles Stokes. Seeking retribution for the Stokes killing, a mob hung Ward from a tree.[17]

Eleanor never forgot local stories and family conversations about brutal attacks against Black Franklin County residents. When racial violence struck one person or family, it struck the entire community, including children. Parts of Eleanor's childhood echoed what blues singer Billie Holiday would in the 1930s famously describe as Black bodies swinging from Southern trees. For Eleanor, anti-Black violence was a constant reminder of her Blackness and the danger of breaching arbitrary color lines. Black murder victims, unpunished culprits, and heartbreaking and haunting scenes of distraught neighbors and friends became part of her collective memory about Louisburg and the American South.

Important lessons about Southern Black life were learned at school. When Eleanor was not assisting her mother with household chores, she and some of her siblings attended either the Episcopal Mission School or the Louisburg Colored Graded School. Established during the Progressive Era, both schools represented the earliest educational institutions for Black children in Louisburg. Hailed as the "best elementary schools in this section of the state" by Franklin County Black educator and Colored Graded School principal George Pollard, the two schools educated children in grades one through eight. "With a good strong force" of women schoolteachers like Estella Hill, one of the women who birthed Eleanor, students were taught literacy, writing, industrial training, and the value of racial uplift and respectability. Black educators emphasized that "politeness, honesty, industry, and thrift and good conduct [made] better citizens of our people."[18] Children were instructed that proper behavior, in part, was essential to promoting images of respectable Black communities and to counteracting racist assumptions about Blacks.

As an eleven-year-old Eleanor devoted her time to domestic responsibilities and formal education, a tragedy struck the Williams household, jeopardizing her educational pursuits and potentially her mental health.

In spring 1929, forty-four-year-old Fannie Belle was diagnosed with pellagra, a disease associated with a dietary deficiency of niacin (vitamin B). Records do not reveal whether Franklin County medical professionals or community healers made Fannie Belle's diagnosis. Pellagra was common among impoverished communities, those unable to consume well-balanced diets beyond cornmeal, molasses, sorghum, and salt pork. These foods were staples for many working-class families. They were inexpensive and needed little preparation. Individuals with pellagra experienced the "Four Ds": dermatitis (skin lesions), dementia, diarrhea, and, if untreated for an extended period, death. Fannie Belle was among the "one hundred thousand [mostly working-class and poor] people in the southern states that [contracted and] died of pellagra during the first four decades of the twentieth century." In 1927, a North Carolina state health officer recorded that at least 659 North Carolinians died from pellagra. A "serious menace to the health of Franklin county," pellagra was treated as a public health emergency, prompting Louisburg's *Franklin Times* to create a weekly column of "Health Suggestions." Often written by county health experts, the column provided residents with facts about pellagra's cause, symptoms, treatments, and prevention. Health professionals advised Louisburg families to eat a diet consisting of fresh meat and poultry, fruit, milk, and eggs. When an individual was diagnosed with pellagra, an improved diet cured the disease within a few months. Financially strapped rural families like the Williamses found it difficult to afford a more expansive diet.[19] They paid the ultimate price for being poor.

Fannie Belle battled pellagra for at least six months. It was undoubtedly a painful time for the Williams family, especially for Eleanor. Alongside her father, brothers, and other family members, Eleanor likely adopted some of her mother's household chores. She also possibly assisted her father, siblings, and female relatives with caring for her bedridden mother. Caring for her mother, she observed how pellagra invaded the older woman's body. The disease ate away at the flesh and mind, covering the sufferer's arms, face, and neck with sores and lesions and causing dementia, bodily weakness, and abdominal pain. And if left untreated, pellagra snatched away one's life.

A few weeks before Thanksgiving, Fannie Belle Egerton Williams died at home on November 11, 1929.[20] She became one of 981 North Carolinians to die from pellagra that year.[21] Amid agonizing sorrow, Black funeral director Dallas H. Blount assisted the Williams family with Fannie Belle's homegoing service. One of several Black undertakers in Franklin County, Blount offered the grieving family consoling words and prepared burial arrangements. A day after Fannie Belle's death, the Williams and Egerton families and friends gathered at the Louisburg Colored Cemetery. Known to Franklin County Black folks as the "Cemetery on the Hill," the Louisburg Colored Cemetery was the only burial site for Black residents in Louisburg.[22] Weeping and holding their family Bibles, the mourners said their final goodbyes to Fannie Belle.

Eleanor would profoundly miss the other woman in the Williams house. Yet Eleanor remained physically and emotionally connected to her mother even in death. Fannie Belle's presence lingered in the Williams home. Memories of Fannie Belle were in the rooms she cooked, cleaned, and died in. Traces of her dwelled in old and faded dresses and worn-down shoes and in other personal belongings, all artifacts Eleanor and her brothers and father inherited.

Witnessing the physical deterioration and death of a parent, especially a mother, is traumatic for a child. Maternal death means the "loss of [an] emotional caretaker" and traveling through the world with a maternal void. Parental death put children like Eleanor at risk for long-term behavioral issues and mental health conditions, including anti-social behavior, depression, anxiety, post-traumatic stress, and dissociative disorder. As formerly enslaved South Carolinian Josephine Bacchus recalled in a 1938 Work Project Administration (WPA) interview, being motherless placed many children in jeopardy for "a heap of roughness [hard life] just on account dat [many] ain't never has mother[s] to have a care for [them]."[23]

Fannie Belle's premature death shifted the Williams's household structure. After her passing, widower John and a community of relatives and friends were left to care for several children: seventeen-year-old saw laborer James Edward Williams, ten-year-old Eleanor, and one-year-old Raymond Williams. Even with the assistance of extended family, Fannie Belle's death forced John to depend on his children's labor. Part of the South's agricultural and domestic labor market forces, Black children's work was critical to their families' economic survival. Mississippi-born writer Richard Wright speaks eloquently in his 1941 book *12 Million Black Voices* about the necessity of children's labor to Southern economies. "Sometimes there is a weather-worn, pine-built schoolhouse for our children, but even if the school were open for full term our children would not have time to go. We cannot let them leave the fields when cotton is waiting to be picked. Hunger is the punishment if we violate the laws of Queen Cotton."[24]

Economic necessity compelled John to withdraw Eleanor from school. Working-class parents' need to prioritize labor over education deferred dreams of formal education for their children. And for some families, labor obligations continued a multigenerational cycle of illiteracy. Eleanor's education ended in the sixth grade. Her expansive household labor was central to the family's survival, making it possible for her father and James Edward to work outside the home as sawmill laborers at one of Franklin County's thirty sawmills.[25]

Leaving school was conceivably difficult for Eleanor. School withdrawal was another major change and loss in her young life. School disruption meant leaving behind friends and women teachers like Estella Hill, the woman who delivered her into the world. Moreover, school interruption shattered many children's educational dreams of what prominent African American scholar W. E. B. Du Bois described as a "longing to know" and advance in their studies.[26] For young girls, educational disruption jeopardized possible, yet narrow, paths to higher education and labor beyond household work and other low-wage jobs. Any educational visions Eleanor had for herself slipped away when she left school. But her dreams of formal education would not die. Those dreams would be instilled in her offspring. Yet Eleanor may have still been optimistic about her future and the possibility of pushing beyond her family's socioeconomic circumstances and the confines of Jim Crow segregation.

With the support of her sister-in-law Laura Silver Belle Alston Williams and a small network of women relatives, an eleven-year-old Eleanor became acquainted with her new role as primary caregiver in the Williams home. Born in 1908, Laura Belle was a native North Carolinian and married Eleanor's older brother, Zollie Williams, in 1928, a year before Fannie Belle's death. A young woman herself, Laura, in her early twenties, was at least ten years older than Eleanor. She was more than a sister-in-law to Eleanor.[27] Laura was a mother-like figure to the young girl, engaging in what Black feminist scholar Patricia Hill Collins refers to as community mothering, or "othermothering." This form of elastic kinship was an expansive idea about childrearing and survival. Othermothers cared for non-biological children as if they were their own, providing them with shelter, clothes, food, and love. They demonstrated a commitment to vulnerable persons within their communities.[28] Juggling the physical demands of household duties in her own home and her work as a laundress, Laura Belle instructed Eleanor on her new responsibilities. Laura Belle's giving of her time placed her in Black women's long tradition of philanthropic efforts, offering her physical presence and domestic skills for her family and for a greater good.[29] Laura Belle taught her sister-in-law/surrogate daughter about working-class Southern Black women's historic laboring patterns, those everyday work traditions that were never done in isolation and that economically sustained Black women and their families for generations.

As a skilled laundress, Laura Belle likely taught Eleanor how to properly wash and dry clothes, suggesting that the physically taxing household chore could be performed alone at home, at an employers' house, or in their communities among other "negro girls marching through the street carrying enormous bundles of soiled clothes upon their heads."[30] Washing clothes was an all-day affair, involving tin washtubs, batting blocks, cast-iron pots for boiling water, and home-made lye soap and starch. The arduous process of producing clean and fresh-smelling garments included soaking, scrubbing, boiling, wringing out hot and cold water, and pinning garments to clotheslines or barbed-wire fences. Performing laundry work with older women relatives, girls like Eleanor would have learned about the labor benefits of the occupation and observed new conditions and possibilities for Black women's wage labor. Unlike domestic workers, laundresses were independent laborers. They created client-based services. Black laundresses controlled their labor, avoiding abusive white families and exploitative labor conditions. Having labor autonomy, women selected their clientele and negotiated labor hours, locations, and wages with Black and white clients. With flexible work schedules, laundresses like Laura Belle carved out time to care for themselves and family members like Eleanor.[31]

Laura Belle and other surrogate mothers may have given Eleanor some of her first lessons in cooking.[32] Eleanor's love for food and cooking was birthed in women's kitchens, sacred spaces Black women and girls employed to express and share inner thoughts about life, love, and kinship. Despite the Williams family's limited food supply, Eleanor developed a deep appreciation for Black Southern culinary production and would share those foodways with her future children. Imaginably, food was important to Eleanor. Food had power. Its smell, appearance, and taste were pleasurable and nourishing to the body, strengthening it to contest the degradations of oppression aimed at harming Black bodies.[33] Food sustained life, and not having it jeopardized life. And Eleanor knew all too well the deadly consequences of not having access to quality and adequate amounts of food.

As cultural transmitters, Southern Black women gave young girls master lessons in food preparation and cookery, keeping alive the memories and recipes of generations of family members. They shared secret family recipes, those committed to memory and written down on tattered bits of paper, and perhaps even cooking techniques from the first published cookbook by a Black woman: Abby Fisher's 1881 cookbook, *What Mrs. Fisher Knows About Southern Cooking, Soups, Pickles, Preserves, etc.* Attentively listening to and watching their mothers, grandmothers, and other culinary teachers move around their kitchens and gardens, Black girls learned how different ingredients blended, how to can and preserve vegetables, how to creatively transform fresh foods and limited rations into tasteful culinary art, and how to prepare and season chicken, fish, collard greens, homemade biscuits and cakes, and one-pot meals. When cooking one-pot meals, girls like Eleanor discovered that such dishes not only allowed them to complete household chores while food simmered on the stove for hours but lessened daily meal preps and fed families for several days.[34]

Caring for her father and brothers was another important aspect of Eleanor's household responsibilities. One of her primary tasks was tending to baby brother Raymond, who affectionately referred to his big sister as "Satta."[35] Eleanor raised Raymond until she started her own family. In between sweeping the floor, washing clothes, and cooking, she mothered her two-year-old brother. Parts of her days were spent feeding him, changing his cloth diapers, rocking him to sleep, and cuddling him when he cried, smiled, or needed to be comforted. She cared and loved her little brother as if he were her own baby. Eleanor's mothering and care work for the men in her family was a symbol of love, necessity, and much sacrifice.[36]

Shouldering family responsibility warped Eleanor's childhood. Family death and household labor obligations forced a quick transition into adulthood. As a child quickly moving into womanhood, she was expected to be an adult—to be self-sufficient and to put her family's needs before her own.[37] For Eleanor, there was little to no time to be a young girl, playing with homemade wooden and metal toys and dolls or engaging in other childhood leisure activities. At best, Eleanor could build a pleasure culture around everyday household labor, family life, and playing with Raymond. She could also spend workdays imagining a world where her mother was alive, cooking in the kitchen, or dispensing another critical lesson about Southern

Black girlhood.[38] And the fast-growing preteen could spend time daydreaming about making a decent life for herself—despite already experiencing loss and disappointment.

———

A twenty-something-year-old Eleanor started her own family during the mid-to-late 1930s.[39] Kinship was a possible route toward personal happiness, self-fulfillment, and finding love. A chance at love and romance came with twenty-something-year-old and fellow Louisburg native Ernest Hayes (Hays). A few years older than Eleanor, Hayes, a manual and farm laborer, was perhaps her first romantic relationship. It was easy to understand Ernest's attraction to Eleanor. She was a beauty. Standing at five feet six, she had smooth cocoa brown skin, thick black hair, high cheek bones, almond-shaped brown eyes, and a beautiful smile.[40] Surviving records do not reveal if or when Ernest and Eleanor legally married. If a legal ceremony was performed by a local minister, Eleanor and Ernest, wearing their best attire and before a small gathering of family and friends, exchanged vows in the mid-1930s.[41]

Ernest and Eleanor's union resulted in the birth of their first child on March 19, 1939. The joy of welcoming their daughter was undoubtedly tinged with the sorrow of being unable to share her with Eleanor's now long-deceased mother, Fannie Belle. Eleanor named her baby Fannie Mae Hayes, with all of the grief, yearning, and honor that the name evoked. The African American tradition of passing down names across generations took on special meaning for the young family.[42]

To care for themselves and a new child, Ernest and Eleanor performed backbreaking labor. Physically grueling labor yielded low wages, long hours, and little to no economic advancements or opportunities. Ernest was one of the fortunate Franklin County residents to be employed during the Great Depression. The economic depression of the 1930s hit the county's nearly thirty thousand residents hard. Middle- and working-class families faced home foreclosures, bankruptcy, and unemployment. With US President Franklin Delano Roosevelt implementing a series of public works projects to address nationwide unemployment, Ernest secured a job with the federal government. He was one of the estimated 125,000 North Carolinians employed by the WPA between 1935 and 1940.[43] Ernest was a construction worker, erecting several buildings for the county, including the Louisburg postal office. Depending on how federal officials classified his skill level, Ernest perhaps earned a monthly wage of between thirty-one and fifty-seven dollars. Monthly federal wages allowed the Hayes family to receive a steady income.[44] However, two incomes were needed to keep the Hayes household afloat.

Eleanor labored at Louisburg's white-owned Franklin Hotel. One of several hotels in the county, the four-story brick building was situated in Louisburg's shopping district on North Main Street, a business area that included a bank, funeral home, masonic hall, and the Franklin County Courthouse. Given Eleanor's limited education, she labored as a domestic worker. She devoted endless hours to accommodating the hotel's white middle-class clientele and cleaning the establishment's forty-plus bedrooms.[45] Eleanor's tenure as a domestic worker was short-lived, ending sometime in the early 1940s.

In May 1942, Eleanor's life took a dramatic turn. A singular act of either courage or malicious behavior forced Eleanor to leave her family. The twenty-five-year-old mother was arrested for assault with a deadly weapon, presumably a knife or a gun.[46] The details and circumstances of the 1942 arrest remain a mystery. Current legal restrictions on North Carolina inmate records makes it difficult to ascertain the details of her crime. It is unclear who was assaulted or the reason for the attack.[47] Conceivably, a range of episodes prompted Eleanor to harm another person. Self-protection, defending a loved one, or the desire to intentionally harm another individual fueled a willingness to employ violence against a supposed threat. According to one family member, one perceived danger may have dwelled in the Hayes household. Family rumors intimated that Eleanor was a victim and survivor of spousal abuse.[48] Ernest may have been what blues singer Gertrude "Ma" Rainey called a "Sweet Rough Man," keeping Eleanor's lips and eyes bloody, black, and swollen and her head throbbing. It's possible that defending herself against partner abuse landed her in "that mean old jail."[49]

The 1942 arrest was Eleanor's first encounter with America's penal system. But it would not be her last. Pleading guilty to the assault charge, Eleanor was sentenced to eight months at Raleigh's North Carolina Correctional Institution for Women, commonly known as the Women's Prison.[50]

Established in 1933, the Women's Prison enforced North Carolina's rigid racial code, segregating the prison's Black and white population of over four hundred women. In 1942, the prison incarcerated at least 147 Black women from various parts of the state. Women were admitted to the prison for a myriad of offenses, including sex work, larceny, assault, and murder.[51] Regularly sporting a gray-blue uniform, Eleanor and other caged women, under the guardianship of the state's first woman superintendent, Edna B. Strickland, experienced a regimented daily schedule. Incarcerated women spent hours performing arduous prison labor. Contributing to the nation's expansive labor sector, women, receiving no recompense, did laundry work, cleaned, gardened, canned, cooked, and sewed shirts for the state's nearly ten thousand inmates and the United States Navy. When not performing coercive penal labor, women participated in various educational and vocational programs, including nursing. Limited bodily mobility, constant surveillance, and possible physical and verbal abuse also marked routine prison life.[52]

Incarceration was an unsettling experience, shocking to detainees' mind, body, and spirit. Penal confinement also impacted those outside of prison walls, disrupting familial relationships. The Hayes household was no exception. Those closest to Eleanor became incarceration's hidden victims. Ernest was left to shoulder the economic burden of the household, and left, perhaps with the help of othermothers like Laura Belle, to raise three-year-old Fannie Mae. The couple's relationship did not withstand Eleanor's time in jail. The couple parted, either divorced or unofficially separated, sometime before or during her jail stint or shortly after her prison release.

Carceral confinement temporarily ruptured maternal bonds. Imprisonment hindered Eleanor's ability to care for Fannie Mae, creating a maternal void between mother and daughter and what scholar Sarah Haley calls a form of gender-specific psychic violence.[53] Eleanor understood firsthand the painful emotional void left by a mother's absence. Penal records are virtually silent on incarcerated women's thoughts on maternal separation. Yet family separation and not having the opportunity to mother their children was a traumatic experience for many women. Eleanor perhaps agonized over not caring for her baby girl and worried about her day-to-day well-being: who was feeding her, changing her diapers, and comforting her when she cried. Eleanor, perhaps hoping to pass time and escape the realities of prison life and family separation, daydreamed about an emancipatory future, one that was free from confinement and included family reunification and personal reinvention. Plans for fulfilling expansive ideas about freedom came in 1943.

In 1943, Eleanor was released from prison. The young mother's time and body were hers again. Breathing fresh air and seeing endless stretches of dirt roads and green meadows, Eleanor found that her freedom ushered in new possibilities. One was a dream of leaving North Carolina.

Eleanor imagined freedom in a different city, a place where she could start anew, secure decent housing and employment, and earn enough money to support herself and her daughter. A place where, to borrow from Richard Wright's classic 1945 memoir *Black Boy*, "anything seemed possible."[54] The formerly incarcerated mother visualized living in a geographical setting that was radically different from the one she was born and raised in, and one that was beyond the prison walls she had just been released from. The Louisburg native yearned to leave her hometown, a complicated space that symbolized racial exclusion and violence, family happiness and death, prison captivity, and fractured domestic relationships. Embodying blues singer Bessie Smith's 1924 "Woman's Trouble Blues," a song about migration, isolation, and imprisonment, Eleanor made plans to "leave this town," heading straight for the Northern big city. But migration would be bittersweet.[55]

Exodus from Louisburg would entail leaving behind all that she knew and those she loved. It meant saying goodbye to surrogate mother figures, her father and brothers, and other relatives, all who served as sources of unconditional love. The journey away from Louisburg and her limited funds may have meant temporarily leaving her daughter with Ernest or other close kin. No doubt leaving Fannie Mae, who was still a small child, would have been a difficult decision. Eleanor, like many migrating mothers, also wanted to establish herself in a new city before bringing Fannie Mae north. Her employment and housing circumstances needed to be stable before her daughter's arrival.[56] If Fannie Mae remained in Franklin County with relatives, it's not clear if or when she joined the countless other Black children migrating north to reunite with their mothers.

Better living conditions and happiness in a new city were not guaranteed. Not even survival was promised. Locating a job and affordable housing, finding trustworthy people, and navigating a fast-paced metropolis would not be easy. But Eleanor was willing to leave the only place she ever knew to go to a place that offered newcomers the opportunity to transform their lives. Like other Black Southerners making the decision to leave the South for the "northern promised land," Eleanor was a visionary and a dream chaser. The Southern young woman was ready to fling herself into the unknown, taking a courageous leap of faith. She stood at the forefront of a personal transformation that would significantly alter her life.

Sometime between 1943 and 1945, Eleanor migrated either by train, bus, or car to what Harlem Renaissance writer Wallace Thurman referred to as the "great black city": New York.[57] She joined the nearly five million Black Southerners who trekked to Northern, Southern, Midwestern, and Western urban cities for good jobs and wages and decent housing and to escape the violence of the American South and to leave behind interpersonal strife. A second Great Migration participant, the hopeful Louisburg native joined the approximately two hundred thousand migrants who flocked to the Big Apple during the World War II era.[58] But Eleanor did not head to New York alone. A new love interest, John "Bumpers," another Franklin County resident who would later father at least one of her children, accompanied the young mother to the bustling city.[59] The possibilities of happiness in a different city and with a new companion would be a mixed blend of blessings and disappointments for the Southern migrant.

John Bumpers and Eleanor had a complicated relationship. Known to family and friends as "Sonny-Man," John was a charismatic and handsome farm laborer who was at least twenty years older than Eleanor. Born in the 1890s, the Franklin County farmer was married with at least five children. Married to Lillie-Bell Bumpers since 1922, John Bumpers separated from his wife sometime in the 1930s or 1940s. John and Lillie Bell never divorced.[60] It's unclear if Lillie Bell knew about her husband's new love, a woman five years younger than her only daughter, Dazell Bumpers. Whether Eleanor was aware of John's marital status is also not known. Eleanor likely was aware of John's family situation given that the two were from the same county; and it's possible that Eleanor was one of the reasons for John and Lillie Belle's separation. John and Eleanor never married, but that did not stop her from adopting his last name. Presumably, Eleanor's decision to adopt the Bumpers surname was part of a public performance. Taking John's surname signaled Eleanor's belief in traditional conjugal arrangements and perhaps a desire to legitimize her extramarital relationship.

Whether the couple was legally married or not, Eleanor's expectations of John possibly aligned with mid-twentieth-century middle- and working-class Black women's ideas about marriage and partnership. Mid-twentieth-century Black women expected their partners to provide emotional and sexual fulfillment, romantic love and intimacy, financial support, and faithfulness.[61] John plausibly vowed to fulfill some of those expectations. He offered Eleanor some measure of financial solvency and help with navigating what seemed like the largest city in the world. The older and more experienced man also probably promised family stability and love. Promises of kinship and love were important to Eleanor, especially as someone who had, as a girl and young adult, experienced familial death, separation, and romantic loss. At the same, perhaps romantic love was not the only reason Eleanor was with John. John may have been Eleanor's only chance out of Louisburg. Migration, financial support, and a new life ahead may have been more important than John's marital status or declarations of love. The desire for personal reinvention outweighed promises of love, trust, and fidelity.

For Eleanor, Northern migration was perhaps not primarily about romantic love. It was about self-love. It provided an opportunity to live an anonymous life with a different set of rules—rules of her own making. And New York City was the perfect place to fulfill dreams of anonymity and unconventionality. With over seven million residents living in the city during the 1940s, New York did not have the trappings of small-town living. Eleanor would not have to worry about the entire neighborhood knowing her business or adhering to others' ideas about respectable behavior. Nor would she have to be concerned about meddling relatives' disapproval of her lifestyle, relationship choices, and criminal past. She could articulate and live out her own ideas about respectability, intimate partnerships, and child-rearing. Moreover, New York offered something radically different for dreamers and risk-takers like Eleanor. The nation's leading commercial and cultural capital offered newcomers the opportunity to pursue fuller and freer lives and, like the spring blossoms of Callery pears and Japanese cherry trees in Central Park, the chance to bloom.

CHAPTER 2

NEW YORK, NEW YORK

New York City enthralled Southern migrants like Eleanor. The world outside her and John's Harlem apartment seemed like it never slept. Everything and everybody moved fast, pounding the concrete pavement with a purpose.[1] Growing up in a small town, Eleanor never saw so many tall buildings, busy thoroughfares, fast-moving automobiles and subway trains, and Black businesses. Blacks owned and operated restaurants and nightclubs—like Ed Smalls's Smalls Paradise in Harlem—beauty shops, and churches like Abyssinian Baptist Church on 132nd Street, and African American and Caribbean pushcart vendors crowded Lenox and Eighth Avenues. New York had so many ethnically diverse inhabitants: Italians, Irish, Puerto Ricans, West Indians, and Black folks. The city's Black residents occupied nearly every inch of the densely populated city. "You can walk from 116th street and you won't see four people that you know," noted writer and editor Elmer A. Carter. "You won't see fifteen people that you have ever seen before. This town [New York] is full of Negroes."[2] Indeed, New York City had the largest urban Black population in the 1940s. In 1940, the city's Black population stood at an estimated 458,000 and rose to over 700,000 by 1948.[3]

Eleanor could hardly wait to explore the city's vibrant landscapes. And 1940s New York had much to offer newcomers. They could "take the 'A' train," as advised by the Duke Ellington Orchestra, attend one of the city's prominent Black churches, and shop at one of city's reasonably priced public markets. And if one earned and saved enough money, they could make a purchase at Black department store

Alleyne's in Brooklyn or enjoy an evening at Harlem's Savoy Ballroom or the Apollo Theater.[4]

Most of all, migrants like Eleanor looked forward to engaging in a popular and free city pastime: people watching and street strolling. NAACP leader and Black national anthem songwriter James Weldon Johnson recalled that Black New Yorkers "get a good deal of pleasure and enjoyment out of strolling." Strolling in Harlem did not mean merely promenading along Lenox or Seventh Avenues or 135th Street. "Those streets are places for socializing. It is more like going out for adventure."[5] Well-travelled New York thoroughfares or even the stairway entrance to an apartment building, known colloquially as the stoop, were ideal for observing new places, people, and possibilities.

Listening to and watching strangers claim urban spaces, a wide-eyed Eleanor was sure to receive an informal yet necessary education about city life. Promenading down the street or sitting on an apartment building stoop, Eleanor could study urbanites' graceful and guileful body language and expressions, their fashion and idiosyncrasies, and their use of Spanish, French, and other dialects she had never heard before. She could overhear everything from stirring speeches by Harlem street preachers to neighborhood gossip about well-known Black Harlemites like Dillard "Red" Morrison, notorious 1940s narcotics dealer, and Adam Clayton Powell Jr., New York City's first Black city council member and later congressional leader.[6]

And like other Southern newcomers, Eleanor learned how to move and act like a New Yorker. "To quicken [her] steps, walk faster, hold [her] head up and [her] back stiff and straight, not waving to everyone whose eyes [she] met but instead acting like she, too had already seen and heard it all."[7] The sooner she adopted Northern mannerisms, the sooner she'd fit in. And her new Northern neighbors were skilled instructors, offering master classes on street protocols, hustling, and navigating Jim Crow North.[8]

For all of New York's many wonders, the city was far from what some Southern migrants had imagined. Eleanor never expected to see dilapidated "greasy and rundown" apartment buildings in what Black journalist Roi Ottley called "filthy and evil smelling littered crowded streets" or hear about "helpless Black children suffering from incest and rat bites."[9] Equally startling to the New York transplant was racial exclusion. Newcomers never dreamed of encountering racial segregation in the urban North. Many viewed the urban North as a land of infinite opportunity, a land that was free from segregation, white violence, and the other Southern horrors they had fled. Eleanor and other Southerners quickly discovered that New York, like how Alabama native and civil and human rights leader Rosa Parks would describe 1950s Detroit, Michigan, was the "northern promised land that wasn't," and that racial apartheid was not unique to the American South. In New York, the Louisburg native found no "White Only" or "Colored Only" public signs on water fountains, in restaurants and recreation facilities, or on public transportation. Yet Jim Crow was omnipresent. It was subtle. It was violent. And Jim Crow was inescapable.[10]

Jim Crow was a national problem. Black New Yorkers "faced a regime of racial proscriptions [in the North] that was every bit as deeply entrenched as the southern system of Jim Crow."[11] One Southern migrant reasoned that New York life "was worse than [living] in Mississippi."[12] Racial discrimination was so rampant in Northern spaces that the *New York Amsterdam News* created a 1950s column called "Jim Crow Up North." But the nature of race exclusion in New York and other geographical spaces outside the South was distinct.

Jim Crow North was a complex system of exclusion that was established and maintained by police officers, school board officials, judges, realtors and housing developers, policymakers, and ordinary white urbanites. Northern white politicians, those concerned with a purported culture of poverty, crime waves, and the migration of "transient undesirable Negroes," employed so-called race-neutral city and state policies that upheld segregation and white entitlements. Color-blind policies took shape in the form of strict zoning rules, land-use laws, school segregation, and law and order enforcement. Race discrimination complicated Black city dwellers' demands for livable conditions, decent housing, well-paying employment, quality education, and equitable policing.[13]

Police brutality was a constant source of frustration for Blacks. Because of entrenched systems of inequality and racist police officers,

New York Black communities were over- and under-policed, and not considered worthy of legal protection.[14] The predominately white New York City Police Department (NYPD) brutalized Black New Yorkers. They turned their guns and nightsticks on unarmed Black people, hurled racial epithets at them, raided their homes, and instigated some of the city's most violent riots of the early twentieth century. On August 1, 1943, white officer James Collins arrested thirty-five-year-old laundress Marjorie Polite in the lobby of Harlem's seven-story Braddock Hotel on 126th Street. Polite was apprehended for allegedly disturbing the peace. Witnessing the physical altercation between Collins and Polite, Black World War II soldier Robert Bandy and his mother intervened, demanding that Collins release Polite. Bandy and Collins fought, and Bandy was shot in the arm. Somehow a rumor about a white officer killing a Black soldier spread throughout Harlem and drew crowds of Black residents to the hotel. The false reporting of Bandy's killing, as well as Black New Yorkers' long-standing struggles against city inequality erupted into several days of violence. A horrific incident, the Harlem uprising was one of several racial unrests that occurred in American cities during the smothering summer of 1943.[15]

While inequalities plagued Black New Yorkers' daily lives, Black women migrants like Eleanor were determined to create meaningful lives for themselves and their families.

Eleanor's day-to-day life in mid-twentieth-century New York is shrouded in mystery. She did not leave behind a trail of historical footprints that tracked her movement in the city or revealed her struggles for labor and wage equity, affordable housing, personal happiness, and race, gender, and class equality. Yet existing primary documentation reveals pivotal moments of her life in the Big Apple. Brief episodes of economic hardship, environmental injustice, illness, and family love and loss offer glimpses of Eleanor's interior world. Scenes from Eleanor's life also serve as a window into the public and private lives of many urban working-class and poor Black women, those pursuing personal and familial happiness within the context of municipal inequalities, racialized and gendered oppression, and personal challenges.

For Eleanor and many urban Black women, the pursuit of happiness was a process that was not without emotional labor and cost.[16] Eleanor's broader vision of happiness aligned with working-class Black women's historic quest for full citizenship, bodily autonomy, family security, equitable employment and housing, neighborhood safety, and the longing to have their humanity recognized and accepted. Happiness and pleasure were necessary radical acts of resistance against white patriarchal structures and hierarchies aimed at dehumanizing and devaluing Black women. Imagining Eleanor's pleasure politics, to borrow from historian Robin Kelley, "strip[s] away the various masks [she and other] African Americans [wore] in their daily struggles to negotiate relationships or contest power in public spaces, and [allows scholars to] search for entry into the private world hidden beyond the public gaze."[17] Further, recognizing Eleanor's pursuit of pleasure and happiness is critical to understanding her interior world in the big city and how she may have confronted personal challenges while embracing self-care practices.

Eleanor's happiness was rooted in her ability to financially support and protect her family and a desire to experience love and intimacy. Quotidian moments with loved ones brought Eleanor a sense of happiness, mental strength, and peace of mind. Eleanor and John's partnership was short-lived. Their relationship spanned a few years after the 1945 birth of their only child, Mary Bumpurs. The reason for the demise of Eleanor and John's union is unknown. Perhaps John and his North Carolina wife reconciled. Maybe John did not want to care for another family. Maybe John and Eleanor amicably split. Or perhaps Eleanor ended the affair, wanting no longer to be in a relationship with a married man. Whatever the circumstances for the breakup, the separation resulted in parental abandonment. According to Mary Bumpurs, her father deserted her and her mother, failing to provide financial support for their family. Yet the broken relationship with John did not deter Eleanor from pursuing intimate relationships with other men between 1945 and 1958.[18]

Eleanor did not leave behind evidence detailing her love life or her thoughts about the men in her life. But short- and long-term partnerships outside the institution of marriage produced happy moments for her. Romantic relationships and cohabitations with several male com-panions resulted in the births of two sons and three more daughters: Glenn and James Nelson were born sometime in the late 1940s, and Deborah Bumpurs, Terry Ann Bumpurs, and Keenie Louise Bumpurs were born between 1956 and 1958.[19]

Motherhood was important to Eleanor. As articulated by singer and activist Emma Azalia Hackley, motherhood was "the greatest privilege and responsibility"for Eleanor.[20] Maternal death and loss likely shaped Eleanor's ideas and feelings about motherhood. Losing her mother at a young age, Eleanor desired to give her children all that she never had and all that she ever wanted in a maternal figure: motherly attention, guidance, and love. In many ways, motherhood became a source of happiness and strength for her. "She lived for her children," noted daughter Mary. To the best of her ability, she nurtured and affirmed her children.[21] Mary recalled fond memories of family outings and her mother "playing and joking and dancing" around the house. "We went different places as a family, and she liked to dance with us. She taught us how to do [soul singer James Brown's] mashed potato dance."[22] The children enjoyed their moth-er's impromptu dance lessons; perhaps they found her performance of trendy dances impressive or hilarious. Eleanor's smile lit up the room when she danced. Listening to the mid-twentieth musical sounds of James Brown, Ray Charles, The Supremes, and others soulful Black artists, Eleanor clicked her heels and swung her long arms and legs, and she encouraged her children to dance with her. The family activity of singing and dancing around the apartment demonstrated Eleanor's investment in creating pleasurable episodes for her children. Eleanor's bodily movement also exemplified a sense of joy and release from the daily grind of household duties and motherhood.

Parenting could also be difficult at times. It did not always yield personal satisfaction. The labor and performance of maternal duties could be physically taxing and at times unfulfilling. And mothering, as suggested by writer Nella Larsen's *Passing* character Clare Kendry, could be "the cruellest thing in the world."[23] The day-to-day labor of mothering and self-sacrificing, especially as a single parent, was costly. It denied single mothers like Eleanor the ability to care for themselves, as they were constantly concerned with feeding, sheltering, and clothing their children. Motherhood forfeited visions of self-care practices that promoted physical and emotional well-being. Experiencing the highs and lows of motherhood and single parenthood, Eleanor found pleasure in a childhood chore: cooking.

Cooking was one of the things Eleanor did best. The cultural work of cooking was therapeutic for her. While listening to one of her favorite radio programs such as *Mr. & Mrs. North* or soap opera *Stella Dallas* or humming or singing one of her favorite gospel songs, "Nearer, My God to Thee," she fried fish and chicken, baked peach cobbler and apple pies, and prepared fresh vegetables. As the aroma of buttery biscuits or fried bacon filled the family's Harlem apartment, Eleanor could be transported to Louisburg when her mother, Fannie Belle, and surrogate mother, Laura Belle, were in their respective kitchens talking or singing and preparing turnip greens, salt pork, cornmeal, and more. For many Black women of Eleanor's generation, nostalgic memories about family and food were a source of psychic relief. Personal recollections revived some women's spirits, as well as comforted them during moments of economic uncertainty, family loss, and physical and mental health breakdowns.[24]

Cooking also connected Eleanor to her present. While passing down family recipes and Southern Black culinary practices to her children, the working-class mother used food to express familial care.[25] Cooking was her love language. The Bumpurs children considered her to be a culinary genius. They took pride in their mother's creativity and mastery over food. They appreciated the beautiful mess she made in the kitchen—the countertop covered with seasoning salts, pots and pans of food boiling and sizzling on stove burners, and meats and desserts baking in the oven. From one week to the next, the kitchen countertop was adorned with macaroni and cheese, rolls, candied yams, cabbage, and baked chicken. Smiling and laughing, family members always conversed about "what momma made" and what was the best food on their plate. And they always rushed to the kitchen for second and third helpings.[26]

Reminiscing about her mother's cooking skills, Mary said, "We were poor, but she always fed her children." Eleanor creatively stretched food rations and meals far into the week as the family dined on homemade casseroles, spaghetti, beans, greens and cabbage, rice, and other dishes. Recalling her mother's culinary magic, Mary stated, "Her cooking was so good. No store-bought food which would have been easier and cheaper to feed all seven children. Everything was from scratch. She could make water smell good and she could whip up anything and make it taste good." Eleanor's talent and love of food and cooking were on full display during the holidays. She out-did herself on Thanksgiving and Christmas. Turkey, stuffing, macaroni and cheese, vegetables, and an assortment of cakes and pies decorated the kitchen. Mary recalled, "We had big cooking times for the holidays. We were all together for the holidays. That was a big part of our life"[27]

For Eleanor, cooking was a pleasant and temporary release from the daily grind of single parenthood. But the aromatic smell and delicious taste of Southern-style cuisine could not ease the unspoken frustrations and anxieties that came with motherhood, economic uncertainty, and family heartbreak.

Big dreams for happiness were constant yet fleeting for the Southern migrant. Eleanor dreamed and planned for a better life in New York City for herself and her children to avoid, in the immortal words of Langston Hughes, "drying up like a raisin in the sun, festering like a sore, and sagging like a heavy load."[28] Labor instability, partner separation, and single motherhood deferred Eleanor's chance at happiness again and again. Such ever-present stresses may have also engendered feelings of despair, undermining her ability to care for her children and jeopardizing her mental health.[29]

As a single parent, Eleanor became part of an increasing national phenomenon among working Black women. Caring for all seven of her children in a small Harlem apartment on 110th Street, perhaps without the financial benefit of a partner, Eleanor worked as a domestic worker. She joined the nearly 60 percent of Black women across the nation entering domestic service during the 1950s.[30] No stranger to the arduous labor of household work, Eleanor, like many working-class Black women of her generation, resented backbreaking household labor. Domestic work yielded little pay for long work hours and provided no labor or bodily protections from potential illnesses or abusive employers. Observing the impact of grueling daily labor on her mother's body and on their family, Mary said, "She was always tired. That why we were expected to do chores around the house. She sacrificed for the family."[31] Five days a week, alongside a few girlfriends and fellow domestics, Eleanor cleaned private houses, office buildings, and a few Manhattan hotels. One of those hotels was Manhattan's exclusive Waldorf Astoria Hotel.[32]

Eleanor was a chambermaid at the light-gray forty-seven-story Park Avenue hotel.[33] Donning a black-and-white maid uniform, she scrubbed luxury suites, moved furniture, hung silk and red velvet drapes, and provided guests with fresh white linens and towels. It was a job that guaranteed no fulfillment, economic security, or upward mobility. But working at the midtown hotel had a few perks, including cash tips and celebrity sightings. On any given day a hotel staffer might catch a glimpse of a movie star, radio personality, or someone who graced the pages of *Ebony*, *Jet*, or the *New York Times*. Hotel employees like Eleanor were perhaps excited to share stories about Waldorf guests with family members and friends. Eager listeners would have enjoyed stories about which celebrities were residing and performing at the hotel, and what they looked like in person.

Eleanor would have had plenty of stories to tell. Throughout the 1950s, the Waldorf Astoria bellmen swung the doors open for many luminaries, allowing them entrance into the hotel's massive and majestic lobby. Prominent Black and white politicians, celebrities, and important local community and business leaders hosted dazzling cultural and social events and resided at the city's tallest hotel. In 1951, Black businesswoman Freddye Scarborough Henderson held a dinner and fashion show in the hotel's Starlight Roof, showing attendees, such as political activist Mary McLeod Bethune and Manhattan designer Zelda Wynn Valdes, "five decades of color and fashion." Hollywood legend Marilyn Monroe took up residence in one of the hotel's luxurious three-room suites during the mid-1950s. In April 1955, actress and Academy Award nominee Dorothy Dandridge broke racial barriers at the Waldorf, becoming the first Black artist to stay at the hotel and the first to perform at the hotel's exclusive nightclub: the Empire Room. In May 1956, at the two-year *Brown v. Board of Education* anniversary, civil rights leader Martin Luther King Jr. delivered his "A Realistic Look at Race Relation" speech on the Starlight Roof, reminding his audience of how "old man segregation" lay "on his death bed." And in 1958, the hotel welcomed Ghanaian prime minister Kwame Nkrumah, who would become Ghana's first president.[34]

Sights of world-renowned leaders and celebrities were thrilling to Waldorf employees, but they hardly made up for Eleanor's low pay and dire financial circumstances. As an employee at one of New York City's most opulent hotels, the single mother only earned between seventy-five cents and $1.25 an hour.[35] The average American family income was estimated at $5,105 in 1950; Eleanor and at least 55.7 percent of New York families earned less than $3,500.[36] Living below the poverty line, Eleanor found it difficult to afford rent, utility bills, groceries, and clothes for her family. Real and imagined threats of apartment eviction, and not having enough money for food, transportation, and utilities, were constant.

The Bumpurs household's financial circumstances worsened in the late 1950s. An emergency gallstone surgery at Manhattan's St. Luke's Hospital pushed a forty-something-year-old Eleanor into early retirement, forcing her to depend on Supplemental Security Income (SSI) benefits. For Black women, state and federal assistance was an assorted blend of opportunity and prejudice, possibilities and limitations, and freedom and surveillance.[37] Race, gender, and class politics shaped New York's welfare system and social workers' treatment of welfare recipients. Struggling women requesting and receiving public assistance experienced intrusive regulations, public scrutiny, moral judgment, home inspections, and lack of privacy and respect. Many women were subjected to threats of being cut off from aid, unannounced visits from welfare workers, verbal and physical harassment, and even police arrests while at welfare offices. In 1952, Bronx welfare officials had thirty-eight-year-old Black mother Georgia Stubbs arrested for being "loud and boisterous." Advocating for herself, Stubbs complained about being "pushed around by Welfare Department officials."[38]

Inequalities within the welfare system and the real possibilities of bodily harm, surveillance, and confinement made some women think twice about applying for public assistance. But limited economic and housing options compelled women to seek government assistance.[39] One urban woman turned to welfare "not became I want[ed] to but because conditions and situations forced me on."[40] Extant evidence is less clear on whether SSI benefits were enough to financially sustain the Bumpurs household or if Eleanor received federal assistance for any of her small and adolescent children.[41] Because of the family's economic status, Eleanor's children would have been eligible for federal and state welfare programs including the 1935 Social Security Act's Aid to Dependent Children (ADC). If the Bumpurs were welfare recipients, they joined the hundreds of thousands of poor New Yorkers receiving public assistance during the mid-to-late 1950s.[42]

Despite the family's economic circumstance, the Bumpurs children recognized their mother's resilient effort to care for them. Mary proudly commented that she "raised us to the best of her ability."[43] "Life was not easy for [our] mother who single-handedly made untold sacrifices just to feed and clothes all seven of [us]."[44] And life for Eleanor and her children became even more challenging after a devastating family loss.

Economic instability and debilitating health issues were coupled with heartbreak for Eleanor. She experienced an unthinkable crime when her preteen sons were abducted. Like another urban single Black mother grieving the 1955 lynching of her Chicago teenage son in Mississippi, this transgression shocked Eleanor to her core. It left her inconsolable and her world spiraling out of control. But Northern white hands did not commit this crime. Nor was a brutal system of racial oppression and violence at play.

Sometime in the early-to-mid 1950s, Glenn and James Nelson, Eleanor's only sons, were allegedly abducted by Mr. Nelson, Eleanor's former lover. Recalling the last time she saw her brothers, Mary Bumpurs, who was a preteen when her brothers disappeared, stated that the boys' "father arrived at the Bumpurs' home to pick [them] up to stay with him for the weekend as was his custom." Upon leaving with their father, Glenn and James waved goodbye to the family. The boys "never returned to [Eleanor's] custody." Motivations for the father's actions are unknown. Concerns for the children's economic and emotional well-being, resentment over an unrepairable romantic relationship, or the desire to hurt Eleanor could have sparked parental abduction.[45]

Eleanor was determined to locate Glenn and James, pursuing numerous avenues. She contacted family members, friends, and neighbors asking if they had seen or heard from her former lover and sons. No one heard a thing, and nobody saw Mr. Nelson or the children. Desperate for assistance, the single mother, according to a family member, reported Glenn and James's abduction to the NYPD.[46] Eleanor hoped that local authorities, perhaps collaborating with federal officials and employing 1930s and 1950s federal kidnapping legislation including the Lindbergh Law, would assist her in the recovery of her boys, the same way lawmen had done in the 1956 kidnapping of another New York child. On July 4, taxi dispatcher Angelo LaMarca snatched five-week-old Peter Weinberger from his family's Long Island home. Under the Lindbergh Law, a statute allowing federal agents to pursue kidnappers across state lines, FBI agents became involved in the Weinberger case days after the kidnapping. However, federal assistance was too late for the young victim. LaMarca had murdered the baby.[47]

Evidence of a police investigation into Glenn and James's kidnapping does not exist. It's unclear if police conducted neighborhood searches, interviewed family members, or released teletype notices of Mr. Nelson and the boys. Like any mother, Eleanor hoped that police would locate her children. But she may not have expected much from police. Class politics and racial stereotypes about African Americans limited police assistance. Black New Yorkers were seldom viewed as victims of crime. Instead, police regarded them as perpetrators of urban crime—as dangerous rather than endangered. Presumptive criminality forfeited Blacks' right to legal protections. Despite Eleanor's best efforts, she never laid eyes on her sons again.[48]

Losing the boys rocked the Bumpurs household. Eleanor's grief and suffering was manifested in both visible and invisible scars. New

York schoolteacher Tiffany Rubin, whose ex-partner, a South Korean national, kidnapped their only child and fled to South Korea in 2008, articulates many parents' thoughts about their missing children. "It's like the worst feeling I could ever imagine a person feeling. It's like you're accepting a loss that a loved one has passed away, but they haven't died."[49] Not knowing the whereabouts of her sons tortured Eleanor, sending her into a tailspin of despair and misery.[50] She cried for days, months, and probably even years. Eleanor hoped and prayed for the return of James and Glenn, expressing often to family members how much she missed and loved them.[51] Maternal grief was compounded by material artifacts. Memories of the boys lingered in the Bumpurs home. Their clothes, toys, and schoolbooks were everywhere, small reminders of what was gone and suddenly snatched away from Eleanor and the rest of the family.

Glenn and James's abduction haunted Eleanor. Like enslaved women who continuously lost their children at slave auctions or to deadly illnesses and even murder, Eleanor existed, for short and long periods of time, in a state of mourning.[52] Losing her boys also imaginably generated unexpected emotions for the now mother of five. Eleanor lived in a continual state of fear, worrying about her daughters' well-being around strangers and perhaps even around close acquaintances.[53]

***

Amid heartbreaking family separation Eleanor moved through the world the best way she could. She clung to family and friends, and she kept busy. On the weekends, she occasionally hung out with friends who lived in New York City Housing Authority's James Weldon Johnson Houses in East Harlem. She juggled the daily demands of motherhood and household labor and management. She cooked and cleaned. And she made sure her adolescent daughters, Mary, Deborah, Terry Ann, and Keenie, attended junior high or high school. Education was important to Eleanor, especially as someone whose education was cut short because of her family's economic circumstances. Mary recalls her "mother made us go to school. We went to school, acknowledged the 12 years that the system gives you."[54] Her oldest daughter,

Fannie Mae, who may have migrated from North Carolina to New York sometime in the late 1950s or early 1960s, was married and raising her children in Manhattan. Eleanor, especially after losing her sons, was determined to keep her youngest daughters safe, even if it meant restricting and monitoring their behavior, social activities, and city travels. "She didn't trust us being in the streets, especially being girls," noted Mary.[55] A protective Eleanor questioned her daughters' whereabouts and social circles and enforced nightly curfews. Living in 1960s and 1970s New York City, Eleanor, like many Black parents, had good reason to worry about her children's safety.

Mid-twentieth century New Yorkers' fears of crime were woven into the fabric of city life.[56] The city's homicide rate slowly rose during the post–World War II era, increasing from 4.0 homicides per 100,000 inhabitants in the early 1950s to 7.6 per 100,000 in the early 1960s, and 9.6 per 100,000 by 1968.[57] Throughout the mid-1960s, New Yorkers witnessed an increase in violent crimes. Felonies were up from 8,554 in 1965 to 13,679 in 1966; in those same years, felonious assaults were up from 791 to 1,143, and rapes went from 104 to 127.[58] Gender and age did not shield girls and women from becoming victims of crime. The news media covered the horrific stories of New York rape and murder victims, including the 1960s killings of twenty-eight-year-old white Kitty Genovese and three African American girls—eight-year-old Mary Winters, sixteen-year-old Malvena Braithwaite, and twenty-three-year-old Louise Bynoe.[59] These were the kind of crime stories that kept parents awake at night.

Police violence was another alarming issue for parents. Commenting on the NYPD in his 1963 classic work *The Fire Next Door*, James Baldwin wrote: "It was absolutely clear that the police would whip you and take you in as long as they could get away with it."[60] City streets, subway cars, police vehicles and precincts, and Blacks' homes were sites of violation, abuse, and even murder. In July 1964, two weeks after President Lyndon Johnson's signing of the 1964 Civil Rights Act, off-duty police Lieutenant Thomas Gilligan fatally shot fifteen-year-old Black student James Powell in broad daylight on 76th Street. Powell's killing ignited protests in Central Harlem and Bedford-Stuyvesant for six days. The unrest became part of a series of urban uprisings that swept the nation during the long, hot summer of 1964.[61]

Police assaults and "trigger happy policing," as soul singer Marvin Gaye sang in his evocative 1971 "Inner City Blues," continued well into the 1970s, a decade known in New York City for economic austerity, inflation, unemployment, and the enactment of harsh narcotics statutes. Local drug and anti-crime measures, including New York governor Nelson Rockefeller's 1973 drug laws and "no knock" and "stop-and-frisk" bills, made Black and Latinx men, women, and even children prime targets for excessive and deadly police force.[62] Presumptive criminality—coupled with racialized constructions of Black youth and police surveillance of public spaces—forfeited children's rights to be seen as young and innocent and to occupy and enjoy public spaces and amusements.[63]

On January 27, 1973, Canarsie High School student Rita Lloyd, according to Brooklyn grassroots organization Survival Action Committee, became a "victim of a historically callous police force." Plainclothes officer Robert Milano fatally shot Lloyd in the chest after she and a friend allegedly pointed a sawed-off shotgun at Milano's head.[64] On September 15, 1974, a police bullet struck fourteen-year-old Brownsville, Brooklyn resident Claude Reese in the head as he prepared for a birthday party. The officer believed Reese was committing a robbery and holding a gun. And tragically on Thanksgiving Day in 1976, a police officer, responding to a report of a man with gun, shot fifteen-year-old Brooklyn ninth grader and Cypress Hills public housing projects tenant Randolph Evans in the head at point-blank range.[65]

No doubt, police brutality troubled Eleanor. Migrating to Brooklyn during the 1970s with her teenage daughters, she was surely disturbed by the horrific police killings of Brooklyn teenagers. As local media reported on the police shooting of Black teens, Black mothers like Eleanor worried about their daughters encountering abusive officers. Sadly, they came to understood that age and gender would not shield their children from police abuse—a painful reality that persists today. Girls, like boys, experienced the pain and humiliation of being stopped, harassed, and even beaten by police while walking to neighborhood stores, going to school, traveling on mass transportation, or hanging out with friends.

———

In 1973, the Bumpurs family had their own encounter with the NYPD. On November 1, nearly thirty years after her release from a North Carolina prison, an unemployed fifty-five-year-old Eleanor, along with seventeen-year-old daughter Deborah Bumpurs, came face-to-face with the legal system. Both mother and daughter were arrested in East New York City for menacing, possession of a dangerous weapon, and possession of an unregistered firearm (J. C. Higgins model 101.13). Like her 1942 North Carolina arrest and conviction, the details surrounding the 1973 arrests of mother and daughter are unavailable to the public. When questioned about her mother's criminal history by New York reporters during the 1980s, Mary indicated that the 1973 arrest stemmed from a conflict between her mother and a neighbor. Residing in a rented home on Schenck Avenue in East New York (Brooklyn), Eleanor, according to the police report, threatened "the neighbor or landlord with an empty rifle." Speaking about why Eleanor had the weapon, Mary said, "My mother had that rifle. Never once was there a bullet in it. [She used it] only to scare people away." Mary also indicated that the weapon was needed for neighborhood protection. "If you lived where we've lived, you'd have some protection in your apartment, too."[66] Many New Yorkers including women safeguarded themselves from potential city crime, carrying a variety of self-defense tools, including guns, knives, ball-peen hammers, and pepper spray. "Given that [the city] has active criminals who make their living committing crimes, people are arming themselves," noted Harlem community activist Rev. Oberia Dempsey.[67]

The city's shrinking police force compelled many New Yorkers to shield themselves from urban dangers. New York City's 1970s fiscal crisis had resulted in massive police layoffs. In 1975, mayor Abraham Beame dismissed 5,034 officers, detectives, lieutenants, and commanders from the NYPD's over thirty-thousand-member police force.[68] With fewer cops on the streets, the number of city arrests fell 20 percent between 1975 and 1979; arrests for misdemeanors and violations decreased by 27 percent and 75 percent, respectively. Police drug divisions halted operations on the weekends, and investigations of serious crime, like homicide and rape, became selective.[69]

One wonders what Eleanor thought when police arrived at her doorstep. Did her mind drift back to the day when 1940s Southern lawmen arrested her? Did she think one of her worst fears was happening to her again, losing her freedom and being separated from her family? What would happen to Deborah? And how would police treat mother and daughter? Police presence in Black homes came with unpredictable encounters. Women, many half-heartedly viewing the NYPD as protectors from violence, hardly knew what to expect when officers arrived at their doorsteps. Acknowledging and witnessing firsthand the NYPD's role in agitating racial and sexual violence against urban Black New Yorkers, many wondered whether they would be treated as victims or assailants—whether they would be assisted or assaulted. "There is a pervasive fear that every black person in this city feels when they encounter a police officer. Fear that they will be the next victim of police violence and abuse solely because they are Black," said Queens lawyer and NAACP activist Laura D. Blackburne.[70]

For threatening her neighbor, Eleanor was detained at what would become during the 1980s the notoriously corrupt 75th Brooklyn (East New York) police precinct.[71] She later stood before a Brooklyn judge, pleading guilty to all charges. Eleanor's plea of guilt was not uncommon. At the time, it was typical for working-class and poor defendants to take plea deals in New York City and around the country. In the early 1970s, an estimated 90 percent of all US convictions were by defendants' pleas of guilt; this still remains true today. In the 2010s, an estimated 90 to 95 percent of federal and state court cases were resolved through plea bargaining.[72] A 1971 *New York Times* article suggested that "of about 101,000 defendants found guilty in New York City's misdemeanor courts, more than 98,000 pleaded guilty," making it possible for prosecutors and defense attorneys to decrease their caseloads and avoid lengthy criminal trials.[73] It's unknown whether Eleanor's admission of guilt was sincere or whether she was pressured by a prosecutor or public defender into accepting a plea bargain under the threat of being charged with more serious crimes and with the promise of no jail time. Avoiding jail would have been important to Eleanor. She was a single mother with several minor children at home.

Eleanor was sentenced to a conditional discharge. She served no time in jail, but she still had to comply with court-ordered mandates.[74] Because Eleanor was charged with several misdemeanors, her conditional discharge lasted between one and three years. For those years, the court could, as a condition of the sentence, require Eleanor to pay a fine, make restitution to plaintiffs, perform community service, and stay out of legal trouble. Failure to comply with legal mandates would jeopardize her freedom, resulting in imprisonment at one of several New York penal institutions, including the Bronx's Rikers Island and Westchester County's Bedford Hills Correctional Facility for Women. Eleanor certainly did not want to go back to prison; nor did she want to be separated from her family. She complied with court mandates.

Eleanor's arrest coincided with an important life decision. The sixty-something-year-old mother left Brooklyn, relocating to the Bronx during the mid-to-late 1970s. Eleanor became part of the Bronx's rapidly increasing Black and Latinx communities. Home to Yankee Stadium, the Bronx Zoo, New York Botanical Garden, New York University (now the site of Bronx Community College), and Fordham University, the Bronx accounted for 1,471,701 million residents in 1970. By 1980, there were 1,168,972 residents living in the South Bronx, Hunts Point, Morrisania, and other Bronx neighborhoods.[75] In her new residence, Eleanor witnessed the impact of the city's fiscal crisis on the borough. On the brink of bankruptcy, municipal leaders imposed a program of economic austerity, resulting in budget cuts, limited services, transit fare hikes, massive unemployment, and the end of tuition-free courses at the City University of New York.

Economic austerity took a heavy toll on the Bronx. Landlord arson, industrial relocation, housing abandonment, middle-class flight, and withdrawal of social services and youth programs left an already economically struggling borough in ruins.[76] For national and local politicians, media outlets, and emerging artists—such as hip-hop musician Grandmaster Flash and the Furious Five and filmmaker Daniel Petrie—the Bronx became a "national symbol of urban decline and deterioration" and ecological disinvestment. One journalist noted, "If you walked through areas of the South Bronx, you would be reminded of bombed out Europe of World War II. The devastation is rampant, spreading like a cancer. Row after row, street after street, neighborhood after neighborhood, naked, boarded up buildings stand gutted by fires, fires that destroy people and lives, not to mention property."[77]

Eleanor would have been keenly aware of the Bronx's national reputation and imageries and socioeconomic problems. Local newspapers like the *New York Daily News* and nightly news captured how years of municipal disinvestment and abandonment impacted the borough. And while traveling on Bronx streets to shop or run errands she couldn't help but notice abandoned and burned-out buildings, uncollected garbage, padlocked firehouses and daycare centers, and as another Bronx resident observed, "the sight of [happy] children playing in ragged clothes [in] debris strewn lots that once housed families."[78] Yet Eleanor, like others flocking to the borough, perhaps saw promise in living in what some scholars called "America's inner city" and, what Nuyorican poet Sandra Maria Esteves referred to as potential "amidst hills of desolate buildings and rows of despair."[79] There were possibilities living in the borough that would a few years later birth rap music, breakdancing, and graffiti art, prompting an international cultural movement in what would affectionately be called the "Boogie Down Bronx."

Relocation to the northern borough was about family. Some of Eleanor's adult daughters resided in various sections of the Bronx with their children. Deborah and her family lived on Macombs Road a few streets from the #4 train on Jerome Avenue. Mary and her three children lived on University Avenue, a short distance from the City University of New York's Bronx Community College. It is likely that Eleanor lived with one of her daughters. Some of Eleanor's daughters were pleased with her move to the Bronx. For Mary, it was convenient for her to have her mother closer. She would not have to embark on the hour-long subway ride from the Bronx to Brooklyn, making daily visits much easier. And living in the same borough made it possible for Deborah, Mary, and other family members to care for an aging Eleanor, especially as her physical and mental health began to deteriorate.

Eleanor may have started exhibiting signs of declining mental health in the mid-1970s. Her inability to decipher reality from non-reality was evident during a conversation with Mary. Eleanor informed her daughter that she saw "her dead brothers [from Louisburg] walking through the walls." Eleanor's admission startled Mary, who had never seen her mother experience delusions before. "I knew that was not normal [but] the best I could do was get her to doctors."[80]

Amid legal mandates and relocation to the Bronx, Eleanor cycled in and out of crumbling mental health facilities during the mid to late 1970s.

New York psychiatric institutions underwent massive changes during the 1970s. City budget cuts, urban officials' efforts to reduce mental health patient numbers, and post–World War II medical professionals' ideas about psychiatric care resulted in inadequate mental health treatment and the deinstitutionalization of mental health facilities. Additionally, a series of state and federal laws contributed to decreasing populations in mental health hospitals. In the 1975 landmark mental health decision *O'Connor v. Donaldson*, the Supreme Court ruled that "a state cannot constitutionally confine, without more, a nondangerous individual who is capable of surviving safely in freedom by himself or with help of willing and responsible family members or friends."[81] In 1978, New York State enacted a new Mental Hygiene Law, permitting mental health facilities to hospitalize patients who were considered a danger to themselves or others. Consequently, city mental health institutions raised admission standards, admitting primarily severely violent and incapacitated patients.[82] "We've had to turn away many terribly sick people. Instead of being able to admit the most treatable people, we've had to save the beds for the most violent and disturbed," noted one mental health professional.[83] Between the 1960s and the late 1970s, the inpatient population of New York State psychiatric hospitals plummeted from 78,000 to 26,000 due to release, reduced admissions, and deaths. Between 1974 and 1979, psychiatric facilities discharged over 83,000 adult patients to old-age homes, single-room occupancy hotels, and shelters. And some mental health patients were dumped on city streets. They were left to face the dangers of homelessness, street life, and the NYPD.[84]

Lacking financial resources and healthcare options, the Bumpurs family, perhaps out of desperation, admitted their mother to several Bronx psychiatric hospitals during the mid to late 1970s. Eleanor received eight years of psychiatric treatment at the Bronx Psychiatric Ward (now the Bronx State Hospital) including one commitment, two stays in the Bronx's Lincoln Hospital's psychiatric ward, and at least seven years of referrals to Lincoln Hospital's outpatient mental health clinic.[85] Much of what the public knows about Eleanor's mental health condition derived from 1980s investigative reports conducted by the *New York Daily News*. Due to the absence of the Health Insurance Portability and Accountability Act (HIPPA) and other 1990s state and federal regulations prohibiting public access to individuals' medical health records, *Daily News* journalists secured access to Eleanor's records from mental health treatment providers. Although sharing patient information was permitted in the 1980s, journalists and medical providers violated Eleanor's and her family's privacy. Data sharing and public dissemination of sensitive health records denied the Bumpurs family control and a voice over the disclosure of such documents.[86] Newspaper stories about Eleanor's private medical condition would have a chilling effect on the Bumpurs family. They would have front-row seats to witness how police and city officials used medical histories to villainize and criminalize their mother.

In October 1976, a fifty-eight-year-old Eleanor was hospitalized at Bronx Psychiatric Ward, a mental health facility established in 1955 with over seven hundred beds and known for patient overcrowding, neglect, and poor conditions. At the time the facility was one of thirty-four New York State public hospitals treating mental illness, and it was also known for criminality.[87] According to a 1975 city report, "Burglaries, muggings, assaults, threats and other crimes against patients occurred with regularity in an atmosphere in which the criminally insane roamed the halls with little control and security and patients often left the hospital almost at will."[88] Limited patient supervision contributed to several resident suicides. In August 1976, hospital personnel discovered fifteen-year-old Luis Echevarria hanging in his room.[89]

Excerpts from medical records claimed that Eleanor was "violent," "extremely agitated and aggressive," and a danger to her adult children. She was admitted to the hospital because she "menaced her children with a knife," using the sharp object "to cut evil." Family members informed hospital staffers that their mother "started acting bizarrely, took a knife and [left the apartment and] disappeared for two days. When she reappeared, she stated that she was on a mission to kill her eldest daughter," which may have referred to Fannie Mae Hayes Baker. "She then reportedly slashed her daughter's hand with the knife." While at the hospital, medical staffers claimed that Eleanor "refused to admit that the people who brought her to the hospital are members of her family." She was treated for acute psychosis for two months.[90]

In March 1977, Eleanor was hospitalized at the Bronx facility for a second time.[91] The reason for admittance was alleged family violence. This time "one of Eleanor's daughters" (Fannie Mae) called the NYPD, claiming that her mother "was walking around with a knife—slashing at the air and threatening her [daughters]. She almost cut one of her children." Entitled to full access to city resources and agencies like the NYPD, many urban Black women phoned the police when they needed assistance with family disputes and crises, even though they were wary of the NYPD. Turning to the police for support was complicated for women, yet some like Fannie Mae wanted officers to help them address household emergencies and obtain scant city services, including medical care. The NYPD and family members brought Eleanor to the Bronx Psychiatric Ward without incident— this would not be the case for some New Yorkers suffering a mental health emergency. Their encounters with police would be tragic, ending in incarceration or death.[92]

While these episodes were documented in Eleanor's mental health file, the Bumpurs family refuted claims of maternal violence. "She wasn't perfect but she would never threaten or harm the family."[93] Referring to one of the 1970s incidents, daughter Mary Bumpurs reasoned that her older sister Fannie Mae called the police and concocted the knife and hand-stabbing story to get her mother admitted to the hospital as a mental patient.

Fabrication of Eleanor's violent behavior revealed the family's concerns about their mother's mental and emotional well-being. The falsehood, which carried long-term consequences for Eleanor, also underscored the daughters' desperate attempt to secure medical treatment for their mother. According to Mary, "If you're trying to get help from someone, especially when you see something is wrong, you just don't walk in. There's many times, as we went to the hospital before trying to get help for her, they were saying it was a normal thing. So it [the manufactured story] was the way to get her into the hospital. You got to say she's attempting to do something to someone otherwise she wouldn't have got no help."[94] For some working-class and poor New York families, extracting racist tropes and images of Black criminality, violence, and madness was a strategic way of navigating mental health admission policies and structural barriers that blocked the poor from receiving adequate care.

The Bumpurs children were undoubtedly concerned with their mother's mental health. The daughters watched—to borrow from Black Power leader Malcolm X's reflection on his own mother's (Louise Little) mental health struggles—their "anchor giving way." At times, it seemed like Eleanor was waning before their eyes. Her mental health, like Louise's, "was something terrible that you couldn't get your hands on, yet you couldn't get away from it."[95] The Bumpurs siblings painfully observed their mother's shifting moods, delusions, expressions of sadness, and perhaps even madness.

Coping with their mother's mental health issues was not easy for the daughters. Eleanor's fluctuating behavior and temperament meant unpredictable days for the family. Would Eleanor display signs of sadness or agitation? Would she reveal seeing a deceased relative? Would they have to hospitalize her, or worse, call the police for assistance? But no matter Eleanor's mood, her children did not waver. While starting and caring for their own families and making plans for their futures, the adult daughters made their mother's health and daily care a priority.

With limited medical resources and assistance, Eleanor's daughters did the best they could for their mother, pursuing any treatment they could. Mary recalled, "My mother continued to hallucinate even though she was place[d] on [antipsychotic] medications" such as Thorazine. Approved by the US Food and Drug Administration in 1954, Thorazine, the brand name for chlorpromazine, treated individuals diagnosed with psychotic disorders, schizophrenia, bipolar disorder, hallucinations, and aggressive behavior. When ingesting Thorazine, some mental health patients experienced less nervousness, aggression, and decreased hallucinations. At the same time, the antipsychotic drug had varying side effects, including drowsiness, body tremors, weight gain, dry mouth, tiredness, nausea, constipation, and sleeplessness.[96] Observing the drug's unpredictable effects on their aging mother was difficult for the daughters. But "the best [the family] could do [given limited options] was to make sure she took her medication and get her to the doctor. Because [we] knew that wasn't a normal thing for someone to say they saw someone coming through the walls," said Mary.[97]

The Bumpurs daughters never abandoned their mother, embarking with her on a long journey toward recovery. They became her anchor and lighthouse. They lovingly stood by her side as she battled her illness. This meant spending time with Eleanor, listening without passing judgment to her talk and maybe even rant, and making sure her living necessities were met. Most crucial to their mother's daily life and emotional well-being were patience and compassion.

CHAPTER 3

LIFE AT SEDGWICK HOUSES

At times it was horrible living at 65 Featherbed Lane. The privately owned five-story University Heights Bronx brick apartment building was in severe disrepair, causing enduring injuries, gratuitous harm, and premature death. Hallways and stairwells were sometimes dirty. Wall paint was cracking and peeling. Vermin problems were constant. The boiler was frequently broken. During the early 1980s, building owner Julius Zuckerman of Julius Holdings, Inc., poorly maintained the living spaces, citing that the building's low-income Black and Latinx tenants "who do not pay [the less than $300 per month] rent should not expect landlords to reach into their pockets" to do repairs. And to make matters worse, rent-paying tenants, including Eleanor and her twenty-four-year-old daughter Deborah, braved severe winter months without heat or hot water.[1]

The winter of 1981 was particularly brutal for 65 Featherbed Lane residents and other New Yorkers. The first few days after New Year's Eve brought frigid conditions to the city. New Yorkers "shivered through an unrelenting cold spell," as one local newspaper described the Arctic pall. Record low temperatures dipped 20 degrees below zero and felt colder with gusting winds. Snowy roads caused car accidents, school closures, transportation delays, and even sickness and death. Wearing their warmest coats, boots, hats, and gloves, many New Yorkers arrived at Bronx Lebanon Hospital, Harlem Hospital, and other city hospitals suffering from hypothermia, frostbite, flu, bruises, and fractures from cold exposure and falls on slippery streets. Because the windchill factor made it feel like 30 degrees below in various parts of New York, the National Weather Service issued

frostbite alerts, advising state residents from Syracuse to Manhattan
to cover their faces and hands. It was a harsh winter for the city, but
for the residents of 65 Featherbed Lane it was unbearable.[2]

Frigid apartment temperatures compelled Eleanor and other Featherbed Lane occupants to stay warm however they could manage.
Tenants used portable electric heaters, boiled water on stovetops,
and opened oven doors to heat up their apartments—all fire hazards.
Families drank hot water and piled into beds to stay warm at night,
wearing coats, hats, and gloves indoors. On Christmas Day 1980,
children wore hooded jackets and "sat bundled up in blankets and
huddled against oven doors" while playing with their new toys. "It's
like being outside in here. We have the stove on all day and night,"
said one resident. Sixty-five Featherbed Lane was so cold that "residents [have] a free ice-skating rink. It's in the lobby of their tenement
building. Occupants of the building must slide across a one-inch-deep
sheet of ice to climb icy steps that lead to their apartments."[3] According to tenants, the ice formed "because we had no heat in the building
since last October."[4] Months without heat and hot water became a
life-threatening issue.

The unheated building was a deathtrap. On January 20, the building superintendent and police found the frozen body of forty-seven-
year-old Jessie Smalls. A neighbor of Eleanor's, Smalls was discovered
encased in ice on her ice-covered kitchen floor. The ice had formed
after a water pipe burst, sending water flowing onto the floor. She
likely was knocked unconscious after falling and hitting her head. To
remove her body, police chopped her out of the ice. One officer reported that "her walls were covered with ice. It was colder inside her
apartment than it was outside." Smalls's corpse was so cold that medical examiners could not perform an immediate autopsy. A spokesman for the medical examiner's office said, "She cold, too frozen."[5]

Smalls's death shocked New Yorkers. South Bronx community activist Fr. John Flynn of St. Francis of Assisi offered poignant remarks
about Smalls's death and living conditions, highlighting a system of
national abandonment of the poor. In a 1981 *National Catholic Review* article, the lanky, gray-haired, and black glasses–wearing Flynn,
known to many borough residents as the "People's Priest," wrote:

"Jessie was hostage to a landlord who had not given heat to [95 Featherbed Lane tenants] since Thanksgiving; hostage to a city government which despite hundreds of calls from tenants didn't respond to restore heat; hostage to poverty and a national neglect of the poor that kept her from being able to move from her freezing apartment."[6]

With their lives endangered, Featherbed Lane tenants frequently complained about deplorable building conditions. Their testimonies and grievances countered political rhetoric and national and local news stories that suggested underprivileged African American and Latinx New Yorkers were indifferent about their living conditions and responsible for deteriorating neighborhoods. This was far from the truth. Featherbed Lane residents joined New Yorkers' long-standing fight against inadequate housing. City dwellers, like those living in Soundview's Boulevard Towers in the Bronx, withheld rent money from unscrupulous landlords. In 1981, nearly three hundred families staged an eight-month rent strike, demanding repairs for windows, washers and dryers, stairwells and hallways, and water-damaged apartments. Boulevard Towers tenants placed an estimated $100,000 into an escrow bank account until housing management met their demands.[7] Throughout the city, other renters appeared in housing courts ready to verbally spar with building owners. And some sent complaint letters to elected officials. In a 1977 letter to New York senator Daniel Patrick Moynihan, author of the controversial 1965 "Moynihan Report," leaders of the Lillian Wald Tenants Association wrote of needing "a new elevator and new kitchens and general improvements" at the Lillian Wald Houses in Manhattan's Lower East Side.[8]

Featherbed Lane tenants like forty-five-year-old Thomas Canty informed city workers about substandard buildings. "Every [day] and other week" for several months, Canty, who'd lived in the building for seven years, called the city's Heat Complaint Bureau about cold radiators, the broken boiler, and lack of heat and hot water. He was just one of nearly seventy thousand New Yorkers who called that month hoping to get assistance.[9] Countless complaint calls from Canty and other Featherbed Lane tenants resulted in the city dispatching an inspector to the building. Shocked by building conditions and sympathetic to the tenants' sufferings, the inspector assured residents that the city would fix the boiler and send heating oil. Tenants' dreams of warm showers and baths and not wearing winter clothes to bed were soon dashed. According to Canty, the city "sent the oil, but no one fixed the boiler. Now, we have 2,000 gallons of oil that can't be burned because the boiler is still broken, and our apartments are still freezing."[10]

Featherbed Lane residents were not only concerned about cold indoor temperatures. They faced other environmental hazards. Bronxites lived in fear of losing household items, everything they owned and cared about, and even their lives to a citywide problem: fires. City fires endangered the lives of working-class and poor New Yorkers. Often organized and set by large-scale arson rings involving greedy landlords, insurance adjusters, and unemployed neighborhood youth trying to earn quick cash, fires in commercial and residential properties and in abandoned buildings plagued the city during the 1970s and 1980s. Fires obliterated New York's built environment, leaving already underserved neighborhoods in rubble and ashes. New York City experienced 151,079 fires in 1976, 114,370 in 1979, and 127,876 in 1980. Between the mid-1960s and 1970s, the Bronx lost approximately 43,000 housing units, and between 1970 and 1981 it lost at least 108,000 dwelling units.[11] City fires destroyed the lives of borough residents. Smoke inhalation and blazing infernos injured and claimed the lives of countless Bronxites including twenty-five partygoers at the Puerto Rican Social Club in 1976, four adults and two children in a South Bronx family home in 1978, and the husband and two daughters of Bedford Park resident Maggie Cruz in 1981. "My whole life has become empty," Cruz tearfully told reporters. "I've lost everything."[12]

Some Featherbed Lane tenants never felt safe in their homes. They "live[d] in constant threat of fire," said Eleanor's daughter Deborah, who experienced several fires while living at 65 Featherbed Lane. "There have been three fires in [my] wing of the building during the last three years." According to a 1979 US Senate investigation, fire survivors like Deborah suffered from "a history of three, four, or more burnouts [fires], each of them accompanied by fright, dislocation, and related financial stress."[13] Sadly, the federal report was correct.

Another fire struck 65 Featherbed Lane a few days after New Year's Day in 1981. Families had just come off the heels of celebrating Christmas. They happily opened gifts, cooked big holiday dinners, and shared their New Year's resolutions with family and friends. Many prayed that 1981 would bring family stability and happiness, improved financial circumstances, and well-heated apartments. New Year wishes vanished with the apartment building's worst fire.

Around 2:14 a.m. on January 4, a kitchen fire in a vacant third-floor apartment quickly traveled through one wing of the building. A blaze and heavy smoke curling under apartment doors woke Eleanor, her daughter Deborah, and four-month-old granddaughter as well as other tenants. "Fire! Fire!" "Help!" "Let's go," yelled frightened and disoriented residents. "I thank the Lord for having that smoke woke us up. I thank Him for sparing my children," said one distraught resident. With only the clothes on their backs, over thirty tenants, including small children and older adults, fled the inferno into icy subzero temperatures. "Winds and bitter cold greeted [Eleanor and her family] as they [quickly] fled the burning building." Standing in the cold was excruciating for an arthritic Eleanor. Her body lost sensation. Fingers, arms, feet, and legs mushroomed and stiffened up; muscle spasms constrained her movement, making it difficult for her to quickly move out of harm's way. Despite such piercing physical pain, Eleanor was still grateful. Nobody perished in the fire. All tenants made it out of the building, and like other fire survivors, Eleanor thought: "Thank God I'm living."[14]

Speaking to a local reporter about the fire and being forced into freezing weather, Eleanor said she "hated to stand in the [cold] weather watching the apartment burn. I was shaking so bad I liked to went down to the ground. [All I want] is a warm place to lay my head down at night."[15]

Eleanor's musings about the apartment fire were brief yet powerful. She echoed working-class Black women's long-held visions and demands for livable housing conditions. Whether in housing courts, correspondences to elected officials, letters to newspaper editors, or tenants' association meetings, long-suffering women were transparent about the structural and environmental inequalities and conditions that prevented them from feeling safe in their homes. That included no roaches, water bugs, or "slimy, long, stout and fearless rats."[16] No fires, unheated apartments, windows without bars, or dirty hallways. No lead exposure or poisoning. No peeling paint and falling plaster. No more disrespect and inhumane treatment. And no callous landlords and public housing officials who ignored women's pleas for decent and improved housing. "Under these conditions nobody can live. We are afraid to go to sleep at night. It's terrible," noted one working-class Brooklyn mother.[17] A sixty-five-year-old disabled Bedford-Stuyvesant woman, whose family was reduced to burying human waste in their backyard because of a malfunctioning toilet, believed that "no human beings should have to live like this. The landlord takes our money and never fixes anything."[18] Women desired to inhabit domestic spaces that were well-maintained and affordable and ensured comfort, protection, and survival. They believed they deserved nothing less. Livable housing conditions were not a privilege; they were a right. On the night of the fire, Eleanor's hope for merely having a roof over her head collapsed.

Eleanor lost much in the fire. Soot deposits ruined clothes. Newly unwrapped Christmas gifts, personal identification cards and records, and medications were destroyed. Irreplaceable family mementoes were damaged. Her sense of safety was gone. For the first time in her life, she was unhoused. This was a nightmare that she never imagined for herself or her family. Because of the structural damage to part of the building, Eleanor and other fire survivors were temporarily placed in Manhattan's Red Cross Disaster Unit center at 150 Amsterdam Avenue on 66th Street.[19] The loss of personal and valuable property, sorrow for those injured in the fire, and frustration over housing displacement produced moments of sadness and stress for the Bronx grandmother.

Eleanor's feelings of loss and grief were captured in a moving photograph. *Daily News* veteran photojournalist Harry Hamburg photographed several Featherbed Lane fire survivors including Eleanor, Deborah, and her granddaughter. Taken at the Red Cross Disaster Unit center, Hamburg's photograph of Eleanor, which became an iconic image for New York City's anti–police brutality movement of the mid-1980s and 1990s, offered newspaper readers a stunning visual. As photojournalist Dorothea Lange did in her iconic 1936 Farm Security Administration photograph of Florence "Migrant Mother" Owens Thompson, Hamburg captured the facial expression and body language of a somber and worried woman, humanizing the consequences of the fire for readers. In the black-and-white photograph, Eleanor is wearing a light-colored sweater or robe, perhaps a clothing item she grabbed as she fled from the burning building or one given to her by Red Cross staffers. Eleanor's eyes appear weary, as if she had lost days of sleep. Her lips frown and her arms are folded, a frustrating and defensive look, likely due to losing her home and thinking about the process of securing housing.[20] Observing Eleanor's caramel complexion, viewers would notice faint creases on her forehead, perhaps caused by personal tragedies and decades of encounters with poverty, housing and environmental inequalities, and vexation over the fire. Eleanor's haunting countenance compels onlookers to read in her face unknown life stories of suffering.[21]

The photograph may also reflect Eleanor's frustration with the photographer. Did Eleanor grant Hamburg permission to photograph her? Was she aware of the camera? Did she want her feelings of suffering and loss made visible for public consumption? Imaginably, Hamburg randomly photographed Red Cross clients and selected images for publication that placed a human face on city poverty and environmental hazards. Perhaps refusing to participate in Hamburg's imaging of the poor, a tired and worried Eleanor looked away from the camera, giving a nonverbal cue to leave her alone. Posing for Hamburg or any photographer was probably the last thing she wanted to do. She rejected, borrowing from Saidiya Hartman's work on turn of the twentieth-century urban Black women and girls, the "terms of visibility imposed" on her, making it "impossible to force [her] into the grid of naturalist description or the taxonomy of slum pictures."[22]

Eleanor stared elsewhere. No doubt, she had a lot on her mind. Warming her body with a light-colored garment and sipping hot liquids, she perhaps wondered how long she and her family would have to stay in the shelter. Maybe she wondered if her other daughters knew about the fire and knew that she and Deborah were safe. And she perhaps wondered how she, as a poor older woman, was going to rebuild her life.

Starting over would not be easy. Finding someplace to live, getting new furniture and clothes, and feeling comfortable in a new home would take time. But she had done it before. She had relocated to other parts of the city. And she was among the millions of mid-twentieth century Southern Black women who had journeyed to New York City with little to nothing and, through perseverance, had navigated difficult moments. Eleanor could survive another migration. Her journey toward securing affordable and decent housing occurred during a transitional era for New Yorkers and the nation: the 1980s.

Coming into the 1980s, working-class and poor New Yorkers were still feeling the devastating economic effects of New York's previous decade of austerity. The Big Apple was on the brink of bankruptcy during the mid to late 1970s. A fiscal crisis resulted in budget cuts, limited and slashed public services, massive unemployment, and the 1977 election of mayor Edward Koch. Some Black New Yorkers insisted that the working poor's economic conditions worsened under Koch. Reflecting on many residents' economic conditions under Koch's leadership, Manhattan Borough president David Dinkins articulated that New Yorkers "face a crisis that can be best described as a struggle for survival [and they] have never recovered from the ravages of the city's 1970s fiscal crisis."[23] A pro-business leader, Koch wanted to bring the city out of bankruptcy. He was committed to an economic revitalization plan that prioritized the financial interests of real estate developers and affluent New Yorkers. Koch failed to restore social services that were lifelines for poor residents.[24] Intending to control the city budget, Koch lowered the operating costs of city agencies between 1978 and 1983. Koch cut city spending by an estimated $174 million.[25] No doubt, New Yorkers felt the impact of city cuts. The number of New York City residents living below the federal poverty line increased from 1.4 million in 1979 to 1.8 million in 1985.[26]

Federal budget cuts exacerbated New Yorkers' low economic status. In a 1984 *New Pittsburgh Courier* editorial, prominent civil

rights leader Bayard Rustin penned that poor Americans living under President Ronald Reagan's economic policies "got poorer" while
the rich got richer.[27] "The poor have suffered a serious erosion in
their standard of living."[28] Elected to office in 1980, Reagan embraced an economic vision of American prosperity that drastically
shaped working-class and poor Americans' quality of life. Embracing
supply-side and trickle-down economic theories, the Reagan administration promoted unbridled individualism, personal responsibility,
deregulation, and government tax cuts. Known as Reaganomics, the
economic policies enacted by conversative policymakers lowered
tax rates on wealthy earners and reduced funding for welfare programs. Politicians used federal funds to enrich the nation's carceral
state, pouring federal funds into penal institutions, into the largest
law enforcement system in the world, and into police officers' heavy
occupation in communities of color.

Reaganites waged a war on welfare and the millions of Americans
who depended on it. Black women welfare recipients and their families became public enemy number one. Politicians branded them as
domineering matriarchs and "Welfare Queens" and as unemployed
individuals who took advantage of the welfare system by continuously
bearing children and collecting government benefits.[29]

Derisive portrayals of Black women as unemployed freeloaders were
far from the truth. Nationally, African American women made up 48
percent of total Black employment in 1980 and were 50 percent of
the Black workforce by 1990.[30] Navigating race and gender barriers,
college-educated Black women entered professional fields including
social work, nursing, education, and office management. Working-class
women secured employment positions as municipal laborers, retail
clerks, data processors, security guards, and household workers.[31] And
some women entered the city's flourishing informal labor market, hosting pyramid scheme parties, operating nurseries, and peddling coun-
terfeit designer handbags and one of 1980s most popular toys: the
cherub-faced Cabbage Patch doll.[32] Notwithstanding women's vast
labor contributions, Reaganomics loomed over their lives.

With Reagan's evisceration of the welfare state, the nation's most
economically vulnerable citizens witnessed major cuts in food stamps,

Medicaid, Aid to Families with Dependent Children (AFDC), federal education and workplace programs, and other government programs. Under Reagan's 1981 tax and budget plan, AFDC was reduced by at least 11.7 percent and tougher eligibility requirements were implemented; at least four hundred thousand individuals were cut from the AFDC rolls. The food stamp program was reduced by 18.8 percent, and the duration of unemployment insurance was reduced by thirteen weeks. Federal budget cuts resulted in a 15.3 percent poverty rate in 1984.[33] Federal disinvestment from social safety net programs pushed working-poor Black families further into poverty and deepened their distrust of Reagan.

New York Black activists and politicians viewed the administration's policies as a form of economic violence against the poor and disadvantaged older citizens. The nation's first Black woman congressional leader, Shirley Chisholm, criticized Reagan's economic plan, calling it a "disaster for lower income Americans" and saying that "reduced government spending will reduce living standards for millions of Americans."[34] During his 1985 campaign for Manhattan Borough president, City Clerk David Dinkins said that "Reaganomics has dealt an especially harsh blow to poorer older women. Cutbacks in Medicaid, Medicare, food stamps, S[S]I, and subsidized housing— combined with the still rising cost of living—are presenting women who are 65 and over with increasingly unpleasant 'golden years.'"[35]

Working-class Black New Yorkers had much to say about Reaganomics. They opined to reporters their inability to afford rent, utilities, groceries, clothes, and transportation. And they made clear who was suffering under federal budget cuts. "His economic policies were designed to hurt poor Blacks on the welfare list. He is cutting everything. I can't take my kid to the day care because they had to close down," noted Brooklyn mother and welfare recipient Joyce White.[36]

It's unclear if federal officials reduced Eleanor's estimated annual SSI of $4,170 or how Reaganomics impacted her everyday life. Government cuts certainly would have made it difficult for her to afford basic living necessities. Notwithstanding any possible monetary reductions from her monthly check, Eleanor was a victim of anti-welfare and neoconservative rhetoric that considered welfare recipients to be undeserving of federal assistance. But perhaps like many New Yorkers, Eleanor witnessed the devastating impact of trickle-down economic policies on the city's poorest residents. Watching the local news and reading city newspapers, she would have observed how Reaganomics made it nearly impossible for senior citizens and financially struggling families to afford high city costs, especially in moments of high inflation and a global recession. And as a single mother, Eleanor knew all too well how working people and the poor, according to late cultural anthropologist Vertamae Smart-Grosvenor, "went from a rock to a hard place."[37]

On September 21, 1982, one year after the devastating fire and one month after her sixty-fourth birthday, Eleanor secured housing. She moved into the nation's largest public housing system: New York City's Housing Authority's (NYCHA) Sedgwick Houses on University Avenue.[38] This would be Eleanor's first time living in a NYCHA development; the federal government would be her landlord. She would join the over five hundred thousand New Yorkers residing in NYCHA's 293 properties.[39] Built during the late 1940s under New York City mayor William O' Dwyer, the Sedgwick (Village) Houses consisted of seven fourteen-story, rectangular red-brick high rises designed by famed architect and Museum of Modern Art trustee Gordon Bunshaft. Overlooking the two-hinged arch Washington Bridge and Manhattan's Harlem River, the housing development was established for moderate- and low-income families.[40]

Moving into 1551 University Avenue marked Eleanor's independence. Her daughters had taken her into their homes and cared for her, but it was time for a change. The siblings acknowledged their matriarch's desire for autonomy. According to Mary Bumpurs, Eleanor "lived alone. She was of [the] age that she didn't need us to live with her, she could take care of herself. She could bathe herself, clothe herself, and give herself insulin shots [and] she kept up with her clinic appointments."[41]

Eleanor spent the last years of her life at Sedgwick Houses, a community located in the Morris Heights section of the Bronx and less than one mile from the condemned 65 Featherbed Lane apartment building. On a fixed monthly SSI allocation of $340, Eleanor paid $80.85 in monthly NYCHA rent for a one-bedroom apartment, which included utilities and intercom service.[42] The Sedgwick Houses community was perfect for Eleanor. The apartment complex was centrally located near a few grocery stores and bodegas, a taxicab service business, and several neighborhood parks. The community had an active tenants' association and community center. A political force during the early 1980s, the Sedgwick Houses Tenants Association (SHTA) promoted civic engagement and volunteerism and worked toward improving housing conditions for residents. Speaking on behalf of the housing complex's over eight hundred families, SHTA leaders, such as longtime president James "Jim" Murphy and vice president John Harris lobbied for building and apartment repairs, efficient housing managers and workers, and increased police protection.[43] And the SHTA members, like many public housing activists, demanded to have input on housing policies that impacted their daily lives.[44]

Intending to enhance the quality of life for its tenants, the Sedgwick Houses Community Center and its staff offered retirees and older tenants like Eleanor a range of social programs and activities. In between conversations about family and work, building repairs, and neighborhood happenings, tenants enjoyed card games, arts and crafts, and holiday parties; they dined on free or inexpensive snacks and meals. The Housing Authority also sponsored affordable day excursions. Residents enjoyed trips to popular city attractions such as the Bronx's Yankee Stadium, New York Botanical Gardens, City Island, and Orchard Beach, the borough's only public beach located in Pelham Bay Park.[45] For many residents, structured recreation programs and activities were avenues for social interaction, community, friendship building, and enjoyment with neighbors.

Most importantly, Sedgwick Houses' proximity to several Bumpurs family members made it an ideal location for Eleanor. The housing project was two blocks from Mary and her three children's basement apartment on University Avenue. In fact, Mary could see the Sedgwick Houses from her front stoop, a flat stone platform where she sometimes sat and chatted with neighbors, played with her dog, or leisurely watched Bronxites strolling down University Avenue.[46] Mary and her teenage children, LuDean, James, and Kareem, visited Eleanor several times per week. Walking the short two blocks from their home to Sedgwick Houses, they looked forward to visiting their grandmother, greeting her often with the usual hugs and kisses. While consuming home-cooked meals or store-bought snacks and beverages, they conversed about family matters: paying bills, newsworthy and neighborhood occurrences, and their personal lives. How is school going? How's work? And what are we doing and cooking for the holidays and for so-and-so's birthday? Such questions sparked lively and long conversations between Eleanor and her children.[47] The Bumpurs family also attended to Eleanor's physical needs. They made sure her refrigerator was stocked with groceries. They inquired about her health, accompanied her to doctors' appointments, and picked up her prescriptions, perhaps making sure she was taking her medications. They opened and read her mail, did laundry, and performed light housework. And they made sure Eleanor kept up with her rent and other bills. Sometimes family members paid her rent, delivering it to the Sedgwick Houses management office. Other times, Eleanor insisted, "I [can] go down and take care of it [the rent] myself." During those visits, the family made sure Eleanor had everything she needed until the next visit.[48] Living so close to Mary and her children ensured that Eleanor could rely on them if she fell ill.

Several life-threatening medical conditions complicated Eleanor's daily life. Diabetes, arthritis, cataracts, and hypertension made a once-strong body weak and caused a heart attack in the early 1980s. The debilitating effects of her illnesses resulted in chronic pain and bodily restrictions, including limited mobility and stiffness in her arms and hands. Sometimes performing the simplest task, such as combing her hair, was difficult. A neighborhood friend recalled that "she had no feeling in her hands. She couldn't comb her hair and could not hold objects in her hands. She had a lot of [thick] hair. Some kids [and her daughters] did her hair for her," gently detangling, combing, brushing, and braiding her black and gray hair. Even grocery shopping was challenging for Eleanor. Slowly walking past Mary's apartment to the C-Town Supermarket on University Avenue, Eleanor, on many occasions, requested that delivery boys like fifteen-year-old Orlando Alvarez carry her heavy bags home. "Excuse me can someone carry my bags. I live down the street," Eleanor often said to supermarket staff. Hoping to receive a good tip from Eleanor, Orlando and other young boys "always pushed the wagon [full of fresh vegetables and fruit, poultry, cleaning agents, and insect spray] for her."[49] Eleanor also had a hard time moving her legs. Her long brown legs, which once enjoyed dancing and standing in the kitchen for long periods of time as she cooked, were swollen stiff and painful to move. Richard Scurlock, fiancé to Eleanor's youngest daughter, Terry Bumpurs during the 1980s, said that she "couldn't make no little move to the left or the right. If she was standing in a spot, that's all she could be doing. Standing in a spot. She couldn't make any little jump or anything."[50]

Declining physical health and arthritic pain kept Eleanor mostly at home. She spent a considerable amount of time in her well-kept apartment, watching her favorite television programs, cooking meals, and observing neighborhood happenings from her window. Akin to an urban fire escape or stoop, the apartment window was a critical semi-private space for many working-class city dwellers. It was a prime spot where occupants enjoyed free activities, amusements, and community events without having to leave their front doors. Gazing out the window into the urban landscape from the comforts of their homes, New Yorkers like Eleanor, especially those who were physically confined to their homes, could observe and articulate opinions about street activities, community affairs, and neighborhood folks' public behavior and business. Windowsill watchers—much like the chatty television fictional character "Ms. Pearl Shay" on NBC's popular 1980s TV show *227*—could also unofficially assume the role of neighborhood watchperson and busybody, collecting and distributing community intel and juicy gossip to inquisitive listeners.

Eleanor's living room window gave her a bird's-eye view of University Avenue. Often sitting on a chair and leaning against her windowsill, she witnessed waves of people flowing in and out of the apartment complex. Sometimes for several hours, Eleanor observed children playing and running down the street, the comings and goings of working and party-going residents, neighborhood squabbles,

NYCHA workers busily cleaning the grounds, and folks filing into University Avenue's Featherbed Lane Presbyterian Church. From her fourth-floor window, Eleanor also communicated with her daughters, grandchildren, and friends. Strolling to Sedgwick Houses, Mary "always could see her [mother] out the window." Spotting her mother in the window sometimes stopped Mary "from making the trip all the way upstairs." Brief window conversations with Mary encompassed loving greetings, inquiries about daily food selections and social activities, and making plans to visit one another.[51]

Notwithstanding societal post–World War II perceptions of public housing recipients as idle, unemployed housekeepers residing in poorly maintained living spaces, the former domestic worker took tremendous care of her small apartment. She curated a minimalist and decorative interior.[52] As cultural producers and visionaries, Black women designed their homes according to their evolving visual sensibilities. Black homes, particularly living room spaces, writes author Elizabeth Alexander, were intentional sites of Black self-making. "In the spaces we designate and create, the self is made visible in the spaces we occupy, literal, 'black interiors,' the inside of homes that black people live in."[53]

Apartment 4A was orderly, embodying self-pride, respectability, and Black women's long tradition of home cleanliness. The apartment's pristine appearance exemplified the home of an efficient former domestic worker. Eleanor's living room consisted of small plaid couches, two small tables, a lamp, several vases with real or imitation flowers, a dining table and chair, a wall clock, and a few wall decorations. Like many African Americans of her generation, Eleanor had a picture of slain civil rights leader Dr. Martin Luther King Jr. hanging on her wall. She perhaps was impressed with King's political organizing in New York City. King criticized Northern Jim Crowism and gave his moral support to the nation's and New York City's, where he had largest school desegregation demonstration. On February 3, 1964, nearly a half million Black and Latinx students and over 3,500 teachers walked out of their classrooms. Protesters were denouncing the city's refusal to implement the 1954 Supreme Court ruling of *Brown v. Board of Education*.[54]

The apartment's other rooms were tidy. Eleanor's one-window kitchen was small, but it was well stocked. Appliances, seasoning salts, and food sat on countertops and narrow shelves. Her bedroom was also orderly. Her dresses, blouses, and undergarments were neatly folded or hung in her closet.[55]

Apartment 4A was a refuge for Eleanor. For many Black people, a household space, according to scholar Jennifer Nash, was an "oppositional site in which black subjects cultivate[d] their subjectivity and personhood without [and in spite of] the threat of cultural and social hyper-surveillance or legal terror."[56] In the comforts of her home, Eleanor was free from judgment and any attempts to punish or confine her. Her expressions of joy and creativity, as well as emotional vulnerabilities and physical and mental limitations, were on full display in her home. Eleanor articulated and affirmed her existence and ideas. She laughed out loud, talked to herself, and presumably remembered scenes of Louisburg, childhood play, and sorrow. At times, Eleanor's living space haunted her. She claimed to see her deceased brothers emerging from the cream-colored walls. Eleanor saw older brother Zollie Williams who drowned in Durham, North Carolina, in 1942. She laid eyes on the spirit of two-year-old Spencer Williams who succumbed to pneumonia a few months before her 1918 birth. And she saw one-month-old Johnnie Williams who died mysteriously in 1924 when she was six years old.[57]

Homebound as she primarily was, Eleanor associated with few neighborhood folks but left a lasting impression. Those who knew her well, occasionally spoke with her, observed her slowly walking down University Avenue and described her as friendly. Sedgwick Houses maintenance worker Louis Hernandez described Eleanor as a "quiet woman." "She used to spend her time just looking out the window. I used to say 'hello' or 'good morning,' but that's all. She didn't bother with anybody I know of."[58] Sedgwick Houses resident Florence Peaks described her as a loner and pleasant neighbor. Peaks, who lived in Eleanor's building and on the same floor, observed her leaving her apartment "every Monday morning at about 10. [S]he'd go to the store [to shop and] to cash a bag full of empty soda bottles."[59] One twenty-three-year-old Marine Corps veteran and University Avenue resident sometimes spotted Eleanor slowly walking to and from the grocery store. "I saw her walking and wobbling before. She was carrying groceries, and I asked her if she needed help. She would always say no."[60] Bronx property owner Tony Viar also recalled Eleanor strolling through the neighborhood. "I knew the woman. I own a building on University Ave. She knew a couple of my tenants. She walked to the store with them. She walked minimally. The woman barely could move."[61]

Next-door neighbor and student Sandra Garcia knew Eleanor well. She appreciated Eleanor's generosity and willingness to assist her family. Sandra was jobless, spending her days looking for employment and attending trade school. Recognizing Sandra's economic circumstance and desire to better her life through education, Eleanor offered the Garcia family inexpensive or free childcare services, drawing on a rich tradition of informal networks of mutual aid and community care among poor and working-class Black women. The Garcias accepted Eleanor's offer, entrusting her with the care of their toddler son. Eleanor treated the baby as if he were her own child. Sandra noted that Eleanor "watched my baby while I went to trade school. We also used to talk. I'd ask her if she'd been out, I tell her it's a beautiful day. Sometimes, she went up University Ave. to a Community Center. She was a private person."[62] Victor Garcia, Sandra's husband, also appreciated Eleanor's care of his son. The Bloomingdale's Department store worker said, "She took care of my child, for almost a year. But she had to give it up because she was getting to[o] sick. Sometimes her feet would swell up so bad she could hardly walk. She loved my son. She used to call him Peanut and he used to call her Grandma. [Sometimes] she stopped by [our apartment] and asked about him."[63] Eleanor stopped babysitting for the Garcias several months before her death. Care work aggravated her existing physical ailments.

Eleanor's childcare labor is telling. Her neighborly act of kindness complicates ideas about mentally and physically disabled persons as being unproductive, incapable of caring for themselves and others, and unfit to contribute to their communities or society at large. The Garcias' reliance on Eleanor suggests that she was trustworthy and protective of others. Speaking on Eleanor's mental fitness and her

ability to care for his son, Victor Garcia would later articulate to journalists, "Do you think we'd let a crazy person stay with our son?"[64]

Other friends and acquaintances also described Eleanor as a kindhearted and sociable person. One of those friends was Bronx resident
Helen Lowe, who was a few years younger than Eleanor. Helen lived
a few blocks away from Eleanor, whom she affectionately called "Ma
Bumpurs." Eleanor and Helen had a special relationship. Being from
the same generation, the two senior citizens looked after one another,
recognizing themselves in each other. Black female friendship was vital
to Eleanor's well-being, giving her companionship outside of familial
relationships and a chance to forge meaningful and intimate bonds.
Enjoying one another's company, the two women chatted and laughed
over the telephone several times a week; sometimes they engaged in
brief conversations from their windowsills. If Eleanor was walking past
Helen's building to get to the store or to Mary's house, Helen would
yell, "Hey, Ma Bumpurs." And when neighborhood trees bore green
foliage and colorful flowers, the two friends socialized in the community park. Sitting on one of the park benches, they smoked cigarettes
and enjoyed "vanilla and chocolate popsicles." They commiserated
about their physical ailments, hoping to feel and "wear" what poet
Lucille Clifton called "new bones." Wellness, pain management, and
the difficulties associated with aging were always topics of conversation. Both women suffered from arthritis. Helen noted that Eleanor's
"hands were the same as mine. She had no feeling in them. She kept
her cigarettes and her lighter in this brown leather case. She had the
lighter. She didn't know what it was to strike a match. She couldn't
do it. [Only] kind of matches she could do was big safety matches in
a box. She had no feeling. We used to call each other every day. When
we were all talked out we started to call every other day. Then once a
week. We didn't know what else to talk about but our pain."[65]

A few neighbors told strikingly different stories about Eleanor.
They did not interact with the person who Sedgwick Tenants Association president Jim Murphy called a "quiet, private person who
didn't bother anyone."[66] Nor did they encounter a social or motherly
figure. They claimed to have encountered an older woman who appeared dangerous. One teenage resident described Eleanor as violent

and extremely mobile. "She once ran after a little kid [and] chased him with a knife. And she chased one of my friends with a knife too. She told him to get the hell out of the building." A Sedgwick Houses activist told a similar story. The resident alleged that Eleanor threatened two association members with bodily harm when they attempted to recruit her for membership. When they knocked on the door, she greeted them with "a knife and threatened to 'get them' if they returned."[67] College student Andrea Bierra, who lived on the same floor as Eleanor, described her neighbor as "anti-social." Bierra reasoned that "she seemed sickly and pretty anti-social. I would see her in the hallway or on the elevator and I'd say hello and she wouldn't say anything. She just stared at me."[68]

Conflicting and perhaps even exaggerated public perceptions of Eleanor's behavior represented various aspects of her personality. Flattering and contentious interpretations of Eleanor as a friendly neighbor and as a loner and potentially violent person spoke to her complexities as a human being. Eleanor's behavioral patterns were also evident of shifting mood swings and chronic mental health challenges.

In the early months of 1984, sixty-five-year-old Eleanor experienced several mental health breakdowns. During one episode, Eleanor's twenty-six-year-old daughter Keenie endured the brunt of her mother's illness. "Suffering from auditory hallucinations" and possibly anxiety and dissociative disorders, Eleanor accused Keenie of attempting to harm her and "putting some kind of hex on her."[69] Concerned for her mother's well-being, a nervous Mary acted immediately, taking her mother to the Bronx's Lincoln Hospital. Eleanor's medical treatment and duration at Lincoln Hospital is unknown. Despite family care and medical interventions, Eleanor's mental health continued to deteriorate throughout 1984.

Something drastic happened in July 1984. Eleanor deviated from one of her routine monthly responsibilities. She stopped paying rent on her one-bedroom apartment. This was unusual for Eleanor, as she typically paid her rent on time. Eleanor made her monthly payments like clockwork, bringing it to the Sedgwick Houses management office, which was not far from her apartment building. Her April 1 payment was a few days late, but it was paid. The June 1 payment was on time. Sedgwick Houses managers never received the July 1 payment. Eleanor's daughters and other family members seem to have been unaware of the missing July payment. Barry Carey, assistant housing manager at Sedgwick Houses, and his assistant, Richard Wallach, took notice of the missing payment right away. Wallach and Carey acted immediately, preparing to collect rent money or proceed with NYCHA's standard eviction protocols. Housing officials wasted no time in contacting Eleanor, but discussing the missing payment and future residency at Sedgwick Houses with her would prove difficult.

Eleanor was less than one month behind in rent when nonpayment proceedings began. NYCHA's standard policy dictated that when one of its tenants failed to pay rent, they were issued a fourteen-day notice. On July 3, NYCHA mailed Eleanor the notice, requiring her to pay the rent within fourteen days or face eviction. Eleanor did not respond to the letter. NYCHA's next course of action was a three-day notice; this was a verbal and personal demand for rent payment. On July 18, Sedgwick employee Richard Wallach, who had shown Eleanor and her daughters the apartment back in 1982, personally carried out the three-day notice. Eleanor answered the door, but she did not invite Wallach into the apartment. Instead, she talked with Wallach through the door. "Are there any problems with paying the rent?" said Wallach. "There are some problems with the apartment. Take care of the problems and I will have the rent," responded Eleanor.[70]

Eleanor complained to NYCHA management that her apartment needed several repairs. She claimed the toilet, hallway light, stove, and bathroom sink were broken and that there was a leak in the bedroom. She also informed Sedgwick housing managers that she withheld rent because "people had come through the window, the walls, and the floors, and had ripped her off. They cleaned me out." NYCHA responded to Eleanor's complaints. They dispatched building maintenance workers to the apartment on several occasions, but maintenance workers had a difficult time gaining access to the apartment. Eleanor refused to let workers into the premises and would only communicate through the door, citing repeatedly a need for repairs.

And she continued to withhold the rent throughout the months of July, August, and September, owing NYCHA a little over $400. On August 8, ten days before Eleanor's sixty-sixth birthday, a petition for eviction for nonpayment of rent was served, and a warrant of eviction was issued on September 6. But the eviction did not happen.

Throughout the months of September and October, the NYCHA personnel made numerous attempts to assist Eleanor. Sedgwick Houses managers referred Eleanor's case to Human Resources Administration's (HRA) Division of General Social Services (GSS) on October 9, informing them of her mental health condition and requesting social and financial services. Created in 1966, the HRA aided an estimated 1.5 million New Yorkers during the early 1980s. The agency provided domestic violence survivors, seniors citizens, and underprivileged persons with food stamps, medical care, and shelter.[71] Responding to NYCHA's request, the HRA eventually planned for Eleanor to undergo a psychiatric examination but made no other plans for her.[72]

The pending eviction also resulted in more home visits from Sedgwick Houses managers, written eviction notices, and several phone calls and emergency letters to Eleanor. It's unclear if Eleanor saw or read the eviction notices and letters. It's likely she had no idea that her residency at Sedgwick Houses was in jeopardy.[73] Nearly three months after Eleanor stopped paying rent, NYCHA also sent letters to Terry and Mary Bumpurs, who were listed as Eleanor's emergency contacts.

Letters to sisters Terry and Mary never mentioned rent nonpayment or a possible eviction. Instead, the letters requested that the family immediately contact NYCHA. Dated September 28, correspondences stated: "Please contact Mr. Wallach or Barry Carey regarding your mother. It is a matter of utmost importance."[74] Terry never received NYCHA's letter. The letter to Terry's Bronx apartment on Sheridan Avenue was returned to NYCHA with a postal notation: "addressee unknown." The letter to Mary was delivered. On October 2, Mary contacted Wallach about her mother. However, the nature of their telephone conversation is in dispute. Wallach claimed he informed Mary about her mother's pending eviction. After that phone call, Wallach and other Sedgwick Houses managers claimed they never heard from Mary again. Mary insisted otherwise, maintaining that Wallach never mentioned an eviction. "He only said that she would not open the door for the maintenance man. I'll get to her and speak to her because she wouldn't open her door to strangers."

A few days later, Mary spoke with her mother about the apartment repairs, advising her to allow maintenance workers into the apartment.[75]

On October 12, 1984, Eleanor granted a Sedgwick Houses manager and maintenance worker access to her home. Eleanor opened the door, holding "a large carving knife" in her right hand. The knife was Eleanor's "security blanket," especially when strangers inhabited her personal space. Walking through the apartment, the maintenance worker carefully inspected the hallway and kitchen. "He looked at the [hallway] light, pulled the switch on the light and the light came on. He went into the kitchen and turned on the oven and after a couple of seconds, it came on. [He concluded] that the hallway light and the stove worked fine."[76] Eleanor's bathroom was a different story.

Stepping inside the bathroom, the maintenance man and the housing manager were greeted with a "horrible smell." The pungent aroma was almost enough to knock them off their feet. "The smell was really bad." Surprisingly, the stench was not coming from the toilet. It was the bathtub. Pulling the plastic floral print shower curtain back, the NYCHA repairman was horrified by a startling scene. "A lot of large flies and several cans of human excrement" were in the tub. "Wow! Oh my God! What happened here, Ms. Bumpurs?" remarked the housing worker. Eleanor informed the repairman that "[President Ronald] Reagan and his people had come through the walls and done it."[77] In disbelief over Eleanor's explanation, housing workers informed her that the bathroom's condition was a health hazard. Astonishingly, the men, observing someone who was suffering from delusions, did not help. They quickly exited the apartment, leaving the cans of feces in the bathtub. They immediately informed housing management of the bathroom's condition and their inability to complete the bathroom inspection under those conditions. "I can't get through this [feces] to check out the pipes," stated the maintenance worker.[78]

Faulting President Reagan for the bathroom's condition was telling. Even in Eleanor's seemingly shifting mental state, her comments about the leader of the free world were representative of many African Americans' critiques about Reaganomics and its impact on the poor. Observing the world in which she and other financially strapped citizens struggled to live, Eleanor, like 1982 Pulitzer Prize–winning novelist Alice Walker, "did not admire" Reagan.[79] Perhaps she remembered how the Republican politician and his anti-welfare conservative colleagues identified welfare recipients as "freeloaders" on paid vacations. And perhaps, she never forgot how the then 1970s California governor labeled all poverty-stricken women as "welfare queens," bolstering anti-Black political rhetoric that characterized Black mothers as welfare cheats.[80]

Learning about the bathroom's condition and still not receiving rent payments from Eleanor, Sedgwick Houses manager Barry Carey contacted longtime city marshal Mary Iopollo on October 17. Iopollo was an experienced marshal, processing and enforcing orders from civil courts such as carrying out evictions for a little over twenty years.[81] The city workers discussed eviction procedures, setting a date for Eleanor's expulsion. A week later, NYCHA mailed Eleanor a letter notifying her about the scheduled eviction. "Dear Ms. Bumpurs, you are under a warrant of eviction for non-payment of rent [$417.00]. We regret to inform you that your eviction has been scheduled for Monday, October 29 at 9:00 am."[82] It is unclear whether Eleanor read the notice or even received it. What is clear is that the grandmother became one of the more than 360,000 New Yorkers receiving eviction notices in 1984. That year, according to New York writer Jonathan Mandell, "there were more dispossesses issued in New York City than there were at the height of the Great Depression."[83]

On the afternoon of October 25, 1984, Manhattan psychiatrist and HRA consultant Dr. Robert John and GSS case manager Herman Ruiz arrived at Sedgwick Houses. The city employees were at the housing complex to conduct a psychiatric evaluation of Eleanor for the GSS and NYCHA. Standing in front of Eleanor's dark-green apartment door, John, who had served as a city consultant since 1982, said: "Hello Mrs. Bumpurs. I'm a doctor. We have come to help [you].

We heard that [you] had some problems where [you are] living and we would like to talk to [you] and hear more. Can we talk inside your apartment? We don't want your neighbors to hear what we are discussing." Assessing John and Ruiz's seemingly friendly demeanor, Eleanor cautiously allowed the two men into the apartment. But she also held a long kitchen knife, which she eventually placed on the windowsill. Inside the apartment, Eleanor granted John and Ruiz access only to the living room and kitchen. The bathroom and bedroom were off limits. John and Ruiz looked around and slowly walked around the living room and kitchen area. Both spaces were neat and exhibited the homemaker's minimalist aesthetic.[84]

The city workers posed several questions to Eleanor, whom they deemed "irritable." "Do you do shopping for yourself?" "Do you take care of yourself?" "When is the last time you saw your children?" "Do your children help you like you helped your mother?" Eleanor answered in the affirmative to the first two questions. Responding to the question about her own mother, she said, "My mother [Fannie Belle] died when I was 9." Then she stated that "Reagan and Castro killed [my children]. They live in the building." Glancing over at the knife lying on the windowsill, John asked, "Have you used the knife on anyone?" Eleanor retorted "not recently." Interested in her physical and mental health, John asked, "Mrs. Bumpurs, how are you feeling? Do you sleep okay?" Eleanor dodged John's inquiries about her health, giving him a brief response: "I sleep fine."[85] Her terse responses and refusals signaled attempts at maintaining a level of privacy and protecting her inner world from municipal workers whom she may have considered to be meddlesome.

Determining what questions she would answer, Eleanor shifted the conversation, articulating her primary concern: harassment. She wanted the annoyance to stop. Seeing "people" in her apartment upset her. She was at her wits' end with "Reagan," the "building superintendent," and the "people in the next apartment" trying to invade her space, steal her belongings, and put her "outdoors." For Eleanor, the "outdoors," signified terror, fear, and dread. She did not want to live among the state's estimated forty thousand to fifty thousand unhoused population.[86] Unsettling feelings and imagined threats of violation, theft, and housing dispossession were unending. Day and night "the people" interrupted her life, disturbing her peace. "They trying to turn [my house] into a whorehouse. I'll be alright if you help with that," Eleanor told John. Her comments did not surprise John and Ruiz. They had reviewed Eleanor's housing file and read Sedgwick housing workers' remarks about her hallucinations.

The conversation between Eleanor and Dr. Robert John and Herman Ruiz lasted about thirty minutes. After the brief evaluation, John sat down on a park bench outside the Sedgwick Houses and filled out a "mental status evaluation" form, jotting down his observations of Eleanor. There was no doubt in his mind that Eleanor needed mental health assistance. His short, informal handwritten note to GSS and NYCHA officials concluded that Eleanor "is psychotic" and "does not know reality from non-reality. Her judgment is impaired. She is unable to manage her affairs properly" and "is in need of hospital investigation and treatment." The report to housing and welfare workers also commented on Eleanor's mobility and physical appearance. "Mrs. Bumpurs was fully ambulatory and had no apparent difficulty in moving from the room. We stood during the entire interview, and she did not use a cane or walker. She is a large overweight Black woman and keeps a butcher knife in her possession." But John didn't perceive Eleanor as being a threat to himself or the GSS staffer. "I felt that she was holding the knife defensively, and she made no offensive gesture with it, neither did she threaten us verbally. She was not a danger to herself or others. This [was] a woman who was strongly experiencing, as far as she knew, people coming into her apartment at night, hearing voices, people speaking about herself and being threatened. . . . This was . . . a way of defending herself." John added that Eleanor was "naturally defensive, given the fact that we were two strange men whom she had never seen before in her apartment in a high-crime neighborhood and she was alone."[87]

Dr. John was right about the knife. Holding the sharp object gave Eleanor a sense of safety and protection. The knife was always in her possession. She carried it around the house, especially when she had visitors, or kept it within her reach. It was often positioned on the kitchen table or on the living room windowsill. One family member noted, "It was picked up when it was necessary and if it wasn't necessary it was there where she could see it. It was always within eyesight."[88] Carrying the knife was a symptom of someone who was mentally struggling with paranoia and delusions. It was also perhaps a reasonable protection measure for someone who believed that harm and danger were imminent.

After receiving John's psychiatric evaluation, NYCHA officials continued with the plan to evict Eleanor on October 29, and GSS, not offering Eleanor any city services, planned to have her hospitalized. Neither city agency informed the Bumpurs family about the eviction date or hospitalization. NYCHA was seemingly more concerned with the condition of its property and collecting rent money than with Eleanor's housing accommodations or mental health challenges. Regardless of her mental capacity, NYCHA wanted Eleanor out of Sedgwick Houses. According to city social worker Herman Ruiz, the Housing Authority "wouldn't want her staying in the apartment because she was a health risk [and] because of the excrement in Mrs. Bumpurs' bathtub." As a soon-to-be-unhoused person, Eleanor was on the cusp of becoming one of the over four hundred people NYCHA evicted between January 1 and September 30, 1984.[89]

Scenes of mental instability and a pending eviction were intertwined with moments of happiness for Eleanor. The last week of her life at Sedgwick Houses were filled with love, care, and pleasure. Those days were spent watching some of her favorite television programs, cooking, engaging in window conversations with her friend Helen Lowe, and spending quality time with her family. Eight days before the eviction, on Sunday, October 21, thirty-nine-year-old Mary and twenty-eight-year-old Deborah visited their mother's apartment. The sisters conversed and laughed while they tidied up her place, which according to Mary did not include disposing of buckets of feces. She claimed there were no feces in the bathtub when she visited her mother. Wanting to break up the monotony of the visit, the daughters decided to treat Eleanor to an afternoon outing. A movie and dinner seemed perfect, allowing them, at least for a few hours, a mental diversion and break from their everyday lives. It's unclear what film the women elected to see. But they had a wide selection of films to choose from. Several Hollywood blockbuster dramas, comedies, and action films were in theaters that October. Nearby Bronx theaters including RKO Theater and the Loews Paradise Quad on Fordham Road were showing Charles Bronson's *The Evil That Men Do*, *Ghostbusters*, and *A Soldier's Story*, adapted from Charles Fuller's 1982 Pulitzer Prize–winning play *A Soldier's Play*.[90]

On Sunday, October 28, the day before the scheduled eviction, Eleanor briefly saw her daughter Mary. "I was coming from volunteering work [at the Bronx Republican club] that day and she was looking out the [apartment] window." Standing outside Eleanor's window, Mary warmly greeted her mother, asking her how she was doing. From her windowsill, Eleanor waved at her daughter, saying she was fine. Then, according to Mary, her mother "came off the conversation." Eleanor questioned why Mary "had sent those two doctors to her house," referring to psychiatrist Robert John and a welfare worker Herman Ruiz. A perplexed Mary said, "What two doctors? I didn't send no doctors to your house." Mary had no idea who her mother was referring to. She surmised that her mother was referring to someone from the hospital. Mary told her mother she would come over tomorrow, figuring she would ask about the "doctors" on her next visit. Nodding her head with approval, Eleanor said, "Okay, see you tomorrow."[91]

For Eleanor there would be no tomorrow. The windowsill conversation would be Mary and Eleanor's last.[92]

CHAPTER 4

THE EVICTION

C loudy skies hovered over New Yorkers on Monday morning, October 29, 1984. Local meteorologists predicted occasional showers and a high of 67 degrees. Cooler temperatures provided relief to New Yorkers, given the previous day's unseasonably warm and humid weather of at least 79 degrees. Wearing sweaters and light jackets and coats and carrying their umbrellas, Bronxites traveled around the 174th Street and University Avenue area that morning, hoping to avoid the rush hour. It seemed like a typical Monday. Workers waited for the local BX3 bus and walked down Featherbed Lane and Macombs Road to the Mount Eden Avenue #4 subway station. Gypsy cab drivers cruised streets in search of passengers. Parents escorted their sleepy and crying toddlers into the doorways of the Head Start program at the Featherbed Lane Presbyterian Church. Neighborhood children talked about the upcoming Halloween holiday as they strolled to neighborhood schools. And local grocers and bodega store workers stocked their shelves in preparations for Monday morning shoppers.

Eleanor was also starting her Monday. She rose early from bed, preparing perhaps for Mary's visit. The day before, Mary told her she would stop by the apartment.[1] However the day unfolded, Eleanor hoped it would be an uneventful one.

But it would not be a typical Monday for her. Nor would it be a usual Monday for Sedgwick Houses residents or the City of New York. It would be a Monday that many New Yorkers would not forget, at least not for a while.

Sometime after 9:30 a.m., a crowd gathered in front of Eleanor's fourth-floor apartment door. Emergency Service Unit (ESU) and Hous-

ing Authority police of the NYPD, the city marshal, NYCHA workers, emergency medical services (EMS) technicians, one of Eleanor's
neighbors, and a Department of Social Services caseworker stood
outside 4A. Between ten and fifteen people gathered in the long, narrow hallway, discussing how to remove Eleanor from the apartment.
The small community of state actors discussed "her state of mind, her
size, [and] about the dangers the eviction team faced."[2] They had no
official removal plan but proceeded to knock on the door. "Mrs. Bumpurs, this the Housing Authority and police, please open the door."

It's unclear whether Eleanor heard the chatter and commotion
outside her apartment door. If she did hear it, was she scared? Did
she look through the door's peephole to see what was happening in
the hallway? Whatever was happening in the hallway, Eleanor knew
to mind her business and, as advised by her daughters, "not to allow
strangers into her apartment and not to open the door for nobody"
other than family.[3]

Whatever Eleanor's state of mind may have been, she was probably unaware that her landlord, the City of New York, was evicting
her from the apartment.

The individuals standing in the fourth-floor corridor were on a
clear mission. Their charge was removal. NYCHA officials, the city
marshal, and other municipal workers had a well-organized eviction
plan. They had an ambulance carrier at Sedgwick Houses to transport Eleanor to the hospital. And they even arranged for a moving
company to remove Eleanor's personal property from the apartment
to one of the city's warehouses, which would strip her of her assets.
Furniture, clothes, cherished family photographs, and other personal
material items accumulated over the course of her life would be out
of her possession. Neither NYCHA nor GSS workers considered Eleanor's post-eviction plan. City employees made no concrete housing
or hospitalization preparations for her.[4] Loss of territorial and property rights and access to housing, as well as the city's lack of physical,
mental, and emotional care for Eleanor would leave her abandoned,
without a home, and perhaps exacerbate existing physical and mental health conditions. Eleanor would be discarded like the thousands
of mentally ill New Yorkers who were discharged from city hospitals

without social support, financial subsidies, or stable housing. She would join the steady stream of urban poor families struggling in Ronald Reagan's America and subjected to embarrassing and traumatizing home evictions. Eleanor would become part of an increasing population of poor older women who, according to the New York City Council's 1982 Subcommittee on the Status of Women report, were "neglected by government, the medical profession, [and] social agencies." According to New Yorker and 1984 Democrat vice presidential nominee Geraldine Ferraro, the status of these older women was "downright tragic."[5]

It's unclear where Eleanor would go once evicted or who would assist her. It seemed as if housing and welfare officials hardly cared about Eleanor's post-eviction circumstances. Nor were city employees concerned about how the stigma of an eviction would impact her ability to secure housing in the future. Home expulsion would ignite a chain of hardship. Being evicted, writes award-winning author Matthew Desmond, was like being incarcerated. Evictions carried (and continue to carry) a stigma, one that would be difficult to conceal or escape.[6] An eviction would ban Eleanor from affordable federal housing programs and possibly from other rental opportunities in the city. Landlords would be cautious about renting to someone with a history of eviction. An eviction would sever Eleanor's ties to her community, ripping her away from familiar surroundings and from her neighborhood friends like Helen Lowe and the Garcia family. Housing and welfare workers prioritized removal from Sedgwick Houses over physical and mental wellness and housing security. City workers' inability or unwillingness to assist Eleanor denied her the basic and necessary socioeconomic and housing resources needed to survive and thrive. To make matters worse, housing managers placed the grandmother in another undesirable and life-threatening circumstance: police officers' crosshairs.

Unlike municipal employees, the NYPD, particularly Housing Authority and ESU officers, were not at Sedgwick Houses to evict Eleanor. Nor did they have official orders to secure housing or mental health services for her. "New York's Finest" had a different task. Standard NYCHA procedures required Housing Authority officers to accompany city marshals to all evictions. Additionally, housing police officers were notified that their presence was necessary because NYCHA was evicting a "cantankerous lady, possible emotionally disturbed."[7] According to the NYPD's first Black police commissioner, Benjamin Ward, who mayor Edward Koch appointed to the top position in January 1984, the ESU were at Sedgwick Houses to "preserve peace in the course of the eviction, not to carry out the eviction itself. Eviction is a civil process that is carried out by city marshals." The ESU officers, including John Elter, Leonard Paulson, George Adams, Richard Tedeschi, Stephen Sullivan, and Sgt. Vincent Musac, were at the Sedgwick Houses apartment because they were responding to a call that involved an "emotionally disturbed person with a knife."

Established in 1930, ESU was the highly skilled "heavy weapons" unit of the NYPD. Trained to use a variety of firearms, including shotguns, anti-sniper rifles, and submachine guns, ESU handled and managed city riots, barricaded criminals, hostage situations, and suicide attempts. Since 1979, after the tragic police killings of Brooklyn residents and mentally ill persons Luis Baez and Elizabeth Mangum, ESU officers, those trained in emergency medical services and equipped with restraining devices, such as nets, tear gas, and chemical mace, were tasked with handling emergency calls that involved "violently disturbed persons."[8] It was often said of the highly trained and respected ESU officers that "when a citizen is in trouble, he calls a cop. When a cop is in trouble, he calls Emergency Service."[9] The Housing Authority police called the ESU, believing Eleanor's eviction would be "a messy job." They deemed her violent and anticipated a forced eviction. They worried about their safety, not Eleanor's well-being.

While Housing Authority police appropriately called the ESU officers for assistance, the specialized unit had "no set rules" for handling persons experiencing mental health breakdowns. The 1984 NYPD ESU Operational Policies and Tactics manual had only suggestions for officers, reminding them that "our relationship with the mentally ill is based on society's desire to HELP, not to punish." The department recommended to officers: "Don't be in a hurry, evaluate the situation, keep your own emotions calm and cool, be honest, and avoid force, if possible. These suggestions may prove helpful." Such recommendations were far from helpful for individuals experiencing a mental health crisis.[10]

Over police radio transmission, Housing Authority police informed ESU officers that Eleanor weighed over three hundred pounds and was an "emotionally disturbed person." They also delivered a critical piece of information to ESU officers. Housing cops maintained that Eleanor was a "knife thrower" and that "on several occasions [she] had menaced maintenance men and others with a knife." Even more damaging, someone in the eviction group, possibly Housing Authority police or Sedgwick Houses managers, asserted the unsubstantiated claim that Eleanor had a history of making and throwing a "Carolina pancake" (lye) on uninvited house guests.[11] Throwing corrosive liquids on someone could result in severe skin damage, dissolving bones, and even death. The genesis of the lye rumor is unclear. Nobody could cite an incident when Eleanor hurled lye on someone. Yet this tale traveled among those assembled in the hallway and reached the ears of ESU officers. Thus, ESU officers, in traveling to Sedgwick Houses to assist Housing Authority police, were responding to patently false information. NYCHA spokesman Val Coleman would later state that "the rumor that she had thrown lye on someone is not verified. There is no record of violence in our files."[12]

Constructed narratives about madness and violence further made Eleanor susceptible to inhumane treatment and rendered her invisible.[13] Projections of a poor, chemical-throwing, and immensely strong Eleanor erased her identity as a mother and as a scared woman in need of protection, compassion, and perhaps psychiatric care.[14] Derisive portrayals relegated Eleanor to being a "nobody." Noting how political arrangements, power relations, and economic circumstances transform everyday citizens' lives, scholar Marc Lamont Hill writes that "to be Nobody is to be vulnerable, disposable, abandoned by the state, and unworthy of investment and the most fundamental provisions of the social contract."[15]

Believing Eleanor was dangerous and lethal, the housing police removed one of the door locks after she refused to open the door. The removed lock allowed the heavily armed ESU officers to peer through the door hole, where officers caught a glimpse of Eleanor holding a knife and moving around the living room. They also observed a "cloudy, foggy type of atmosphere" in the living room and smelled a strong odor. They suspected the stench was insect spray, perhaps Raid, but they could not completely rule out lye. According to witnesses, officers shouted out to Eleanor: "We are the police. Come out. We want to make sure that nobody gets hurt. We don't want to hurt you. Don't force us to come. We'll break your door down. We're coming in."

At one point, officers even allowed one of Eleanor's neighbors to assist them in convincing her to vacate the apartment. Thirteen-year Sedgwick Houses resident and fifty-year-old Florence Peaks, who lived on the same floor as Eleanor, was concerned about the large police presence. She asked the city marshal: "[Did] it [take] all those people to get Mrs. Bumpurs out of her apartment." Florence did not know Eleanor well, but the two women always had smiles and kind words for each other when they passed in the hallway or shared the elevator. On occasion, they would briefly talk about their health issues, with Eleanor confiding in Florence that she had diabetes and a heart condition. A compassionate neighbor, Florence did not want to witness her sickly neighbor evicted from the apartment, especially in such a public and demeaning way. "It was a matter of dignity. The whole neighborhood didn't have to know she was being evicted."[16]

Florence approached Eleanor's door. "Mrs. Bumpurs, this is Florence, your neighbor, I live down the hall, please don't let them disgrace or take away your dignity, please give them the apartment. Miss Bumpurs don't do anything irrational. They're talking about taking the lock off the door, they're going to break it down."[17] Neighborly kindness and friendly warnings had no effect on Eleanor. She did not come out of the apartment.

Eleanor defiantly responded to the apartment invaders. She launched a range of verbal retorts. She cursed at them. She yelled. She threatened the strangers with bodily violence. And she refused to open her door or talk to Florence or anyone else. She snickered at Florence, uttering sarcastically, "Huh, I don't have any neighbors. And let them [NYCHA] take the door down, housing has enough money to buy another one." The five-foot-seven woman also issued a warning for anyone threatening to enter her home. Ready to defend herself and her household, Eleanor boldly cautioned the intruders: "If somebody comes through the door we'll see who gets hurt. Go away, if you don't go away, I have something for you. If you come into my house, I'll kill you! Get away from my door. Leave me alone."[18]

Eleanor had good reason not to allow strangers into her home. Although steadily declining, crime was still high in the Bronx. In the borough, reported felonies amounted to 91,614 in 1982, 83,966 in 1983, and 81,794 in 1984. In 1981 there were 30,471 burglaries and the next year 26,844 burglaries, including the robbery of borough president Stanley Simon's residence in the Bronx's exclusive Riverdale neighborhood.[19] Several Bronx neighborhoods, including Hunts Point, Fordham, and Sedgwick Houses' University Heights, experienced an increase in violent crimes.[20] And since the late 1970s crimes against older people, particularly those living in public housing developments, was increasing. According to police officials, older residents were "special targets for the anti-social members of our society," becoming victims of an assortment of crimes including aggravated assaults and burglaries.[21] Sexual and physical assaults, stabbings and murders, and other offenses hovered over Bronxites, making many borough residents think twice about opening their apartment doors to strangers.

Eleanor likely had other reasons for not opening her apartment door. The one-bedroom apartment was a sacred space for the grandmother. The well-kept domestic space offered Eleanor some measure of housing stability. She'd faced displacement before and had at last settled into a home that was just hers, one she cared for and felt safe in. And it was important for Eleanor to have a say in who entered her home. Not allowing strangers inside her home allowed her to assert her autonomy.

Officers were frustrated with Eleanor's refusals. According to several eyewitnesses, ESU officers, those who pledged to show "patience, empathy, and understanding" toward handling persons with mental illness, did not exhaust every possible avenue to coax Eleanor out of the apartment. According to one Sedgwick Houses resident and eyewitness, "Police did not give [her] enough time to calm down. Not enough time to leave her the breathing room to save her life."[22]

On the order of forty-two-year-old NYPD sergeant Vincent Musac, ESU officers Stephen Sullivan, Richard Tedeschi, John Elter, George Adams, and Leonard Paulson proceeded into Eleanor's home. Officer Elter entered first with a six-foot restraining bar, and officers Adams and Tedeschi entered second and third carrying plastic shields. Having handled many "emotionally disturbed" cases without incident in 1984, nineteen-year police veteran and forty-one-year-old decorated officer Stephen Sullivan held the 12-gauge sawed-off pump-action shotgun. The weapon was fully loaded with five rounds of double O buck shots, each shell contained nine pellets, each the size of a .32-caliber bullet. It was just by happenstance that the stocky and dark-haired cop carried the shotgun. Officer Tedeschi initially had the weapon but asked Sullivan to hold it while he tied one of his shoes. After tying his shoe, Tedeschi never retrieved the deadly weapon from Sullivan. Sullivan's favor to his fellow officer would upend the next days, months, and years of his life. Equipped with the shotgun, Sullivan's primary responsibility was to protect the three officers in front of him: Elter, Adams, and Tedeschi. Musac was behind Sullivan and officer Paulson remained at the apartment door.[23]

As if ready to do battle, the officers, with over sixty years of police training combined "went [into the apartment] like it was a dope raid. They didn't treat her like she was an old woman," recalled one witness.[24] Officers were not raiding an apartment for narcotics or storming a battlefield, yet the six ESU officers employed the same level of intensity and military tactics to restrain and remove an older woman from her home. Sullivan and his fellow officers' entrance into apartment 4A was swift and forceful.

Once inside the apartment, police observed Eleanor sitting on a stool in the living room, holding an eight-to-ten-inch butcher knife in her right hand. They were fixated on the knife, telling Eleanor to "please drop the knife." At the same time, Eleanor witnessed several strange men entering the apartment wearing protective vests, gas masks, and goggles and carrying plastic shields, clubs, a six-foot restraining bar, and a 12-gauge shotgun. According to Bronx district attorney (DA) Mario Merola, the officers "must have been quite a sight for [Eleanor], who had imagined that people were after her, coming through the walls and floors to get her. Here were six men, dressed like spacemen, carrying bizarre equipment and pleading with her to drop her knife."[25] Eleanor had no idea who these individuals were or their reason for being in her apartment. She was terrified by uninvited strangers removing locks from the door and entering her beloved home. The forced entry confirmed Eleanor's suspicions and worst nightmares, that apartment invaders, like national political leader "Ronald Reagan and his people," were there to harm her; such imminent danger called for self-protection and open rebellion. Staring down the apartment invaders, Eleanor was ready to stand her ground. She was willing to place her body on the line to safeguard her home.

But Eleanor also wanted to live. Live to see another day. Live to see her daughters and socialize with Helen Lowe and other friends. Eleanor wasn't ready to die—at least not on that day and not in that way.

The violent apartment confrontation only lasted between thirty and forty-five seconds. Armed with the doubled-barrel weapon, Sullivan fired two shots at Eleanor, claiming that the knife wielding woman was attempting to slash another ESU officer. "I feared for his life. I thought she was going to chop his head off." According to several witnesses standing outside the apartment, "The shotgun blasts were loud and sounded like a bomb went off in the building." The blast was so loud and frightening that the small crowd of people in the hallway emptied the corridor. "Nobody was there, nobody was there. People ran away into the stairwell." The first shot struck Eleanor in her right hand, the hand holding the knife. The powerful blast blew off three fingers. The index finger was gone, the middle finger was attached by a fragment of skin, and most of the thumb was gone. Presumably, the right hand was inoperative. Sullivan, standing about two feet from Eleanor, shot her again because she allegedly was waving the knife. The second shot penetrated Eleanor's chest, shattering her ribs and ripping open her lung.[26]

Feeling the heat, pain, and power of the second shot, Eleanor "looked very surprised. She looked up, crossing her arms over the wound [and bloodstained night gown]" as if she were gently embracing herself and trying to stop the blood flow from her body. "She then went into the kitchen and slowly slumped against the wall and fell down to the floor." Blown-off limbs, bone fragments, and the long kitchen knife were on the linoleum floor. Shattered and mangled bones and bodily tissues and a large pool of blood were evidence of the shotgun's destruction to Eleanor's thick, brown body.[27]

Emergency medical technicians and paramedics rushed into the apartment. They spent approximately twenty minutes aiding a semi-conscious Eleanor. Despite serious gunshot injuries, miraculously Eleanor was still alive. She had massive chest and hand wounds and suffered significant internal bleeding. Still unclear about who the intruders were and what was happening to her, a confused Eleanor resisted the technicians. While in tremendous physical pain, "she kept fighting us off and flopping around, resisting our attempts to stabilize her," said one EMT. According to one police officer, she yelled and cursed at that the paramedics, saying "get off of me you motherfuckers."[28] She attempted to remove the oxygen mask from her face and inadvertently pulled the intravenous line from her left arm. A wounded Eleanor also uttered nonverbal expressions. She moaned and groaned, motioning bodily discomfort and perhaps cries for her daughters.

Successfully stabilizing Eleanor, the medical unit placed her legs in "mask trousers—wrappings that can be inflated to force blood back into the body cavity and packed wounds in her chest and right hand with 4-by-4-inch gauze pads." The medical team then removed a critically wounded Eleanor from her home. She would never return to 1551 Sedgwick Houses.

A handful of cops moved around Eleanor's apartment. They searched the living room looking for the knife. They inspected the kitchen, looking for the boiling lye that housing officials claimed Eleanor was cooking and planning to throw on them. Nothing was boiling on the small stove. The kitchen was clean and orderly. Seasoning salts, small jars, cans of nonperishable food, and appliances occupied the space. Officers did smell a strong chemical odor, a sulfur-like scent, but no lye was discovered. Instead, they located several cans of Raid roach spray.[29] Eleanor was not boiling lye to throw on anyone. She was waging a deadly war against cockroaches, those pestering insects crawling from apartment to apartment in search of shelter and their next meal.

Having heard the gunshots that ripped through Eleanor's body, neighbor Florence Peaks cried, "Oh my God, they've killed her. They didn't have to shoot her." Florence believed that NYCHA could have found another way to evict Eleanor, an alternative method that did not involve police. While standing in the hallway with housing officials and welfare workers, Peaks claimed that she informed them that "if [they] had waited a half hour [after 9:30 a.m.] [they] could have locked Eleanor out of the apartment. Every Monday morning at about 10 [she goes to the store]." Hearing the ear-splitting sonic booms, Rosalee Thomas, who lived on the twelfth floor and was an eyewitness to some of the confrontation, sobbed uncontrollably, saying "How could they do that? She was an old lady. There was so many of them [cops]." Peaks, Thomas, and other neighbors had never heard such sounds, nor seen such a sight. It was like a scene out of a horror movie or World War II, according to building maintenance worker Louis Hernandez. Part of the fourth floor and the building elevator was covered with blood, and the stench of gunpowder and bodily fluids thickened the air. "Blood was all over the place. Everywhere there was blood. Blood was in the hallway and as they carried her to the elevator, it was dripping all over the place."[30]

Shocked and inconsolable Sedgwick Houses residents observed a ghastly scene as Eleanor was carried from the building. "When they brought her out [of the apartment] it was horrible. She had a big hole in her chest. One of [her] hands was blown off," recalled one neighbor. Having a front-row seat to the horrific scene from their apartment windows and from standing inside and outside the building, several tenants said that the NYPD, EMS workers, and NYCHA had no regard for Eleanor's life or her wounded body. In their view, city workers publicly violated and dehumanized their neighbor even after shooting her twice. "The way they carried her out the building was terrible. It was a very bad thing to see them carrying her out like that, like an animal," noted one grieving onlooker.[31]

Granting her little respect and bodily privacy, Eleanor's bloody body was exposed and on full display for Sedgwick Houses residents.

Eleanor's next-door neighbor thirty-nine-year-old Victor Garcia, who witnessed the shooting through his door peephole, believed that police and EMS "did not care about her. They carried her out of the building with no clothes on. She was naked. Naked . . . They didn't even cover her up. She was naked for everyone to see. She had a big hole in her chest. One of her hands was blown off. They didn't even put her in an ambulance. They put her in the back of a Housing Authority car." Overwhelmed by the shooting and sight of Eleanor's body, Garcia cried. Observing the scene from her window, another Sedgwick Houses resident recalled that Eleanor's nightgown barely covered her. "Her [shoulders and] breasts were exposed" and "blood poured" out of her body.[32]

Unclear about the details and circumstances of the police shooting, residents could not understand why police and so much weaponry were needed during an eviction proceeding—especially for an older woman. Housing tenant and community activist Mildred Johnson said, "This [eviction] was never a thing for the police to get involved with. What were they going to do, put her in the street?"[33] Sedgwick Houses Tenant Association leader James Murphy noted that "usually an [eviction] involves a housing assistant, one police officer and a marshal. Not all these police that were here. [And] they're not supposed to handle anybody physically. They're not supposed to put a hand on them."[34] Even though Mildred Johnson, James Murphy, and other residents did not know Eleanor well, the Sedgwick Houses community prayed for her survival. But judging by the amount of blood in the hallway and elevator and Eleanor's massive chest wound, chances of recovery appeared slim.

Sometime after 10 a.m., Eleanor arrived at the South Bronx's Lincoln Hospital. According to the hospital director of the emergency medical residency training program, the emergency room surgical section head, and the *Daily News* medical columnist Dr. Harold "Oz" Osborn, Eleanor, who went into cardiac arrest, was barely alive when she arrived. She "was without spontaneous breathing and a pulse and bleeding profusely." She had lost well over half of her blood volume. Her right hand "was a bloody stump with the thumb and index finger completely missing and the fourth and [fifth] fingers were all crumped over and sort of dangling down by pieces of skin that weren't fully attached to the hand." Eleanor had few signs of life, but Osborn and a team of doctors and nurses were determined to save her. Working over an hour, Osborn and the medical team "put a breathing tube in her, gave her oxygen and fluids, tried to stop the bleeding from the big wound in her chest," and performed open-heart massage to keep her blood circulating. Tremendous medical interventions and attempts to resuscitate Eleanor were futile. "We finally had to pronounce her dead." Doctors declared Eleanor's death at 11:27 a.m., nearly two and half hours after the botched eviction.[35] Eleanor's death saddened Osborn. He would never forget attempting to save her life, considering her death to be "the most disturbing case that I have dealt with in more than 15 years of medical practice." Weeks after Eleanor's death, Osborn would relate to reporters that he "hadn't been able to sleep since seeing the many gunshot wounds."[36] Her death made a tremendous impression on him.

Eleanor wasn't the only one given medical care that morning. As the Lincoln Hospital medical team vigorously tried to save Eleanor, officer Stephen Sullivan was hospitalized at the Bronx's Abraham Jacobi Hospital. Although the former marine showed no signs of physical injury, standard NYPD policy required that officers involved in shooting incidents undergo a basic medical evaluation. A health assessment was necessary due to the possible range of physical, emotional, and cognitive behavioral responses some officers experienced in the moments after a deadly shooting. Fellow officers described Sullivan as being "in shock." Physiological attention was also warranted given Sullivan's limited experience discharging his service weapon. Sullivan fired his gun three times throughout his entire career. The first time was in July 1983 when he killed a ferocious Doberman pinscher during a Bronx drug raid. That same year in October, Sullivan shot the car tires of seventeen-year-old Lucille Petrocelli during a police chase on the Bronx's Grand Concourse. The 1984 Sedgwick Houses shooting was the third time Sullivan had fired his weapon. It was his first kill.

A medical practitioner checked Sullivan's heart rate and blood pressure. Doctors determined that his vital signs were normal. Sullivan was released with a clean bill of health. Flanked by NYPD officers, Sullivan walked out of Jacobi Hospital, believing that shooting Eleanor was the appropriate course of action to safeguard fellow officers' lives. This was what Sullivan, Sgt. Vincent Musac, and the other five officers—John Elter, Leonard Paulson, George Adams, Richard Tedeschi, and Stephen Sullivan—conveyed to NYPD top brass and investigators and Patrolmen Benevolent Association union lawyers during hours of questioning about the shooting. For Sullivan, the killing of an older, disabled woman seemed of little consequence. He purported to superiors and later to journalists that he was "just following the training and doing [his] job." After answering the higher-ups' questions, Sullivan was given time off from work. He left the city, heading to his Lake Carmel, Putnam County, home to his wife and two teenage children.

Eleanor's killing would not be of little consequence to her five daughters and ten grandchildren. Learning about NYCHA's attempt to evict their mother for a little over $400 and about the gruesome shooting would be gut wrenching and unsettling. It would change their lives.

PART II

Protest

CHAPTER 5

"THEY SHOT A GRANDMOTHER!"

Between 11 a.m. and 11:30 a.m. on Monday, October 29, Mary Bumpurs and her nineteen-year-old daughter, LuDean, walked the two blocks from their basement apartment to the Sedgwick Houses. Mother and daughter planned on spending part of the day with Eleanor, watching television, checking in about the apartment repairs, and discussing the mysterious "doctors" who came to visit Eleanor a few days ago. Mary had not been to her mother's apartment in a few days, and she informed her mother that she would pay her a visit that day.

Arriving at Eleanor's building, Mary and LuDean noticed an active neighborhood scene on 174th and University Avenue. It seemed relatively early in the day for University Avenue to be so busy and noisy. Several ambulances, countless NYPD officers, and scores of neighbors crowded the street and the apartment complex's courtyard. "I had seen all of the emergency trucks and the ambulances and I said, 'Oh, God, somebody is sick in here,' so we walked up to the building. We continue to see more crowds of people, thinking, what is going on. Everybody was talking, looking around and pointing at the [1551] building," Mary recalled. Some of the neighbors were gazing up at the building, pointing their finger toward the fourth floor. That was Eleanor's floor. "I hope everything is okay," a slightly worried Mary told LuDean.[1]

Mary and LuDean made their way through the commotion and into the building. Stepping off the elevator, mother and daughter walked into chaos. Parts of the hallway floor were covered with blood. Gunpowder saturated the air. Police swarmed the small corridor. According to Mary, "We see a big bunch, a lot of police and I'm saying what is going on and then an officer comes out of my mother's apartment."[2]

A frantic Mary prayed Eleanor was safe. Her mind and heart were racing as she stood outside her mother's apartment. She wondered why police were coming in and out of the apartment, thinking, What happened inside the apartment? Where was her mother? Was she sick? Was she safe? As a nervous Mary approached the damaged apartment door, police officers prohibited her from entering the apartment. "I attempted to get into my mother's apartment, I was physically blocked by two officers. All the police were standing outside, ransacking the house. One officer came out and put his arms around my shoulder and proceeded me down the hallway."[3]

He told Mary the unthinkable. "Your mother has been shot and she's been rushed to the Bronx's [Lincoln] Hospital." Mary yelled, "Shot! What you mean she's been shot, for what reason?" The officer, either not sure or ordered by his superiors not to disclose the details of the shooting, bypassed Mary's questions. Nor did he indicate that a police officer shot Eleanor. Police departments' withholding of information about officer-involved shootings, especially from victims' families, allows law enforcement agencies and city officials to construct and control a narrative—to protect officers or in some cases orchestrate cover-ups. Remaining silent on Eleanor's shooting, the officer offered Mary and LuDean a ride to the hospital. Scared and confused, mother and daughter accepted the ride.[4]

Shortly after Mary and LuDean arrived at the hospital, emergency room surgeon Harold Osborn, who had worked tirelessly to preserve Eleanor's life, informed Mary that her mother had succumbed to a gunshot wound to the chest. Mary recalled the moment: "The doctor was holding my hand. He said, 'Well, don't get so upset.' I said, 'What do you mean don't get upset? My mother is gone and you are telling me not to be upset. You must be crazy. Why did this happen?'" Dr. Osborn had no answers for Mary. He didn't know why Eleanor was shot or who shot her. What made Dr. Osborn's shocking news about her mother real was viewing her body, a traumatizing and unwanted endeavor that put grief-stricken onlookers like Mary at risk for post-traumatic stress disorder. "He took me in where my mother was lying and I looked at her, and I just kissed her."[5] The sight of a hospital sheet covering her mother's wounded thick, brown body powered Mary's swift exit from the hospital room. It was a devastating sight, and one she would never forget.

Learning of her grandmother's death, LuDean, a City University of New York freshman and Mary's oldest child, tried to comfort her inconsolable mother. She didn't know what to say; nor could she believe the news. "My grandmother didn't hate anybody. She wouldn't hurt anyone unless they tried to hurt her. The police are covering up." Eleanor's death would heavily weigh on LuDean, particularly as she was deciding on a career path. Much of her adult life LuDean dreamed of being a police officer, where she would be one of a small percentage of Black women police officers. In 1984, white officers represented 81.1 percent of the NYPD, with Black and Latinx officers representing just 10.2 percent and 8.3 percent, respectively.[6] In 1983, there were 387 Black women on the force.[7] In 1984, the NYPD had an estimated 1,827 women in its estimated 19,206-member force.[8] Despite the NYPD's racial composition, LuDean wanted to serve the citizens of New York and be an agent of social change. "I want to be on the streets protecting people," she said. The optimistic college student desired to "change things around" by improving the dynamics between police and Black New Yorkers. But now LuDean would have "second thoughts about becoming a cop" and taking the New York City and Nassau County police entrance examinations in November and December.[9]

Still unclear about the apartment eviction and the details of the shooting, Mary had the painful task of informing family members about Eleanor's death. Mustering up the strengthen to articulate the unthinkable, Mary uttered the words "She's gone. They said a police officer killed her." Terry Ann Bumpurs, one of Eleanor's younger daughters, collapsed to the ground after hearing about her mother's death. The words *shot* and *dead* were overwhelming and catastrophic to penetrate the membrane of the psyche. Daughter Deborah Bumpurs said, "I can't believe my mother was murdered. I don't know why but I know she was murdered." Other devastated family members left their homes and headed straight to the Bronx's Forty-Sixth Precinct. The precinct patrolled various sections of the Bronx, including Eleanor's University Heights and Morris Heights communities. Family members demanded to know what happened inside the apartment. Speaking to and yelling at officers, Eleanor's family asked, "Why was my mother being evicted? Why did they have to kill her? Couldn't they have found another way?" Front-desk officers, knowing very few details about the Sedgwick Houses shooting, offered the family a general statement. They indicated that the NYPD would investigate the shooting. Unsatisfied and not surprised with the officers' response, Eleanor's relatives left the precinct angry and dejected.[10]

The Bumpurs family weren't the only New Yorkers learning about Eleanor's shocking killing. Within hours and days of the deadly eviction, the story about a police officer killing a disabled, poor Black grandmother quickly spread throughout the city, eventually becoming a national and international story. Local journalists and cameramen rushed to Sedgwick Houses to report on the incident. Sedgwick Houses tenants and other New Yorkers were discussing what happened to that "poor old lady." New Yorkers' initial responses to the killing, captured in newspaper stories and opinion columns, heard in everyday conversations at bus stops, beauty salons, barber shops, churches, and at community meetings, exposed the city's long-standing social issues and racial tensions. Eleanor's killing laid bare many white New Yorkers' disdain for Black people and other racially and ethnically diverse urbanites and poor people. At the same time, urban citizens' thoughts about Eleanor's killing made clear a desire for legal justice for the grandmother and underscored their long-held struggle to combat government disinvestment and anti-Black police violence. Residents' impassioned neighborhood and kitchen table conversations about municipal neglect, police brutality, and human compassion fueled the makings of one of the city's most significant social justice campaigns of the decade. Eleanor's death became many New Yorkers' call to action, compelling them to take part in citywide legal justice protests.

"Murder! Murder! Murder!" "This makes no sense! It's a damn shame how they killed that old lady!" yelled some Sedgwick Houses tenants. On Tuesday, October 30, 1984, one day after her killing, Eleanor's relatives, neighbors, friends, journalists, Bronx high school students, and countless others crowded into the Sedgwick Houses Community Center for an evening meeting. This was one of the first of many community meetings and protests held for the grandmother who lived in apartment 4A.

Sedgwick Houses residents had much to say about Eleanor's death at a meeting organized by Sedgwick Houses Tenants Association (SHTA), including asking why a grandmother was gunned down the night before. Seated in her chair and anxious to be heard, thirty-five-year-old tenant and Girls Scout leader Leila Crittendon stated: "How [could] an armed police force shoot and kill a defenseless grandmother[?] I don't understand and it doesn't seem right." The deadly eviction did not sit well with Crittendon and other Sedgwick Houses tenants who were mad as hell. "Someone needs to tell us why this happened. Why were the cops trying to evict an old lady[?]" shouted several residents. Elevating her voice above the chorus of concerned tenants, Mary Bumpurs, standing in the back of the room with LuDean, sister Terry Ann, and other family members, yelled: "You don't murder someone for 96 bucks. My mother was killed by an officer with vengeance in his heart." Mary and the residents were directing their anger and questions toward NYPD spokesperson Deputy Police Commissioner Alice McGillion, NYCHA district manager Ralph Williams, Forty-Sixth Precinct police captain Andrew Dillon Jr., and several plainclothes officers and Housing Authority officials.[11]

Captain Dillon drew the most ire. In his brief remarks to attendees, the high-ranking officer made it clear that the meeting was not a press conference. Police did not intend to answer all of residents' questions. "We are not here to talk about the particulars of the shooting. I'm not going to discuss that with you. Our purpose here is to inform the community that the NYCHA, NYPD and Bronx District

Attorney's Office are conducting full investigations into the shooting." New York City mayor Edward Koch's office was also compiling an official city report on Eleanor's death. "How long will that take[?]" yelled one resident. "I don't know," replied Dillon. Residents did not want to wait weeks for the release of city reports. They wanted answers now. The crowd was unsatisfied with Dillon's remarks. Nor did they appreciate his unsympathetic tone. Incensed by the NYPD and NYCHA officials' unwillingness to address their concerns, Sedgwick tenants lustily booed police and housing officials, calling them "legalized gangsters [and] cold-blooded liars" who covered up the truth. Frustrated with the crowd, Dillon, surrounded by plainclothes officers, quickly walked out of the crammed community center.[12]

Pouring salt on the community's open wounds, a NYCHA official, hardly thinking or caring about the emotional and psychological impact of the shooting on residents, chastised and blamed Eleanor's family and extended community for her economic predicament and death. "If you folks had acted earlier, Mrs. Bump[urs] wouldn't have been five months behind in her rent payment." Police and city officials' assertion that family and community neglect resulted in Eleanor's dispossession and death became an ongoing refrain. And it was a charge that the family would incessantly refute. Meeting attendees responded swiftly to the NYCHA official's callous statement: "What did you say!" "That some bullshit." "Housing killed Ms. Bumpurs." Defending their dead neighbor and her grieving family, Sedgwick Houses residents told the administrator to "shut up [and] get the hell out of the meeting." The housing worker, along with Housing Authority police, did leave the heated meeting, offering tenants neither apologies nor answers. Residents left the hourlong meeting with more questions than when they had walked in. They also left the meeting motivated to act.[13]

Outraged with police officers' and NYCHA's behavior and lack of empathy for the Sedgwick Houses community, SHTA president and long-time Bronx resident James Murphy penned a letter to NYCHA's long-serving chairman Joseph Christian. A World War II veteran, Christian was appointed by Mayor John Lindsay to oversee the country's largest public housing authority in 1973. Stating that "the tragic event of October 29 is of great concern to tenants," Murphy demanded accountability, reprimanding NYCHA personnel. He wrote: "We, the tenants of Sedgwick Houses, respectfully request the suspension of the Sedgwick Houses manager and immediate answers to several questions: Who was responsible for authorizing such extreme measures to be taken, when in fact, less fatal action is taken when responding to hardened criminals, proven fatal animals, and other dangerous elements. Why wasn't the clergy or neutral mediator brought into this situation before deadly force was applied? We want to make sure that this is the last time this happens." It is unclear if Christian or any housing official responded to Murphy's letter. However, Murphy and the SHTA would continue to question NYCHA about the eviction, demanding to "get down to the bottom of what happen[ed]."[14]

Eleanor's killing struck a nerve with the housing complex's over eight hundred tenants. For years and decades, tenants lived, raised children, and socialized in and around the public housing development. Despite neighborhood erosion, arson, and increasing street crime, many residents felt safe living in Sedgwick Houses. For some, feelings about neighborhood and apartment safety changed on October 29. Scenes of heavily armed and militarized police occupying the complex, a blood-stained hallway, Eleanor's half-naked body, and a gunshot blast weakened their sense of security. The traumatic incident left many feeling stressed and fearful that such unspeakable violence could happen again—within their own homes and community. For them, Eleanor's forcible eviction and police shooting did not feel like a singular attack. It felt like an assault on the entire community. Residents' collective grief and anger over police abuse ignited a public health crisis within the Sedgwick Houses community.

In recent decades, scholars and mental health professionals maintain that exposure to police violence takes a toll on Black mental health. Witnessing or reading about police violence, men, women, and even children experience communal trauma, a lost sense of safety, and an increased state of hypervigilance.[15] Hearing about Eleanor's death, many Sedgwick Houses residents were traumatized and scared about increased police presence and surveillance in their community. Some were afraid to leave their apartments.[16] Sensing residents' fears,

Sedgwick Houses senior center crafts instructor Lola Greaes noted that since Eleanor's killing "things are slow here, at the center, people are afraid now."[17] And other tenants feared the possibility of police forcibly removing them from their homes. Communal fear and sorrow also cultivated a sense of community closeness, inspiring some Sedgwick Houses tenants to be more vigilant about caring for their neighbors, especially the oldest ones.

Long-time University Heights and Sedgwick Houses tenants like the Yorks were devastated. Sitting at their dinner table after a long day of work, the couple "couldn't even eat dinner. [We] were too upset. Mrs. Bumpurs didn't seem to be the type who could harm a fly."[18] Sixty-year-old Margaret Freeman feared for her fellow residents. "I hope it won't happen [again.] We have a lot of senior citizens in there."[19] In an exclusive interview with *Daily News* brash-talking columnist Jimmy Breslin—known for his raw, gritty, and intimate writings, including columns on the 1970s "Son of Sam" serial killings—Helen Lowe, one of Eleanor's close neighborhood friends, tearfully recalled the last time she saw and talked with her dear friend. The two women briefly spoke days before the eviction. Talking to Breslin from her third-floor apartment windowsill, Lowe, staring through her large glasses at the black-haired and thick-browed Breslin, expressed her shock about Eleanor. "I can't believe it. The last time I saw Ma Bumpurs was on the Wednesday before this thing happen. She was on her way to the [C-Town supermarket on University Avenue]. She stopped right outside on the sidewalk of my building and I called down [from the window] to her and said, 'Hi Ma.'"[20]

The cigarette-smoking Breslin wasn't the only journalist walking around Sedgwick Houses questioning residents about the impact of Eleanor's death on them. A few days after Eleanor's killing, the Bronx Media Collective—consisting of ten to twelve students from the South Bronx's Regional High School, veteran teacher and journalist Dennis Bernstein, and writer-filmmaker Chela "Connie" Blitt—wrote, directed, and filmed *Eleanor Bumpurs: 12-Gauge Eviction*. Under one hour, the well-researched film is one of a few investigative and student-produced documentaries on the Bumpurs killing. Personal and geographical connections to the University Heights area inspired students to cover one of the Bronx's worst cases of police brutality. Some students resided in Sedgwick Houses. Some had occasionally spotted Eleanor in the neighborhood. And several students had the unfortunate experience of witnessing "the commotion in the neighborhood and [hearing] the gunshots." Deeply troubled by the community tragedy, the young filmmakers and journalists were eager to understand why the NYPD was at a housing eviction and why an officer shot Eleanor.[21]

Building upon the civil rights and cultural activism of high school students and filmmakers such as William Greaves and Spike Lee, local documentarians and reporters used film to spotlight their neighbors' thoughts and emotions as well as the growing call for community mobilization.[22] Featuring a creative blend of hip-hop music, cartoon drawings, role playing, narration, poems, and speeches from Bronx activists and prominent Black Power activists such as Malcolm X, the film puts a human face on community suffering and rage. Using a variety of camera shots and angles, they filmed crying neighbors, a contentious Sedgwick Houses tenants meeting, a candlelit vigil staged at 1551 University Avenue, and Eleanor's damaged apartment door. One student who resided in Eleanor's building led his classmates to her door, where they positioned a 35-mm camera and assumed the roles of Eleanor and the police officers. Taking up the entire camera frame, a close-up shot shows an open hole where a cylinder lock used to be. Police pushed out the cylinder during the eviction. A single camera shot inside the broken keyhole gave viewers a small-scale view of Eleanor's living room. Natural light cascades into the room, making it possible to see several pieces of furniture and leaving viewers to imagine the brutal confrontation between Eleanor and police.

Candid interviews with neighbors made *Eleanor Bumpurs: 12-Gauge Eviction* a compelling documentary. Interviews with working-class residents were some of the first testimonies documenting Bronxites' views about the killing and the NYPD's actions. On the streets, in bodegas, at neighborhood meetings and protest rallies, and around the Sedgwick Houses area, students, equipped with cameras, microphones, and writing materials, spent countless hours posing questions and talking with public housing tenants, Eleanor's relatives and friends, local store merchants, and religious and political leaders. High schoolers asked, "Did you know Mrs. Bumpurs?" "Did you ever see her?" "What did you think about what the police did to her?"[23]

Standing in front of Sedgwick Houses among a small crowd of tenants, neighbor Deborah Kirby told student interviewers exactly how she felt: "They [the community] are all in an up-rage. We are all one. We are all God's children. It's sad to see someone get killed like that, especially a sixty-six-year-old woman. That lady old enough to be my mother or grandmother. It's a shame." Rosalee Thomas, who lived on the twelfth floor of Eleanor's building, told the students, "I saw all these cops. So I went down to the fourth floor to watch. She was an old lady." Like many folks, Thomas was baffled over the need for a specialized SWAT team to expel Eleanor from her apartment. "There was so many of them [cops]. Are you telling me five cops can't take one knife away from an old lady?" An unnamed resident, who requested anonymity for fear of police retribution, told filmmakers that police had more empathy for animals than for Black people. "A couple of weeks ago a dangerous animal escaped from the Bronx Zoo, and they captured it with a sleep dart and brought it safely back to its cage in the zoo. Around here cops treat black folks worse than zoo animals. They'll risk their white skin to save an animal, but they'll murder us on the spot."[24] One man, standing next to his friend, who happened to be Mary Bumpurs, noted that Eleanor's killing had politicized him, igniting within him a strong desire to advocate for legal justice. "There are many Ms. Bumpurs in the city. But this case, for me, was the straw that broke the camel's back. And I decided I want to do something."[25]

New York's finest were also featured in *Eleanor Bumpurs: 12-Gauge Eviction*. Students interviewed several white and Black Housing Authority and police officers. Placing microphones and cameras in officers' faces, students boldly asked, "What happened? Why did NYCHA want to evict and throw a grandmother onto the streets? Why did police shoot her?" The officers offered the teenage interviewers a range of unsatisfying answers: "We can't comment on that." "The NYPD is conducting a full investigation."[26]

A creative work about community pain and outrage, *Eleanor Bumpurs: 12-Gauge Eviction* would garner much media attention.

Student filmmakers were featured guests on radio programs on the liberal-leaning station WBAI, among others, and profiled in New York's popular *Newsday* publication. The documentary even premiered at Harlem Week's film festival and other local venues.[27]

Sedgwick Houses residents were not the only New Yorkers troubled by Eleanor's killing. Growing media coverage of the deadly eviction set off a firestorm of anger and sympathy throughout the city. Wide-ranging opinions about the NYPD's use of excessive and deadly force were articulated in heartfelt and passionate letters to newspaper editors, newspaper opinion pieces, street interviews with journalists, and correspondences to city and state lawmakers and housing officials. Big Apple residents were "completely outraged, horrified, frightened and saddened" over the Sedgwick Houses incident.[28] Outpouring emotions over what many called a "murder" had much to do with Eleanor's race, gender, class, age, and physical and mental abilities. It had much to do with the sheer brutality of forced displacement and her lack of bodily protection. And New Yorkers' anger over the killing was about bearing witness to yet another tragic incident that involved Black women and police. "It is another case," according to National Black United Front (NBUF) activist Dave Walker, "of brutal attacks against Black women of this city by the N. Y. P. D."[29] The police abuse and killing of Black women was an all-too-familiar part of New York City's long history of racial violence.

Frightening encounters with the NYPD and its various law enforcement divisions, including the Transit Police Department and NYCHA, were an incessant issue for Black women during the 1980s. New York's rapidly transforming socioeconomic and political landscape—including fluctuating crime rates, an increasing unhoused population, a drug epidemic, and societal beliefs that Black households were sites of criminality—drove women's encounters with police. Black women's interactions with police increased as New York City mayor Edward Koch expanded the NYPD's presence and power. Addressing the city's wars on drugs and social disorder and answering citizenry demands for neighborhood protection, Koch hired more officers and sanctioned the NYPD's focus on street-level drug dealing and quality-of-life offenses, such as vandalism, sex work, and gambling.[30]

Police officers physically and sexually attacked women on city streets and subway platforms, in police cars and precincts. They dragged women by their hair down flights of steps and along rough, dirty pavements, pummeled them with their fists and batons, and hurled racial epithets and vile language at them. Beyond the public gaze, police assaults occurred in women's most sacred spaces: their homes. Those interior areas, according to writer Elizabeth Alexander, "go far, far beyond the limited expectations and definitions of what black is, isn't or should be."[31]

Police home attacks were distinct forms of gendered state and racist violence against Black women. It was a kind of violence that upended their intimate lives, and according to anthropologist Christen Smith a "kind of spiritual terror—an attack not only on the body but also the psyche and refuge of the soul."[32] Invasive police raids and visits, according to one police brutality victim and mother, were the "worst thing that ever happened" to Black families. Wearing combat tactical gear and carrying military-grade weapons supplied by state and federal agencies, cops busted down front doors, damaged furniture with their nightsticks, and destroyed clothes and other family belongings. Apartment foyers, kitchens, living rooms, and bedrooms became sites of human violation. And, for some women like Eleanor, spaces called home became killing grounds. With no regard for women's privacy, property, and legal rights, the NYPD and other state and federal officers conducted some of late-twentieth-century New York's largest and most violent paramilitary raids.

On April 19, 1980, Harlem residents living at 92 Morningside Avenue experienced a horrifying three-hour predawn police raid. More than fifty heavily armed officers tore through the apartment building. Police were in search of Black Liberation Army leader and Clinton Correctional Facility for Women escapee Assata Shakur (formerly Joanne Chesimard). Convicted of several crimes, including first-degree murder, Shakur escaped from the New Jersey facility in 1979, prompting a nationwide search. Police, who believed tenants were harboring Shakur, broke down apartment doors, pointed military-style weapons at sleeping tenants, and dragged startled and half-dressed residents out of their beds. Agents subjected women tenants, including Columbia University graduate student and political activist Ebun Adelona, to a demeaning physical search. They forced women to "lift their [clothes] to bare their upper legs to agents looking for a scar that Chesimard is supposed to bear." In pursuit of Shakur, agents ransacked several apartments. According to Adelona, "They pulled out my linen, the bathroom door was off the hinges, and my sofa was in the middle of the floor. It was a terrorizing experience."[33]

On October 18, 1984, just weeks before Eleanor's killing, an army of at least three hundred FBI agents and NYPD Joint Terrorism Task Force officers raided the Brooklyn and Queens homes of lawyers and political activists Viola Plummer, Colette Pean, Yvette Kelly, Ruth Carter, and other members of the New York Eight Against Fascist Terrorism (New York 8+). Their political activism made them targets for what historian Ashley Farmer referred to as "the government's decades-long surveillance and harassment campaigns against Black [women] activists."[34] Invading women's homes, police and FBI agents manhandled and arrested women. "They even battered their children, knocking one fifteen-year-old girl to the floor, handcuffing her, and putting a gun to her head." Employing the 1984 anti-crime and preventive detention legislation, federal officials, including Southern District of New York (SDNY) prosecutor Rudolph Giuliani, arrested activists for conspiring to use murder, kidnapping, and arson to rob armed trucks and to facilitate several prison escapes.[35] Giuliani charged the group with the Racket Influenced and Corrupt Organization (RICO) statute, a 1970 law he successfully used to jail New York mobsters and Wall Street tycoons.[36] Federal officials claimed the New York 8+ were violent terrorists planning armed robberies and jailbreaks for political activists Sekou Odinga and Kuwasi Balagoon, two men convicted of the deadly 1981 Brinks robbery in Nyack, New York. Deemed threats to national security, Plummer, Pean, Kelley, and Carter were denied bail and prosecuted in a federal court in 1985.[37]

These police home invasions were shocking to the public. Yet Eleanor's story was unique. Her death consumed New Yorkers, bringing many residents to a breaking point. "This is the worst case of police killing in a long history of police killings. They have killed children as young as eleven years old and now they have begun to kill grandmothers. All decent citizens ought to be outraged by this unspeakable crime," noted Brooklyn minister and activist Herbert Daughtry.[38] Bronx public school teacher Lillie Mae Robinson was devastated. "It angered many of us in the community," said Robinson.[39] "She was treated as if she were on the FBI's Ten Most Wanted list," Manhattan resident Donna Singleton told *Daily News* reporters.[40]

Eleanor's killing became a high-profile police brutality case, receiving citywide media coverage. Black, Latinx, and white newspapers including the *New York Amsterdam News*, the *New York Times,* and the *City Sun* offered the reading public attention-grabbing black-and-white photographs and thought-provoking editorials. Like Eleanor's Sedgwick Houses neighbors, New Yorkers had much to say about her death.

New York Amsterdam News reporter and photojournalist James "Jimmy" Gilbert's "Roving Camera" column highlighted several Harlem residents' thoughts about the shooting. Legal secretary Delores Sistrunk told the *Amsterdam News* staffer that "this incident has really struck something within me. The excuse the police gave for killing her doesn't ring true. It seems to me that it wouldn't take six policem[e]n and a 12-gauge shotgun to evict a 67-year-old senior citizen. If it happens to her it could happen to my grandmother." Schoolteacher Marv A. Douglas questioned the NYPD's tactics and inability to deescalate mental health situations. "Surely, they could have handled the situation differently. Realizing that the woman was emotionally disturbed, the officers should have changed their plans and sought help from other agencies or personnel. They should have studied her case history before they set out to evict her."[41]

Amsterdam News reader Carolyn Davis articulated a range of emotions. She did not talk with Gilbert. Instead, she penned a blistering letter titled "Where Is the Black Pride?" to the newspaper. Davis did not mince words about the "latest and most horrible tragedy to affect the Black community." Nor did she did shy away from critiquing city officials, the NYPD, Eleanor's adult children, Black political leaders, and the broader African American community. Davis blamed Eleanor's death "on all of us." "All I can feel is anger. I'm angry at her relatives, the police department, the murderer, the HRA, and the public in general. It's a scandal and a shame." Davis also questioned some prominent Black leaders' seeming silence on Eleanor's death. "I wonder where all of our so-called 'Black leaders' were hiding. Where was [former civil rights activist and 1984 US presidential candidate] Jesse Jackson, the NAACP, [and Nation of Islam leader Louis] Farrakhan? They have something to say about everything else. We need them now."[42] Uttering the feelings of some New Yorkers, Davis also commented on her willingness to employ lethal violence against any police officer who harmed her family. "I don't know how anyone else feels about it, but if it had been my grandmother, the policeman that shot her would not be alive today." Davis's remarks echoed writer June Jordan's feelings about the 1978 police killing of Brooklyn businessman Arthur Miller. Jordan recommended lethal violence as a strategy against police killing. Jordan's "Poem about Police Violence" suggests a life for a life; for each incident of police murder, members of the Black community slay an officer.[43]

Meanwhile, *Village Voice* writer and photographer Anthony Barboza invited some of the nation's most prolific artists to share their opinions about the shooting. Olu Dara, a jazz musician (and father of 1990s hip-hop emcee Nas), personalized Eleanor's killing, stating "she may as well as have been part of my family." Photographer and 1971 *Shaft* filmmaker Gordon Parks connected the shooting to how white society employed violence to control Black bodies: "To me this is an example of the hatred and the need to impose their inner violence upon black people." Soul singer Stevie Wonder, who five years prior held a benefit concert raising $45,000 for police brutality victim and California mother Eula Mae Love, encouraged *Village Voice* readers to see themselves in Eleanor and other police brutality victims. "How many of them are you and me?"[44]

Newspapers outside New York reported on Eleanor's tragic story. The *Detroit Free Press, Pittsburgh Courier, Chicago Defender, Los Angeles Sentinel,* and popular magazines such as *Jet* covered the case, offering American readers details about the shooting. *Los Angeles*

104 TELL HER STORY

Sentinel Black journalist Betty Pleasant's weekly "Soulvine" column compared the New York incident to the fate of California's Eula Love. In a brief editorial titled "Shades of Eula Love," Pleasant maintained that the Bronx murder was a replay of the 1979 police shooting of the thirty-nine-year-old working-class widow and mother of three. On January 3, two Los Angeles Police Department (LAPD) officers were at Love's Orchard Avenue house because she allegedly attacked a city worker over an unpaid utility bill. LAPD officers emptied between seven and nine rounds of bullets in Love's body after she allegedly attacked them with a knife. She died in front of her children.[45]

The botched eviction sent shockwaves beyond US borders and throughout the international community. Foreign newspapers, particularly those in Canada, heavily covered the case, raising awareness about the Bronx expulsion. Canadian newspapers such as *The Province, The Winnipeg, The Vancouver Sun*, and the *Gazette* offered their citizenry a window into their longtime political ally's disconcerting issues with race and policing. Global news editorials about the way shotgun bullets mutilated Eleanor's body, as well as photojournalists' images of her inconsolable family tugged at readers' hearts.

Global citizens emotionally connected to Eleanor, in part, because she was a mother. Urbanites, especially Black and Latinx New Yorkers, saw Eleanor as someone who could have been in their family—namely, one of the most important figures in their lives: their mothers and grandmothers. Older Black women like Eleanor, those born during the period of Jim Crow segregation, were highly respected. Having endured the burdens of race, class, gender exclusion, white violence, and labor exploitation, Black mothers were viewed by younger generations as sources of wisdom and strength and instillers of family traditions and values. They were essential to the survival of their families and communities. Black mothers were unique figures who everyone loved, protected, and revered—and whether biologically related or not, Black folks laid claim to elderly women. "Mrs. Bumpurs was someone's mother. Now she's everyone's mother," voiced *Amsterdam News* editor William A. Tatum.[46] Even NYPD commissioner Benjamin Ward, who defended officer Stephen Sullivan's deadly actions, saw his Brooklyn mother in Eleanor's face.

In an interview with *MacNeil/Lehrer NewsHour* journalist Charlayne Hunter-Gault, Ward said that it would have been difficult for him to shoot Eleanor. "Mrs. Bumpurs looked like my mother. My mother was that kind of large woman. I wouldn't have shot that woman."[47]

Financially struggling New York women, those hit hard by economic inflation and Reaganomics, related to Eleanor. They knew all too well the realities of poverty and joblessness and the unsettling consequences of late and missed rental payments. For many, the possibility of losing their homes, seeing their personal belongings piled on street sidewalks, living in overcrowded welfare hotels and shelters, or sleeping on streets among the city's rapidly growing unhoused population was frightening.[48] One Bronx resident who had fallen behind in rent payments prayed that she would not end up like Eleanor: "I hope this will not become a practice with the police."[49] Real fears and nightmares of apartment evictions and police guns compelled late-paying renters, "especially grandmothers, [to] hurry up and pay up" their rent.[50]

For many New Yorkers, Eleanor became the poster child for various socioeconomic and political issues plaguing the city. They reasoned that the attempted forced eviction and the police killing were the consequences of reduced city services that aided the poor, unemployed, and older populations. "Her murder smacks of systematic racism, police terror, and contempt for Black lives. Once again the police came into an oppressed community heavily armed. This time to evict a senior citizen from a federally funded housing project at a time when thousands are already homeless, and she was gunned down for the crime of being poor," noted members of the Eleanor Bumpurs Justice Committee, a Bronx grassroots group dedicated to securing legal justice for Eleanor.[51] Moreover, folks connected the NYCHA, NYPD, and other city agencies' handling of Eleanor's expulsion to municipal inefficiency and neglect. City abandonment was at the heart of the eviction, causing Eleanor to slip through the cracks. And if Eleanor could fall through the cracks, any New Yorker could.

Societal framings of Eleanor as a maternal symbol would mobilize political activists. Racial and ethnically diverse residents would join social and legal justice campaigns for Eleanor, becoming politically active for the first time in their lives. Seasoned activists would use the Bumpurs case to shine a light on the urban poor's long-standing struggles against municipal neglect, policing, and racial inequality.

Anti-police-brutality New Yorkers were not the only ones talking about Eleanor's killing. White New Yorkers also voiced opinions about the apartment shooting. Some wept for Eleanor. Others, however, commended Sullivan's deadly actions while articulating racist and sexist stereotypes about Black women. Their varying sensibilities spoke to ongoing conversations within New York white communities about urban poverty, policing, and Blackness.

White New Yorkers from all social and political spectrums had thoughts about the Sedgwick Houses killing, including statements like "I cried for her!" "Stephen Sullivan was a hero." "Everyone with a sense of decency is saddened." "I think Stephen Sullivan did us all a favor." In the local press and in letters to elected officials, New Yorkers articulated a range of opinions about Eleanor Bumpurs and the NYPD officer who shot her. Reading popular city papers, some progressive-leaning white people were moved by reports on the events leading up to the shooting. They viewed Eleanor as a victim, a term and status historically denied to Black bodies and often reserved for whites. Carrying the status of victimhood came with the privilege of believability, compassion, and legal and social protection. Many white people identified the Bronx grandmother as a victim of police brutality and a casualty of a multi-tiered system of race and class oppression.

In letters to newspaper editors, white New Yorkers candidly voiced their sadness over Eleanor's story. After reading several *Village Voice* articles about the Bumpurs case, Manhattan resident Penelope Andrew expressed grief and anger about "this violent, ignorant act." She wrote, "I cried. I am not black and I am not poor—but I am angry. I am outrage[d], and I am not going to forget what has happened to Mrs. Bumpurs. I want to do something!" Perhaps eager to join emerging 1980s anti-brutality campaigns, Andrews wanted to put her money where her mouth was. She proposed establishing a monetary fund in honor of Eleanor, asking *Village Voice* editors: "What would be involved in starting a memorial fund in Mrs. Bumpurs's name? Are there [any] active and/or legal recourses?" Across the Hudson River in New Jersey, Harriette Carpozi, another *Village Voice* reader, was shocked by "the cold-blooded murder of Eleanor Bumpurs." Carpozi wrote to the weekly: "I am nauseated and appalled at the ruthless ignorance of our supposed law system. Racism has got to stop!" Feeling vengeful, the Garden State resident even hoped to "see God Almighty wring the neck of the thoughtless, heartless officer who used his cold heart instead of his warped brain in a bloody cop-out bullet!"[52]

In a letter to Manhattan city clerk David Dinkins, a white former NYCHA police officer expressed a surprising view about officer Stephen Sullivan. His opinions departed from many of his brothers in blue. He wrote that Sullivan's actions were inappropriate. For him, the shooting had nothing to do with racism or class politics or the preservation of officers' lives. He uttered thoughts officers rarely voiced about themselves or about one another, reasoning that Sullivan was scared and made a grave mistake. "The fatal shooting of Eleanor Bumpurs was a terrible tragedy. [It] should never have taken place. The shooting took place because of a yellow-bellied police officer, who panicked and overacted. Mr. Sullivan, without question, overreacted, and Mrs. Bumpurs' death should never have occurred."[53]

Such critiques sharply departed from a significant cross section of white men and women who overwhelming supported Sullivan. Pro-Sullivan sentiments ignited a series of scathing public narratives about Eleanor and inspired some of the NYPD's largest political protests.

Just as a justice-seeking campaign for Eleanor was emerging so was one for Stephen Sullivan. Many white people quickly came to Sullivan's defense. Well-known WNBC television journalist Gabe Pressman was one of those defenders. Considered "the indefatigable dean of New York's television reporters," Pressman was a respected veteran newsman, covering the hoopla of city politics and city crime from the 1950s until his death in 2017. Pressman reported every story the city had to tell, including the 1984 police killing of a poor Black grandmother.[54]

The esteemed news personality used his massive media platform to advocate for Sullivan, reserving what writer Kate Manne calls "himpathy" for the officer. Pressman distorted the framing of Sullivan's violence against Eleanor, ignoring her victimhood and imagining Sullivan as both sufferer and lifesaver. He praised the father of two and decorated officer, the "real" victim who in a matter of seconds made a difficult decision that protected the lives of his fellow ESU officers. During a 1984 NBC *Late Night News* broadcast, Pressman acknowledged Sullivan's commendable police service. He informed millions of viewers that the officer had a history of heroism, citing his rescue of a distraught man about to jump from a bridge and successful confrontation of a man swinging a baseball bat. "If Sullivan is guilty, he should be punished, but [my] research shows Sullivan to have an exemplary record, having received six Excellent Police Duty Awards, two meritorious Duty, and one unit citation."[55] Having the support of popular media personalities like Pressman was beneficial to Sullivan. Pressman's opinions reflected and amplified the thoughts of conservative white New Yorkers and those who would eventually participate in mass protests for Sullivan.

Much of Sullivan's support came from whites who lived outside of New York City, those from suburbs such as Westchester, Nassau, and Putnam Counties. These enclaves were predominately composed of middle- and working-class Irish, Jewish, Catholic, Italian, and Polish families, who were typically Republicans or conservative Democrats. They unapologetically preached the conservative politics of the day. Many were anti-liberal, anti-Black, and anti-immigrant. As Reagan supporters, they backed welfare reductions, law-and-order measures, and the police. Speaking about his overwhelming support within his Putnam County community, Sullivan noted: "I had a lot of support—a lot of letters and cards. I even had a Mass card and a nun praying for me. [Outside this community,] they've called me a murderer and a killer. But I've had nothing but good words."[56] In both right- and left-wing newspapers and on conservative talk radio programs like Bob Grant's show, white- and blue-collar white men and women wrote letters to editors and phoned into radio shows, expressing their unapologetic defense of Sullivan.[57] They championed what Sullivan and all white men represented to them: comfort, protection, and authority. Such characteristics were tethered to their identity and privilege.

Many whites unsurprisingly employed the Bumpurs case to voice their unshakable confidence in and respect for the NYPD. Based on their extensive and amicable personal experiences with law enforcement and their perceptions of urban crime, white New Yorkers viewed the NYPD as protectors of law-abiding citizens, as frontline soldiers in the fight against urban crime, and as enforcers of robust crime-control measures. Many saw cops, especially those who were white male officers, as self-sacrificing and hardworking public servants who deserved to return to their families at the end of the day. Adopting a pro-police stance, whites did not readily accept purported claims of police wrongdoing or brutality, especially allegations made by New York's racially and ethnically diverse populations. They did not believe, as concluded in a 1983 congressional hearings report on policing in American cities, that racism was a "major factor underlying complaints of police brutality in New York City."[58] For them, police brutality was not pervasive or systemic. According to one New Yorker, "Sure, there's an occasional question about police conduct, but our cops are the best in the world. It's tough dealing with the worst elements of society. Their heroic acts never get the publicity given [the] occasional incident of brutality."[59] Complaints of police violence were interpreted as an anti-police strategy, one intended to contest police authority and prevent law enforcers from performing their duties—which included occupying supposedly dangerous Black and Brown communities like the one Eleanor lived in. This line of thought, writes historian Kali Gross, spoke to the "profound alliance between white citizens, law enforcement, and the American justice system; it is a mutually constitutive allegiance that privileges and maintains whiteness, and the ideologies of white supremacy therein in part, by policing and criminalizing black [men and] women's bodies via an expansive carceral regime."[60]

White people did not consider Sullivan's shooting of an elderly woman to be excessive. They made endless excuses for why it was necessary to kill Eleanor, signaling a broader problem: the exoneration

of state violence in cases against nonwhite people and a lack of empathy toward Black people killed by the state. "He did what he had
to do. If I were him, I would have done the same thing," voiced one
New Yorker. Others made similar comments. "If someone weight-
ing 270 pounds rushed at me with a knife, I wouldn't stop and ask
her if she had arthritis. I'd defend myself the best and quickest way
I knew how. If Officer Sullivan hadn't done the same, his wife would
be a widow."[61] Manhattan attorney Brian Graifman stated, "The
Bumpurs shooting illustrates one thing: don't go charging after police officers with a knife."[62] Some white New Yorkers even worried
about the apartment shooting's long-term impact on Sullivan's mental health. "Think of the poor cop who made the decision to shoot
[her]. He has to live with that."[63] Sympathy for Sullivan was also
coupled with anger.

Whites directed their scorn at the dead. Statements about Eleanor were racist, sexist, and fatphobic. They demonstrated a disdain
for the poor, especially those receiving state and federal assistance.
For many, welfare recipients like Eleanor were public enemy number one. White people's feelings about Eleanor conjured stereotypes
of urban poor Black mothers living "high off the hog" on taxpayers'
dime. As then California governor Ronald Reagan said, welfare recipients were "wearing fur coats, driving fancy cars, and eating T-Bone
steaks with food stamps while us[ing] eighty names, thirty addresses,
fifteen telephone numbers to collect food stamps and Social Security. Her tax-free cash income has been running at $150,00 a year."
Anti-welfare advocates embraced a politics of disgust toward Eleanor
and the city's more than eight hundred thousand welfare recipients.
They believed that public assistance receivers refused to pull themselves up by their own bootstraps and were freeloaders and hustlers
who scammed hardworking taxpayers and the federal government
out of money.[64]

Disdain for welfare recipients lessened sympathy for Eleanor.
Many white New Yorkers failed to see Eleanor or her children as
victims of urban poverty, race discrimination, or police violence. Instead, Eleanor became symbolic of unfit single motherhood—a parent who made poor lifestyle choices, relied on welfare to support her

family, and passed down to her children a culture of poverty. "Why didn't her family of seven grown children pay her rent? Why did they let things get so bad, are they on welfare also!?" wrote newspaper letter writers, voicing cruel and inconsiderate remarks about Eleanor. Her name appeared in the same sentence as "welfare cheat," "many children," and "overindulgent mother." Even more egregious, city folks who knew nothing about Eleanor's personal life or financial circumstance claimed that she was a longtime welfare abuser. "She used public assistance as a way of life. She got fat on our tax dollars. What did she do with the money welfare was sending her each month?"[65]

Callous public commentary about Eleanor's economic circumstances promoted conservative ideas that poor people were undeserving of access to public resources and that federal policies centered on eliminating economic safety net programs were necessary. Reading white newspapers' public opinion sections, many Black New Yorkers, especially journalists, found the comments about Eleanor to be despicable, prompting some to pen counternarratives.[66]

While perusing the comment sections of several white newspapers, *Amsterdam News* columnist Abiola Sinclair was stunned by white New Yorkers' views on Eleanor and her family. Comments like "fat," "Sullivan was just doing his job," and "the cop was right" angered her. Sinclair spilled her emotions onto the pages of the *Amsterdam News,* penning an editorial for her "Media Watch" column. She censured certain white New Yorkers, including TV journalist Gabe Pressman, calling them "racist" and highlighting how Pressman's praise of Sullivan "gave comfort to whites who hate Bumpers." Sinclair went on to say that she was "hurt at the unkind and insensitive letters sent concerning" Eleanor.[67] Fellow Brooklyn journalists and newspaper founders Andrew Cooper and Utrice Leid were also incensed but not surprised about whites' bigoted comments. As longtime observers of city affairs, they recognized how negative racial images reinforced false and stereotypical portrayals of African Americans and bolstered anti-Black rhetoric and violence. Having the attention of Black New Yorkers, particularly those residing in Brooklyn, Cooper and Leid used their newly established newspaper, the *City Sun*, to counter de-monizing press accounts about Eleanor.

Founded in the summer of 1984, the fifty-cent weekly informed its readers that it was suspending its regular editorials on Black New York life, the Caribbean and Africa, culture, and sports. Instead, *City Sun* editors and staff dedicated an entire edition to the Bumpurs story, showing "the outrage of the community and the passion that it feels on this [Bumpurs killing] and related issues." Not to be drowned out by scathing editorials about Eleanor, the *City Sun* "decided that the full force of the community should be expressed."

Sixteen pages long, the *City Sun's* November 7–13 edition fea-tured a gripping front-page headline: "Speaking Truth to Power: The Shame of The City." Editors solicited expert, opinion, and eyewitness accounts from various community members, including David Dinkins, civil rights activist Rev. Wendell Foster, NYPD veteran Alton Waldron, *Village Voice* writer Jack Newfield, and Baruch College professor Juanita Howard. With this impressive slate of writers, politicians, and ordinary residents, "no one will be able to say they didn't know the full depth of the impact of this callous killing on us all. We offer this entire issue to those who say they are interested in eliciting testimony from the Black community about the murder of one of its own."[68]

Raising public awareness about Eleanor's story, the *City Sun* was also committed to upending police violence. They encouraged read-ers to join New Yorkers' long-standing fight against "wanton acts of violence perpetrated against our fellow citizens by officers and rep-resentatives of the law enforcement community."[69] Using the Bum-purs story to mobilize political action, editors created a "A Petition to Stop Police Brutality and Violence Now." Taking up a full page in the November issue, the petition creators "deplore[d] the killing [of] Mrs. Eleanor Bumpurs at the hands of New York City police offi-cers, and we deplore every other such act that has violated. . . . We deplore the rash of recent killings by police of citizens of inner-city neighborhoods and condemn those responsible for this careless disre-gard for human life." The appeal called for legal action against those involved in Eleanor's eviction. "We insist that: firing [of] all persons involved in Mrs. Bumpurs's death—including police officers, the city marshal, and Housing Authority personnel; an investigation of the shooting by an impartial and non-law-enforcement panel; and that the full weight of the law, and the full weight of administrative censure, be brought against all persons directly and indirectly involved in this unforgiveable tragedy."[70]

The *City Sun*'s commitment to offering readers critical and thought-provoking editorials on Eleanor's killing did not go unnoticed. Readers praised the newspaper. One reader commented that the *City Sun* should "be commended highly for the manner in which it continues to cover the recent atrocity of the New York Police Department which was perpetrated against Mrs. Eleanor Bumpurs."[71] Another reader said: "I was truly proud of the paper because of the compassionate way in which it presented the story, but also because it took an unprecedented stand journalistically in making a statement of the outrage I believe the Black community and entire city felt as a result of this killing."[72]

New Yorkers had much love for Eleanor. And that love, support, and belief that her life mattered provided the impetus for public action. Their loud voices became the makings of a movement, one that the city had not witnessed before. A racially and ethnically diverse coalition of labor and religious leaders, students, scholars, cultural producers, neighborhood advocates, and activists against police brutality would not, as Mary Bumpurs stated, "let this case be swept under the rug. No, not this time. We have to keep it going so people don't forget, because just like it was my mother, it could have been someone's mother."[73] New Yorkers did not forget about Eleanor. They deemed her worthy of community mobilization.

CHAPTER 6

SAYING GOODBYE TO ELEANOR

A few days after their mother's killing, the Bumpurs family struggled to prepare for one of the saddest days in their lives: Eleanor's homecoming and burial services. Arranging funeral services was difficult for the working-class Bronx family. Nothing made sense to Fannie Mae, Mary, Deborah, Terry, and Keenie. It was hard to comprehend what had happened to their mother and what was happening to them. Being Black New Yorkers, they were all too familiar with police harassing and attacking nonwhite residents on streets, at places of residence, and in subway cars. Some of them remembered the horrific story of transit cops brutally beating young graffiti artist Michael Stewart on a subway platform in 1983. But this police assault hit home. In a haze of confusion about Eleanor being snatched away, some family members did not have the emotional bandwidth to plan a funeral.

Money was also an issue for the family. The Bumpurs daughters could not afford the over $1,800 in funeral costs—nor did Eleanor or her daughters have life insurance policies. Limited and fixed incomes, cycles of unemployment, and poverty prevented the family from affording monthly life insurance premiums. The working-class family was not certain as to how they would afford a minister, casket, flowers, funeral programs, clothes for Eleanor, burial fees, and other associated expenses. But assistance was on the way.

Eleanor's killing shocked New Yorkers to their core, compelling many to offer the family their time, resources, comforting words, and money. One heartbroken community member was Bronx councilor and veteran civil rights activist Rev. Wendell Foster. An Alabama native and founding pastor of the United Church of Christ in the Morrisania section of the Bronx, Foster became the first Black and independent city official in the Bronx in 1978, representing the Ninth District, which included Highbridge, Morrisania, and the South Bronx. The politician and pastor aided the Bumpurs family during one of the most difficult moments in their lives.[1]

Sedgwick Houses residents informed Foster about Eleanor's death. Located on the Bronx's Grand Concourse, Foster's office was inundated with telephone calls and letters about Eleanor. Writing on the day of the shooting, one concerned Sedgwick Houses tenant wanted Foster to investigate Eleanor's killing. The letter stated: "This entire matter warrants not only a complete, in-depth investigation but some form of criminal action taken against the police involved. It is inconceivable that a senior citizen, age approximately 67, can place the NYC Police Department in a life-threatening situation, with a knife, to the extent of warranting the killing. Please help, Councilman Foster. I trust that you will take the appropriate action necessary."[2] Like his Bronx constituents, Foster was outraged about Eleanor's killing. "It's just unbelievable. It doesn't make sense. They were going to put her on the street, an old lady. Maybe that's why they felt they could shoot her. They thought she didn't matter. But she did matter. No one can explain to me to any satisfaction that she deserved to die."[3] Foster even compared the NYPD's lack of care for Eleanor to their handling of a fifty-pound pit bull terrier mix that killed a two-month-old baby. Two weeks before Eleanor's killing, Harlem infant Coral Robinson was tragically mauled to death by the family pet. "Police skillfully and professional restrained [that] vicious dog. Yet they had to kill this woman [Eleanor]. They handled the animal better than they did a person and the city should do what it has to so that it never happens again."[4]

Several brief correspondences also draw Foster to the Bronx tragedy. Foster did not personally know Eleanor or any members of the Bumpurs family. But their last name was familiar to him. One year prior to Eleanor's killing, Mary, after attending one of the councilor's free housing clinics at the United Church of Christ, handwrote him several letters. Frustrated and saddened with seeing abandoned and boarded up apartment buildings and neighborhoods destroyed by the Bronx's infamous blazes of the 1970s, Foster and his staff offered housing workshops to hundreds of Bronx residents. These residents turned to Foster, hoping to escape dilapidating structures and obtain affordable housing. Foster and his invited guests of housing officials and other municipal workers offered attendees insight on NYCHA's application process and encouraged Bronxites like Mary to advocate for better housing conditions.[5]

At her wits end with residing in her basement apartment, the young mother turned to the Bronx councilor, requesting assistance in securing public housing and available city services. She also explained her long journey toward obtaining a "nice place to live." "I am a registered voter and a citizen of these U.S. states. I think something can be done to help me. I am a single parent. I have three children one, 18yrs, my two sons which are 16 [years] and 10 [years] of age. I live under substandard [and] over crowed conditions. I have been trying to find an apartment for the last 10 yrs. I have applied in the section 8 programs. I have applications anywhere there have been housing coming up." Mary further explained that her basement apartment was hazardous to her children's health. "I have a very sick child. My youngest [son] suffers from asthma." Poor ventilation, earthen floors, mold, and perhaps lead exposure exacerbated her son's existing health conditions. "It's a must that I move from here. I truly hope you can help me and my children."[6]

Like the hundreds of housing request letters from borough residents, Mary's poignant plea for decent living conditions moved Foster and his staff. But there was little the councilor could do for the Bronx mother. Foster could not resolve Mary's housing situation; nor could he secure for her an apartment in one of NYCHA's properties. But Foster did what he could, which was forward Mary's letters to the NYCHA and request that the housing agency assist her. Mary and her family remained in the decrepit basement apartment. It would be years before she could move. One year later in 1984, the Bronx councilor and Mary's paths crossed again—in an unfortunate way.[7] And this time, he was determined to help her.

Foster and his church and office staff raised funds and arranged Eleanor's wake and funeral services. This was not the first time that Foster and his congregation of dedicated parishioners performed beneficent acts for grieving working-class Bronx families. They gave those in need money, time, prayers, and love. Speaking to a local reporter about the church's community service efforts, he commented: "These are our brother[s] and sister[s] in Christ and this is a service I am committed to render and glad to be able to. We've rallied to a number of tragedies." On April 16, subway transit police sergeant Carrol Braxton fatally shot nineteen-year-old Daniel James Evans while he was riding a Bronx subway train. Braxton claimed that the Park West High School graduate had a rifle. Foster and United Church of Christ members arranged Evans's funeral service, covering burial expenses for his widowed mother.[8]

According to Foster, "Nothing was done about making funeral arrangements to bury Mrs. Bumpurs. The funeral director needed $1,800 to make the arrangements and I discovered that the family could not come up with a dime. [They] simply did not have the money." Foster's church did what it's always done. They started making funeral arrangements at J. Gibson Funeral Home on East Tremont Avenue. "The funeral director [James S. Gibson] was gracious enough to extend credit and we went on the good faith that the money would be raised and we would be paid."[9] Donations for Eleanor's funeral—including the casket, embalming, hearse, limousine, clergy honorarium, cemetery charges, music, and pallbearers—were raised through Foster's Bronx Disaster Fund (BDF), a grassroots interfaith Bronx organization formed in 1981. In the tradition of Black philanthropic societies, the BDF financially assisted working-class New Yorkers, especially during times of bereavement.[10] In 1982, BDF raised funds for four Bronx children who were left parentless after a tragic automobile accident. New Yorkers opened their hearts and wallets for the children, sending thousands of dollars to the BDF.[11] For Eleanor, the BDF and other local donors followed suit. They pulled together to give her surviving family the support and care the city had not.

Monetary contributions poured in for Eleanor. Pooling their resources, Foster's Christ Church members, Sedgwick Houses residents,

and other kindhearted persons assisted in paying for Eleanor's homecoming services, making it possible for the family to grieve and not
worry about money. New Yorkers mailed twenty-dollar, fifty-dollar,
and one-hundred-dollar checks to the BDF's 169th Street office in
the Bronx. During Reverend Foster's Sunday morning church services
and weekly Bible study meetings, supporters reached into their purses
and wallets, giving crisp and wrinkled one-, five-, and ten-dollar bills
as well as spare change. Several other Bronx churches also made
generous donations. In between singing spiritual hymns and reading
biblical scriptures, parishioners dropped their tithes and donation
money into church offering plates and baskets. The Beck Memorial
United Presbyterian Church made a financial contribution toward
Eleanor's funeral arrangements. BDF partner, the Seventh-Day Ad-
ventist Church on 169th Street and the Grand Concourse, raised over
$1,000. On behalf of some Sedgwick tenants, Sandra Garcia, Elea-
nor's next-door neighbor, gave the Bumpurs family $137 in "crum-
pled" bills. Others reached into their pants and coat pockets and
donated what they could. One man handed Mary five dollars during
a candlelight vigil, "telling [her] this is all that I have."[12] The BDF
even received donations from incarcerated men, those perhaps thinking about the well-being of their own mothers and grandmothers.
In a November 1984 letter to Foster, New York's Sing Sing Correctional Facility supervisor of Volunteer Services Martin Goodman
expressed that "several of the inmates [at least twenty-five] wanted
to contribute their funds to the [Bumpurs] family and/or the funeral
of Mrs. Eleanor Bumpurs. They feel this is the least they can do."
Scraping together wages earned from countless hours of exploitative
prison labor, over twenty-five men contributed $83.50 to help lay
Eleanor to rest.[13]

Monetary love gifts, both big and small, made it possible for the
bereaved family to bury Eleanor with respect, dignity, and honor.
Because of the violent nature of Eleanor's death and disparaging
comments printed in some local newspapers, the family wanted her
funeral to be special. A homecoming service full of beautiful floral
bouquets and crowds of family and friends expressing declarations
of love would be a fitting gesture for someone who cared for others.

On a partly sunny and chilly Saturday afternoon on November 3, 1984, scores of weeping family members, friends and neighbors, community and religious leaders, and politically active celebrities such as actors Ruby Dee and Ossie Davis crowded into the Bronx's Gibson Funeral Home. Every seat was filled in the small one-story brick church. David Dinkins, Bronx city councilor Wendell Foster, and Brooklyn Congressman Major R. Owens were among a handful of city and state politicians who attended Eleanor's funeral. Mayor Edward Koch and NYPD commissioner Benjamin Ward were noticeably absent. Both officials extended condolences to the family in the media and promised that an official city report on Eleanor's death was imminent. Brooklyn pastor Herbert Daughtry and clergymen from various denominations throughout the city gathered at the church, offering attendees prayers, biblical scriptures, and much needed comfort. New York broadcast journalists, reporters, and photographers such as Lester Holt and Jimmy Breslin assembled into the church, hoping to get a comment or an interview from mourners. White college student, *City Sun* freelance photojournalist, and future 2002 Pulitzer Prize recipient Nancy Siesel quietly stood in the funeral home, taking pictures of the somber occasion.[14]

Siesel's and other photojournalists' images of Eleanor's funeral would challenge misconceptions about Eleanor—that she was disconnected from her family and her community. In fact, Eleanor was tethered to a network of family and friends who loved her. Photographs from the funeral showed that Eleanor was "somebody," echoing 1984 US presidential hopeful and civil rights leader Jesse Jackson's popular 1971 poem titled "I Am – Somebody." She was somebody's neighbor. She was somebody's close friend. She was somebody's mother. And she was becoming an entire city's grandmother.

Eleanor's New York and North Carolina families, dressed in black and white dresses, suits, and hats as they sat in the reserved front pews, holding hands. They listened to loving testimonials about "Ma Bumpurs" and hymns such as "Amazing Grace." Some relatives walked up to the open casket and leaned inside, brushing their lips gently against Eleanor's cheek or forehead. Mary gently guided her young son, nieces, and nephews to the casket, consoling and hugging them.

Other relatives stoically looked at Eleanor in casket. And some took funerary images of Eleanor with their Polaroids, intending to show pictures to those who could not attend the funeral.[15] Although mourning, Mary and her siblings were pleased with the funeral turnout. So many distant relatives, friends, neighborhood folks, and strangers came to pay their respects to Eleanor and support the family during one of the darkest chapters in their lives.

For the over one hundred funeral attendees, the silver-haired matriarch was more than a victim of housing inequality, poverty, environmental injustice, and a fractured mental health system. And she was certainly more than one of New York's latest victims in a rash of police killings. Eleanor was a self-sacrificing woman who possessed a compilation of life experiences—all of which would fail to capture the media or the public's interests. At the funeral, relatives and friends, wiping their tears and attempting to control their cries, reminded attendees that the way Eleanor lived was equally as important as how she died. Viewing Eleanor in the open "casket with her best Sunday Baptist Church [dark-colored striped dress and] white gloves [holding] a large red rose," they remembered her joys, wanting onlookers, especially those who never met Eleanor, like former American Negro Theatre actor Ruby Dee, to know her the way they knew her. Eleanor had an affinity for cooking for her family. She loved flowers, their shape, colors, and smell. As a young person, she enjoyed dancing to the classic sounds of soul singers like B. B. King and Muddy Waters. She listened to mid-twentieth century radio series such as "Stella Dallas" and "The Adventures of the Thin Man." And more than anything else in the world, Eleanor fiercely loved her children. "Lord knows she loved her children. They were her life." Heartfelt testimonials wove together a powerful narrative that unveiled Eleanor's interior world, one marked by a lifelong battle against poverty and a constant struggle for family stability and happiness, despite the challenges of single motherhood, the abduction of her own two sons, and illness. "God knows the hard times she had," said Harlem's Memorial Baptist Church minister Louis Grant who gave a touching eulogy for Eleanor.[16]

Mourners also spoke truth to power. Clearing their throats, they passionately voiced opinions about the police violence that ended Eleanor's life and their commitment to bringing continued awareness to urban inequalities and police brutality against Black and Brown New Yorkers. They vowed not to let Eleanor's killing be in vain. And some vowed to let the world know what happened to Eleanor. "We must act with the same sense of outrage as they did in Poland to protest the torture and killing of [Polish Roman] Catholic priest [and trade union supporter] Jerzy Popieluszko on October 19, 1984. That act has gained international attention. We have to do the same," stated Foster. Funeral attendees promised to "fight" for legal justice for Eleanor and all New Yorkers who lost their lives to police violence. Native New Yorker Ruby Dee, who had a long history of political activism from emceeing the 1963 March on Washington to being an outspoken critic of South African apartheid, hoped that Eleanor's tragic death "would be a coming together for all of us. When I was growing up in Harlem, I used to see evicted people's furniture out in the streets. Now I see the story has not changed much."[17]

In a dark-brown sandalwood coffin decorated with white and red flowers and ribbons, Eleanor Gray Bumpurs was laid to rest in an unmarked grave at the Frederick Douglass Memorial Cemetery in the Oakwood neighborhood of Staten Island. The family, witnessing NYPD Stephen Sullivan's supporters' contempt for Eleanor and understanding that white supremacy stalked and tortured Black bodies even in death, concealed Eleanor's resting place, hoping to deter any attempts to desecrate her grave site.

Eleanor lay among her kinfolks. Established in 1935 for African American New Yorkers, the Frederick Douglass Memorial Cemetery's purpose was to "lessen sorrow by creating around the death an atmosphere of beauty and inspirations" and "to halt indignities to Negro dead," those racially excluded from city cemeteries. The historic burial site was the final resting place for prominent early and mid-twentieth century Black race reformers and entertainers, including 1920s actress and blues singer Mamie Smith, and for poor New Yorkers whose kin could not afford plots or headstones. Offering

Eleanor final prayers and placing flowers on her grave site, the Bumpurs children and their extended families and friends walked out of the seventeen-acre cemetery as if they did not want to leave Eleanor behind. On the grassy and concrete walkways to parked cars, they emotionally broke down, weeping and consoling each other, knowing that their lives were forever changed.[18]

The sudden loss of Eleanor turned her family's worlds upside down. Their pain was unfathomable, and that pain was compounded by how she died. "To lose your mother in that kind of a way, that's pretty painful," said Mary. The Bumpurs siblings and extended family agonized over the brutality of their mother's death, struggling to make sense of it. Granddaughter LuDean expressed, "How and why did this happen to her? She would not hurt anyone."[19] Police killings, borrowing from historian Kidada Williams's discussion on the aftershocks of lynching on African American families, were "horrible both for what it did to the people killed and to their surviving kin." As a particular form of homicide and premature death, police killings "denied victims and their relatives the opportunity to experience a good [and perhaps even a natural] death."[20]

Police killings generated terror far beyond that of the primary victim. Due to media narratives, city and police reports, courtroom testimonies, and crime scene photographs, police killings, for many families, conjured images of loved ones dying alone and afraid, pleading for their lives, and enduring indescribable physical pain. A few weeks after Eleanor's funeral, the Bumpurs family came face-to-face with the horrors and brutality of the apartment confrontation between their mother and police. On November 27, Sedgwick Houses managers and the NYPD permitted the family to enter their mother's apartment. They did not know what to expect and were not sure if they could emotionally handle being in that space, but they had a job to do. Their mother's clothes, Bible, family photo albums, and other valuable belongings needed to be packed up. NYCHA wanted Eleanor's possessions removed as quickly as possible. Housing workers were preparing to scrub the floors, paint the walls, and remove any trace of the bloody confrontation between police and Eleanor so they could lease the apartment to another family. Financial profit and returning to the everyday business of property and rental management outweighed family trauma.

Opening the damaged forest-green apartment door, daughters Mary, Deborah, and Terry, and grandchildren Kareem Parker (Mary's twelve-year-old son), Sherice Baker (Fannie Mae Hayes's nineteen-year-old daughter), and Terry's fiancé, Richard Scurlock, walked into a gruesome scene, one that brought them to tears.

What was once a space where the family gathered for birthdays, holidays, and celebrations was now a grisly crime scene—left exactly as it had been the day Eleanor was killed. Seemingly, no one from NYCHA or the NYPD cared enough to think about the condition of the living room before granting access to the Bumpurs family. No one thought how this scene would add to the family's emotional and mental toll. Once again, the City of New York failed the Bumpurs family. Coming face-to-face with the gory space would cause another deep pain to the family; and in that space they would bear witness to the long tradition of state neglect and violence.

The floor was covered with "giant gauze pads stiffened with dried blood." A silhouette of Eleanor's body was exhibited against part of the kitchen wall. Beneath Eleanor's beloved Martin Luther King Jr. portrait were buckshot holes in the wall. Eleanor's small chairs and coffee tables were shoved aside and overturned. And the apartment had a pungent odor. It reeked of gunpowder and blood.[21] The living room's condition horrified and saddened the family. Struggling to complete the task of retrieving their mother's belongings, the family was startled by another sickening sight. Small bits of flesh and bone fragments were scattered in the corners of the floor and in the cracks of the dark linoleum. And one of their mother's severed fingers lay in the living room among the debris.

The family screamed and cried, shaking their heads in disbelief. "Oh my God, what is that?" "Didn't anyone have the sense to clean up?" asked a visibly shaken and angry Mary. The family grappled with what to do with their mother's dismembered finger. Should they call NYCHA or the Bronx District Attorney's Office, letting them know about their discovery? Should they remove the finger from the apartment? Refusing to touch their mother's severed limb, the family "left it right where [they] saw it."[22]

Discordantly, their mother's small bedroom was untouched. The bedroom was just as Eleanor had left it and how the family remembered: everything was in its place. Bedding sheets and pillows decorated a queen-size bed. Colorful dresses, favorite and comfortable housecoats, underwear, and socks were properly placed in dresser drawers and hung in a small closet. Sitting on their mother's bed and looking at the bedroom's immaculate condition, the daughters and grandchildren thought about what to do with their mother's clothes. Mary wanted to donate Eleanor's clothes to the Salvation Army. Oldest sister Fannie Mae had a different opinion about her mother's belongings. She wanted to keep her mother's dresses, desiring to feel emotionally connected to Eleanor. Mary deferred to her sister's wishes. The family also wept over media stories about Eleanor's mental health. Stories the family knew somewhat to be true yet did not want to be public or used to justify the NYCHA and the NYPD's actions. "Look at how neatly these clothes are folded," Deborah said as she ran her fingers over her mother's shirts and dresses. "Is that the way an emotionally disturbed person behaves?" asked Deborah. One of the youngsters, perhaps unaware of his grandmother's mental health history, also questioned the "psychotic" charge. "How can they say that mammy was mentally disturbed when she kept this apartment so neat?"[23]

As the family collected their mother's personal items, they conceivably thought about how she fought for her life and how she died in that apartment. Brief flashes and memories of family gatherings and daily episodes of love and laughter were interrupted by scenes of violation, violence, and death. "It was an assassination, plain and simple," said Mary.[24]

The family received a stack of condolence cards and handwritten letters from neighbors and strangers around the country, which eased the difficulty of the apartment visit. While sitting on their mother's bed, a distraught Deborah read aloud sympathy cards that were stuffed in Eleanor's mailbox. Collectively, the letters conveyed love and encouragement to fight for justice. Letter writers from New York and as far away as Texas and North Carolina reassured the daughters that the "City of New York is with you," "God is with you," and "we will fight with you." "This should have never happened" and "I'm keeping your family in my prayers" were inscribed in several letters. Many correspondents also articulated contempt for the NYPD, city social workers, and officials, including Mayor Koch and Commissioner Ward. Supporters were incensed about the City of New York's refusal to provide an elderly woman with mental health issues with appropriate city services, medical care, and the assistance needed to sustain life. High-ranking NYPD officers' refusal to immediately terminate Stephen Sullivan from the police force or arrest him for killing Eleanor also did not sit well with writers. In supporters' minds, the City of New York failed Eleanor. Having little to no faith in the legal system, some believed that politicians and prosecutors like those in the 1983 Michael Stewart case would do "absolutely nothing" about Eleanor's killing, as one New Yorker wrote. "They just allow them to kill us. No justice."[25]

Imaginably, the grief-stricken Bumpurs family found some comfort and strength in letter writers' expressions of care. They took comfort in knowing that New Yorkers and part of the nation were mourning with them. It was moments like these, those filled with overwhelming encouragement from strangers, that the siblings understood that community support would sustain them through intense public scrutiny, ongoing state violence, and municipal neglect.

Having suffered such a devastating loss, the Bumpurs siblings would have to locate or create care practices and strategies to manage the daily routine and challenges of everyday life and cope with perpetual anti-Black and state violence. While struggling to maintain their households and attend to their mental health, these working-class women lacked access to services that would address the stresses of exposure to police and state violence. Poverty coupled with 1980s deinstitutionalization hindered the grieving Bronx family from receiving professional medical and mental healthcare. To make matters worse, civilians involved in police shootings were sometimes disqualified from receiving aid from New York's victims' compensation program.

Created in 1966, New York's Crime Victims Compensation (CVC) program assists financially strapped "innocent crime victims" and their families. The state typically covers burial and funeral costs, lost wages, property damage, medical bills, and counseling expenses. In 1983, New York State's Crime Victims Board received an estimated nine thousand claims and made awards to 3,301 victims for a total expenditure of $8.8 million in compensation. That year, crime victims requesting financial support from the CVC for funeral costs received $1,500 each, the maximum award for burial expenses. The state's burial amount coupled with generous donations from community members would have certainly been enough to cover Eleanor's funeral. But Eleanor and her daughters were not seen as crime victims or victims of police brutality. They did not receive CVC benefits. Rev. Wendell Foster thought this was a travesty, articulating to *City Sun* reporters: "Do you know that after the city killed her it refused to bury her?"[26] The state did not acknowledge the family's loss or grief nor that city workers harmed and killed Eleanor. Official city reports produced a few weeks after Eleanor's funeral would suggest that the "knife-wielding" senior citizen and her family played a "contributing role" in circumstances leading up to the eviction. The city officials' interpretations of the eviction and perceived family neglect overrode any claims of victimhood or innocence, thus making the Bumpurs family ineligible for CVC funds and services, including mental healthcare.[27]

Three decades after Eleanor's killing, the late New York activist Erica Garner articulated the importance of mental health services for working-poor families and victims of police brutality, pointing out how economic disparities blocked access to costly mental health treatments. Garner's words, especially as an adult daughter who lost a parent to police violence, rings true for Mary and her family. In a 2018 interview with *Democracy Now* host Amy Goodman, Garner said, "When you deal with grief, when you talk about grief and you talk about how regular families deal with it, you know, families have problems, trouble coping with it [police violence]. Mental health is very important for families that's put in my position, black families

SAYING GOODBYE TO ELEANOR **127**

that's on public assistance, that doesn't have the income to get therapy for $300 an hour, because how are we supposed to cope with this if we don't have someone to talk to, someone professionally to talk to because this is trauma."[28]

Without the benefit of processing the aftershocks of police brutality with medical professionals, Eleanor's daughters weathered the stresses of police violence and family loss the best way they could. Family, close friends, and an emerging community of anti–police brutality activists became their lifelines. What's more, Mary Bumpurs, the woman whom city officials and police would later describe as irresponsible and money hungry, undertook a miraculous feat. She pulled hope out of despair and courage out of hopelessness.

Protest leaflets, newspaper clippings, and scattered papers with the personal and office phone numbers of David Dinkins, Wendell Foster, and other city activists and politicians lay on the furniture throughout the small basement apartment. The space where Mary Bumpurs and her children ate, socialized, and slept was slowly transforming into a site of political activism. According to Mary, her mother's killing radically shifted her life.[29] The catastrophic October 29 incident compelled Mary to embark on an uncharted personal and political crusade. Family obligation also compelled Mary. Because oldest daughter Fannie Mae was suffering from life-threatening illnesses, including diabetes and asthma, Mary, as the second-born daughter, took on the responsibility to represent the family. According to Mary, her big sister expressed to her: "You're next in line. She [Eleanor] needs somebody to speak for her."[30]

Overnight, the thirty-seven-year-old unemployed public assistance recipient stepped into New York City's long-standing activist circles, becoming the family spokesperson. Mary went from primarily caring for her three children and pets and volunteering at the Bronx Republican club to delivering passionate speeches at anti–police brutality rallies around the city. Mary became a dynamic full-time activist, organizing a protest campaign that altered the face of New York City's anti–police brutality movement of the 1980s. This campaign inspired the rise of the African American Policy Forum, the Center for Intersectionality and Social Studies' #SayHerName campaign and other influential political movements that center the stories of Black women and girls harmed, traumatized, and killed by police and state violence. Yet stepping into the role of family activist was not an easy decision for the Bumpurs family's new matriarch.

Mary was a reluctant activist. The discomfort of public mourning and the labor of juggling political activism with that of parenting and caring for her grieving family made Mary hesitant about being the face of an emerging social justice movement. As her private and public worlds were rapidly changing, the Julia Richmond High School graduate questioned her ability to be an activist. In between child-rearing, actively combing classified ads for jobs, applying for public housing, and handling her mother's affairs, would she have the time and energy to crisscross the city, attending and speaking at protest rallies? An inexperienced activist and orator, she wondered if her tell-it-like-it-is attitude and style, very much akin to the powerful oratory style of civil rights leader Fannie Lou Hamer, could inspire mass political mobilization. Mary questioned if she was the appropriate person to represent the family. She was not college educated. She was on public assistance. And she would have to take a crash course in civil rights activism.

Thrust into a whirlwind of national attention, Mary would have to, as journalist Matt Taibbi writes about Erica Garner's journey from working mother to political activist, "learn about the media, politics, civil law, and especially the criminal justice system."[31] And like many grieving Black women before her, Mary would have to assume multiple roles as an activist. The burden of being a public advocate, community organizer, and gatekeeper of her mother's legacy would fall on her shoulders.

The Bronx mother was unsure if she could project a public persona of grace, strength, and respectability. There were times when grief consumed her, engendering feelings of anger, sadness, and isolation. In the days and months following her mother's killing, Mary, on many occasions, felt like 1980s and 1990s Brooklyn and Bronx mothers Carrie Stewart and Margarita Rosario. In the aftermath of her son Michael Stewart's brutal beating and death, Stewart, at times, did not have the emotional or physical capacity to face the public. She did not always feel up to talking with media personalities, answering repeatedly the same invasive questions about her son and trying to convince the public that Michael's life had value. Although the Stewart family came from "a family of fighters for Black rights," Stewart declined many media and demonstration requests, citing the emotional strain of such appearances. Rosario, founder of the Parents Against Police Brutality organization, felt the same way. After a hail of over twenty police bullets killed her eighteen-year-old son, Anthony Rosario, and nephew Hilton Vega in 1995, Rosario said that her "pain kept bringing her down. [I wanted only] to submit to my bedroom."[32] The physicality of mourning exhausted Stewart and Rosario. Their grief matched what novelist Chimamanda Adichie called "an affliction not merely of the spirit but of the body, of aches and lagging strength."[33]

The consequences of contesting state and police power concerned Mary. She worried about the impact of her political engagement on her family. Taking on urban officials, the NYPD, and its powerful fraternal order was potentially dangerous for the Bumpurs family and put them at risk of not only decades-long state surveillance campaigns that targeted politically engaged African Americans but also police and city officials' coordinated efforts to discredit and smear her—just as they had done with other state violence victims.[34] According to Bumpurs family members, they witnessed how their unabashed critiques of the NYPD resulted in the police targeting of nineteen-year-old Hunts Point Terminal worker James Roy Bumpurs. Seven months after his grandmother's death, Mary's oldest son, James, was arrested, becoming entangled in New York City's expanding jail population. Taking in the fresh spring evening air, James, sitting on a rusty dark-brown fire escape with a few friends, was arrested on a gun possession charge. Using her "rent money to keep [her] child of out jail," Mary paid James's $250 bail. She was adamant that arresting officers "planted the gun to try and frame him. The arrest is payback. They're jerkin' me around because of my mother. Because I asked for justification because of what they did to my mom." Mary believed that the NYPD would use James's criminal history to project public images of dysfunction and her failings as a parent.[35]

Challenging police violence and New York's broader political structure meant going up against city agencies' attempts at making "cases against police officers vanish in blizzards of political excuses and unintelligible legalese." Such "bureaucracies," according to writer Matt Taibbi, are intended to aggravate and emotionally drain justice-seeking families, "grinding them down over time until they become dispirited and give up."[36]

Mary was not sure if she was ready to face the reprisals that flowed from contesting state power. The single mother had good reason to worry about retaliation. Historically, New York Black women's brazen critiques, activism, and testimonies against police violence and repression were greeted with a broad range of retaliatory tactics from police and their white supporters. Their day-to-day movements were monitored. Their home phones were tapped, and they received harassing phone calls. In 1978, Florence Miller, Crown Heights Brooklyn resident and wife of businessman Arthur Miller, who was killed by a police chokehold, experienced firsthand the consequences of pursuing legal justice for her husband. Florence and her four school-age children were stalked by unknown persons. They endured sleepless nights due to "the most disturbing and cruel harassment." The Miller family received constant offensive and terrorizing phone calls. Callers maliciously uttered: "I'm glad he's dead" and "Can I speak with your husband?"[37]

The Bumpurs family were victims of the same kind of ugliness. As Eleanor's tragic story quickly garnered national media attention, Mary and her children received a series of vulgar and frightening telephone calls at all times of the day and night. Sometimes harassers would hang up without saying anything; other times they spewed coarse insults and racial epithets like the n-word. Breathing heavily into the phone, anonymous male callers would hiss angrily, "Your mother had it coming." Stalkers threatened the family with violence, warning there would be hell to pay if they did not stop criticizing the NYPD and their mother's killer, Stephen Sullivan.[38] The harassing calls alarmed the family. They wondered about strangers watching them and knowing where they lived, and they worried about their safety, hoping that callers would not make good on their threats of violence. But the family did not back down.

Mary and her children typically hung up the phone on unknown callers or kept the phone off the hook, causing them to miss important calls from family, friends, and activists. Sometimes Mary, standing up for her family, met fire with fire. She pushed back on callers, cursing them out and articulating pinned up rage at their disrespect, hatefulness, and racism. "Shut the hell up. And don't call this house no more." Verbal resistance did little to halt offensive phone calls. At one point, continuous harassment forced Mary to disconnect her home phone entirely.[39]

Vile telephone calls laced with racial slurs did not intimidate Mary. Nor did the threat of police reprisal or bodily violence dissuade her from contesting police brutality and pursuing legal justice for her mother. She understood that the journey toward police accountability would be an uphill battle, that it would be one of the hardest endeavors of her life. But it was something she had to do for her mother and her family. Mary could not let scathing media stories and NYPD and NYCHA narratives about housing expulsion, Black motherhood, and familial relationships go unchallenged. She could not stand by knowing that Stephen Sullivan would remain on the police force, retain his city pension, and possibly evade legal prosecution. The emerging Bronx activist refused, as scholar Tina Campt writes about the practice of refusal, "to accept the status of black disposability and the mundane regularity of black death."[40] The thought of no one being held responsible for her mother's death infuriated Mary.

A brokenhearted and angry Mary used what feminist writer Audre Lorde called a "well-stocked arsenal of anger" as "a powerful source of energy serving progress and change."[41] Anger and sorrow became transformative political fuel. Love and devotion to her mother motivated Mary's resilient fight for justice—the kind of love that encourages one to fight even when they are afraid and even when the battle appears dangerous. And guilt perhaps powered Mary's journey toward justice. She may have harbored feelings and questions about her inability to protect her mother from housing dispossession and deadly violence. Could she have persuaded her mother to leave the apartment? Could she have talked with police, letting them know that her mother was not a violent person, but rather an elderly woman afraid of strangers and terrified that someone would try to break into her apartment? And perhaps Mary could not shake the thought of knowing that she was merely two blocks away from her mortally wounded mother, an agonizing fact she'd have to live with forever.

Like civil rights activist Mamie Till-Mobley, mother of 1955 lynching victim Emmett Till, Mary "took the privacy of [her] own grief and turned it into a public issue, a political issue."[42] Following the paths of Black Brooklynites Annie Evans Brannon and Carrie Stewart, mothers of 1976 and 1983 police brutality victims fifteen-year-old Randolph Evans and twenty-five-year-old art student Michael Stewart, Mary refused to conceal her suffering. A devoted daughter and sibling, she made a pledge to her mother, family, and herself. She promised "to make it [her mother's life and death] mean something. As long as I have enough strength left, I'm going to fight. An injustice was done to me."[43]

Mary was determined to tell the world what police violence and city bureaucracy did to her mother, and what it did to the Bumpurs family. "They hurt a lot of us. And it's not fair. There's no way they can ever justify it and give us anything." Mary was committed to upending the horrific violence that snatched her mother's life and shattered the lives of so many other New York families. "They're not going to get away with what they did. All I want is justice. I don't want no other family to feel this kind of pain."[44]

A commitment to justice provided the daughter-activist with the much-needed strength to fight the NYPD and other emissaries of anti-Black violence. Personal endeavors toward contesting police violence also engendered the city's first "say her name" campaign.

CHAPTER 7

SAY HER NAME

S ome students were nervous, adjusting their clothes, practicing
their lines, and experiencing butterflies in their stomachs. Others were excited, smiling and happily thinking about their big
moment. Students were preparing for their radio debut. They could
hardly believe they were going to be on the radio like New York
rappers Run-DMC, Doug E. Fresh, Roxanne Shante, and LL Cool J.
But despite feeling nervous and excited, the students were ready to
let New Yorkers and listeners around the nation know how they felt
about Eleanor Bumpurs.

On July 17, 1985, South Bronx middle schoolers took center stage
in citywide tributes memorializing Eleanor. Inspired by the police
killing that rocked their borough and perhaps encouraged by their
community and politically engaged parents and teachers, creative
Black and Latinx preteens from the Paul Laurence Dunbar Junior
High School 120 dedicated their poetry to Eleanor. Recorded at the
Cauldwell Avenue middle school with longtime radio producer David Nolan, students "shared the best of their work, from rap to more
serious poetry" in a segment called "What Eleanor Bumpers Means
to Me." Since Eleanor's killing, WBAI, a progressive radio station established in 1960, consistently publicized the Bumpurs case. Radio
personalities kept its millions of listeners abreast of upcoming demonstrations and legal developments, interviewed activists involved with
the case, and showcased the music, writings, films, and other cultural
productions inspired by Eleanor's death. A few months prior to the
student performances, New York scholars and WBAI Radio Pacifica
Women's Department broadcasters Blanche Wiesen Cook and Susan

Heske produced a three-part radio series on the Bumpurs case.[1] Thousands of WBAI listeners from New York to California tuned in to hear Cook and Heske's program, and now radio audiences did the same for the young poets.[2]

Student poems poignantly shined a light on several weighty issues. Stepping up to the radio microphones, students recited from the pages of their black-and-white composition notebooks and loose-leaf binders what was in their hearts and minds. Poems conveyed messages of community loss and expressed empathy for Eleanor's grandchildren, as they shared in the devastation of losing a grandparent.[3] Their recollections represented the voices of an understudied community of police brutality survivors and witnesses: children. Urban youth voices are important to understanding how anti-Blackness and police violence shaped children's experiences living in the city, illustrating the broad range of human suffering and loss.

Junior high school students' moving radio tribute was part of citywide memorials and demonstrations launched in Eleanor's name. From the Bronx to Harlem to Brooklyn, city folks organized street protests, established grassroots organizations, performed songs and poems, and embarked on letter writing campaigns to elected officials. Crowds of protestors, displaying the Black Power salute, chanted "Justice for Eleanor Bumpurs" in churches and courtrooms, on college campuses, and behind prison walls. And community activists articulated what many New Yorkers demanded: city investigations into Eleanor's eviction, legal action against Stephen Sullivan, and the city to be held accountable for Eleanor's death; this meant public admission of police and city wrongdoing.

Citywide activism for Eleanor signified a watershed moment in New York City history. Expansive political mobilization around the Sedgwick Houses killing represented, at least since the civil rights and Black Power eras, the city's first anti–police brutality campaign centered on a Black woman. This emerging 1980s social justice movement was an early iteration of what legal scholar Kimberlé Crenshaw would in 2014 call the #SayHerName campaign, a movement dedicated to bringing visibility to violence against Black women and girls. Like contemporary #SayHerName advocates, New Yorkers of previous decades brought public awareness to Eleanor's killing. They placed the police killing of a disabled Black grandmother at the center of conversations about race and class oppression, inadequate city services, and racialized state violence. New Yorkers used Eleanor's story to spotlight poor and working-class Black women's living conditions. And they made visible women's long struggles for city services and their experiences as victims of state-sanctioned brutality and municipal neglect.

Protests for Eleanor were part of dynamic 1980s Black diasporic movements aimed at eradicating race, gender, labor inequality, global apartheid and oppression, and police violence. They were also part of national anti–police brutality campaigns for police accountability and justice campaigns for victims and survivors of abuse. As Eleanor's supporters rallied on the steps of Manhattan's city hall and on busy Bronx and Brooklyn thoroughfares, citizens in Los Angeles, Miami, Norfolk, and Philadelphia battled against unfettered police repression. People across the country, according to journalist and activist Charles E. Cobb, were frustrated with the "total disregard for black life among the nation's police, who have adopted an attitude of shoot first and ask questions later."[4] Thousands of urban citizens descended on city streets, orchestrating rallies over the police slayings of Californian Eula Love (1979), seventy-three-year-old Virginian Laura Kelly (1980), twenty-year-old Floridian Nevelle Johnson (1982), and members of Philadelphia's Christian Movement for Life (1985), a Black liberation organization.[5]

Interborough demonstrations for Eleanor were situated in New York City's intense climate of 1980s political activism. Socioeconomic and political issues from around the city and world captured New Yorkers' attention, inspiring many to employ mass protests, strikes, and boycotts to address a range of injustices, including deteriorating public schools, federal cuts to social programs, the AIDS epidemic, inadequate labor conditions for city employees, South Africa's apartheid system, and the international nuclear arms race. On April 1, 1980, over thirty thousand transit workers and Transport Workers

Union (Local 100) members halted the city's 1,800-mile subway and bus systems, the Long Island Railroad, and four private bus lines. Through a twelve-day strike, workers orchestrated the nation's largest transit system protest, affecting over three million city subway and bus riders. Transit workers battled the Metropolitan Transportation Authority leadership and city officials for improved labor conditions and increased wages.[6]

On June 12, 1982, one million people flooded Central Park's Great Lawn for one of the largest peace rallies in American history. Protestors demanded an end to the Cold War arms race, the abandonment of nuclear weapons, and the redistribution of government resources from military to human needs.[7] Throughout the 1980s, New York political activists, students, and labor and religious leaders participated in transnational anti-apartheid and anti-brutality movements against the South African government. Challenging fascism, white supremacy, and anti-Black violence, New York college students, including Columbia University's Coalition for a Free South Africa organization, called for their universities' full divestment from firms operating or conducting business in apartheid South Africa. Students organized rallies, petition drives, and hunger strikes and protested at South African embassies and consulates in Washington, DC, and Manhattan.[8]

The Big Apple had its own problems with racism, white terror, and state-sanctioned violence. Several incidents of white terrorism and police brutality signaled that New York City was becoming what Brooklyn activist and preacher Rev. Al Sharpton called the "capital of racial violence." Sometime after midnight on June 22, 1982, Black city transit worker Willie Turks and two other Black coworkers were leaving a bagel shop in the predominately white community of Gravesend in Brooklyn. Upon seeing the Black outsiders, fifteen to twenty white men and teenage boys brutally attacked the three Black men. Thirty-four-year-old Turks was severely beaten and later pronounced dead at Coney Island Hospital.[9] In a separate incident on September 28, 1983, twenty-five-year-old Pratt Institute student Michael Stewart died after being in a coma for thirteen days at Bellevue Hospital. Eleven Transit Authority police officers had hogtied and viciously beat Stewart for scrawling graffiti on the 14th Street subway station wall. Weeks after Eleanor's killing, Cora and Alan Simmons's two-family house, located in a predominately white section of the Bronx, was firebombed by members of the Ku Klux Klan (KKK). Assailants warned the couple that the "KKK will burn [the entire house down] if n—rs return. KKK does not play."[10] And on August 23, 1989, one of New York City's hottest days that summer, sixteen-year-old high school student Yusef Hawkins was attacked by a mob of white teens in Bensonhurst Brooklyn who then shot him to death.

The unimaginable violence inflicted on Willie Turks, Michael Stewart, the Simmons family, Yusef Hawkins, and other racially and ethnically diverse citizens enraged New Yorkers, revealing what Abyssinian Baptist Church pastor and activist Calvin Butts deemed "an alarming rise in racial violence and racially motivated police misconduct."[11]

———

Raenice Goode, Carol Lucas, and other Bronx residents were eager to pursue legal justice for Eleanor. Listening to local radio and television news broadcasts and talking about Eleanor's killing with their family and friends, they observed the chilling effect of Eleanor's killing on their Bronx community and on the Bumpurs family. They witnessed ordinary citizens wipe their tears, heard the feelings of outrage in their voices, and saw the pain and hopelessness in their eyes as the officer who killed Eleanor remained on the police force and received overwhelming support from white New Yorkers. They'd witnessed firsthand the struggles for equality, dignity, and improved living conditions. They had grown weary of attending funerals and reading stories about others killed by the NYPD. The frequency of police killings was becoming too much to bear. "Civil rights hasn't improved anything for blacks. This kind of thing happens all the time," remarked Raenice Goode.[12] Yet they, along with countless other New Yorkers, refused to sit idly by and wait for the wheels of justice to turn. In November 1984, Goode, Lucas, and other urban working-class activists took an important step in the journey toward securing justice for Eleanor.

Remembering the impassioned speeches and cries for equality and justice echoed at Eleanor's funeral, Bronx activists established

the Eleanor Bumpurs Justice Committee (EBJC). A grassroots organization, the EBJC was the first social justice organization launched
on behalf of Eleanor. The EBJC comprised a diverse group of work-
ing- and middle-class urbanites, including public housing organizers,
welfare rights advocates, socialists, labor union leaders, anti–police
brutality organizers, and members of the Bumpurs family. The organization was a blend of first-time activists, veteran civil rights organizers, Black Power movement members, and progressive organizers,
representing a broad coalition of grassroots community groups and
national political organizations, such as the Young Lords, National
Association for the Advancement of Colored People (NAACP), North-
west Bronx Community and Clergy Coalition, and Sedgwick Houses
Tenants Association. These groups tirelessly worked to improve the
quality of life for Bronx residents, addressing a variety of socioeconomic, political, and environmental issues such as unemployment,
city fires, dilapidated building structures, inadequate health facilities,
drug addiction, economic injustice, and police brutality. Mary Bumpurs, an active EBJC member, appreciated the group's vast community
and political ties and knowledge, as well as their deep commitment
to her family. She praised EBJC activists for "steadily staying on the
case" for justice.[13]

Working-class Black women Raenice Goode, Carol Lucas, and
Elizabeth Abrahams Ramirez were among EBJC's talented and effec-
tive grassroots leaders. They were at the forefront of New York social
justice movements. At Manhattan city hall meetings and Bronx community gatherings at schools and churches and even on city streets,
they raised their concerns and voices about poor housing and school
conditions, environmental hazards, and the elimination of safety net
programs that were lifelines for many Bronxites. Like previous generations of New York Black women freedom fighters (Ella Baker,
Audley Moore, Mae Mallory, and Marvel Cooke), they struggled for
police reform and abolition, legal protection, and livable conditions
for all city dwellers. And like many 1980s Black women community
organizers and leaders, Goode, Lucas, and Abrahams Ramirez stood
ready to defend Eleanor's name and all urban Blacks against state and
police violence and other oppressive forces. With women at the helm,

the EBJC emerged as a grassroots organization committed to what 1960s civil rights activists like Ella Baker identified as "participatory democracy." "A style of inclusive, consensus-oriented democracy," participatory democracy, writes Baker biographer Barbara Ransby, "opened organizational doors to women, young people, and those outside of the cadre of educated elites."[14] EBJC women like Raenice Goode, Carol Lucas, and Elizabeth Abrahams Ramirez modeled this style of leadership, understanding the value of "getting people involved." In recruiting prospective EBJC members, Lucas said, "we need to make community people feel like they're wanted, that they're important, and teach them to be organizers. They are the one that will push the Bumpurs case forward."[15]

Always pictured in local newspapers with a smile on her face, Raenice Goode was a veteran leader. Originally from South Carolina, the soft-spoken thirty-nine-year-old single mother played a pivotal role in several important New York initiatives. Known to family and friends as Cookie, Goode was an active member of the Bronx School Board 9 and, in partnership with Rev. Wendell Foster, was instrumental in the renaming of the Bronx's University Avenue. In January 1989, a few days before the sixtieth birthday of slain civil rights leader Martin Luther King Jr., city council members changed the name of the avenue north of Fordham Road to Dr. Martin Luther King Jr. Boulevard. Years later, Goode would become pivotal to another significant project, one that forced New Yorkers to confront its dark history with slavery. In 1993, after construction workers unearthed the African Burial Ground, a six-acre cemetery containing over fifteen thousand skeletal remains of enslaved and free Africans in Lower Manhattan, Goode and other New York activists, politicians, and intellectuals—including future New York governor David Paterson, Schomburg Center for Research in Black Culture director Howard Dodson, and renowned scholar John Henrik Clarke—successfully lobbied federal agencies to make the site a national historic landmark.[16]

EBJC member Elizabeth Abrahams Ramirez was no stranger to community work. As a young leader and future New York City public school teacher, Abrahams Ramirez was an NAACP member and known for hosting neighborhood block parties for pleasure and political and socioeconomic purposes. At these community gatherings, participants enjoyed a shared meal and discussed community conditions as children and young adults played double Dutch jump rope, skully, basketball, and local DJs were playing the latest R&B, hip-hop, and Latin music. Two months prior to Eleanor's killing, Abrahams Ramirez successfully organized a block party in the Bronx's Highbridge section on 172nd Street, an area situated in Eleanor's neighborhood. The party served as an opportunity for her to talk about city politics and her candidacy on the Democrat ticket for "Female" District Leader in New York's 76th Assembly District. Like many of her Bronx neighbors and supporters, Abrahams Ramirez was a woman of faith, partnering political activism with religion. She was an active member of Rev. Wendell Foster's Christ Church, joining Foster and other parishioners' planning of Eleanor's funeral.[17]

Carol Lucas's activism was similarly inspired. She was committed to "improv[ing] the quality of life for Black Bronxites." Lucas was part of working-class New Yorkers' enduring welfare rights movement, serving as the vice president of the Welfare Action Coalition, an organization that lobbied for city and state welfare systems to be more responsive to welfare recipients' economic needs. Lucas staunchly opposed the Reagan administration's economic policies and federal budget cuts. In 1982, she joined over ten thousand New Yorkers to protest the National Conference of Christians and Jews "Humanitarian of the Year" award recipient: Ronald Reagan. They lambasted Reagan as an anti-humanitarian, condemning the "slash spending on human needs, lavish tax breaks on the very wealthy, starving education programs, and creating wide-spread unemployment."[18] Lucas's involvement with the EBJC would lead to a close friendship with Mary Bumpurs.

Upon establishing the Bronx organization, Goode, Abrahams Ramirez, Lucas and other EBJC members had a laundry list of demands and goals. Their primary objective was legal justice for Eleanor. In countless letters to city officials and during media interviews, EBJC members unapologetically called for the NYPD commissioner Benjamin Ward to terminate Stephen Sullivan. They also wanted (1) the tough-talking Bronx County district attorney Mario Merola to convene a grand jury and charge Sullivan with homicide, (2) NYCHA and welfare workers to be held responsible for mishandling the eviction, (3) a federal probe into Eleanor's killing, (4) Mayor Edward Koch to immediately release the multicity agency report on the eviction, and (5) Governor Mario Cuomo to appoint a special prosecutor, an individual removed from local politics and interests, to investigate Eleanor's expulsion and killing. Mayor Koch promised New Yorkers that his administration would conduct a comprehensive investigation into the Bumpurs case and that the report would be released in mid-November. Activists were eager to read how the Koch administration would explain the deadly eviction.

The EBJC members and some city and state Black lawmakers reasoned that a special prosecutor was the best chance for a thorough and fair investigation into Eleanor's death.[19] Because incidents of "police brutality among minorities was of epidemic proportions," New York assemblyman and 1984 Democratic National Convention speaker Albert "Al" Vann urged the governor to appoint an independent prosecutor to conduct an extensive and immediate investigation.[20] Brooklyn assemblyman Roger L. Green agreed with Vann. In 1985, Green, who was the chairman of Albany's Black and Puerto Rican Legislature Caucus, wrote a two-page letter to Governor Cuomo, advising him to appoint "a special prosecutor immediately to investigate charges of police misconduct in New York State against Eleanor and other Blacks and Hispanics. [This will] restore the faith and dispel perceptions of racial bias."[21]

Calls for a special prosecutor signaled a lack of faith in city prosecutors and the NYPD. Activists did not trust city leaders or the police to hold themselves or each other accountable. "We can't expect the police department to do a thorough, objective investigation of one of their own," noted city clerk David Dinkins.[22] Nor could city activists expect borough prosecutors to prosecute police officers. There was and continues to be an inherent conflict between police and prosecutors. In a 2014 op-ed, Albert Vann's former legal staffer and then New York City public advocate Letitia "Tish" James, speaking about a Staten Island grand jury's decision not to indict the police officer that placed Eric Garner in a deadly chokehold, acknowledged the close working relationship between police and prosecutors. "Our justice system allows district attorneys to be charged with the great responsibility of prosecuting the very same police officers they work side-by-side with every day and whose union support they seek when running for reelection. It's unrealistic to expect even the best district attorney to be absolutely impartial in cases where they are asked to prosecutor a police officer."[23]

Governor Cuomo rejected activists' demand for a special prosecutor. Speaking on Cuomo's behalf, Lawrence Kurlander, a political appointee and the state's director of criminal justice, noted "there is insufficient basis to supersede the District Attorney [Mario Merola] and appoint a special prosecutor."[24]

More broadly, the EBJC members, after spending considerable time with Mary and witnessing her family's heartbreaking pain, desired to upend police violence, a battle that New Yorkers had long fought. Such violence had claimed too many lives and ripped apart too many families. Having a front-row seat to the Bumpurs family's grief, the EBJC wanted no other family to experience a loss from police brutality.[25]

The EBJC employed a myriad of political strategies to advance their agenda. One tactic was consciousness-raising. Members organized petitions and letter-writing campaigns to city and state officials and politicians and encouraged media outlets, particularly African American, Latinx, and left-wing newspapers and radio stations to cover the Bumpurs case. Keeping Eleanor's story in the media was critical to galvanizing supporters and increasing awareness about legal developments and upcoming demonstrations. The EBJC activists hoped that sustained coverage in newspapers and on radio programs including WBAI and WLIB, "the nation's first all-Black all-news and information radio station," would convey their primary objective: to see Stephen Sullivan indicted, prosecuted, and jailed. In a letter to *Amsterdam News* editor-in-chief Wilbert Tatum, EBJC activist and League of Revolutionary Struggle (LSR) activist James "Modibo" Baker extended a "sincere thanks" to the Harlem-based newspaper for covering the case. "We cannot stress enough the importance of the role media can play in determining the outcome of this case. We trust that the Amsterdam will continue to provide the necessary coverage that this case so rightfully deserves."[26]

Grassroots mobilization and interracial coalition building served as another political tactic for the EBJC. Activists believed that broad and diverse community engagement was critical to their justice-centered campaign. Viewing police violence as a cross-cutting issue, they encouraged "Black, Latino, Asian, poor and working-class communities to join [the EBJC] and together fight against injustice, police violence, [and] murder and terror against helpless civilians."[27] "It is important for organizations to work together. This is what we [the EBJC] stress," said Carol Lucas.[28] For EBJC activist Gary Aweta, coalition building and neighborhood mobilization was a path toward community protection and against state violence. Commenting on the NYPD's "invasion" of Eleanor's home, Aweta surmised that "the only reason they [police] came into that community with a shotgun is because they knew they could get away with it. If they knew that they would be met with strong opposition coming into a housing project with a shotgun, they wouldn't have done it that way."[29]

Building broad multiracial and political alliances, the EBJC partnered with activists advocating for tenant and senior citizens' rights, moratorium on evictions, and the creation of a non-police controlled Civilian Review Board. They received support and resources from established grassroots civil rights, religious, and legal groups such as the New York Civil Liberties Union, City-wide Coalition for a Moratorium Against Evictions, Chinese Progressive Association, and League of Autonomous Bronx Organizations for Renewal—and from labor unions, including the Social Service Employees Union and American Federation of State, County and Municipal Employees (Local 420).[30]

The EBJC formulated its strategic plans for justice at the Bronx's Beck Presbyterian Memorial Church. Between full- and part-time jobs, parental duties, and other political work, EBJC members convened twice a month at the old Gothic- and medieval-style church. Allowing the EBJC to use their facilities, church leaders and parishioners actively supported the Bumpurs family. Under the leadership of Rev. Winston Clarke, a former New York City Department of Corrections employee, the congregation contributed financially to Eleanor's funeral services and became one of the many city churches to join the Coalition for Justice for Eleanor Bumpurs (CJEB).[31] The CJEB was a community-based organization established by Bronx clergy members, comprising over thirty labor, political, cultural, and religious organizations. EBJC members sat in the castle-like church, strategizing over how to circumvent the NYPD's efforts to "sweep the case under the rug" and planning protest events.[32] They designed pamphlets and flyers to circulate around the city and at political demonstrations, authored newspaper editorials for the *City Sun* and the *Amsterdam News*, discussed which members would speak at tenant association meetings, churches, and political events, and wrote letters to city, state, and federal officials, including SDNY prosecutor Rudolph Giuliani. They insisted that the 1983 Ronald Reagan appointee conduct a federal investigation into Eleanor's killing. Giuliani and federal authorities would initiate a federal probe in December 1984, investigating whether Sullivan and the NYPD violated Eleanor's civil rights. Mary and other EBJC members also spent hours making sure they had enough protest paraphernalia to distribute to supporters.

One of EBJC's popular protest items was a red, black, and white pinback button. The button featured a widely seen image of Eleanor: the *Daily News* photograph taken in the aftermath of the horrific 1981 apartment fire. It's unclear why EBJC activists or the Bumpurs family selected a distressed-looking Eleanor for the photograph. Surely, the family possessed other pictures of their mother. They could have selected a photograph of Eleanor that the public had not seen before—perhaps an image of Eleanor smiling or being surrounded by her daughters or grandchildren, experiencing moments of love and pleasure. One possible option was a mid-twentieth-century studio portrait of Eleanor, which the family gave to the *Daily News* a few weeks after her death.[33] The photograph is stunning. Eleanor exudes confidence, grace, and beauty. Flashing a glowing smile, Eleanor is wearing a light-colored sleeveless dress and her dark black hair is pulled away from her face, highlighting her shimmering brown skin, almond-shaped eyes, high cheek bones, and full lips. Positioning her body like a *Jet* magazine "Beauty of the Week" model, Eleanor's hands and manicured nails are on her hips and her head is slightly tilted. Eleanor's self-portrait illuminates signs of bodily adornment and captures a blissful moment in her life. Another possible option for the protest button was a 1980s photograph the Bumpurs family gave to the *Amsterdam News* after Eleanor's death. This image features a bright-eyed and smiling LuDean leaning over and embracing her grandmother; a seated Eleanor appears content and enjoying her granddaughter's affection.[34] The decision to use the 1981 *New York Daily News* image for the button was perhaps strategic. The EBJC may have hoped that the image would evoke an emotional response from the public, playing on the "everyone's grandmother" sentiment. At the same time, the EBJC used the pin to convey two messages. Circling Eleanor's image in bold black lettering were the phrases: "Stop the Rise of Police Violence" and "Justice for Eleanor Bumpurs."

The Eleanor Bumpurs pinback button would become part of many New Yorkers' everyday attire. Traveling to work, school, and participating in anti–police brutality rallies, men, women, and children proudly paired the colorful social justice pin with trendy 1980s fashions and accessories. Eleanor's face was affixed to athletic tracksuits, denim jackets, wool coats, scarves, professional attire, and Kangol hats.

Political activists wrote letters and made phone calls to city council members, local ministers, and state leaders. For their rallies, they rented a mic, mixer, an amplifier rack, speakers, and other audio equipment from local Bronx audio visual businesses. Anti–police brutality organizers posted protest event fliers in community centers, church vestibules, apartment building hallways, and bodegas throughout the city, and activists such as EBJC members made sure they had enough "Justice for Eleanor Bumpurs" buttons, placards, and other protest paraphernalia to distribute to participants during the first wave of demonstrations in November 1984.

With the support of numerous clergy, political leaders, and social justice organizations—such as *Black Nation: Journal of Afro-American Thought,* the Bronx NBUF chapter, Tenant Political Action

Committee, River Park Tenants Association, Highbridge Tenants Association, and *UNITY/La Unidad* newspaper (League of Revolutionary Struggle)—the EBJC cosponsored and participated in a weekend-long series of protests and memorials. These were some of the first direct-action events held for Eleanor. Demonstrations were intended to mobilize New Yorkers and disrupt media narratives that portrayed Eleanor as an abandoned elderly woman. "They thought there was no one to stand behind her whatsoever," said Mary.[35] That surely was not the case. Her family and a broad cross-section of New Yorkers stood behind Eleanor. The initial wave of political protests for the grandmother proved that she belonged to a community that was willing to fight on her behalf.

On Saturday, November 17, for nearly four hours, over two hundred New Yorkers braved thirty-degree temperatures to "stop racist attacks on the Black community" and "demonstrate against the brutal murder of Eleanor Bumpurs."[36] One participant noted, "We are out here because we just can't sit by and let them get away with dismissing this case as though it was just another killing of a black person."[37] Around noon on a busy shopping day, just a week before Thanksgiving, EBJC members and protestors gathered at Alexander's Department Store on the Grand Concourse in the Fordham Road section of the Bronx, one the Bronx's busiest shopping districts. In 1984, the area had several MTA subway lines, small bodegas and electronic shops, a bookstore, theater, Fordham University, restaurants, and countless clothing shops—it was an ideal location to launch one of the first protest marches for Eleanor. The Fordham Road area was also within walking distance of activists' intended destination: the NYPD's Forty-Sixth Precinct.

Located at 2120 Ryer Avenue and 181st Street, near the Grand Concourse, the Forty-Sixth Precinct was home to officers implicated in Eleanor's killing. Serving the central part of the western Bronx, the Forty-Sixth Precinct also employed cops accused of killing Bronx resident Louis Rodriguez and Harlem resident Peter Funches, a mentally disabled Vietnam veteran, in 1979. Both men mysteriously died while in police custody at that precinct. No charges were brought against the officers.[38] Wearing their "Stop the Rise of Police Violence: Justice for Eleanor Bumpurs" buttons on their winter coats, EBJC organizers and participants, stopping traffic, marched down the Grand Concourse singing protest songs, yelling "Justice for Eleanor Bumpurs," and carrying placards that read "Indict Killer Cops," "Stop Evictions Executions," and more. Their rousing chants and steady flow down the busy Bronx thoroughfare caught the attention of bystanders and windowsill watchers who yelled words of encouragement and admiration. "Justice for Eleanor Bumpurs," "We're with you," and "Arrest the cops," yelled some onlookers. In response, protestors encouraged shoppers, apartment window spectators, and other onlookers to join them. "C'mon man, get out here and walk! It could be your grandmother next. It'll happen to you. You ain't safe. Nobody's safe."[39] The Fordham Road demonstration inspired a burst of action among shoppers, workers, and bystanders.

A heavy police presence greeted demonstrators when they reached the police station. Armed officers were stationed in front of and around the precinct building and on the roof. On that day, the well-guarded precinct resembled a military base. Speaking on the substantial police presence, East Harlem union activist Estela Vazquez said, "They [the police] think we are here because we like to talk and shout. They think we're here to treat them like they treat us. But we're here to let them know that we're going to put an end to this kind of murder."[40] Armed uniformed and plainclothes officers couldn't stop an impressive slate of speakers from delivering fiery and emotionally charged speeches on anti-Black rhetoric and violence. The event's speakers, including Brooklyn minister Herbert Daughtry, accused New York lawmakers and police of condoning pervasive racism and brutality against non-white New Yorkers.

A well-connected activist, Daughtry was part of New Yorkers' enduring struggle for race, gender, and class equality. Throughout the post–World War II era, Daughtry fought for equality in public education, campaigned to secure the release of South African liberation leader Nelson Mandela, and served as Jesse Jackson's special assistant during his 1980s presidential bids.[41] In the late 1970s, Daughtry along with other activists, including Jitu Weusi and Samuel Pinn, established the National Black United Front (NBUF), an organization at the forefront of New York's anti–police brutality campaigns. During the 1970s and 1980s, NBUF activists organized street demonstrations and memorial services for New Yorkers lost to police violence, including fifteen-year-old Randolph Evans, Brooklyn businessman Arthur Miller, and graffiti artist Michael Stewart.[42] And under Daughtry's leadership, the NBUF did the same for Eleanor. A gifted orator, Daughtry told Bronx protestors: "This is a most brutal act by the people we pay to protect us. We are gathered here today to lift our voices in unison so that the city fathers will hear our unified protest. We are all fired up and we won't take anymore. We demand an independent body, a civilian-composed review board, to monitor and investigate police actions in the killing of Mrs. Bumpurs and charges of police brutality throughout the city."[43] Daughtry also had words for the Patrolmen's Benevolent Association (PBA). Founded in 1892, the PBA was and is the nation's largest municipal police union, representing rookie and veteran officers, detectives and administrative staffers, sergeants and lieutenants, and other high-ranking cops. The veteran civil rights activist censured the union for its long history of ignoring police violence against civilians and protecting abusive cops. "If the PBA had acted earlier, Michael Stewart, Clifford Glover, Rick Borden Luis Baez, Randolph Evans, Arthur Reyes and Mrs. Bumpurs, all of whom were killed by police, would be alive today."[44]

Former Southern Christian Leadership Conference organizer and Commission for Racial Justice associate director Benjamin Chavis echoed Daughtry's sentiments, encouraging protestors to unite to fight against the pervasive issue of police violence. "Because it is November and because the air is cold, do not underestimate our anger, do not underestimate our rage. Eleanor Bumpurs lies in her grave because of racism of New York City. We must leave this rally more determined than ever before to unite Blacks and Hispanics with progressive Whites to change New York City."[45] Tenant rights and union organizer Estela Vazquez connected Eleanor's killing to unaffordable housing and the city's increasing insensitivity to the poor and said that all working-class New Yorkers were at risk of city neglect and state violence. "[People] are finding fewer and fewer affordable places to live. Even when they find somewhere to live they are hard-pressed to afford the skyrocketing rents. How the police acted in this situation has to be condemned. I am here to tell you that if we don't move quickly to put a stop to this, they will have us all out in the streets by whatever means necessary, with dogs or with guns."[46]

Several protests and memorials followed the Fordham Road demonstration. On Sunday, November 18, House of the Lord Church (HOLC) pastor Herbert Daughtry held a special memorial service for Eleanor.[47] Established in Brooklyn during the 1940s, the HOLC under the leadership of Daughtry served as a religious and political center for Brooklynites, feeding parishioners' spiritual appetites while serving as a site for the political mobilization of New York's Black freedom movement.[48] The Atlantic Avenue church was no stranger to hosting memorials, prayer vigils, and political demonstrations for grieving families.[49]

Sponsored by the New York Metro Black United Front and African Peoples' Christian Organization, two groups founded by Daughtry, this memorial service for Eleanor welcomed more than 150 attendees. While tired and recovering from the previous day's protest on Fordham Road, several Bumpurs family members were in attendance. Prominent civic, political, and religious figures such as Democratic Congressman Major Owens were also at the HOLC event. Representing Brooklyn's Eleventh Congressional District, Owens was one of the few congressional leaders to publicly express indignation over Eleanor's killing. "It was cold-blooded murder. There can be no excuses when you kill a grandmother. There is not enough outrage in the community. This does not happen to whites. In the darkest days of the civil rights movement in the Deep South, I can't remember a black grandmother shot in her living room for refusing to pay rent," said Owens.[50]

Through heartful songs, prayers, and testimonies, memorial attendees paid tribute to Eleanor, offering the Bumpurs family words of solace. Parishioners even collected more than $1,000 for the family. Overwhelmed by attendees' generosity and love, Mary, with her two children and other relatives by her side, expressed the Bumpurs family's appreciation to "the poor people of the City of New York" for their tremendous kindness. Mary also thanked local religious and political activists and Bronx residents for assisting the family with funeral costs. "They [the police] killed my mother, but they wouldn't give me a penny to bury her. It was the poor people who paid for that. They gave [whatever they could], crumpled bills and [raised over $500]. If we stand together this won't have to happen again." The outspoken daughter also censured city officials, particularly NYPD commissioner Benjamin Ward. Mary called the top cop "ridiculous and a robot," noting his indifference toward her mother. "He did nothing to help [my] mother."[51]

Weekend-long tributes and protests ended with the "March and Rally for Justice for Eleanor" on Monday, November 19. An evening march, the event began with a candlelight vigil at Sedgwick Houses and ended at the Bronx County Courthouse on 161st Street and the Grand Concourse. The courthouse's stone steps, sidewalks, and surrounding neighborhood was a central location for those involved in the Bumpurs case so it made sense to end the rally there. EBJC and other activists frequently assembled at the building, demanding legal justice for Eleanor. Similarly, NYPD officers, PBA union members, and civilians would stage demonstrations at the courthouse, shaking their heads and fists and howling to the sky in support of Stephen Sullivan. The city building also housed the office of Bronx district attorney Mario Merola, the city's longest-serving prosecutor at the time. That November, Merola and his team of assistant DAs were investigating Sullivan's killing of Eleanor for potential prosecution.

City councilor Wendell Foster, Fr. John Flynn of St. Francis of Assisi, and members of the newly established Coalition for Justice for Eleanor Bumpurs organized the November 19 demonstration. Like the EBJC, the CJEB called for a "thorough, independent investigation" into Eleanor's killing. The progressive Bronx organization also demanded an end to the eviction of senior citizens and for the police to stop branding poor people of color as dangerous and mentally disturbed. They advocated for the creation of citizens' liaison committees to work with the police. Hoping to gain mass participation for the protest, the CJEB members circulated thousands of leaflets, posting them in Bronx churches, barbershops and beauty salons, supermarkets, and around the Sedgwick Houses neighborhood; some stood in front of subway stations passing out flyers. CJEB organizer Reverend Foster used his personal and political networks to spread the word. He personally phoned and mailed flyers and letters to local media outlets and members of the Black press, fellow ministers, and city and state lawmakers. Foster sent letters to fellow city council members Mary Pinkett and Enoch Williams, New York State Assembly member Aurelia Greene, and American Federation of State, County, and Municipal Employees (AFSCME, District Council 37) leaders Elaine Espeut and Lillian Haskins-Hope. A savvy city official, Foster also employed his political status to raise public and media attention about the march.[52]

At a special press conference on November 15, Foster boldly stood outside mayor Edward Koch's office at city hall, criticizing New York politicians' public silence on Eleanor's death. Flanked by Herbert Daughtry, NAACP New York State president Hazel Dukes, city clerk David Dinkins, Bronx minister John C. Flynn, and other political and clergy leaders, the council member told reporters and passersby that "everyone who believes in justice [should] come out and march with us to show this should not have happened. A Black life in this city and country has no value. Had the killing taken place in Poland, the Soviet Union, Cuba, it would be headlined nationally in the United States, the United Nations would be talking about it as well. Yet most of the human rights and women's groups have not condemned the killing. [I] question whether there would be such silence if other than minorities were involved."[53]

Interestingly, Foster, in his passionate speech, specifically called out feminist activist and former New York Congresswoman Bella Abzug and New York's women's rights groups. The Bronx leader questioned why Abzug and other women activists had not offered public statements on the fatal shooting of an elderly poor woman. Foster wondered, "Was it her race? Was it her status as a poor and mentally ill woman" that prevented the Bronx-raised Democrat from publicly addressing the Bumpurs case?[54] Foster's comment reflected some Black New Yorkers' critique about certain elected officials. He, like many, were frustrated with city and state officials' failure to

publicly address nonwhite urbanites' ongoing claims of police brutality. It is unclear if Abzug responded to Foster's remarks or if she
publicly commented on the Bumpurs case.[55] But many city feminists,
scholars, and women's rights organizations did publicly acknowledge
Eleanor's tragic death.

In a 1984 letter to the *New York Times*, National Organization
for Women New York City chapter president Barbara Rochman and
Bronx chapter president Geraldine Miller reasoned that "Bumpurs's
tragic death" was connected to systemic issues of income disparities for older women, and that "city officials must [ensure] that the
needless death of Bumpurs cannot happen again to another woman
in New York City."[56] Other feminists took to the streets in Eleanor's
name. Several days after Foster's press conference, nearly one thousand queer activists, feminists, and anti-militarist groups such as the
Women's Pentagon Action gathered around Manhattan's Wall Street
area for the "Not in Our Name" (NION) demonstrations on November 18 and 19, the same weekend as the first wave of protests for
Eleanor. Although the NION protests were scheduled before Eleanor's killing, organizers dedicated the demonstration to her. Headline
speakers, including Black women from the African National Congress
and the Coalition to Save Medgar Evers College, discussed women's
global struggles, linking Eleanor's killing to that of poor women's everyday experiences with economic inequalities and state-sanctioned
violence.[57]

Raising awareness about the November 19 march paid off. New
Yorkers came out in droves. Enduring cold temperatures in the twenties, hundreds of residents, student activists, senior citizens and labor
and community leaders made their way down University Avenue and
the Grand Concourse to the courthouse. They carried protest slogans
and placards that illustrated their disdain for urban inequalities and
compared New York's racial climate to that of South Africa's caste
system. In unison, they loudly chanted "Koch and Cuomo, you can't
hide. We charge you with genocide."[58] Neighborhood youth activists,
including members of New York's vigilante group the Guardian An-
gels, carried a makeshift coffin made from soda cartons and draped
with an American flag. Other participants like seventy-six-year-old

Bronx resident Mary Y. Cumming, who lived four blocks from Bumpurs, carried political signs that said: "Save Your Mother: Don't Call a Cop," "Apartheid in the Bronx," and "Sullivan Wanted for Murder." Concerned about the violence in her community, Cumming told a local reporter, "We want peace and quiet in our neighborhood. You can't have it if people are being shot like this." A group of hospital and other municipal workers from AFSCME Local 420 held a banner reading: "The elderly and sick are in need of health care – Investigate the case of Eleanor Bumpurs."

All gathered at the courthouse, demonstrators attentively listened to speakers in the cold for one and a half hours. The windy cold air could not keep marchers away from such an important event. Invited speakers—such as Bronx Community College president Roscoe Brown, Bronx borough president Stanley Simon, New York State Assembly members Georgia Davis and Roger Green, Asian American activist Mae Ngai, Abyssinian Baptist Church pastor Calvin Butts, and NYPD officer and Black Guardians president Marvin Blue—encouraged marchers to stay on the "battlefield" for justice and human rights, not just for Eleanor, but for all of the nation's poor and vulnerable. Speakers demanded that city officials hold the entire NYPD accountable for Eleanor's death. "We're not going to let this case die. We demand that the city officials responsible for issuing the orders that led to this unforgivable tragedy discipline their police officers immediately. Nothing we can do and nothing anyone can do will bring (Mrs. Bumpurs) back. We want justice. If the city administration is incapable of disciplining its own men, then it, too, must go in the interest of justice for all citizens," said Wendell Foster.[59]

Weekend protests for Eleanor Bumpurs invigorated participants. New Yorkers emerged from demonstrations motivated to continue supporting the demand that Stephen Sullivan be arrested for murder and that city officials release the multi-city report on the Sedgwick Houses killing. Activists would have to wait years before witnessing police accountability in the Bumpurs case, but they did not have to wait long for the city report. On Monday, November 20, 1984, mayor Edward Koch and members of his administration released the highly anticipated report to the public.

Reporters and cameramen from the *New York Times, Amsterdam News,* the *City Sun,* the *New York Post,* and various other media outlets crowded into city hall's historic Blue Room. As members of the press arranged their microphones and cameras and prepared their questions, Mayor Koch, NYPD commissioner Benjamin Ward, New York City Health and Hospital corporation chairman Victor Botnick, and New York City's Human Resources Administration commissioner George Gross entered the room. The Koch administration scheduled the live press conference to announce the release of the multi-agency report.

For weeks, the Bumpurs family, activists, journalists, and many New Yorkers had eagerly awaited the city's official account of the deadly eviction. Many were curious about how city officials and top police brass would frame the eviction and shooting and wondered which city agencies would be blamed for Eleanor's death. In the Bumpurs family's hearts and minds, they knew who was responsible for their mother's death: the housing officials who called the police on their mother, the cops who stormed into the apartment, and, as Congressman Major Owens, put it: the "trigger-happy cop who gunned her [Eleanor] to death."[60] The family hoped that Koch administrators would publicly acknowledge the NYPD and NYCHA's wrongdoings, but their hopes were dashed, as the city's findings spun in surprising directions. The city report did not point the finger at one individual or city agency. The voluminous report implicated several individuals.

Compiled by trusted mayoral aide Victor Botnick, the report, titled *The Eleanor Bumpurs Case,* did not primarily focus on the NYPD's actions on October 29. The report covered the actions of multiple city agencies including the HRA, NYCHA, NYPD, and the Department of Mental Health, Mental Retardation and Alcoholism Services. Divided into four sections, the report centered on "events leading up to the shooting, existing procedures and protocols of each involved city agency, whether the appropriate procedures were followed by each agency and, if not, where did the gaps exist, and recommendations for future cases." On answering the critical question of who or what city agencies were to blame for Eleanor's death, Botnick maintained that the deadly eviction was a byproduct of "a series of mistakes, lapses, and failure in communication, and other circumstances that combined unpredictably to precipitate the tragedy."[61] The city report also concluded that several individuals and one city agency was responsible for Eleanor's tragic killing.

The HRA took the fall. The City of New York blamed several high level HRA welfare (union and nonunion) workers for Eleanor's death. According to HRA Commissioner Gross, who had been head of the agency and its twenty-four thousand employees for only a few weeks, welfare supervisors, directors, and caseworkers failed to provide Eleanor with the appropriate social and psychiatric services.[62] "In this case there is no doubt that H.R.A.'s procedures were not followed and not followed in substantial ways."[63] Weeks before the October 29 eviction, NYCHA, believing that Eleanor "appeared to be somewhat out of touch with reality," requested that HRA pay Eleanor's rent with an emergency income maintenance grant. The monetary grant would have prevented the eviction. It was not unusual for the city to provide emergency assistance to public housing tenants facing eviction. In 1983, the city paid an estimated $20 million in such assistance. But in Eleanor's case, the HRA did not issue the grant. The request for the grant "was never transmitted to the income maintenance people at HRA. It slipped between the cracks," according to Botnick.[64] Negligence, inefficiency, and psychiatrist Robert John's brief assessment of Eleanor four days prior to her death informed city workers' decision not to transfer her case to the appropriate HRA staff. After reviewing John's report, welfare workers believed that eviction and hospitalization was the best course of action. "If welfare caseworkers and their supervisors had followed established procedures and protocols Bumpurs' back rent would have been paid and the eviction would have been avoided. It was at this point that the most serious error in judgment was committed by GSS staff," wrote Botnick.[65]

Being denied city services was not new for poor urban Black women like Eleanor. Historically, city leaders and welfare workers had a lack of concern for women's living conditions. As state actors, they used their authority to determine and distribute what resources and services women were entitled to and needed to live. Racism, sexism, and class prejudice combined with bureaucratic breakdowns resulted in city neglect and women not receiving the resources they needed to survive. Women were allotted limited access to social, health, and financial services and relegated to deplorable housing units. And some women were denied these services entirely. This municipal abandonment, a form of state violence, revealed an unsettling reality about women's quotidian lives: Black women were never far from housing insecurity, economic and health inequities, environmental hazards, and state-sanctioned harms and death.

For their negligent and careless approach toward Eleanor and her economic circumstances, the HRA reprimanded some of its employees. The Botnick report indicated that "for their serious error in judgment" two city officials, Bronx borough manager of the GSS Marie Franco and director of HRA's East 181st Street office in the Bronx Eleanor Walton were relieved from their supervisory positions on November 9, 1984. In a November 15, 1984, memo to HRA deputy administrator Bobbie Poussaint, Walton, who had worked for the city for over twenty years, responded to the report, acknowledging the HRA's blunders. "We did not spell out a plan on the proper form even though our only plan was to help Ms. Bumpurs. An assessment was initiated but not completed and we did not assess the ability to pay the rent for her. The procedure was not followed."[66]

Marie Franco and Robert John refused to capitulate. They took issue with the report's findings. Speaking about her demotion and $1,500-a-year pay cut, Franco felt she "was scapegoated. I feel very sorry for the poor woman. It seems like I killed her. But I couldn't have shot her from [my office in] Brooklyn. We made errors but one mistake doesn't lead to another and to a killing."[67] Robert John was dismissed from his consulting position with the city. *The Eleanor Bumpurs Case* report cited that John "should have taken action to have Bumpurs hospitalized" before the eviction. The Park Avenue psychiatrist challenged the report's characterization of his handling of the Bronx case. In a November 15, 1985, memo to Mayor Koch, John wrote: "I believe that my examination, diagnosis, and recommendation were ethical, professionally expert, and I reject aspersions to the contrary. I acted properly. I'm satisfied that within the limits of my understanding and my interview and professional experience, I feel quite satisfied that I did the right thing. I've been unjustly treated."[68] Strongly disagreeing with his termination, John would take legal action against the city and the HRA. In 1985, he sued the city for $3 million in punitive damages and $670,000 in compensatory damages. He also demanded that his contract with the city be reinstated.[69]

HRA went beyond admonishing city employees. The agency would implement a series of new guidelines in April 1985. New procedures targeted vulnerable populations, namely persons living with mental health conditions and families experiencing economic precarity. Under the guidelines, all impending expulsions from city-owned buildings or NYCHA properties would be referred to HRA at least thirty days in advance. HRA would guarantee past due rent for welfare clients living in public housing, and no welfare recipient would be evicted for nonpayment. HRA's policy changes would prevent the evictions of 1,354 persons in 1985.[70]

The city report not only laid the housing tragedy at the HRA's doorstep but also faulted Eleanor and her daughters. The Koch administration maintained that Eleanor was a violent person with a troubling history of lawlessness, citing her 1940s and 1970s arrests and imprisonment. Part of the Botnick document, the five-page police report stated that "a routine run of fingerprints turned up that Eleanor Bumpurs served 8 months in Raleigh N. C. in 1942."[71] Shockingly, the multi-agency report intimated another claim. Without a shred of evidence, city officials charged Mary and her sisters with elder neglect and maternal desertion. They asserted that the family's lack of concern for their mother's daily physical and emotional well-being and their failure to respond to alleged eviction notices jeopardized her housing circumstance and her life. Botnick wrote that "had the family responded and involved themselves with the Housing Authority and HRA these tragic events may have been avoided." The city hall special assistant was referring to NYCHA and city workers' emergency letters and telephone calls to daughters Mary and Terry Ann, informing them several weeks before the eviction to contact Sedgwick Houses workers about their mother. Blaming the Bumpurs family for their own tragic loss publicly shamed them and served to dismiss housing workers and the NYPD's role in Eleanor's death.

The Koch administration absolved the NYCHA and NYPD of any wrongdoing. The NYCHA "reacted in a reasonable, responsible, and concerned matter and followed all outlines, procedures and established protocols." Interestingly, Botnick did not find fault in NYCHA's false narratives about Eleanor or in providing police with erroneous information. Housing officials' false accounts of Eleanor throwing lye and brandishing a knife resulted in the presence of a militarized police unit at the eviction.

City officials supported the NYPD, highlighting that the apartment killing was "atypical" for police. In the first nine months of 1984, "the Police Department responded to 13,358 calls for assistance involving emotionally disturbed persons, 592 of them serious enough to warrant calling the Emergency Service Unit and none of these resulted in a death. But Mrs. Bumpurs did die and one such death is one too many." Mayor and NYPD Commissioner Ward also backed Stephen Sullivan's split-second decision to shoot Eleanor.[72] Coming on the heels of a critical 1984 congressional report on policing in New York City that indicated "racism was a major factor in New York police community relations," Koch made clear to reporters that "Mrs. Bumpurs had died not, it appears, because of brutality but because of something much more complex." Her death was a byproduct of "a chain of mistakes and circumstances that came together in the worst possible way, with the worst possible circumstances."[73]

Ward articulated that the police officer violated no rules but followed faulty procedures. The "killing of Mrs. Eleanor Bumpurs was justified by procedure."[74] The city did not recommend disciplinary action for Sullivan or any other officer involved in Eleanor's attempted eviction. Nor did city officials recommend that the NYPD amend its policy regarding persons living with mental disabilities. But Ward, facing mounting public pressure to hold the police accountable, revised the NYPD's "faulty" policies for handling persons experiencing mental health breakdowns. In his report to Koch and Botnick, Ward wrote that "the Department takes seriously this commitment to review its policies and procedures so that a tragedy such as the death of Mrs. Bumpurs does not recur."[75]

On November 9, one week after Eleanor's killing, the NYPD leadership made several personnel and departmental policy changes. First, Sergeant Vincent Musac, who ordered five officers to enter Eleanor's apartment, was transferred out of the ESU. Musac was reassigned to the NYPD's Harbor Division, which had less contact with the public. Second, the NYPD revised its 1970s policy on confronting "emotionally disturbed" citizens.[76] The new policy instructed officers not to confront "an emotionally disturbed person believed to be armed or violent . . . to the extent that the person poses no immediate threat of danger to any person. No further action will be taken until the Precinct Commander or Duty Captain arrives and evaluates the situation." Finally, the NYPD implemented nonlethal methods when confronting persons living with mental illness. Such measures included following the department's hostage negotiation procedures and using nonlethal methods of restraint, such as mace, tear gas, nets, restraining bars, shields, and Taser gun.[77]

But revised NYPD policies would change little for some persons living with mental disabilities. Excessive force continued to be many officers' first response when encountering this vulnerable population. Even with an arsenal of nonlethal devices at their disposal, NYPD officers killed several persons with mental health illnesses after Eleanor's 1984 killing. In 1987, Nicholas Bartlett, a twenty-seven-year-old army veteran and street vendor, was shot six times after supposedly wielding a pipe at police. A year later, thirty-nine-year-old Transit Authority bus cleaner Alfred Sanders was shot eight times after allegedly lunging at cops with a knife.[78]

Mayor Koch appreciated the NYPD's incremental changes. Yet his public defense of Sullivan and the NYPD was not surprising. Mayor Koch was pro-police. "The cops are doing everything that we could ask of them. They would do even more if we made more resources available to them," Koch told a *New York Times* journalist.[79] PBA union president Philip Caruso praised Koch for his support of the police. "No one, no mayor in recent history, has been more supportive of police supporters. No one has been more aggressive in terms of law enforcement on all the issues—drugs, the death penalty and putting more police officers on patrol."[80] While tasking officers with fighting city crime and arresting nonviolent citizens deemed disorderly, Koch provided little oversight of the NYPD. He ignored widespread police misconduct and citizens' complaints of brutality, which were considered acts of wrongdoing by the 1983 congressional hearings on urban policing and later in the 1994 *Mollen Commission Report*. The mayor's unwavering support of "New York's finest" was, in part, shaped by the PBA's political influence over its members and politically conservative white voters. Union leadership encouraged members and supporters to participate in local elections, challenge police reform, and endorse pro-police politicians.[81] It was in Koch's best political interest not to critique the NYPD's handling of Eleanor Bumpurs. He would need the PBA's endorsement for his third mayoral campaign in 1985.[82]

The Eleanor Bumpurs Case report incensed many New Yorkers. They did not appreciate city officials backing the NYPD. At the same time, some were hardly shocked by the city's findings and its protection of the police. Similar to how James Baldwin interprets policing in his 1972 book *No Name in the Street*, African Americans living in the 1980s understood that Stephen Sullivan was not "compelled to answer to these natives for anything he does; whatever he does, he knows that he will be protected by his brothers, who will allow nothing to stain the honor of the force."[83] The demonization of the Bumpurs family was deeply troubling and part of a strategic and coordinated effort to publicly slander Eleanor and her daughters. Many nonwhite New Yorkers, having suffered and struggled against decades of city inequality and police lawlessness, were frustrated with the Koch administration's refusal to admit that the fatal housing expulsion was an act of racist police violence. "The city's official report loses credibility by its omission. The officer who pulled the trigger escaped blame and punishment. A psychiatrist and a social worker are disciplined, but the officer who shot this poor woman does not even receive so much as a reprimand," said Herbert Daughtry.[84]

Hours after the release of the report, over four hundred Harlem residents confronted Koch and twelve city commissioners, including

Commissioner Ward, at an already-scheduled town hall meeting at Harlem's Bethune School on 134th Street. This was Koch's ninety-fourth town hall meeting since taking office in 1973 but only his second in Harlem. When introducing Koch to the audience, New York Councilor Frederick Samuel chided the mayor for not coming to Harlem sooner. "Why didn't you come sooner? This is a troubled community." The predominately Black audience was eager to talk with Koch and city officials about a host of issues plaguing their neighborhoods and daily lives: inadequate housing, inadequate public education, street crime, unemployment, and gentrification. But the ongoing problem of police repression, Eleanor's killing, and the controversial report dominated the over ninety-minute meeting. Appearing at the podium, Koch began his remarks with the Bumpurs case. "The City of New York accepts the responsibility because we believe that city personnel failed to comply with the procedures that were put into place. I know there will always be a question whether or not if she (Bumpurs) had been white, would she be subjected to the same kind of action. And was this an act of racism. We will never know. We will never know." Audience members immediately interrupted Koch. In unison, attendees shouted, "No, no, we know," "Police killed that woman," "Murder," and "Sullivan's butt belongs in jail."[85]

The Social Service Employees Union (SSEU) also took issue with the report. Offering welfare workers as sacrificial lambs while justifying police officers' use of excessive and deadly force did not sit well with the ten-thousand-member union. Defending HRA workers Marie Franco and Eleanor Walton, Stuart Leibowitz, longtime union organizer and vice president of the SSEU, criticized HRA's new commissioner. "The union deplores that HRA Commissioner George Gross is allowing the HRA to be scapegoated for the death of Eleanor Bumpurs. HRA workers do not shoot people. Eleanor Bumpurs should never have been killed. The mayor is castigating HRA while the police, whose procedures and personnel were responsible for the death of Mrs. Bumpurs, are exonerated. We are outraged by the dual standard."[86]

Shifting the blaming away from the NYPD, the Koch administration dismissed the officers' harmful and deadly actions. Instead, the city put forth public narratives that Eleanor and other people with mental health illnesses were dangerous and responsible for their own bodily harms and demise, and that cops like Sullivan worked hard to protect and preserve New Yorkers' lives. "They [the NYPD] place the highest value on life," said Benjamin Ward.[87]

No one was more shaken and hurt by the Koch administration's assertions than the Bumpurs family. *The Eleanor Bumpurs Case* report intensified the Bumpurs family's pain. The expansive carceral regimes that neglected and brutally snatched Eleanor's life were continuing to wreak havoc on the lives of her family. City officials were using everything in their political toolbox to excuse the NYPD, while fabricating narratives about Eleanor and portraying Mary and her sisters as negligent daughters. State actors, including police union leaders and members of the powerful PBA, advanced city officials' public rhetoric about the Bumpurs family, manufacturing propaganda intended to promote police heroism, mobilize support for Sullivan, and vilify Eleanor. Mounting public attacks did not deter Mary. She struck back, contesting disparaging city reports and police accounts and offering counternarratives that illuminated her mother's humanity.

CHAPTER 8

DAUGHTER-ACTIVIST

Mary was fuming. As a family member read the city's report to her, "she could barely hold back her torrent of disgust." Sitting at home in her living room, Mary repeatedly shook her head, rolled her eyes, and sucked her teeth in disagreement with the multiagency report. She couldn't believe that Mayor Koch, Commissioner Ward, and other city leaders were publicly calling her mother "psychotic" and "delusional" and suggesting "had the family responded and involved themselves with the Housing Authority and Human Resources Administration, these tragic events may have been avoided." "What are they talking about? This is nonsense," snapped Mary. She viewed the city's account of her mother's killing as "cruel" and as a way for city officials to shift blame away from police. Without hesitation, she said, "This is a cover-up. Plain and simple. I did not know anything about my mother's eviction. I would have used my own rent money to save my mother from being thrown out. They are not interested in the truth. They are firing all these social workers and directors when the man who shot my mother has yet to speak. Don't try to run that psychotic game about my mother on me. It doesn't matter if she was crazy or not crazy. She did not deserve to die for not paying her rent."[1]

The report's reference to Eleanor's criminal past and incarceration also stunned Mary. "I knew nothing about an arrest in North Carolina. How could this be true?" The revelation, if true, was embarrassing and painful as well as confusing. The North Carolina incarceration was a mysterious and unsettling claim the family would have to publicly address.[2] Media outlets would have many questions about the 1942 arrest, endeavoring to show Eleanor's history of violence and lawlessness. But regardless of Eleanor's secret imprisonment and regardless of what city officials said and what journalists printed, the Bumpurs family intended to fight for their mother. And much of that fight would fall on Mary's shoulders. It would be her responsibility to rehabilitate her mother's image and defend her family against detractors. And one of the family's enemies was the largest police union in the nation.

While grappling with the report's troubling assertions, Mary and her family faced another challenge: preparing emotionally for the upcoming holiday season, particularly Thanksgiving. Typically, the Bumpurs family came together for Thanksgiving. They prepared food, played games, and listened to music. Sharing memories of her family's holiday traditions with an EBJC member, Mary recalled, "We had big cooking times for the holidays. That was a big part of our life."[3] But the 1984 Thanksgiving holiday would be different for Eleanor's children. On that day, both pain and joy would be in tandem. No doubt, the family would be grateful to be in community with each other. But it would be difficult for the family to celebrate being thankful. That month they had buried their Eleanor, cleaned her bloody apartment, and had been blamed by the Koch administration for the deadly eviction. And a surprising visit from a city leader would not make Thanksgiving any easier.

Like previous holiday gatherings, the Bumpurs family—including Eleanor's daughters, grandchildren, and a few friends—gathered at Mary's basement apartment. While the family looked forward to spending time with each other and eating some of their grandmother's favorite dishes, they mourned the empty chair at the dinner table and the life that was suddenly and violently taken away from them. It would be difficult without Eleanor sitting there, observing and smiling or affirming and gently critiquing the various homemade and prepackaged dishes they were hurriedly preparing.[4] No doubt, some family members wished their mother was alive to see and taste all the delicious food and to reflect on their blessings as a family.

Just as hostess Mary was putting the finishing touches on her Thanksgiving dinner of turkey, sweet potatoes, stuffing, cranberries, cake, and cider, she received several unexpected visitors.[5]

Interrupting moments of familial laughter, Mayor Koch and his assistant, Victor Botnick, appeared at Mary's apartment door. This surprise visit made an already difficult holiday more intense. "I was here cleaning up the house and [cooking and] all of a sudden, the telephone rings and it's a representative of the mayor's office and said he was in the building. Before I knew it, there was the mayor at the door and shaking my hand. He [and members of his staff] came to my house in the [Bronx], with his condolences." This was perhaps the first time that Koch had met Mary and her family. He didn't attend Eleanor's funeral. Nor had he, according to Mary, extended to the family "one word of sympathy. I guess it [was] just a minor thing to the city. Just another person shot."[6] Aside from sympathetic remarks, Koch also offered the family a small white box containing "two dozen chocolate chip cookies from [the mayor's official residence in Manhattan] Gracie Mansion." Delivering cookies to New Yorkers during the winter holidays was a tradition for Koch. Ever since entering the mayoral office in 1978, Koch and his aides spent the early hours of Thanksgiving and Christmas delivering several hundred freshly baked "all-American" chocolate chip cookies to city employees, sick and elderly citizens, and the unhoused, orphaned, and incarcerated. According to Botnick, "Normally on holidays, the Mayor and I go out and visit city agencies. We were in the Bronx and since I am the one who did the report, the Mayor asked me if I knew where the daughter lived, and I said yes."[7]

Cookies in hand, Koch "apologized for the actions of city workers. We can never bring your mother back, but hopefully, we can learn something." Immediately responding to Koch, Mary, with her family in the background silently observing the conversation, thanked the mayor for his visit. "Thank you for the visit and cookies. But my mother should not be dead over an incident like this. It makes no sense."[8]

While she had the mayor's attention, Mary informed him of her daughter LuDean's desire to become a police officer. Perhaps with a heavy heart over her grandmother's killing, LuDean took the Nassau County police exam in early November. She was also scheduled to take the NYPD officer test in December. Despite some family members' "grudges against all cops," LuDean said she had "nothing against cops just the one" who killed her grandmother. "He should have had more common sense to know when to pull the trigger. He's been a cop for 19 years." After hearing LuDean's career plans, Koch wished her well.[9]

Mary also made a request. She used the opportunity to briefly discuss her employment situation with the mayor. High inflation, federal reductions in welfare spending, and a sluggish labor market complicated the single mother's efforts to secure employment and afford basic necessities. "I have been unemployed for the last three years, doing volunteer work. Can the city help me?" She likely hoped Koch or one his aides would help her locate and secure employment within city government. The mayor listened to Mary yet made no promises. Koch informed her that "he would try to help her with [her] situation."[10] City employment never came for the mother of three. Mary would only receive public opposition from the Koch administration.

Neither Mayor Koch's visit nor his Gracie Mansion cookies moved the Bumpurs family. Mary viewed Koch's twenty-minute visit as a publicity stunt and disingenuous performance. The brief visit was met with eye rolls, teeth sucking, and even a few expletives. The family found the unannounced visit audacious. How could Koch enter their home, offering "condolences" and "apologies," especially after his administration publicly blamed the family for the eviction and their mother's death? Mary would later articulate that the mayor's gesture had no effect on her decision to take on the NYPD and pursue legal action against the city. "I'm suppose[d] to be a fool, don't understand that he's sweetening up my mouth so I won't talk or I won't fight this thing? So, old Koch brings me two dozen chocolate chip cookies, to let me know that I'm what, a chocolate chip little 'n_gger'? He didn't sweeten my tongue up enough to stop me from fighting for what was mine."[11]

That November, Mary secured the legal services of George Stone, an attorney at the Manhattan law firm Burke, Storm, and Silverstein.

The next month, the Bumpurs family would file a $10 million wrongful death lawsuit against the City of New York and the New York City Housing Authority.[12]

After Koch's unexpected visit, the Bumpurs family turned their attention back to what was important—eating their Thanksgiving dinner. A beautiful *New York Post* photograph captured the occasion. Dressed in their casual clothes or Sunday best attire, they tenderly pulled one another close and congregated around Mary's couch, allowing twenty-seven-year-old freelance photojournalist and future 2001 Pulitzer Prize winner Jim Estrin to photograph them.[13] The Thanksgiving picture accompanied *New York Post* reporters Richard Esposito and David Ng's article on the family.[14] Estrin produced a stunning image of family love. The striking black-and-white photograph was a fitting visual against the Bumpurs family's detractors, those politicians, police officers, and city residents who claimed Mary and her family abandoned Eleanor.

The Patrolmen's Benevolent Association union was one of the family's toughest foes. With the possibility of Sullivan facing criminal charges for killing Eleanor, the PBA, under the leadership of former NYPD officer Philip Caruso, took an active role in the vilification of Eleanor. Even in death, Eleanor was not safe from the police, who continued to brutalize and punish her, impugning her character and stripping her of her humanity.

In December 1984, the estimated eighteen-thousand-member PBA launched a well-orchestrated smear campaign against Eleanor. The PBA leadership used paid radio commercials, television, and newspaper ads to censure the deceased woman. Their broader objective was to defend Sullivan, shape public opinion about the shooting, and delegitimize anti–police brutality movements. The PBA had a long history of employing mass media and other strategies against city and state politicians, community activists and journalists, and ordinary New Yorkers who alleged police misconduct, criticized police procedures, or called for reform initiatives.[15] Taking to the airwaves in the mid-1960s, the PBA public relations director Norman Frank, commonly known as "the voice of the PBA," paid thousands of dollars to public relations agency Cole Fisher Rogow to curate billboards, radio and television advertisements, and other media opposing changes to the police controlled Civilian Complaint Review Board.[16]

Twenty years later in 1983, the PBA paid approximately $16,240 for a full page in the *New York Daily News*. On behalf of the union, Caruso issued a scathing letter to *Daily News* journalist Jimmy Breslin. Caruso criticized Breslin's editorials on the 1983 firing of twenty-five-year-old Puerto Rican police officer Cibella Borges, dubbing them "irrational, biased, and irresponsible." In several thought-provoking columns, Breslin, the self-described "street reporter" questioned NYPD commissioner Robert McGuire's decision to terminate Borges. McGuire dismissed Borges for posing nude in Larry Flynt's pornographic *Beaver Hunt* magazine, saying her "modeling activities [were] well below acceptance standards of personal and professional behaviors." Borges had posed for the magazine in 1980, before becoming a cop; her risqué photographs appeared in the magazine's 1982 issue, one year after she joined the police force. Breslin charged the NYPD with hypocrisy, racism, and favoritism, arguing that white male officers were treated with leniency for disreputable and immoral conduct. Whiteness and male privilege shielded officers from disciplinary actions for alcoholism, moonlighting as security guards at questionable after-hours bars, and purchasing "girlie magazines with their badges."[17] For pointing out the double standard, Breslin found himself on the business end of the PBA's ire.

In July 1983, the PBA paid $50,000 for radio and television airtime to oppose the 1983 congressional hearings on police brutality. Chaired by Detroit congressman John Conyers, the hearings were sparked by nationwide incidents of excessive and deadly police force. Held in Harlem and Brooklyn during the fall and summer, the New York hearings were part of several 1980s federal probes on policing in Los Angeles, Miami, and other American cities.[18] Carried on several New York radio stations and television channels, the 1983 commercials presented "the officer's side of the story in the current controversy over police brutality." Attempting to raise New Yorkers' consciousness about the perils of police work, the advertisements drew attention to what many NYPD officers called a "silent yet deadly issue."[19]

PBA ads asserted that officers were not perpetrators of crime but casualties of "brutal acts." While traversing New York streets, entering dangerous locations, or pursuing alleged law violators, cops were subjected to civilians' ferocious attacks, which the public hardly knew or cared about. In a 1983 *New York Times* op-ed article, Caruso, consistently defending and protecting the rights of police officers since winning the PBA presidency in 1980, maintained that "there is police brutality in New York City. It is widespread and it is pervasive. It is occurring on a daily basis. It is the brutality that is directed against police officers. [Those risking their lives for the citizens of New York are subjected] to an alarming number of shootings, stabbings, and other vicious attacks." The police union used the Bumpurs case to buttress claims about civilian attacks, rendering a troubling yet unsurprising picture. Eleanor was branded a perpetrator, and the real victims were said to be the NYPD officers who stormed into her apartment.[20]

The PBA paid more than $30,000 for ads about Eleanor. PBA advertisements appeared in several local newspapers including the *New York Post* in mid-December just as New Yorkers were scanning city papers for holiday ads and discounts. Titled "Police Brutality?," the ad gave a handful of "facts" about the "best trained, most efficient, most professional officer[s] in the world." Showing four small images of police officers giving assistance to those in life-threatening situations, "Police Brutality?" praised NYPD officers for "devoting their entire careers to the saving of lives." Without naming Eleanor, the black-and-white ad demonized her and the thousands of other New Yorkers battling mental illness. "The handling of an emotionally disturbed person is one of the most dangerous police assignments. This year, NYC police officers have responded to 13,000 emotionally disturbed person calls with only *one* civilian fatality. Many officers have been killed or maimed by violent gun-toting, knife-wielding, and lye-throwing psychotics." Praising the NYPD for its dedication to protecting citizens from urban crime and violence, the ad demanded of New Yorkers: "Respect your police. They've earned it."

The PBA radio commercial did not pull any punches. Aired locally for eight weeks, the advertisement directly identified Eleanor. Because of the ad's highly inflammatory content, at least four local stations refused to air it. The radio commercial, which also appeared in print in some newspapers, featured a male voice announcing, "Brought to you by the New York City Patrolmen's Benevolent Association. We're upset about the handling of the Eleanor Bumpurs case. Many have been quick to condemn the police because of the fatal shooting. People demonstrated in the streets because they'd been led to believe that she was an arthritic grandmother who couldn't possibly harm anybody." Other parts of the advertisement targeted Eleanor's mental fitness and body weight, claiming both were deadly liabilities. "The police had no knowledge of Mrs. Bumpurs's violent history, and no one has been stating what really took place before those shots were fired. This 300-pound woman suddenly charged one of the officers with a 12-inch butcher knife, striking his shield with such force that it bent the tip of the steel blade. It was as she was striking again that the shots were fired. [The officers] had no chance to subdue her—no chance."[21]

References to Eleanor's physical appearance were intentional. The PBA wanted audiences not to imagine an arthritic and elderly woman fighting for her home and life. The fraternal union wanted listeners to visualize a physically intimidating and strong woman who could move her body in threatening ways, justifying the use of deadly force. The *Daily News*, perhaps unintentionally, buttressed PBA claims that Eleanor was a danger to NYCHA personnel, police officers, and anyone that entered her apartment on October 29. The newspaper mirrored late nineteenth- and early twentieth-century urban culture that used racist illustrations and caricatures of Black women to offer social commentaries on the links between Blackness and criminality and white vulnerability.

Shortly after Eleanor's death, the *Daily News* published a damning cartoon titled "Eviction Day Scene." Presumably based on NYPD reports, the black-and-white illustration shows the living room altercation between Eleanor and police. The drawing depicts a menacing and mobile-looking large woman, dressed in a black housedress and armed with a large knife. With anger in her eyes and mouth wide open, she is aggressively lunging toward six police officers. The picture paints a repulsive image of wildness and monstrosity, an individual evoking fear in others—even in experienced, well-trained, and armed cops. Eleanor is imagined as the antithesis of womanhood, lacking all civility and restraint. The cartoon villainizes her, bolstering city reports, police testimonies, and some public opinion that she was far from a sickly woman in need of protection. "Eviction Day Scene" erases the possibility that Eleanor or any woman who looked like her could be in fear of losing her life. Instead, the artwork presents Eleanor as a threat to police authority and white men's lives. These depictions erased Stephen Sullivan's culpability, resurrecting twentieth-century ideas that murdered and physically or sexually assaulted Black women were either unworthy crime victims responsible for their own misfortunes or not victims at all.[22]

Incessant mentions of Eleanor's "large" and "fat" body were damning. One Brooklyn political activist noted, "They made this woman seem like she was some kind of beast; some kind of deranged woman, and they kept referring to the fact that she weighed 300 pounds as if it were a crime to be 300 pounds."[23] Fixating on Eleanor's figure was a way to publicly fat shame and degrade her, suggesting that her physique failed to conform to normative beauty and weight standards for women. Her "fat" body demonstrated that she was irresponsible, gross and unattractive, and lazy—a person who lacked self-discipline. Her size meant she lacked the moral authority to be a victim. Media campaigns centered on racism, poverty, fatness, and ableism were discursive anti-Black tools used to deny Eleanor dignity, protection, and public sympathy—even in death.[24] Further, Eleanor's hyper-visible body became a site of debate and scrutiny for conversations about Blackness, poverty, and capitalist ideas about productivity.[25]

Swift backlash greeted the PBA's insidious tactics. Already distrustful of the NYPD, Black political activists criticized the union's efforts to shift public attention away from Sullivan's actions. Brooklyn minister and community organizer Michael Amon-Ra called the ads "vicious."[26] An *Amsterdam News* writer commented that the PBA has "stooped to a new low. The ad is so inflammatory and so frightening that a casual listener would believe that the New York Police

Department, rather than Mrs. Bumpurs, was the victim of murder. We continue to hear the stories recounting Eleanor Bumpurs' life of poverty, children, psychotic episodes, violence. All these recountings are setups."[27] Even the *Daily News*, despite publishing the controversial "Eviction Day Scene" illustration, took issue with the provocative ads. "It is natural enough for the Patrolmen's Benevolent Association to rise vigorously to the defense of its members in connection with the fatal shooting of Eleanor Bumpurs. But the PBA is out of line in letting that defense take the form of a radio-ad blitz. The PBA's attempt to prejudge the case in paid-for commercials is not what a union is for."[28]

Eleanor's supporters also reasoned that the PBA's release of ads was calculated. PBA media promotion coincided with an important legal development in the Bumpurs case, a development that activists had prayed and worked for. That December, Bronx district attorney Mario Merola began the grand jury process, selecting twenty-three persons to decide whether there was sufficient evidence for a trial. The decision to convene a grand jury was not hard for Merola. A Bronx prosecutor since 1972, the outspoken Democrat had a long history of indicting police officers, which made him unpopular with the NYPD and the PBA. Speaking about the decision to convene a grand jury in the Bumpurs case in his 1988 autobiography, Merola wrote, "It's long been the policy of my office to put before a grand jury all cases of police actions that result in someone's death. That policy is part of the reason that cops have disliked me so much."[29] No doubt thrilled with Merola's actions, Mary and other Bumpurs supporters believed that media ads were an attempt to shape jurors' decision whether to indict Stephen Sullivan. Bumpurs family lawyer George Stone said of the ads, "We don't approve of their [PBA] to use the mass media to influence a grand jury proceeding."[30]

PBA spokesman Dennis Sheehan disputed theories about the ads' timing. The police "do a terrific job day in and day out. We feel the public should know about it. And we want to set the record straight about this case."[31]

Mary joined the resounding chorus of voices condemning the PBA's public attacks. Without the assistance of a public relations firm or money for media ads, she launched a publicity campaign of her own.

Mary Bumpurs at the casket of her late mother, Eleanor Bumpurs, with various grandchildren.

Benjamin Ward, the first African American New York City police commissioner.

David Dinkins at his office.

Bronx district attorney Mario Merola says the indictment of New York City police officer Stephen Sullivan completes the Eleanor Bumpurs investigation unless there's new evidence, on February 1, 1985.

A spectator is removed after a courtroom demonstration at the Bronx Supreme Court on February 27, 1987. Inside the court, Emergency Service Unit officer Stephen Sullivan heard Justice Fred Eggert pronounce him not guilty of criminal charges in the killing of Eleanor Bumpurs.

New York City police officer Stephen Sullivan speaks to the press with the Patrolmen's Benevolent Association president, Phil Caruso, right, on April 13, 1985.

Ruby Dee and Ossie Davis arriving at the funeral for Eleanor Bumpurs on November 3, 1984.

Fanny Bumpurs, daughter of Eleanor Bumpurs, is pictured in her Bronx apartment on February 1, 1985.

Mary Bumpurs, daughter of Eleanor Bumpurs, speaks to the press on November 20, 1984.

Police officers stage a demonstration in support of indicted NYPD officer Stephen Sullivan on February 8, 1985. Sullivan fatally shot Eleanor Bumpurs.

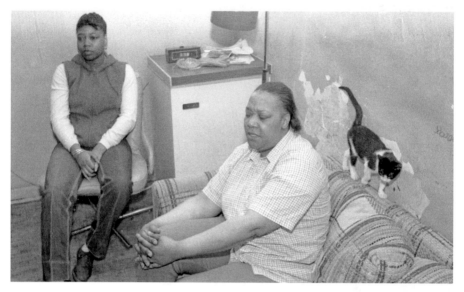

Mary Bumpurs, daughter of Eleanor Bumpurs, is pictured in her apartment in the Bronx on April 13, 1985, after NYPD officer Stephen Sullivan's charges were thrown out of court.

Mary Bumpurs on January 31, 1985, during a press conference in New York City.

Mary Bumpurs outside the funeral for her mother, Eleanor Bumpurs, on November 3, 1984.

New York City mayor Edward Koch.

Eleanor Bumpurs protest button.

Mary organized in defense of her mother, insisting that monstrous portrayals of Eleanor were far from the truth. "She wasn't perfect, but she had struggles just like everyone else," Mary said frequently to reporters.[32] Mary conveyed to the public that her mother was a complicated person with everyday problems. In radio, television, and newspaper interviews and in public talks at churches and political rallies, the devoted daughter poured out her heart for her mother. She presented to New Yorkers nuanced narratives of the woman who raised her. Life-affirming stories illuminated maternalism, personhood, and humanity and invalidated pathological notions of Black motherhood. Such stories demonstrated Mary's commitment to tending to the dead. And fighting and caring for the dead, as scholar Christina Sharpe eloquently writes in her groundbreaking study about Black life and white supremacy, was often a difficult task. It was "hard emotional, physical, and intellectual work that demand[ed] vigilant attendance to the needs" of the deceased.[33] The difficult labor of tending to the dead was also a daring endeavor. For Mary, it meant revealing moments of Black intimacy against a sprawling backdrop of carceral and anti-Black projects that specialized in dispensing suffering and death. But like poet Audre Lorde's moving words, Mary had "come to believe over and over again that what is most important to me must be spoken, made verbal and shared, even at the risk of having it bruised or misunderstood."[34] She spent the latter part of 1984 and much of 1985 giving interviews to journalists, television and radio broadcasters, and fellow activists.

EBJC member Modibo Baker thought the League of Revolutionary Struggle's (LRS) trilingual leftist newspaper *Unity/La Unidad* was a fitting venue for Mary to share her mother's story and discuss the shooting from the family's perspective. A radical activist and frequent contributor to Black and left-wing publications, including the LRS's *Black Nation Magazine: A Journal of African American Thought*, Baker reasoned that the bimonthly newspaper elevated the stories and voices of police brutality victims. And *Unity/La Unidad* contributors, including Baker and Asian American activist Mae Ngai, heavily covered the Bumpurs case, criticizing Stephen Sullivan for killing Eleanor and the PBA for its derisive media ads.

In 1985, Baker sat down with Mary for an exclusive interview for *Unity/La Unidad*. Mary felt comfortable talking with the devoted EBJC member; the two comrades had become friends while organizing EBJC events. Along with other EBJC members, they spent hours discussing everyday life and the latest city happenings—from family life to the weather to the shocking December 1984 New York City subway shooting of four Black men by white subway rider Bernhard Goetz. Mary trusted Baker, knowing that her opinions and family histories were in good hands. Fear of her words being misrepresented and scrutinized or sensationalized for readers did not cross her mind. Through the *Unity/La Unidad* interview, Mary affirmed her mother's existence, voicing her historical silences and giving her personal story emotional life and power.

Intending to offer audiences a window into Eleanor's interior life, Baker asked Mary to "give us some family background. Tell us what your mother was like. The Human Resources Administration investigation into the case, and the media, claimed that your mother was 'emotionally disturbed.' Is there any foundation to these allegations?"[35]

Comfort and friendship made it easy for Mary to answer some of Baker's questions, but she did not disclose everything. "Let me clear up a couple of things because in the papers they showed my mother as being psychotic or something or other." The newly minted activist offered *Unity/La Unidad* readers mental pictures of Southern tobacco fields, white violence, and Black migration. Mary also described Eleanor as a loving homemaker who experienced cycles of poverty, medical challenges, and limited access to decent labor. "My mother had seven children. She came from a very large family of 20, and she was the only girl. My mother came from North Carolina. She worked in the fields for other people who owned these lands. She left [the South because of] white people coming into your area and beating you up and killing you and there was nothing done. When she was 21, she came to New York [and despite the ups and downs of life] my mother raised us for love. Never to hate anyone."[36]

Mary was less forthcoming in addressing Baker's inquiry about her mother's mental health. Publicly discussing her mother's long-standing mental health challenges was difficult. It was even more trying to talk about the family's struggles to care for Eleanor and the stress and heartache they endured loving their mother through her illness. Mary certainly did not want to relive those moments, and the shame and stigma associated with having a mentally ill parent was an embarrassing topic to publicly disclose. "Is that something you would want to publicize?" Mary told another reporter when confronted with questions about her mother's mental fitness.[37] Mary decided that this aspect of their family's lives wasn't for media consumption. Her mother's mental health was private. Family memories of behavioral outbursts and hallucinations, hospitalizations and medications, and stories about her mother seeing and conversing with dead relatives and world leaders like President Ronald Reagan and Fidel Castro did not find their way into Mary's interview with Baker or in any public speeches.

Even though Mary was fully aware of her mother's mental health issues, she pushed back on allegations of her mother being "psychotic" and "emotionally disturbed." She took issue with her mother being labeled "crazy" and how city workers employed the term and other offensive language to justify her eviction and the use of excessive and deadly police force. She told Baker: "I knew her (Eleanor) for 39 years and she was never crazy to me."[38] "The best I can do is say that if this woman went crazy, she went crazy the instant those men [police officers] went in on her."[39] Mary skillfully reframed conversations about Eleanor's well-being, focusing instead on her mental fitness and her ability to care for herself despite numerous ailments. "My mother was ill. She had severe arthritis, heart disease, diabetes. She was able to give herself two insulin shots a day and she kept all her clinic appointments so how could she be crazy?"[40]

In future interviews and public conversations about her mother, Mary carefully navigated between testimony and a veil of secrecy, employing what historian Darlene Clark Hine calls a "culture of dissemblance." "Only with secrecy could Black women [like Mary] accrue the psychic space and harness the resources needed to hold their own in the often one-sided and mismatched resistance struggle."[41] Omissions and silences enabled Mary to construct and have authority over her mother's story while concealing less flattering family histories. Mary understood that her mother's complicated past would be used to reinforce media falsehoods and as fodder for state actors, the NYPD and PBA, and Stephen Sullivan's defense attorney and supporters. A limited public narrative was also suitable for a grieving daughter. Brief flashes of Eleanor's life offered a version of a complex and painful family narrative that Mary could emotionally handle when speaking to activists, supporters, and media personalities.

But no matter how hard Mary wanted to conceal certain aspects of her mother's life, she would not be able to hold those secrets for long. As journalists' stories and city reports of admittance into Bronx hospitals and family violence became catchy news headlines, Mary bravely weathered the rapid waves of public scrutiny and judgment. But she did not endure strangers' stares, finger pointing, and scathing newspaper comments about family dysfunction alone. Her "fighting family" stood right by her side.

Most New Yorkers had never met the Bumpurs family before Eleanor's killing, but some attended Eleanor's funeral, praying and mourning with the family. Many more read the countless newspaper editorials about the shooting. And others marched down busy Bronx streets during the first wave of protests for Eleanor in November 1984. Kindhearted New Yorkers became staunch social justice warriors for the Bumpurs family. Mary called this community of caring and brave New York men, women, and children her "fighting family." This was a group of seasoned city and state politicians, neighborhood activists and students, and ordinary urban citizens who were frustrated with decades of increasing police power, militarization, and violence. They took Mary, who they described as a "powerful force," under their wings.[42] They readily assisted Mary in navigating a new reality as an activist, advising her about the ins and outs of movement work, being in the public eye, and coping with the uphill battle toward judicial justice.[43] Their compassion and unwavering support were, in part, crucial to her healing process. "Rarely, if ever, are any of us healed in isolation," writes author bell hooks. And for Mary, "Healing [was] an act of communion."[44]

Respected preachers Wendell Foster and Hebert Daughtry were members of Mary's newfound family. Entering her family's lives at a time of tremendous loss, Foster and Daughtry made a commitment to assist the Bumpurs family until justice prevailed or as long as the family needed them. Establishing close partnerships with Mary, the two city preachers brought to the Bumpurs case well over forty years of community and political organizing in the city. They offered the Bumpurs family access to their long-standing political networks and financial resources and to what prominent civil rights lawyer Benjamin Crump called the "mediasphere."[45] Like the skillful political strategies of renowned religious activists—including Dr. Martin Luther King Jr. and Harlem anti-drug activist Oberia Dempsey—Foster and Daughtry employed their wide-reaching community status to keep the Bumpurs story in the media and to pressure city officials to hold police and municipal workers accountable for Eleanor's death. Both men became important channels of emotional and spiritual support for Mary. They were never short on prayers, Bible scriptures, and life lessons. Further, Foster and Daughtry ushered Mary into Black New Yorkers' enduring political movements against race, gender and class discrimination, state-sanctioned terror, and the public vilification of Black women and girls.

Foster and Daughtry spent hours schooling the young mother about the city's troubling history of police violence and urban activists' relentless crusade against it. At Daughtry's House of the Lord Church, a haven and political training ground for families that had experienced police violence, Mary received emotional support, spiritual counseling, and learned how to become a political activist. Foster and Daughtry connected Mary to a special community of Black and Latinx New Yorkers, those who tragically lost fathers, mothers, sons, daughters, sisters, and brothers to police beatings, bullets, and chokeholds—those families that were, according to LoLisa Miller-Bradford, daughter of 1978 police brutality victim and Brooklyn businessman Arthur Miller, "destroyed and ruined and broken by [police violence] and the system."[46] Together, these working-class families, borrowing from Gwen Carr, mother of police chokehold victim Eric Garner, "changed mourning into movement, pain into purpose, and sorrow into strategy."[47]

The families of Brooklyn ninth grader Randolph Evans, twenty-five-year-old Michael Stewart, seventeen-year-old prep school student Edmund Perry, and others became part of Mary's "fighting family."[48] The daughter-activist joined a resilient network of multiracial and ethnic police-brutality survivors, forging relationships and systems of support to collectively upend police violence and find meaning out of personal tragedy. Mary formed kinships with people who endured comparable traumas and understood the pain of coping and living with police killing. They related to Mary's grief and identified with the residual effect of anti-Black state terror.[49] And like considerate family members, they cared for Mary and each other, especially during difficult times. Phone calls, cards and handwritten letters, and hugs and kisses at gatherings comforted family members dealing with deceased loved ones' birthdays, Thanksgiving and Christmas, death anniversaries, legal disappointments, public harassment, and moments of loneliness. Loving words and gestures also came when new cases of police killings brought families back to the day state violence irreversibly altered their own lives. Shared experiences of loss, sadness, and anger fostered enduring bonds among many New York families. Blossoming friendships also cultivated new political partnerships.

Amid household and family responsibilities, Mary appeared at community forums, political rallies, and protest marches with other New York women grieving their own family members. Mary and these other activists gathered at public events to discuss their family's experiences with police violence. Channeling the words and spirit of civil rights leader Mamie Till-Mobley, they wanted to "let the people" hear and see what the NYPD did to their loved ones and to their families. Their testimonies about police violence and family loss reflected Black women's collective storytelling tradition. In the 1930s, Scottsboro mothers traveled the world with radical left activists, raising awareness about their imprisoned sons in Alabama. Appearing at the 2016 Democratic National Convention to endorse presidential nominee Hillary Clinton, Sybrina Fulton, Georgia congresswoman Lucy McBath, and seven other "Mothers of the Movement," those who had lost children to gun and police violence, used the national stage to share personal stories of loss, love, and hope. And in recent years, Emerald Garner and Lora Dene King, daughters of 2014 and 1991 police brutality victims Eric Garner and Rodney King, have been in conversation with one another, discussing the impact of paternal injuries and death on their lives.[50]

In the streets, church halls, and community centers, and inside and outside city courtrooms, Black women stood holding hands, embracing one another, and wiping each other's tears. Survivors watched and listened as their newfound sisters delivered heartfelt speeches. They described how police killings murdered their souls, causing mental and emotional anguish and undoing dreams of family stability and happiness.[51] They gave voice to their loved ones' interior lives, bravely echoing the words of contemporary New York political activist Gwen Carr: "Our loved ones were much more than a news headline. [They] were people with hopes and dreams like anyone else and we all agreed that they deserved to be remembered for more than just their violent ending."[52]

One of Mary's fellow activists was Harlem schoolteacher and community organizer Veronica Perry. The two women often attended and spoke at the same political events. On September 24, 1985, Mary and Veronica appeared at the Communist Party's Spartacist forum "From Soweto to Harlem: Smash Racist Terror!" at Harlem's Memorial Baptist Church.[53] The New York Communist Party had an extensive history of fighting against police brutality. Viewing it as an impediment to African American citizenship and "creating a unified opposition front to capitalism," the party organized anti–police brutality demonstrations and reported on high-profile and lesser-known cases of police violence in their publications.[54] Throughout the late twentieth century, the *Workers Vanguard*, the biweekly newspaper of the Spartacist League, published New Yorkers' horrific stories of police abuse, harassment, and murder. In November 1976, the *Workers Vanguard* informed readers of the tragic Thanksgiving Day killing of fifteen-year-old Cypress Hills Housing Projects resident Randolph

Evans. White NYPD officer Robert Torsney shot the Black teenager from East New York in the head at point-blank range after a brief encounter with him.[55]

Six years after the Bumpurs case, the left-leaning newspaper covered the story of another disabled Black woman killed in her apartment. "The murder of a black mother in her own home invoked instant memories of the 1984 SWAT-cop shotgun murder of Mrs. Eleanor Bumpurs, a black Bronx grandmother whose 'crime' in racist America was to be behind in her rent." *Workers Vanguard* writers were referring to forty-one-year-old Bronx mother Mary Mitchell. In November 1990, twenty-five-year-old NYPD officer Arno Herwerth shot Mitchell in the chest at point-blank range, claiming she "seized the officer's nightstick, swinging it at him like a baseball bat." An emergency call to police over a domestic disturbance between Mitchell and her adult daughter had brought Herwerth to the Mitchell home.[56]

Under the editorship of Marxist activist Noah Wilner, the newspaper placed Mary, Veronica, and other "victims of racist terror" stories of abuse, murder, and degradation at the center of global conversations on state violence. Those harrowing accounts were on full display at Spartacist League forums.

The "From Soweto to Harlem: Smash Racist Terror!" forum featured remarks from 1985 Spartacist Party mayoral candidate Marjorie Stamberg, Spartacist Party candidate for Manhattan Borough president Ed Kartsen, and Mary and Veronica. This event may have brought Mary and Veronica together for the first time, but it certainly was not the last time the two women would share a stage. Upon seeing one another, Mary and Veronica warmly greeted each other, sharing smiles and words of encouragement. No stranger to speaking before large audiences, Veronica, who was chair of Manhattan's District 3 School Board, spoke eloquently to attendees about her son who was shot four months earlier. On June 12, 1985, a plainclothes white cop killed honor roll and college-bound student Edmund Perry outside Morningside Park near Columbia University.[57] Seated behind the Spartacist forum's banner and next to co-panelists Marjorie Stamberg and Ed Kartsen, Mary listened to Veronica's loving words about her son's promising yet short life.[58] Veronica refuted media and police reports that Edmund was a troubled Harlem teen and a thug looking to rob others. "He was none of things that newspapers said he was. He never had problems at home, in school or in the street." Veronica described Edmund as the epitome of academic promise. The Harlem youth was a gifted and athletic high school senior who attended New Hampshire's prestigious Phillips Exeter Academy. "My son," said Veronica, "was a very special and unique individual, that he had earned scholarships that sent him to the best places that this world has to offer." Perry had been offered academic scholarships from Ivy League schools, including the University of Pennsylvania and Stanford University. "He had touched so many people in a positive manner."[59]

Mary empathized with Veronica's feelings of hopelessness. Their loss was the same. Their anger and pain were the same. And their quest for justice was the same.

Taking a deep breath, Mary began her remarks at the forum with expressions of sorrow and gratitude, telling the audience about the difficulties of living without her mother, especially as the one-year anniversary of her death approached. "Good evening to everyone. It's not easy standing before you or anyone else, since what happened to my mother almost a year ago. But through the grace of God, and I have to say that—if it wasn't for Him, I won't be standing here or anyplace else."[60] Her speech was peppered with brief stories about her mother's Southern upbringing, particularly childhood lessons about white supremacy and about not harboring hatred toward whites. "She sat and she told us all the dreadful things that happened to her in her lifetime. But she did not instill hatred in us," for Eleanor knew, as writer James Baldwin put it more than half a century ago in *Notes of a Native Son*, that it was important to keep her children's "heart[s] free of hatred and despair."[61] Eleanor taught Mary and her siblings that it was important to extend mercy to those even if mercy isn't extended to them. Mary explained: "It was for us to come to that conclusion by ourselves, which I am standing here to say, no, I can't. I won't find time to hate anyone. Because that's a big word." Mary did not despise white people. Yet she despised those officers who killed her mother. And she was highly critical of the NYPD, making parallels between white domestic terrorist groups and "New York's finest." Historian Keisha Blain writes that there is "a link between the activities of the Ku Klux Klan (KKK) and the NYPD, emphasizing the historical legacies of racist violence in the United States and the role law enforcement played in maintaining it."[62] The "Ku Klux Klan is in disguise in the blue uniform [and] We Will Not Stand for KKK in Blue Uniforms," reasoned Mary.[63]

Parts of Mary's speech were hopeful. Feelings of sorrow and vexation were interwoven with a message of collective power. Even against a backdrop of scathing public portrayals and accusations of family dysfunction, she, embodying the words of one of her mother's heroes, Dr. Martin Luther King Jr., "never lost infinite hope," especially in New Yorkers. Mary was optimistic about the efforts of urban activists, writers, artists, and ordinary citizens in combatting police violence and securing legal justice for police brutality victims. She told forum participants to "keep the strength," citing that their fortitude was inspiring and kept her going. "As long as you keep the strength, I'll keep the strength. I've been fighting. I'm going to continue on fighting, because there was an injustice done to me." Mary was hopeful about a transformative future, one where the collective struggle for freedom and fairness and police accountability produced a just world for all Americans. "I believe as a people we will overcome whatever this system has become today."[64]

Mary would continue to appear at social justice demonstrations and forums with Veronica Perry and other "fighting family" members, raising public visibility about the human toll of police violence on families. Such gatherings became a way for Mary to pay forward the same kindness others gave her. Just as New York's broad network of surviving families supported and attended marches and rallies on Eleanor's behalf, Mary readily did the same for those bearing the scars of police brutality.

Christmas decorations adorned Mary's basement apartment. Colorful lights and garland and a few gifts were neatly positioned under the artificial tree. In between protest rallies, newspaper interviews, and meetings with family attorney George Stone, Mary prepared as best she could for Christmas in 1984. She pondered what she would cook and if she would host guests at her house. This year she wanted little from her family; knowing they were safe was enough for her. All Mary really wanted for Christmas and the New Year was justice for her mother. And Mary wanted to see 1984 quickly drift away. She had hopes for 1985. She prayed that a Bronx grand jury would indict Stephen Sullivan for killing her mother. An indictment would be one of the best Christmas gifts she could receive. And she hoped Sullivan would lose everything: his job, his pension, and his freedom.

PART III
Justice

CHAPTER 9

THE INDICTMENT

E leven African Americans, ten Whites, and two Latinxs sat inside the Bronx County Courthouse with its "elegant eighteen-foot ceiling, dark-wood walls and ornate balustrades." Twenty-three grand jury members listened to the Bronx County assistant district attorney Laurence "Larry" Lebowitz's presentation of the evidence. Working at the Bronx DA's office since 1978, Lebowitz was considered one of Mario Merola's top ADAs. For nearly four weeks, the grand jury was shown fifty exhibits and images of Eleanor's apartment floor plans, medical reports, police documents, and NYCHA eviction letters. They did not see the gory pictures of Eleanor's body or images of her severed fingers. The Bronx DA's office chose to leave out the inflammatory materials. "We didn't want the jurors to let their emotions dictate their decisions. We wanted them to act on the facts. So we didn't enter into evidence the pictures we'd taken of Mrs. Bumpurs's body," said Merola. Instead, jurors heard thirty-three witness and expert testimonies from Sedgwick Houses neighbors, housing and welfare workers, NYPD officers, and the person at the center of the case: Stephen Sullivan. A man of few words, Sullivan testified twice before the grand jury, expressing no "remorse," "apologies," or "sadness" about the killing. Describing his encounter with Eleanor, he was stoic and matter of fact, sticking to the story that "Eleanor had a knife in her hand after the first shot and kept coming."[1]

Determining Sullivan's legal fate did not come easy for the jury. They deliberated for five hours. According to Merola, "After hearing evidence most grand juries only take about ten minutes to make up their minds to indict or not to indict." Five hours was unusual.

"That's almost unheard of. [This] grand jury [took its time with the case], recognizing the complexity of the case."[2]

On January 30, 1985, three months after the deadly eviction, the grand jury articulated what the Koch administration had failed to admit. They reasoned that a crime had been committed on October 29, 1984, and that officer Stephen Sullivan should stand trial for that crime. The panel indicted the nineteen-year-veteran ESU officer on a second-degree manslaughter charge, citing he "allegedly recklessly caused the death of another person by shooting her with a loaded shotgun." If held criminally responsible for Eleanor's death, Sullivan would face a maximum of fifteen years in prison. The grand jury's decision was significant. The judgment departed from official city reports and investigations that absolved Sullivan and the NYPD of any wrongdoing. The grand jury's verdict also came with a surprising critique of city bureaucracy. Merola told reporters that the jury "was angry at the way the whole thing had been handled. They decided they couldn't blame Sullivan without blaming everyone else who'd been involved in the eviction of Eleanor Bumpurs." The jury could not legally hold Mayor Koch or other city officials responsible for Eleanor's killing.[3] Yet they wanted to express that bureaucracy and neglect resulted in unlivable conditions and ultimately death. A scathing two-page report to Mayor Koch accompanied the grand jury's one-line indictment statement.

Signed by jury foreperson Eliza Giles, the report blasted several welfare and social services departments within the Human Resources Administration, citing that inadequate "procedures and actions" contributed to the deadly eviction. "Certainly, the forced removal of an elderly woman from her $96 per month apartment should occur only as a last resort." Giles affirmed mayoral aide Victor Botnick's twelve-page city report that a series of bureaucratic blunders and "serious errors of judgment" led to the eviction. "The actions of the Human Resources Administration in this matter are evidence of an agency which appears to have many arms but no head. It was apparent from the evidence that there was little, if any, effective communication between the New York City Housing Authority and the Human Resources Administration." The NYPD was also mentioned in the letter. Giles called for "additional training or stricter guidelines" on the use of deadly force. She also acknowledged the "positive steps" the NYPD had already taken in amending its policies concerning the use of shotguns with mentally ill citizens.[4]

A few days before Sullivan's indictment, Commissioner Ward issued new shotgun guidelines. The police use of the weapon would require the authorization of an officer of the rank of captain or above. Exceptions to the policy would include incidents where an individual experiencing a mental health crisis had a gun.[5] In addition to the NYPD's revised 1984 policy on implementing nonlethal methods when confronting persons with mental illnesses, Ward spent an estimated $45,000 on fifty Taser guns for Emergency Service Unit cops. The handheld electronic device, carrying 55,000 volts of battery-powered electricity, would allow ESU cops to immobilize persons experiencing a mental health crisis.[6]

Mayor Koch acknowledged the grand jury's letter, asserting that the NYPD and city officials "are doing all in our power to insure that the tragedy which befell Mrs. Bumpurs does not befall others."[7] Proving Koch's point, city and police officials noted that "new rules for dealing with the emotionally disturbed prevented another Eleanor Bumpurs case [and] are leading to possibly fatal delays when cops are called to help deranged people barricaded inside their homes."[8] In the aftermath of revised police guidelines, the NYPD was quick to publicize that they used nonlethal methods to remove several mentally ill women from their apartments without incident.[9] One of those women was twenty-nine-year-old Bronx Black mother Renee Green.

A mother of two, Green was in and out of Bronx Lebanon Hospital's psychiatric clinic in early November 1984. She was denied in-patient hospitalization. Medical professionals did not consider her suicidal or homicidal, but a horrific household incident suggested otherwise. On November 29, Green held her three-year-old son Clayton Simmons, three-month-old daughter Dorothea Simmons, and infant nephew Clinton Davis at knifepoint in her apartment. After a nearly two-hour siege, ESU police and hostage negotiators gained entrance into the home without the use of weapons. Officers apprehended Green and saved her daughter. Babies Clayton and Clinton were not so lucky. The blade of a sharp kitchen knife mortally wounded their tiny bodies. Green was charged with two counts of second-degree murder.[10]

The grand jury decision to indict Sullivan sparked a two-year battle to bring the Bumpurs case to trial. Occurring against the backdrop of New York's highly charged racial climate, this judicial fight was a mix of legal highs and lows for the Bumpurs family, political activists, NYPD advocates, and, more broadly, city residents. Given the city's increasing and tragic string of mid-to-late 1980s police brutality, white violence, and legal cases, New Yorkers paid close attention to the legal justice system's handling of the Bumpurs case. For many, the 1985 indictment was not only about the prosecution of Sullivan. Police brutality also would be on trial, as would the city bureaucracy that reinforced and entangled poor urban women like Eleanor into pervasive patterns of race, gender, and class discrimination. Thus, city residents became interested in how the city's criminal justice system would treat the death of a poor and elderly Black woman.

Stephen Sullivan was arraigned on January 31, 1985. Wearing a beige trench coat, blue sweater, and gray slacks, he appeared with his attorney Bruce A. Smirti, PBA president Phil Caruso, and other PBA officials and cops by his side, before Bronx Supreme Court justice Vincent Vitale. Sullivan stood stone-faced, shocked, and silent as Judge Vitale and court officers powered through the brief proceeding. Confident in his split-second decision to shoot Eleanor, Sullivan pleaded not guilty. Although facing a serious criminal charge, Sullivan, at the recommendation of ADA Lebowitz, was released without bail, pending a future court hearing. Race and class privilege, combined with Sullivan's exemplary police record, made his release possible. Considered trustworthy, Sullivan was not deemed a flight risk or a danger to New Yorkers. Planning to ensure that Sullivan did not spend one day in prison, Smirti, a former Nassau County ADA turned private defense attorney who represented countless PBA union members, filed a motion to dismiss the indictment. The motion argued that "the evidence before the Grand Jury was not legally sufficient to establish the commission by the defendant of the offense charged (Manslaughter 2) or any lesser included offense."[11]

News of Sullivan's indictment was greeted with mixed sentiments. Black New Yorkers, especially Eleanor's Sedgwick Houses neighbors, were stunned by yet pleased with the indictment. "I'm so happy that he was indicted. The whole building should be jumping for joy. [The police] were wrong. They shot her twice like she was a dog. Then they took her out with no clothes on," said twelve-year-old Sedgwick Houses resident Caridad Mali. Sedgwick Houses Tenants Association vice president John Harris called the indictment "fantastic," saying it's "about time action was taken against the officer."[12] For seventeen-year-old Sedgwick Houses tenant and Bumpurs family friend Tony Johnson, the indictment came as a surprise. "They said he [Sullivan] shot her twice. I don't think he needed to do that . . . but I didn't think they were going to indict him." Andre De Jesus, who rented Eleanor's apartment months after her death, was "totally surprise[d] but glad." Bronx resident and mother of three Denise Sampson "believed he would not be indicted, maybe a firing. I thought they would reassign him. But I'm glad that somebody is taking responsibility."[13]

African Americans like Johnson, De Jesus, and Sampson had good reason to doubt that the legal system would hold Sullivan accountable. History had shown them, according to *New York Amsterdam News* reader D. H. Russell, that the "judicial system [could not] deliver justice to us when our [Black] person is violated by whites, be they police or individuals."[14]

Legal justice for Black victims and survivors of police violence seemed out of reach. This is because officers' brutal actions against Black citizens were not considered violent. Scholar Robyn Maynard convincingly argues that the "state is granted the moral and legal authority over those who fall under its jurisdiction, it is granted a monopoly over the use of violence in society, so the violence is generally seen as legitimate."[15] During the 1980s, few NYPD officers accused of brutalizing and killing nonwhite persons faced legal and professional repercussions. The NYPD decriminalized their actions. City officials such as police commissioners and internal NYPD investigators often

sanctioned officers' use of excessive or deadly force. Cops' use of violent tactics against citizens was vehemently defended by police unions,
fraternal orders, and a segment of the civilian population. Few abusive
officers were suspended from their jobs or indicted for their actions.
If city prosecutors and grand juries did indict police officers, many
were charged with less serious criminal violations; they were legally
defended by police union lawyers, and they were often acquitted by
predominately white juries. For instance, the MTA's Patrolmen's Benevolent Association raised and spent more than $300,000 in legal
fees to defend the six transit police officers charged in the 1983 death
of twenty-five-year-old Brooklyn artist Michael Stewart.[16]

Historical legal, institutional, and social impediments—including
close alliances between police and prosecutors and several 1980s New
York State and US Supreme Court (USSC) cases—made it difficult to
prosecute police officers accused of brutality and murder. New York's
People v. Benjamin (1980) and USSC cases *Tennessee v. Garner* (1985)
and *Graham v. Connor* (1989) established the constitutional standards
for police use of force.[17] Legal statutes give cover to abusive officers,
allowing them to evade accountability and civil liability. Decriminalization of police brutality bolsters Blacks' belief that legal justice
is a pipe dream, and that police are legally untouchable. Police-
sanctioned violence also suggests that a dual system of justice exists:
one for cops and another for everyone else.[18]

The Bumpurs family had much to say about Sullivan's indictment.
They had long prayed for this legal development, yet they had not
anticipated a manslaughter charge. An indictment of murder was always the hope. One of Eleanor's youngest daughters, Terry Bumpurs,
was happy about the indictment. Sitting in her Bronx apartment, she
heard about the indictment while watching the morning news. "I
couldn't believe my ears." Like many Black New Yorkers, Terry was
surprised that the Bronx DA brought the case before a grand jury. "I
had every doubt that this man would be tried. Somebody is finally
doing something about police shooting innocent people and covering
it up." For Terry, the indictment even on a manslaughter charge was
a step toward "some justice for our mother. I feel much better. I'm
very happy, very pleased to know that some justice has been done."[19]

Ecstatic about the news, Terry immediately called her sister Fannie Mae Hayes. Fannie was also "happy" about Sullivan's indictment. But tragically, Fannie would not live to see the entire legal process. Eleanor's oldest daughter would die four weeks after the announcement of the indictment. On February 27, 1985, the forty-seven-year-old Manhattan resident perished from complications of heart disease and diabetes.[20] The Bumpurs family would find themselves mourning again, planning another funeral at the Gibson Funeral Home. While Fannie Mae suffered from chronic health conditions, perhaps her mother's killing and disparaging media portrayals about the family brought on additional anxiety and stress and contributed to her death. Like the premature deaths of twenty-year-old activist Erica Garner in 2017, who lost her father Eric Garner to police violence, and Bronx resident Venida Browder in 2016, mother of former Rikers Island detainee and suicide victim Kalief Browder, Hayes's death signaled the hidden repercussions of state-sanctioned violence on surviving families' mental, emotional, and physical health. "The long-range trauma police brutality causes," notes anthropologist Christen Smith, "can be as deadly as a bullet." For Black women, "the pain of loss kills with heart attacks, strokes, depression, and even anemia in the weeks and years after lethal police encounters."[21]

Mary felt differently about Sullivan's legal charge. Like her older and younger siblings, she was pleased with the criminal indictment. She prayed for an indictment but feared it would not happen. "I'm surprised that something did take place," she said. The Bronx activist, however, was not "satisfied" with the second-degree manslaughter charge. Mary wanted Sullivan to be charged with first-degree murder. Quoting from Deuteronomy 19:21, Mary proclaimed "a life for a life." At a press conference held at Brooklyn's House of the Lord Church, Mary, sitting with Rev. Herbert Daughtry and Black United Front coordinator Michael Amon-Ra, further expressed her disappointment with the manslaughter charge. A frustrated Mary told reporters: "The killing of my mother in such a state was something beyond mere manslaughter. Nothing will ever bring her back. I don't want him back out on the streets. Like [convicted 1970s New York City serial killer David 'Son of Sam'] Berkowitz, you should put him in a corner and let him sit there. I feel he should be sitting in jail for the rest of his life. If it wasn't for the press coverage, my mother would have been just another person killed in New York. I'm just sorry it took my mother for people to realize a lot of rats are out there."[22]

Bumpurs family advocate Herbert Daughtry commented on the felony indictment, commending and censuring the District Attorney's Office and the grand jury for its work. "We greet this decision with mixed emotions. On the one side we are pleased that this decision has been rendered. We do commend the D.A. Merola and we would urge that other district attorneys do likewise. Perhaps he [Merola] should conduct a crash seminar." Daughtry, like many other activists and civil rights lawyers, also reasoned that the manslaughter charge gave the impression that the Bronx DA's office was not committed to securing justice for Eleanor. He believed that the appropriate legal charge was murder. "We also think that the charge was insufficient when you consider the crime that was committed. A life was taken with two shots from a shotgun, which was totally unnecessary."[23] Prominent attorneys and activists William Kunstler and Ronald L. Kuby agreed with Daughtry. In a 1985 *Amsterdam News* opinion piece about police violence, Kunstler and Kuby wrote that "there was ample evidence to warrant [a] murder charge in the [Bumpurs] case. When one acts with 'depraved indifference to human life' and those acts cause death of a human being, murder has been committed."[24]

City officials expressed varying opinions about the legal development. Not surprising, Koch was disappointed with the grand jury's decision, articulating his sympathy for Sullivan. "I believe that the people on the Sullivan grand jury who indicted him were not bigots, were not racists, were not malicious. I just happen to disagree with them. I accept [the] grand jury outcomes. Not that I necessarily agree with what they do. I can differ. [They were] wrong in indicting Sullivan. I would be surprised if he were found guilty."[25] While Koch had much to say about Sullivan's indictment, he also publicly voiced strong opinions about a Manhattan grand jury's decision on another controversial shooting. This incident occurred on the New York City subway. Like the Bumpurs case, this incident sparked nationwide conversations and debates about race and crime, public safety, self-defense, and disorder in American urban cities. On December 22, 1984, two months after Eleanor's death, thirty-seven-year-old electronics expert Bernhard Goetz shot and wounded four African American teenagers (Barry Allen, Troy Canty, James Ramseur, and Darrell Cabey) on a downtown train. Carrying an unlicensed .38-caliber revolver, Goetz claimed he acted in self-defense when the teens attempted to rob and assault him. A few days after the bloody subway incident, Koch said, "This city will not tolerate vigilantism. That's the difference between the wild West and a civilized society."[26] Dubbed the "Subway Vigilante," the "Death Wish Gunman," and a "subway hero," Goetz fled New York City after the shooting and later surrendered to state police in Concord, New Hampshire, on December 31. Goetz was charged with attempted murder and several firearm offenses. On January 25, 1985, five days prior to a Bronx grand jury's decision in the Stephen Sullivan case, a Manhattan grand jury refused to indict Goetz on attempted murder charges. But Goetz was indicted on the lesser criminal charge of weapons possession.[27]

Speaking on the grand juries' legal renderings in the Goetz and Sullivan cases, Koch articulated that the Manhattan grand jury was "right" in exonerating Goetz but "wrong" in indicting Sullivan. Koch, at some point, changed his mind on the subway vigilante case. He believed that both men should not have been indicted. Although one case involved a police officer and the other a civilian, the incidents involved two white men acting in purported self-defense, allegedly safeguarding the lives of others from dangerous and "deranged" individuals—who happened to be African Americans. Koch's 1985 bid for reelection likely motivated his stances on both cases. His public defense of Goetz and Sullivan boded well with city voters, particularly whites who believed that the "city was out of control," that cops were heroes, and that Eleanor and the four Black men targeted and shot by Goetz "got what they deserved."[28]

NYPD Commissioner Ward shared Koch's views on Sullivan's indictment. He disagreed with the grand jury's ruling, saying, "The guy who shot her was a nice, suburban, Irish police officer from out of town. He didn't live in the city. Sullivan did not violate police guidelines. I don't see how Sullivan was indicted."[29] But Ward's feelings about Sullivan's indictment did not prevent him from making several controversial decisions concerning the officer's employment. Just several days after the indictment, Ward suspended Sullivan without pay on February 1. A day later, Ward reinstated Sullivan, placing him on modified administrative duty pending the outcome of the criminal trial. Stripped of his gun and shield, Sullivan was assigned to the Tactical Assistance Response Unit. His new responsibilities included setting up and monitoring electronic surveillance equipment for investigations and providing technical help to hostage negotiating teams.[30] Explaining his change of heart, Ward reasoned that "the grand jury's one-sentence indictment does not, in and of itself, provide a basis for changing my original preliminary finding that Sullivan acted within departmental guidelines. Under our system of laws, an indictment is an accusation, not a finding of guilt or innocence. Only a public trial will ultimately determine whether Officer Sullivan is guilty or innocent. He is entitled to his day in court."[31]

Ward also cited two separate 1981 cases as justification for placing Sullivan on modified duty. That year, NYPD officers William Baker and Carol Esserman shot and killed two men: one African American and the other white. Both officers claimed their lives, as well as the lives of their fellow officers, were threatened. On March 28, off-duty officer Baker killed white twenty-two-year-old Yonkers weightlifter Robert Endersbee. Several days later, thirty-six-year-old plainclothes officer Esserman fatally shot forty-two-year-old Bronx resident and Five Percent Nation member Robert L. Greene. Baker and Esserman were indicted for the shootings. In the aftermath of the incidents, NYPD Commissioner Robert McGuire did not suspend Baker or Esserman but placed both on modified duty. The two officers were reinstated to full duty after their acquittals.[32]

Notwithstanding the Baker and Esserman cases, Ward's decision to reverse Sullivan's suspension was perhaps motivated by the PBA leadership and rank-and-file officers. The PBA rebuked Sullivan's indictment and suspension. By suspending Sullivan, Ward risked the possibility of losing officers' respect. And at that time, the newly appointed commissioner could not afford to lose support from New York's law enforcement community. The top cop was already facing public scrutiny for questionable conduct. In April 1984, controversy arose when Ward was on vacation and unreachable during the Palm Sunday massacre, in which a Brooklyn family, including two women and eight children, were gunned down in their home.[33] Another controversy loomed over Ward. A 1984 city report accused Ward of being a "heavy drinker" and an adulterer when he was city corrections commissioner in 1983. The city's Department of Investigation report claimed Ward used his Rikers Island office as a motel for "late night and weekend trysts with a female guest." Ward admitted to cheating on actress Olivia Ward, his wife of over thirty years.[34]

Critiques over Ward's reinstatement of Sullivan flooded in. New York City Council president and 1985 mayoral candidate Carol Bellamy disapproved of Koch and Ward's handling of the Bumpurs case. Bellamy articulated that Ward's decision to "reinstate [Sullivan] could undermine public confidence in the department's ability to police itself." For some Black New Yorkers, Ward's unwavering support of Sullivan was disappointing. His backing of Sullivan was interpreted as an act of betrayal, especially for those who hoped he would use his position as commissioner to address police brutality and minoritized communities' distrust of law enforcement.[35] Mary had no faith in Ward. She called him a "fool," believing that the commissioner was more concerned with protecting police than Black people. He "doesn't care about the slaying of a black woman. I'm damn mad about it. As far as I'm concerned, Ben Ward is the biggest fool in the world. He is just saying that he doesn't give a ____ about a black woman being killed. He just doesn't care." Mary insisted that Ward "resign immediately because he has demonstrated his arrogance toward Black people. If the victim had been a Caucasian woman, the police commissioner would not have acted this way." Thirty-year-old Brooklyn National Youth Movement founder Alfred "Al" Sharpton also had words for Ward. The Baptist minister, who would become a renowned civil rights leader and political pundit, resurrected historical images of submissive Black caricatures, suggesting that Ward "be nominated Uncle Tom of the year."[36]

Amid news of Sullivan's indictment, federal officials announced a major investigation into the Bumpurs case. The federal probe centered on exploring allegations of a coordinated effort to mask police brutality and to falsify how many bullets struck Eleanor's body. A day after Sullivan's indictment, on February 1, 1985, SDNY prosecutor Rudolph Giuliani launched an eight-month criminal investigation on the city's chief medical examiner Dr. Elliot Gross. Appointed to the top medical position in 1979 by Mayor Koch, Gross directed one of the busiest medical examiner's offices in the country, conducting over twenty thousand autopsies a year during the early 1980s.[37] When Giuliani launched the investigation, Gross was already the subject of several city and state inquiries. Both Koch and Governor Cuomo investigated allegations that Gross committed improprieties in handling autopsies of Michael Stewart, Eleanor Bumpurs, and other persons who died in police custody.[38] A four-part *New York Times* series maintained that Gross was biased toward the NYPD. He produced misleading autopsy reports to protect police from possible criminal liability.[39] Speaking on the Gross probe, Giuliani stated, "The purpose is to see if someone should be indicted for federal crimes."[40]

Black political pressure prompted Giuliani's investigation. Black United Front and NAACP leaders and Black city and state lawmakers urged federal authorities to investigate the Office of the Medical Examiner (OME). They had long been suspicious of the OME, viewing the agency as an extension of an abusive and corrupt police state. They asserted that structural gaslighting functioned to shield the NYPD from legal scrutiny and deny the real causes of death.[41] In a 1985 letter to Giuliani, NAACP leaders wrote that "allegations against Gross may be only the tip of the iceberg of a conspiracy among law enforcement officials and others at the highest levels of government to violate the civil rights of blacks and other minorities in our city."[42]

In Eleanor's case, Gross revised the original autopsy report. Eleven-year associate medical examiner Dr. Jon S. Pearl performed Eleanor's autopsy, recording that the cause of death was "homicide" from "two shotgun wounds to the chest, hand, and lung." Reviewing Pearl's report, Gross ordered the pathologist to change the findings to "shotgun wound of chest and lung, shotgun wound of hand without the [gun-shot] number," suggesting the possibility that a single shot, not two, hit her. The modified autopsy findings bolstered NYPD reports and Sullivan's story that two shotgun blasts were fired at Eleanor; the first shot missed the hand holding the knife, and the second shot struck her chest. Cops argued that the second shot was necessary to stop a knife-wielding Eleanor from harming anyone in her path; therefore, Sullivan should not have been indicted.[43]

Across the city, NYPD officers said they were "gratified" with Sullivan's job reinstatement but were "hot as pistols" over his indictment. They viewed the indictment as an attack on all police officers. PBA president Phil Caruso reasoned that the indictment was a miscarriage of justice, saying, "Here's a cop who was given a shotgun and told to go in and protect his buddies under department guidelines. [He is] being made a scapegoat for society's failure to deal with a tragedy of this magnitude."[44] Caruso also took aim at Merola. Caruso claimed that the fifteen-year-career district attorney did not support the NYPD, that he had a history of indicting police officers, and that Sullivan was his latest victim. "Mario Merola has a consistent track record where he has indicted police officers for doing their jobs. He should stop fighting cops and start fighting crime."[45] The cops, according to Merola, "were furious because I'd gotten the first homicide conviction against on-duty cop [Thomas Ryan in 1977] in the city's history, and I hadn't hesitated to prosecutor cops in the years since."[46]

Caruso was not alone in his critique. One NYPD detective saw it as "another Merola indictment and it's not the first Merola indictment of a cop, and it's not the last one that won't hold up in court."[47] Sergeants Benevolent Association president Peter J. Mahon said, "Sullivan is a dedicated police officer. It is sickening to see Sullivan made the scapegoat for the alleged failure of the Police Department, the Human Resources Administration, and our urban society."[48] PBA Nassau chapter president Wayne McMorrow voiced his support of Sullivan in "An Open Letter to the Citizens of New York City." Printed in the *Daily News*, the full-page letter emphasized that Sullivan is a "highly trained and highly decorated member of the New York City Police Department. This indictment never should have occurred. Officer Sullivan was indicted for appropriate actions during a highly dangerous situation. His conduct was not only procedurally sound, but morally correct."[49]

A broad network of law enforcement fraternal orders and wartime veteran groups also publicly supported Sullivan. At least ten thousand legionnaires of Brooklyn's Kings County American Legion suggested that Sullivan's lawyers make a motion to examine the grand jury minutes to dismiss the indictment for insufficiency and for justice.[50] Established in New York City in 1953, the NYPD Emerald Society, an Irish American fraternal order, proclaimed Sullivan's innocence. They even invited the indicted officer and fellow Emerald Society member to serve as its honorary marshal for the 1985 St. Patrick Day's Parade in New York City.[51] The Emerald Society's support of Sullivan extended beyond a parade invitation. The fraternal order raised money for Sullivan's legal defense, contributing $520 toward legal expenses.[52] Police fraternal orders' philanthropic endeavors allowed indicted officers like Sullivan to draw from legal defense funds and even police union money to afford and sustain lengthy legal battles.

Advocacy for Sullivan also came from white women, particularly the wives of NYPD officers.[53] In a 1985 *Daily News* opinion column, Rose E. Baker, wife of an indicted cop, empathized with Sullivan and his family. "As the wife of a police officer who was indicted for shooting an assailant, my heart goes out to the family of Sullivan. [The media] indicts good officers like Sullivan yet make[s] heroes out of citizens who shoot them in the back. Take heart Sullivan family. Sullivan will be exonerated but what a price to pay in outrage, mental anguish and precious time. You will emerge from this stronger, more confident and wiser."[54] Sullivan drew support from Dobbs Ferry resident and widow Mary Beth Ruotolo who lost her husband, NYPD officer Thomas Ruotolo, in a 1984 shooting. She was pleased that Sullivan preserved the lives of his fellow officers, saying, "I feel very strongly about this. I thank God every day that we didn't have to go through another hero's funeral . . . that Sullivan's wife and his partner's wife didn't have to live through that."[55] Overwhelming support and love for Sullivan also came from Maureen Sullivan, his spouse of over ten years. As her husband's freedom hung in the balance, the Putnam County woman would make frequent court appearances with her husband, never leaving his side.

The NYPD came out in full force for their "brother in blue." Rookies, veterans, detectives, lieutenants, and other high-ranking officers orchestrated massive demonstrations in support of Sullivan. On February 4, 1985, a few days after Sullivan's indictment, all 252 of the city's ESU police officers (Sullivan's unit), requested unit transfers. The job they loved was no longer serving their needs. They cited "dissatisfaction with working conditions." Officers were fearful of performing their duties and being charged with a crime. Officers saw themselves in Sullivan. One ESU officer said, "Steve Sullivan only did his job and he was indicted. That could have been any one of us in Sullivan's place."[56] Not completely surprised with the officers' actions, Caruso said, "Our own elite troops of the Emergency Service, who perform beyond the call of duty—all have requested a transfer. I never thought it would come to such dismay and disappointment where police officers don't know where they stand under the law."[57]

Three days after the mass transfer requests, officers staged another protest, one that demonstrated police unity and resistance against the indictment, Black political activism, and legal efforts that questioned and challenged their authority. This "protest," according to one city official, "expressed great anger and polarization that had been brewing in the city."[58] It stunned New Yorkers and became a pivotal moment in the city's and the NYPD's histories.

Not even a breezy twenty-nine-degree temperature could stop more than five thousand predominately white off-duty officers on February 7 from attending one of the city's largest police demonstrations of the mid-1980s. Dressed in warm coats and hats and carrying American flags and protest banners, off-duty officers belonging to various police precincts and fraternal orders throughout the state— including the PBA, Detectives Endowment Association (DEA), NYPD Hispanic Society, and Housing and Transit Police Authority—staged a ninety-minute protest outside the Bronx County Courthouse and DA Merola's sixth-floor office window. Unbeknownst to the officers,

Merola wasn't in the building. Anticipating police protests over the indictment, Merola spent days after the announcement working from his second office in another Bronx courthouse building across the street from the main courthouse.

On February 7, off-duty cops staged an astonishing scene outside the Bronx courthouse. They screamed and chanted and carried placards reading: "Ayatollah Merola," "Merola is an EDP—an Emotionally Disturbed Prosecutor," "B. Goetz is a hero," and "Sullivan is a Saint." Inspired by the demonstration, some Bronx courthouse officers who were inside the building, hung out the windows and waved in support as the protestors chanted, "Merola must go." According to some courthouse employees, the protesters' "shouting was so loud that it rattled the windows of the courthouse."[59] One group of men, enacting early-to-mid-twentieth-century scenes of racial violence and terror, imitated a lynching scene. Cops carried a dummy dressed in a police uniform and wearing a black shroud over its head and a noose around its neck. A note pinned on the dummy's chest read, "Merola's idea of justice."[60] Articulating the thoughts of law enforcers, DEA president Edward Blasie told the crowd: "We stand united as we have never stood before. We will not sit by idly and watch as Officer Sullivan is made a convenient scapegoat."[61]

Officer Sullivan did not attend the Bronx courthouse protest, but he read about the history-making demonstration. Reportedly, he was "very pleased and touched" with the outpouring of support.[62]

Not all NYPD officers requested unit transfers or attended the Bronx rally. Nor did all cops support the PBA's stance on the Bumpurs case or issues of police brutality. The Guardians Association broke ranks with the PBA leadership and their white fellow officers. Established in 1943, the Guardians Association, a fraternal and civil rights organization representing African American and Latinx officers, backed Commissioner Ward's decision to place Sullivan on modified police duty. They wanted to see Sullivan prosecuted for killing Eleanor.[63] Representing nearly five thousand Black police personnel during the mid-1980s, NYPD detective and Guardian Association president Marvin Blue noted that "the killing of Mrs. Bumpurs once again shows the insensitivity of some officers in dealing with citizens in minority communities. We feel the indictment charge is proper. We have a grandmother who was lost."[64] The Guardian's and PBA's opposing opinions on Sullivan's professional and legal fate was not surprising. The two organizations had a long history of conflict, particularly over issues of race. Discriminatory hiring practices, race and gender exclusion within the NYPD, and the beating and killings of Black children were points of departure for the fraternal orders. Guardian members did not appreciate how the PBA gave financial assistance and public support to abusive and murderous cops.

During the 1970s, clashes over the police shootings of two unarmed Black boys nearly resulted in Guardian Association members pulling their membership and dues from the PBA. "Blacks put more than $500,000 in dues into the PBA each year. With that money, we could get our own attorney and life insurance—the only benefit we derive from the PBA," noted Guardian Association president Sgt. Howard Sheffey. A veteran police officer since 1956, Sheffey urged Black officers to disassociate from the PBA after the union posted bail for white officers accused of murdering nine-year-old Queens resident Clifford Glover and fifteen-year-old Brooklynite Randolph Evans. In 1972 the PBA paid the $25,000 bail needed to secure Thomas Shea's freedom after he shot Glover in the back. Six years later, the PBA did the same thing. The union raised Robert Torsney's $40,000 bail after he shot Evans in the head on Thanksgiving Day.[65] Guardian members disapproved of the PBA's use of their membership dues to finance positions they staunchly opposed. With the Bumpurs case, the Black fraternal order publicly acknowledged what they knew personally to be true—that police brutality and harassment against the city's marginalized communities was pervasive and that an independent review board should investigate all incidents of police violence, including those cases within the NYPD.[66]

The Guardians were not the only New Yorkers at odds with the NYPD and PBA. The police union's unwavering support of the accused and militarized police power incited public critique and even violence. On February 15, one week after the Bronx's largest police protest, two unknown white women, carrying a mysterious bag, walked into a Manhattan building on 250 Broadway, across the street from city hall. They rode the elevator to the PBA headquarters on the twenty-first floor, entered a women's bathroom, and quickly placed several unknown objects above the ceiling tile and under a sink. The contents of the bag were discovered eight days later. Shortly after 1 a.m. on February 23, a woman called the Broadway building, advising the on-duty security guard to quickly evacuate the building: "There's a bomb." Minutes later, a loud boom shook the twenty-first floor. The women's bathroom exploded, filling the air with flames, smoke, dust particles, and dangerous gases. The powerful force of five to ten sticks of dynamite blasted out a bathroom wall, ripped sinks from the wall, ruptured water pipes, and knocked out elevator service. The blast also heavily damaged the PBA's reception area. Destruction to part of the floor left two maintenance workers uninjured but shaken up. Minutes after the explosion, an unidentified woman called New York's Associated Press office and left a recorded message, explaining what had just happened. "Tonight, we attacked the Patrolman's Benevolent Association to support the demand of Black communities across the country to stop killer cops." The female caller made it clear that the police union was targeted because of the Bronx police rally and "murders" of Eleanor Bumpurs and Michael Stewart. "The 10,000 racists [police] are not worth one hair on the heads of Eleanor Bumpurs and Michael Stewart."

A political group, identifying itself as the Red Guerrilla Defense, claimed responsibility for the bombing. FBI agents identified the organization as the Red Guerrilla Resistance. Founded in the 1970s, the underground left-wing group orchestrated a string of 1980s bombings at the Israeli and South African Embassy offices in Manhattan and at the US Capitol.[67] In an organizational statement about the PBA bombing, Red Guerrilla Resistance reasoned that their actions were "correct and just. The cops are the frontline enforcers of a system of colonization of Black, Puerto Rican, Mexican-Chicano, and Native American peoples. They provide the funds and legal defense of killer cops."[68]

Sullivan's indictment polarized New Yorkers. Political activists, city officials, police, and ordinary residents employed media outlets, mass protests, and even political violence to express their varying thoughts about the indictment. At the same time, many greeted the Bronx grand jury decision with optimism, viewing the indictment as the first step toward legal justice for Eleanor and recognition that Eleanor's life mattered. Others were disappointed, interpreting the potential prosecution of a veteran cop as a travesty of justice and as a war on cops. Public commentary on the legal matter would continue throughout 1985 and 1986, especially as the indictment made its way through New York's judicial system.

On April 12, 1985, supporters and opponents of Sullivan's second-degree manslaughter indictment received a surprise. After reviewing hundreds of pages of grand jury minutes and testimonies, Vincent Vitale delivered a serious blow to the prosecution's case against Sullivan. The Acting Bronx Supreme Court justice dismissed the indictment. This was a ruling that would spark a more-than-two-year legal battle within New York's criminal justice system. Borrowing from historian Kali Gross's analysis on Black women and the legal system, the dismissed indictment reflected the "legacies of an exclusionary politics of protection whereby black women were not entitled to the law's protection, though they could not escape its punishment."[69]

In a fourteen-page decision, Vitale empathized with the Bumpurs family, calling Eleanor's death "a tragedy in the most profound sense of the word." Yet the Bronx judge agreed with Smirti: The DA's office had "insufficient" evidence to charge Sullivan. The defendant "acted in conformity with the procedures of his ESU. There was no proof or evidence before the grand jurors upon which they could determine that the defendant acted outside the scope of his authority or that his actions did not conform to the specific mandates of his job."[70]

Vitale's ruling sparked a joyous courtroom display. Sullivan and his supporters were elated. Unable to hold back their emotions, they yelled and cheered and high-fived. They hugged and patted Sullivan on the back, saying, "Yeah!" "All right!" and "That's what I'm talking about!" ESU officer Steven Dodge, who worked with Sullivan for several years, was ecstatic for his friend and colleague. "I feel my faith in the criminal justice system has been restored. Steve didn't deserve this," said Dodge. No one was more thrilled about the dismissal than Sullivan. He was relieved at not having to endure a criminal trial and thankful that he did not have to worry about losing his freedom. Sullivan immediately rushed to a courthouse phone to call his wife. Hearing Maureen's voice, Sullivan simply said, "It's over. It's finally over." Sobbing over the good news, Maureen replied, "Thank God." Sullivan also relayed his happiness to numerous reporters. "I'm very excited. I'm happy. I was doing my job. I think I handled it properly. It's been very hectic for myself and my family. I just want to have a couple of beers and take my wife away for a weekend." When asked if he would have handled the Bumpurs situation differently if it meant avoiding killing someone, Sullivan said he viewed the shotgun blasts that ended Eleanor's life as a necessary means to an end. Sullivan coldly responded: "I'd do the same exact thing again. If it [killing someone] happens, it happens. It's a job. . . . Police never take liberties with people's lives."[71] The bullets that ripped through Eleanor's body, ending her life and shattering a family, still seemed of little consequence to Sullivan.

Mayor Koch and Commissioner Ward were also pleased with Vitale's decision. "My position always was that he should not have been indicted in the first place since he was carrying out police regulations. He has now been exonerated," said Koch. "So all's well that ends well." More sympathetic to the Bumpurs family than Sullivan or Koch, Ward believed that Vitale's ruling was "consistent with the Police Department's initial inquiry. But I don't expect any police officers to be celebrating a victory. As I have said many times in the past, I sincerely regret the death of Eleanor Bumpurs."[72]

Coincidently in April, city officials announced another important decision regarding the Bumpurs case. They cleared medical examiner Elliot Gross of "falsifying or obscuring autopsy reports or death certificates" and insisted that there was no evidence of collusion between Gross and the NYPD.[73] Months later, federal authorities would follow suit. In September 1985, they would clear Gross of alleged civil rights violations in a dozen controversial autopsy cases, including Eleanor's killing. "There is no evidence to sustain any (federal) charges against Dr. Gross. This matter is closed," said Giuliani.[74]

The dismissed indictment devastated those advocating for legal justice for Eleanor. Anti–police brutality activists were already disappointed with the grand jury's decision to forgo a murder charge in favor of second-degree manslaughter. For many, the sacked indictment took away any sliver of hope that Sullivan would be held accountable for Eleanor's killing. Blasting Vitale's decision, one political activist expressed what many New Yorkers felt: "It's a sad day for New Yorkers. This is truly a sad day for all of us. We must insist on justice for all!"[75] In a 1985 *New York Times* op-ed article, Dr. Harold H. Osborn, the doctor who had tried to save Eleanor's life, wrote, "Judge Vitale's dismissal of the indictment can only be regarded as a sad ending to an extremely troubling case."[76] For many New Yorkers, the legal dismissal signaled a lack of empathy for Eleanor and a disregard for poor people and Black life. It intimated what anti–police brutality activists and ordinary Black New Yorkers had long believed—that there is no justice for poor people and that the legal system did not believe that Eleanor's life and death warranted protection or legal justice.[77]

As for the Bumpurs family, they were heartbroken. Family members burst into tears after hearing the words: "insufficient evidence" and "dismissed." New York's criminal justice system had completely let them down, taking away their chance to witness Sullivan's prosecution. EBJC members and other political activists consoled an emotional Mary and her family. While wiping their tears and rubbing their backs, activists made clear their feelings about Vitale's decision. Angrily, they yelled "murder" and shook their fists at the judge. Mary joined her comrades. She voiced her outrage about the dismissed indictment, emphasizing how race and class denied Black citizens legal retribution. "The judge and the Police Department are saying, if you're poor, if you're black, then there's no justice. The law doesn't stand for us. . . . All I want is some justice. We have to keep it going so people don't forget, because just like it was my mother, it could have been someone else's mother." Despite Judge Vitale's disappointing ruling, she further affirmed her commitment to see Sullivan behind bars. Personal misgivings about a historically adversarial and exclusionary judiciary system did not weaken the promise she made to her family: "I'm in this battle till the very end. He took my old woman's life, and they throw it out. They're not gonna kill my mama and get away with it. Somebody is going to pay. The judge said he read all hundred-odd pages of the grand jury minutes and then he said that even though 23 people came up with an indictment, he was going to throw out the charges. I don't see how he could say that. They can't just throw it out like that. I won't let it happen. I want an appeal."[78]

Appealing Vitale's verdict was also on DA Merola's mind. Justice Vitale "failed to deal with crucial aspects of the case. We have an obligation to present it to the Appellate Division," contended Merola.[79] On April 15, Merola filed a legal appeal with the State Supreme Court's Appellate Division. To the appellate judges, Merola wrote "PLEASE TAKE NOTICE that the People of the State of New York appeal to Appellate Division, First Department from the part of an order of the Supreme Court, Bronx County which granted defendant Stephen Sullivan's motion to dismiss Indictment No. 394 on the ground of legally insufficient evidence before the Grand Jury."[80] It would take an entire year before the Appellate Division rendered a decision on the appeal.

Urban activists refused to sit idly as appellate justices discussed and debated Merola's appeal. They redoubled their efforts in seeking justice for Eleanor by organizing tributes and protests, letter campaigns, and media interviews.[81]

A month after Vitale's ruling, activists from East Harlem, commonly known as "El Barrio," or "Spanish Harlem," organized a special tribute for Eleanor. On Sunday May 19, 1985, Puerto Rican and Dominican activists, taking advantage of the beautiful sunny day, held an outdoor "Post-Mother's Day Memorial Service" on 117th Street between Park and Lexington Avenues. New York Latinx communities' support of justice campaigns for Eleanor signaled the longstanding alliance between Black and Brown communities over racial injustice issues. Organizers wanted New Yorkers and the world to know "that the people who live in East Harlem El Barrio care about what happened to Mrs. Bumpurs. She deserves respect and remembrance."[82] Guest speaker Mary paid a touching tribute to her mother. This was a hard day for Mary and her family. It was their first Mother's Day without their matriarch. Surely the family missed the tradition of bringing Eleanor fresh flowers and small gifts and gathering in her apartment for lunch or dinner. Mary's short speech was reflective of the moment. Honoring her mother, Mary's heartful stories of maternal love and sacrifice brought smiles and tears to attendees' faces. Not surprising, she also mentioned how the family was faring after the dismissed indictment. The family is "not good with that decision. But we are still fighting."[83]

Members of Mary's fighting family kept Eleanor's story in the press. The EBJC let "the public know that [Eleanor Bumpurs's] tragic and unnecessary death has not been forgotten." They wrote letters and gave interviews to newspaper editors and reporters, keeping them abreast of legal developments and upcoming demonstrations. One special event was held on October 29, 1985. That evening, the EBJC held a commemorative program on the one-year anniversary of Eleanor's death. Nearly two hundred people jammed into the Bronx's Miracle Revival Church to "remember [and honor] Bumpurs."[84] The remembrance was an emotional but serious event, featuring musical selections from Bronx playwright and director Titus Walker and husband-wife duo Jaribu and Ngoma Hill of Serious Bizness. Founder of the Ujamaa Black Theater in 1977, Walker, a former Medgar Evers College student, performed "Revolution," a song dedicated to "Mrs. Eleanor Bumpurs."[85] Connecting Eleanor's killing to histories of global oppression, Serious Bizness belted out the Eleanor-inspired song "Old Glory." Using her powerful and melodic voice, Hill sang about Eleanor's killing and New Yorkers' unapologetic fury over that slaying."[86]

Songs about loss and political struggle encouraged attendees to keep their spirits up and continue the fight for legal justice for all victims of police repression.[87] Soul-stirring music was accompanied with rousing remarks from Dr. Harold Osborn, the Lincoln Hospital emergency room physician, Bronx councilor Wendell Foster, attorney C. Vernon Mason, and Mary. Still emotionally processing her mother's death and Sullivan's dismissed indictment, Mary told attendees, "It's been a difficult year. But I keep fighting for justice. Things are not what they seem. It could happen to any one of you, as it happened to me." Mary's friend and EBJC member Carol Lucas closed the program, stating, "We have to struggle, we have to organize, we have to educate the people."[88]

The EBJC members also spent hours writing letters to city and state officials, requesting a federal investigation and the reinstatement of Sullivan's indictment. EBJC member Albert DeNully wrote US attorney for the Southern District of New York Rudolph Giuliani. DeNully petitioned the Southern District to investigate the Bumpurs case. "As a result of Justice Vitale's decision, the Eleanor Bumpurs Justice Committee is calling upon your office to investigate the circumstances surrounding Eleanor Bumpurs' death for possible violations of her civil rights. The actions of Stephen Sullivan denied Eleanor Bumpurs life, liberty, and the pursuit of happiness. We feel the involvement of the federal government is warranted." Recognizing the collective power of the urban citizenry, EBJC members invited New Yorkers to join their letter-writing efforts. In an *Amsterdam News* editorial, activist Modibo Baker encouraged readers to "Let your voice of outrage be heard. It is urgent that the community act now to continue the fight for justice for Eleanor Bumpurs." Some New Yorkers participated in the EBJC's letter writing campaign and sent letters to court of appeals chief justice Sol. M. Wachtler in Albany, demanding that Sullivan stand trial.[89] Existing primary documentation does not reveal if court officials received or read EBJC members' letters. Nevertheless, a year after Vitale's decision, the Appellate Division ruled on the dismissed indictment.

Appellate Division justices Leonard Sandler, David Ross, Bentley Kassal, and Ernst H. Rosenberger did not all agree on the 1985 indictment, but the four-panel members rendered a decision. On April 1, 1986, the appellate court upheld Bronx Supreme Court justice Vincent Vitale's ruling. In a three-to-one vote, the justices ruled that criminal liability could not be imposed on Sullivan, who "in good faith" believed his first shot missed Bumpurs and that "his brother officers continued to be in imminent danger. Law enforcement officials may not be stripped of their ability and right to take fair and reasonable protective measures necessary under the circumstances, particularly in their own defense."[90]

Justice Ernst Rosenberger disagreed with his colleagues, emphasizing the importance of grand jury decisions. In a nine-page dissenting opinion, the American Civil Liberties Union and Legal Aid Society advocate and former civil rights attorney for the 1960s Freedom Riders wrote:

> A review of the District Attorney's instructions reveal that they were adequate and proper. I dissent and would reverse the order, which based upon an inspection of the grand jury minutes, dismissed the indictment which had charged the defendant with Manslaughter in the Second Degree. The grand jury remains the exclusive judge of the facts with respect to any matter before it. In this case, Criminal Term [Bronx Criminal Court/Vitale] substituted its own evaluation of the inferences to be drawn from the evidence for that of the grand jury, thereby usurping the grand jury's function as finder of the facts.[91]

The appellate court ruling added another layer in the Bronx eviction case, generating a mix of emotions and legal highs and lows for the Bumpurs family, political activists, NYPD advocates, and city residents.

Not again, thought Bumpurs family supporters. To patiently wait a little over a year for a court ruling and then receive another setback was crushing. Political activists were livid with the appellate court's verdict, "demanding that D.A. Merola appeal this decision in the highest state court." Merola agreed with activists. He, too, was frustrated with the lower courts' rulings. Justices "rejected the indictment. They'd decided to act as judge and jury, throwing out the charge on the grounds of insufficient evidence. I [Merola] had no choice [but] to challenge both decisions. It was important that this issue be aired before the public that everyone have his or her day in court. So I'd take it to [the state's highest court]," the court of appeals.[92] Merola filed the appeal in April 1986. It would take nearly eight months for the Bronx DA's office to hear back from the high court.

Days, weeks, and months after the appellate court's ruling, political activists descended onto the streets of Brooklyn, Manhattan, and the Bronx. On April 4, 1986, the eighteenth-death anniversary of civil rights leader Martin Luther King Jr., EBJC members and Brooklyn political activists organized a Michael Stewart/Eleanor Bumpurs Justice Committee protest. Event organizers urged "people of goodwill and consciousness to take a day off from work, school and shopping and march for justice in the spirit of Dr. King and keep the memories alive of those who died unjustly at the hands of this city's police force. We will be marching in the spirit of Dr. King, Nelson Mandela, Mr. Stewart and Eleanor Bumpurs." Carrying banners and placards and photographs of Michael and Eleanor and other murdered police victims, marchers assembled at Brooklyn's House of the Lord Church (HOLC), making the long trek across Atlantic Avenue and the Brooklyn Bridge and past the Manhattan offices of district attorney Robert Morgenthau and Governor Cuomo. The march culminated in a rally at city hall.[93]

In October 1986, Mary and her family attended another HOLC event. Herbert Daughtry and the Michael Stewart Justice Committee, including Irene Davis and NBUF organizer Charles Barron, planned a candlelight service for families of police violence. The event brought families together to honor the memory of individuals lost to police violence and to commend the social justice work of families left behind. Love and hope lingered in the air as activists paid tribute to Annie Evans Brannon, mother of Randolph Evans who was killed on Thanksgiving Day in 1976; Carrie and Millard Stewart, parents of Michael Stewart; Ronnie Groce, son of Dennis Groce, killed in 1986; Veronica Perry, mother of Edmund Perry, killed in 1985; and Mary. Families were gifted small houseplants, which, according to Barron, represented life and growth.[94] Mary and her family would need positivity as they awaited the court of appeals' ruling.

On November 25, 1986, a few days before the Bumpurs family would endure another Thanksgiving without Eleanor, the court of appeals rendered a decision. In a six-to-one decision, New York State's high court reversed two lower court decisions that vacated the second-degree manslaughter indictment. The justices determined that "the facts [medical testimony] could support a finding of an unnecessary shooting."[95] In the lone dissent, chief justice Sol Wachtler wrote that Sullivan should not have been charged with reckless shooting: "In my view, the indictment charging the defendant with a reckless shooting is a compromise with no support in evidence." Instead, Wachtler argued that the evidence presented to the grand jury warranted more serious charges of second-degree murder or first-degree manslaughter.[96] Judge Wachtler's dissenting opinion affirmed what Eleanor's advocates and other civil rights lawyers had been articulating throughout the legal process: that Bronx prosecutors should have charged Sullivan with murder.

Defense attorney Bruce Smirti phoned Sullivan about the ruling. Naturally, Sullivan was disappointed with the court's ruling, but he was ready to have his day in court. Attorney Smirti ensured his client that "he was ready to try the case. I've been ready for two years." He also told Sullivan that going to trial, having his personal and professional life scrutinized would not be a "pleasant experience" for him or his family. In a telephone interview with a Westchester County reporter, Sullivan elaborated further on going to trial. "I'm actually looking forward to a trial." The court proceeding would give Sullivan, whatever the outcome, a sense of finality. "This has been going on for a long time and it will be good to get it over with." Sullivan was confident that a jury or judge would clear him of any wrongdoing.[97]

In Black neighborhoods across the city, "the mood was one of jubilation as word spread that the state's highest court had ordered Sullivan to stand trial."[98] Judicial appeals and "mass pressure from the community," according to EBJC member Modibo Baker, was instrumental in moving the Bumpurs case forward. "That is what finally brought this case to trial."[99] Another EBJC activist, Carol Lucas, said the "court decision was the best Thanksgiving present I could have gotten. I'm excited about it, but I know that this is just the beginning of the fight."[100] Some political activists were cautiously optimistic about the court's decision, viewing it as "the beginning of confidence in the system, but there's a long way to go. While we hail [the decision] as a victory and a step in the right direction we are still left with the nagging question: Will Sullivan be tried for the crime he committed?" Still advocating for a special prosecutor to investigate and prosecute the case, community organizers had little faith in the Bronx DA's office to "diligently and vigorously prosecute Sullivan with the full weight of his office."[101] And even with the court of appeals's decision, activists were concerned that Sullivan's lawyer would waive a jury trial and push for a change of venue. Moving the trial out of the Bronx would lessen the chances of African Americans and Latinx serving on the jury.

The Bumpurs family was thrilled with the court decision. They would finally have their day in court. Trial dates were scheduled for early January 1987. For them, the reinstated indictment represented a step toward longed-awaited justice and recognition that their mother's life mattered. While hugging and kissing her youngest son, Kareem Parker, Mary told reporters, "Thank God. There is a God. I'm gonna get what I asked for. All I want is justice. I've been praying the whole time that God would listen because he knows what happened to her. It was unjust the way things went down. I want satisfaction. I lost all I had with my mother."[102]

The criminal trial would be bittersweet for the Bumpurs family. Getting the case to trial was a major victory. Witnessing Sullivan face criminal prosecution was a blessing. The family understood that many surviving families would never have a chance at justice. Harlem resident Shirley Roper, mother of former army veteran and 1983 police victim Kenneth Thompson, never saw the inside of a courtroom. Roper was heartbroken when a Manhattan grand jury determined that three officers "justifiably used deadly force" against her only child. Mary's "fighting family" member Veronica Perry's dreams of legal accountability for her son's killer exploded in 1986. That year, a Manhattan grand jury cleared twenty-four-year-old plain-clothes NYPD officer Lee Van Houten of fatally shooting Edmund Perry. Thirty years after Eleanor's death, Gwen Carr, mother of 2014 police brutality victim and Staten Island resident Eric Garner, who infamously uttered the phrase "I Can't Breathe" eleven times before dying, would also feel the pain of legal injustice. In 2019, Carr noted that her family still "can't breathe" or have peace of mind because city and federal prosecutors failed to charge the police officer implicated in Garner's death.[103] A police officer facing prosecution for killing a Black woman would be the exception, not the rule.

Sitting in the courtroom and listening to trial proceedings would not be easy for Mary and her family. They would have to relive October 29, 1984, all over again. A front row seat to varying narratives about their mother's killing would be gut-wrenching. Loved ones would have to bear witness to legal strategies and testimonies intent on vindicating Sullivan and discounting Eleanor as a credible victim. They would have to see graphic images of their mother's mutilated body. They would have to withstand one-dimensional accounts that conjured images of a poor Black woman with a history of mental illness, incarceration, and violence. Daily trial attendance would entail hearing the details of their mother's last moments of life, as well as cruel allegations of family dysfunction and neglect. Such insensitive and, what the family deemed, fictious stories would be hard to hear. Through it all, the Bumpurs family would have to maintain courtroom etiquette and embody an outward performance of respectability, one that pushed back on anti-Black stereotypes of unruliness. No matter how Sullivan's defense attorney, police, and other witnesses characterized their mother, the Bumpurs family could not respond. No loud weeping. No outbursts. The presiding judge and court officers would not tolerate open rebellion. Boisterous behavior would be met with a warning or swift removal from the courtroom. Sitting quietly and observing the different ways state actors devalued their mother's life was their charge, and that would be difficult to do.

CHAPTER 10

THE TRIAL

I n late January 1987, a thick envelope arrived at the *Amsterdam News's* Harlem office on Frederick Douglass Boulevard. Addressed to editor-in-chief Wilbert Tatum and the rest of the staff, the package was sent from the Attica Correctional Facility, a maximum-security men's prison in Wyoming County, New York. Carefully opening the envelope, newspaper staffers discovered a duplicate copy of a hand-written petition; the original document had been addressed and sent to the Bronx District Attorney's Office. On the paper were the hand-written signatures of 102 incarcerated men. Organized by imprisoned activist and frequent *Amsterdam News* letter writer Charles "Kenya Nkrumah" Montgomery, the petition spoke of the men's "outrage and concern over the killing of Eleanor Bumpurs."[1] No strangers to political activism or state-sanctioned violence, the Attica men, building from post–World War II radical and anti-carceral movements, wanted "to let [DA Merola and] the public know that there are people in prison who are concerned about this case and want to see Sullivan brought to trial for his unjust killing of Bumpurs." Petitions were also sent to the city's largest Black radio station and one of the nation's first all-Black, all-news radio station, WLIB. Under the ownership of prominent New York City African American and Caribbean American business-men and politicians, including former Manhattan Borough president Percy Sutton, the station was highly respected for its acclaimed news and public affairs department, garnering over twenty-eight thousand listeners during every fifteen-minute period throughout the 1980s.[2]

Understanding the *Amsterdam News* and WLIB's expansive reach within New York's Black communities, the Attica men hoped that well-respected and popular journalists and radio personalities, like Peter Noel and Kae Thompson, would inform newspaper readers and radio listeners about their call for the "expeditious, diligent and vigorous prosecution" of Sullivan.[3] *Amsterdam News* staffers obliged the Attica men. In their January 31 edition, investigative journalist Peter Noel, who wrote extensively about 1980s New York police brutality cases, including the Eleanor Bumpurs and Edmund Perry killings, penned an editorial titled "Inmates Want Cop in Prison." Making the front page, the editorial offered New Yorkers excerpts from the petition and brief and dramatic scenes from the highly anticipated *State of New York v. Stephen Sullivan* criminal trial. In every corner of New York, eyes were on this trial.

The *People of the State of New York v. Stephen Sullivan* was set for January 12 at the Bronx Supreme Court. White Bronx resident and Supreme Court justice Fred W. Eggert presided over the trial. The former World War II United States Army captain and Fordham University Law School graduate was assigned the case because he was a "senior and experienced judge" who, many Bronx Supreme Court judges believed, would ensure a "fair hearing for the defendant and the Bumpurs family." According to Burton B. Roberts, chief administrative judge for the New York Supreme Court, Eggert was ideal for the high-profile case. He did not face the political pressure of reelection or reappointment; after serving over ten years on the bench, Eggert would retire at the end of the year.[4] Bronx ADA Laurence J. Lebowitz represented the State of New York. The Emory University Law School graduate was the perfect prosecutor for the case. Lebowitz served as the DA's homicide bureau supervisor at the time of the shooting; he conducted the preliminary investigation, and he successfully presented the case before a grand jury. As the case's lead prosecutor, Lebowitz also on occasion met with Mary in the DA's office, keeping her abreast of legal developments and preparing her to take the witness stand.[5]

The PBA union lawyer Bruce Smirti defended Sullivan. Under legal advisement, Sullivan elected for a bench trial, preferring to place his liberty in the hands of Justice Eggert rather than a jury. The New

York State constitution affords criminal defendants the right to a jury trial or bench trial. Defense counsel Smirti, who in later decades would represent dozens of NYPD officers accused of murder, manslaughter, assault, burglary, and conspiracy, reasoned that "a judge will be much more likely than a jury to understand the defense that the shooting was justified. The average lay person might find it difficult to understand why the police were there in the first place, and why a shotgun was employed."[6]

In recent decades, it has become common for officer-defendants, especially those involved in high-profile shooting cases, to waive their right to a jury trial. In several publicized cases of the 1990s, 2000s, and 2010s, Black, Latinx, and white officers indicted on manslaughter and murder charges for killing Baltimore native Freddie Gray (2015) and New Yorkers Anthony Baez (1994), Sean Bell (2006), and Deborah Danner (2016) left their legal fate in the hands of judges. Compared to juries, judges are believed to be familiar with law-enforcement procedures, better equipped to analyze complex legal issues, and less likely to emotionally react to victims' assaults or deaths. And jurists, according to well-known New York criminal defense lawyer Ronald L. Kuby, "have an emotional bias for police." Police officers often fare better when a judge is ruling on their cases; this was certainly true for officers involved in the killings of Gray, Baez, Bell, and Danner.[7] Bench trial jurists acquitted officers involved in those cases.

New York's contentious racial landscape and the 1986 killing of Michael Griffith in Howard Beach also shaped Sullivan's decision to go before a judge. On the evening of Saturday, December 20, 1986, one month after Sullivan's indictment was reinstated, twenty-three-year-old construction worker Michael Griffith, Griffith's thirty-six-year-old stepfather and former army veteran, Cedric Sandiford, his twenty-year-old cousin Timothy Grimes, and Florida native Curtis Sylvester were driving from Brooklyn to Queens. The four Black men were sightseeing and enjoying one another's company. Unfamiliar with their surroundings, the men got lost and their car broke down in Howard Beach, a predominately working- and middle-class Italian American community of Queens, an insular area known to Blacks as racist. "They don't want Blacks in [that] neighborhood," noted one

middle-age Black janitor who worked in Howard Beach.[8] Sandiford
and Grimes walked through Howard Beach, searching for the nearest
subway station back to Brooklyn. Sylvester decided to stay with the
car, wanting to protect the vehicle from potential thieves. The plan
was to return to Brooklyn, borrow a car from a relative or friend, and
return to Queens to pick up Sylvester. The unwelcomed presence of
African Americans in the white neighborhood prompted a "mob like"
group of about a dozen white teens. The teenagers harassed, chased,
and assaulted Griffith, Sandiford, and Grimes. Screaming "let's kill the
n—s," the teenage "wolfpack" beat the Brooklyn men with tree limbs,
tire irons, and baseball bats. Running for his life, a battered Griffith
was chased onto Queens's busy six-lane Belt Parkway. Attempting to
escape his attackers, a terrified Griffith dodged speeding traffic. But
his legs were not fast enough to avoid white motorist Dominic Blum.
Unknowingly, Blum, a Brooklyn court reporter not with the attackers,
struck Griffith, throwing his body between 75 and 125 feet.[9]

Commenting on the Howard Beach case, Smirti noted: "I had
thought about a nonjury trial well before this. But Howard Beach
is a factor that has to be considered. Because of the climate now in
the city, I don't want people perceiving this [Bumpurs' killing] as a
racial case."[10] But for New Yorkers, particularly African Americans
and Latinx, Eleanor's killing was all about race. They insisted that
race, gender, and class prejudice shaped the ways city welfare agencies
and the NYCHA and NYPD treated Eleanor. Black and Brown New
Yorkers' interpretation of Eleanor's killing mattered to Sullivan and
Smirti. Both the defendant and his counsel worried about the pros-
pect of having a jury trial, one that would reflect Bronx's multiracial
population. They believed that working-class Black and Latinx jurors would be sympathetic to a poor Black grandmother and question the veracity of a police officer. Sullivan and Smirti were right.
Nonwhite New Yorkers empathized with Eleanor. Many were wary
of the police. And many could relate to having been abused and violated by the police. Their mind and bodies bore the memories and
scars of, as James Baldwin put it, "the thunder and fire of the billy
club, the paralyzing shock of spittle in the face," and "what it is to
find oneself blinded, on one's hands and knees, at the bottom of the

flight of steps down which one has just been hurled."[11] Traumatic experiences with officers and living with ongoing police terror would likely shape Bronxites' perceptions of Sullivan's actions. They would likely reason that Sullivan's shooting of Eleanor had nothing to do with protecting another officer but had everything to do with white officers' troubling views of Blackness and poor people of color. Such perceptions left Eleanor and anyone who looked like her vulnerable to police abuse and death.

New York activists were not surprised by Sullivan's bench trial decision. Yet they were still upset. They understood the close professional alliances between police and officers of the court. The EBJC feared that Eleanor would not receive justice. "We want a jury trial, not a backroom, Bronx-style sellout with the judge deciding everything, without the people being able to participate and hear everything that happened," remarked EBJC Carol Lucas.[12] The Bumpurs family was also distrustful of the nonjury trial. "How can you get justice without a jury?" said Mary.[13] For the daughter-activist and others, a jury trial would grant the Bronx community a voice in Sullivan's prosecution. A nonjury trial would mute that critical voice, excluding Bronx residents from the judicial process. For a community with justifiable suspicions about the justice system, the bench trial was one more occasion for skepticism.

Everybody was nervous on January 12. Mary and her family rose early, ate breakfast, dressed warmly for the wintry mix of wind, cold, and possible flurries and made the short trip from their University Avenue apartment to the 161st Street Bronx courthouse. They weren't sure what day one would bring, but they hoped ADA Laurence Lebowitz would fight hard for their mother. Miles away in Putnam County, Stephen Sullivan, dressed in a black suit, white shirt, and light-colored tie, also made the commute to the courthouse. The NYPD officer was "looking forward to [the] trial." He was certainly aware that his freedom and his family's future were on the line. But "he wanted the trial to be over."[14] With their legal documents, witness lists, and pads of prepared questions and exhibits in tow, Sullivan's attorney, Bruce Smirti, and ADA Lebowitz were also anxious that morning. Both men wanted to present to Justice Eggert the best legal arguments possible: ones that would demonstrate Sullivan's guilt or innocence.

By 8:30 a.m., 161st Street was jam-packed. A flock of journalists, political activists, and "a blue rank of white faces wearing silver badges" lined the courthouse steps and the street, waiting for courthouse officers to open the doors at 9:00 a.m. Once doors opened, spectators quickly rushed into the building, making their way to the fourth-floor courtroom and hoping to secure a seat to witness what would be one of New York City's most important criminal trials of 1987.[15]

The oak-paneled courtroom was packed throughout the six-week trial. Well over one hundred family members, political activists, friends from both sides, NYPD officers, and journalists crowded into the courtroom to hear witnesses testify about the Bronx eviction and police killing. Because of limited space, many trial attendees were denied entrance into the courtroom. But they were determined, as advised by Mary and other EBJC members, to "pack the court every day!" Making themselves comfortable for opening summations and lengthy witness testimonies, they sat on the floor and on wooden benches in the hallway and leaned their bodies against the corridor's marble walls, trying to listen to trial proceedings. Whether sitting inside or standing outside the courtroom, spectators noticed that the trial was an emotionally charged and intense proceeding.

Wearing their "Eleanor Bumpurs Justice" pins, EBJC members and other political activists interrupted opening statements and even witness testimonies. They specifically targeted Smirti. He narrated the story of a military veteran, a hardworking and decorated police officer, "a hero cop that risked his life every day to protect New Yorkers." Smirti argued that Sullivan shot Eleanor to "protect the life of a brother officer when his life was imminently threatened by a psychotic woman." Sullivan shot Eleanor twice, firing the second shot because the first had no effect on Eleanor. Although Sullivan pulled the trigger, Smirti contended that other factors contributed to Eleanor's death. Her death was a byproduct of failing city agencies, paramedics transporting her to the hospital thirty minutes after the shooting, and her own actions. She "lunged at him [Sullivan] with a 10-inch knife knowing fully well that he was heavily armed," and after being shot she removed two "intravenous devices" from her arm, complicating paramedics' efforts to provide medical aid to her.[16] To add insult to injury, Smirti made inflammatory statements about Eleanor's children. Referencing the Koch administration's *Eleanor Bumpurs Case* report, Smirti maintained that Mary and her family failed to respond to notifications from NYCHA workers about their mother's deteriorating mental condition. "Her death might have been averted if members of the deceased's family had complied with their family obligations."[17]

Smirti's assertions were greeted with a cascade of jeers. "Liar," "Cover-up," and "Convict Stephen Sullivan! Stephen Sullivan murder," shouted Bumpurs's supporters. Determined to maintain an orderly courtroom, Judge Eggert immediately rose to his feet, informing spectators that "there will be no demonstrations or shouting as we heard. I know there are emotions on both sides. Try to contain them, whatever side you are on."[18] Protestors ignored Judge Eggert's warnings. They refused to be silent, objecting to any legal rhetoric and attacks against Eleanor and her family. Spectators were not concerned about being removed from the courtroom or, worse, being arrested for contempt of court. After several verbal outbursts, "five men walked to the front of the courtroom . . . and unfurled a white sheet with a portrait of Mrs. Bumpurs on it. Holding the portrait aloft, the men left the courtroom quickly to the applause of some of 100 spectators."[19] Courtroom disruptions were not limited to the first day of the trial. Outbursts erupted throughout, causing delays, the need for additional court officers, and Judge Eggert's self-removal from the bench until order was restored.[20]

Prosecutor Lebowitz's opening statements garnered no protests. However, some EBJC members and other activists would critique Lebowitz's courtroom performance and question his ability to successfully prosecute Sullivan. Many did not have faith in Lebowitz. In his introductory remarks, Lebowitz, like Smirti, blamed city welfare agencies for failing to provide Eleanor with sufficient social and psychological services. But the Bronx ADA placed Eleanor's death solely on the defendant. "The people will show beyond a reasonable doubt—indeed I suggest beyond all doubt—that the defendant's first shot did not miss but hit Mrs. Bumpers' hand shattering the knife and disarming her, making the second shot—the fatal shot that struck her breast and killed her—unnecessary. In firing that second shot," he added, "the defendant acted recklessly, in that his conduct was a gross deviation from the normal standard of conduct one would observe on that circumstance." For the duration of the trial, the two attorneys offered Justice Eggert and courtroom attendees contrasting arguments, views, and witness testimonies on one important question: Was Sullivan justified in firing a second shotgun blast at Eleanor?[21]

Fifty lay and expert witnesses appeared before the court. For weeks, courtroom testimonies from medical professionals, police officers, NYCHA employees and consultants, city social workers, and Eleanor's neighbors voiced conflicting impressions about Eleanor's personal, physical, and mental health histories and on events leading up to eviction day. They differed on whether Sullivan was justified in firing two shots at Eleanor and how many seconds there were between the shots. Two of the trial's most anticipated testimonies came from Mary Bumpurs and Stephen Sullivan.

Spectators were eager to hear the daughter-activist's testimony. She would be the only family member to appear before the court. Court observers were likely curious about what Mary would say about her mother and her family and interested in witnessing her courtroom demeanor. Would she crack under the pressure when answering tough direct and cross-examination questions? Would her anger and grief get the best of her, causing an emotional breakdown and tears? How would she respond when she came face-to-face, for the first time, with the defendant? Would she express a few choice expletives toward defense counsel and the man she believed had "hate in his heart" or would she maintain courtroom decorum, focusing only on answering lawyers' questions? Such questions were laid to rest when Mary appeared before the court on January 27.

Mary walked slowly toward Justice Eggert's bench, taking the witness stand next to him. Mary was a bit nervous appearing before the judge, court officers, and spectators. She had never been a trial witness before, and now she was a key witness in a high-profile case and on the trial of the man who killed her mother. She knew defense counsel Bruce Smirti's cross-examination would be aggressive. His job was to confuse her, twist her words, open her family's lives to scrutiny, and paint an image of a neglectful daughter who allowed her mother to live with feces in her tub and who was now looking for a payout from the city. Yet nobody—not Smirti, Stephen Sullivan, or the NYPD and PBA—could prevent Mary from using this moment to pursue justice for her mother. After several conversations and trial prep sessions with ADA Lebowitz, she was ready.[22] She was ready to look into the eyes of the man who took her mother's life. Firmly raising her right hand and taking the witness oath, a composed Mary, looking directing at Lebowitz and projecting her voice so no one in the courtroom could miss a word, uttered, "My name is Mary Bumpurs. I am the daughter of Eleanor Bumpurs."[23]

Mary's testimony had nothing to do with Sullivan's legal culpability. Her testimony contextualized her mother's medical history, revealed her last conversations with her mother, and explained what the family knew about delinquent rent payments and NYCHA's plan to evict Eleanor. Mary's testimony refuted defense counsel Smirti's claim that her family abandoned Eleanor.

"Did you know that your mother did not pay rent for July, August, September, and October? Did you receive any notification about an eviction? Did the Housing Authority ever contact you?" Mary insisted, like she had done previously in media interviews, that the family knew nothing about the eviction. "We knew nothing about being four months behind in rent. Nobody from the Housing Authority or from Social Services Administration contacted us about that." Mary admitted that Sedgwick Houses managers did contact the family, but it wasn't about housing expulsion. Listed as one of two emergency contacts on her mother's NYCHA housing application, Mary told the court that "she had received a [brief] letter, [on October 1, 1984], a month before the eviction date asking that she call the Sedgwick Houses management on a matter of "utmost importance." The next day, on October 2, a concerned Mary, while at her volunteer job at the Bronx's Republican Club, telephoned the management office. Housing assistant Richard Wallach answered the phone. Glancing between Judge Eggert and ADA Lebowitz, Mary testified that Wallach "said my mother wouldn't open the door for the maintenance man, so I told him, all right, I'll get to her and speak to her because she wouldn't open her door to strangers, that's out. He did not mention back rent or eviction. The first I knew of it [eviction] was the day she died."[24]

Under oath, Wallach told a different story. He implied that Mary was lying. Recalling the phone call with Mary, the housing worker of over ten years asserted that Mary knew everything. She was aware of her mother's nonrental history, and she knew about the pending eviction. "I explained to her the possibility of an eviction to her mother. She said she knew nothing about it and she would talk to her mother and get back to either me or [another housing manager] the following day. She never got back to me." Another witness testimony advanced Wallach's assertion, disclosing a troubling allegation about the family's knowledge about the rent payments. Court witness and former NYCHA bookkeeper Joan Alfredson claimed that a female family member, perhaps one of Mary's sister or her daughter, LuDean, went to the housing management office and "tried to pay half of what [Eleanor] owed." Alfredson turned down the payment. She could not accept partial payments without a supervisor's written approval. Mary denied NYCHA workers' charges.[25]

The man at the center of the case testified on February 5. This was Sullivan's first time giving the public a full account of the shooting. On the advice of PBA leadership and his lawyer, he rarely gave media interviews, maintaining a low profile as the story became international news. This testimony would be an opportunity to defend his actions on October 29, 1984, and explain why he should not go to jail. Dressed in a gray suit and yellow tie, Sullivan detailed his extensive experience and training as an ESU officer and the events surrounding the apartment shooting. The crux of Sullivan's eighty-minute testimony was about the two shotgun blasts. "I fired one round and apparently I missed because it had no effect whatsoever on Miss Bumpurs, she kept slashing and slashing [at one of the officers]." Mimicking how he fired the second shot, Sullivan, given the actual killing weapon, hoisted the unloaded shotgun to his hip and squeezed the trigger, pumping the cartridge chamber. "I fired a second round then she stopped. She stopped and took about three or four more steps and went into the kitchen and slumped against the wall and fell down."[26]

Watching an emotionless Sullivan reenact shooting Eleanor, the way he held the gun, aimed the weapon, and pulled the trigger, was too much for Mary. She rose from the seat and left the courtroom, pushing past court officers and hallway spectators. Greeted by news cameras and reporters, Mary, surrounded by loved ones and supporters, articulated her impressions of Sullivan's testimony. As usual, she did not mince words. Courtroom respectability was over. "He is lying. It's all lies. This was a real woman they shot away like a common animal! And she's being kept from justice by a brotherhood of lies! That's the brotherhood of liars. No cop wants to go to jail. This is not the first time they killed somebody."[27]

Trial attendees poured into the courtroom on February 17. This was a pivotal day for ADA Lebowitz and defense attorney Smirti. Both men presented their well-rehearsed closing arguments to Justice Eggert. Like opening trial remarks, final summations were met with loud remonstrations. Portions of Smirti's statements sparked courtroom commotion. In hopes of saving his client from a fifteen-year residency at one of New York's penal institutions, defense counsel argued that Sullivan "went to [Sedgwick Houses] to make peace, not break the peace." Smirti placed Eleanor's death not on Sullivan's hands but at the feet of Lincoln Hospital doctors who failed to save her life, the welfare workers who allowed "red tape and snags in the city bureaucracy" to deny her housing security and empathy, and a "callous" family who didn't care enough to pay the late rent.[28] Smirti devoted a considerable amount of time to attacking the credibility of one of the prosecution's star witnesses: Mary. Labeling the daughter-activist an opportunist, Smirti claimed that she was not concerned about her mother's physical, emotional, and mental health. "Her only interest is profiting from her mother's death. She is a liar and would lie because she's anxious to get money for herself." Smirti was referring to the $10 million lawsuit Mary and her siblings filed against the city.[29]

Black activists quickly came to Mary's defense. Smirti could hardly get a word in without being interrupted. Hecklers booed and yelled: "Convict Stephen Sullivan" "Justice for Eleanor," "Lies" and "Stephen Sullivan, murderer!" Courtroom attendee Rev. Herbert Daughtry used the chaotic moment to make a statement about police violence. Amid loud chants of "Sullivan's Guilty" and other sayings, Daughtry read a list of names of Black New Yorkers killed in police custody, exposing a pattern of police violence against nonwhite citizens. "Eleanor Bumpurs, and so many more like Dennis Grice, Michael Stewart, Luis Baez, Arthur Miller, Randolph Evans, and Clifford Glover. All lost to police brutality," said Daughtry. Courtroom protests lasted twenty-five minutes, forcing Justice Eggert to call for order. Banging his hardwood gavel, Eggert shouted, "Order, Order, Order in the court. Please leave the courtroom. Everyone vacate the courtroom." Gavel banging and directives were futile. Activists defied Eggert's orders, refusing to leave the courtroom or quiet down. "We are the people of the State of New York, and we are not leaving," screamed one man. "Bring out the shotguns and shoot us all," screamed another. Unable to control his court, Eggert ordered eleven court officers to form a human barricade between himself and protestors. The beleaguered judge called a recess and slipped quietly into his chambers until the courtroom was clear. He hoped a delay would allow court attendees to cool down.[30]

After the short recess, court officers permitted spectators to return to the courtroom. They quickly filed into the room, and Justice Eggert soon followed, taking a seat on his bench and giving attendees a stern warning about courtroom decorum. "I do not believe in a closed courtroom," he said, but Eggert threatened to close proceedings to the public if anyone interrupted Smirti or Lebowitz's closing arguments. "I will not tolerate more demonstrations."[31] This time attendees complied with Eggert's directive. Both Smirti and Lebowitz completed their summations without incident.

ADA Lebowitz challenged opposing counsel's attempts "to place [Eleanor's death] elsewhere. The fact is that she did not deserve to be shot to death." In response to the defense argument that Sullivan was following NYPD training and procedure, Lebowitz called the "elite cop" a "robot." "He would have fired again, until he got the result he was programmed to expect," said the ADA. Lebowitz drove home the argument that Sullivan made a "gross error" when he fired a second gunshot blast at Eleanor. "For a man trained for 19 years to make a mistake is a gross deviation of the standard of care that should have been exercised in this case." He must "stand and face the music when you do wrong."[32]

After hearing closing arguments, Justice Eggert announced that he would announce his decision at the end of February.

On February 26, 1987, Justice Eggert rendered a verdict in the *People of the State of New York v. Stephen Sullivan*. Sullivan's legal fate would finally be decided. Nearly two years and four months after one of the Bronx's most infamous housing evictions and police shootings, the criminal prosecution of Sullivan, which captivated New Yorkers' imaginations for weeks, would come to a close. The packed courtroom was tense as attendees waited for Eggert to enter. Throughout the six-week trial, many wondered: Would Sullivan, as the Bumpurs family and activists hoped, be convicted of second-degree manslaughter and given the maximum fifteen-year prison sentence? Or would Sullivan, as his family, fellow officers, and advocates hoped, be acquitted? However Eggert ruled, one side of the courtroom would not be satisfied with the decision. No matter the verdict, the courtroom would be filled with a mix of relief, sorrow, and anger.

In anticipation of violence and protests, the Bronx Supreme Court took extra precautions on verdict day. Additional court officers were positioned inside and outside the courtroom. Nearly three hundred uniformed and plainclothes NYPD officers patrolled the courthouse and the surrounding 161st Street and Grand Concourse neighborhoods. Several police helicopters flew over the courthouse, scouting neighborhood streets for possible lawlessness and disorder.[33] Even before Justice Eggert uttered "guilty" or "innocent," there was commotion.

Outside the courtroom, political activists chanted, "We say guilty, we say guilty" through the hallway. Inside the courtroom, Bumpurs's supporters were agitated over the limited seating space. With an eighty-person capacity, courtroom seats were reserved for off-duty police officers, Bumpurs's and Sullivan's families and advocates, and journalists. According to trial attendee and *Unity* newspaper journalist and activist Mae Ngai, "very few seats were given to African Americans. True to the cowardly racism that has marked the case from the beginning, Eggert did not want to face the people." Hoping to resolve the space issue, EBJC organizer Modibo Baker demanded that Justice Eggert move the proceedings to a larger courtroom; a bigger space would accommodate the hundred spectators who had hoped to being admitted into the room and who were standing and sitting in the hallway. "Your honor may I have one moment please? There are still a lot of people waiting to get in here. . . . These people have been waiting two years for this. We have exceeded the legal capacity of this room." Baker's request was ignored by Justice Eggert; yet Baker continued to insist on a room change despite Eggert's warnings to be quiet. Frustrated with Baker's lack of decorum, Eggert ordered his removal from the courtroom. As six court officers forcefully ushered the former Black Power activist out of the courtroom, Baker could be heard yelling, "You have turned a deaf ear on democracy and justice." Hallway spectators respected Baker's righteous indignation, nodding their heads in agreement and displaying the 1960s Black Power clenched fist salute.[34] Pushed onto the street, Baker continued to rant about Eggert and his decision to deny hundreds the opportunity to witness the verdict. He joined the other hundred sign-waving demonstrators who gathered on courthouse steps, chanting, "No Justice, no peace!"[35]

As the courtroom calmed, Justice Eggert read parts of his twenty-three-page ruling. Dressed in a three-piece brown suit, a nervous Sullivan, rubbing his hands and tapping his foot, listened to Eggert's words. With her hands folded in her lap, Mary also carefully listened to Eggert, hoping that justice for her mother would prevail. "This was the toughest case I ever tried," said Eggert. The prosecution "failed to prove beyond a reasonable doubt that Sullivan's second shot was legally unjustifiable and that the officer's actions had been a gross deviation from the standard of conduct a reasonable police officer would be expected to follow." Eggert acquitted Sullivan of second-degree manslaughter and criminally negligent homicide.[36]

Sullivan's acquittal received a ripple of applause. Family members, NYPD officers, PBA members, and city officials praised Eggert's decision.

Across the city, Sullivan's supporters cheered, hugged one another, and some even had tears in their eyes, rejoicing that a "good cop" was not made a "scapegoat" for the city's troubling social issues. Hearing about the verdict over a police radio broadcast, one cop patrolling Manhattan's Greenwich Village said, "This is great. It makes it worthwhile to be a cop again." Popular New York radio talk show host Bob Grant—who believed that Merola's case against Sullivan was a "cockamamie, unnecessary prosecution and a diabolical plot [designed] to lynch [the defendant]"—was pleased with the legal outcome. Taking to the airwaves, the right-wing veteran shock jock characterized Eleanor as violent and disposable and as a leech on society, telling his more than 150,000 listeners that "Stephen Sullivan did us all a favor." NYPD Commissioner Ward, who consistently defended Sullivan throughout the exhaustive legal battle, was "glad it's over. I'm not surprised by the outcome. It's exactly the outcome that I would have predicted." Within a day of the verdict, Ward restored Sullivan to full police duty, returning to him his badge and gun. Ward would also offer Sullivan a career opportunity, demonstrating how agents of the state benefit from maintaining and implementing carceral logics that specialized in bodily injury and harm, incessant regulation and containment, and excessive policing. Months after the acquittal in May, the commissioner promoted Sullivan to detective. Speaking to reporters about Sullivan's promotion, Ward said, "I saw no reason not to promote him. We never did find any violation of our guidelines, although we did find that our guidelines needed tightening up."[37]

No one was more elated over the verdict than Sullivan. A difficult period in his personal and professional life was finally over. As soon as the verdict was announced, a relieved Sullivan was whisked immediately out of a back door in the courtroom, avoiding hallway spectators and journalists. He headed straight to the PBA's lower

Manhattan office on Broadway. The PBA leadership planned a press conference for Sullivan; it was his first press interview. The exonerated officer—surrounded by his attorney, PBA president Phil Caruso, fellow officers (some of the officers who had entered Eleanor's apartment with Sullivan), and his wife, Maureen—told reporters from local media outlets: "I was very happy, very pleased. It's been trying, a trying time. I had no doubt about it. Like I said before, I never felt that I was guilty. It was a job I had to do, and I don't think I'd change it at all." Even after the verdict, Sullivan was still unfazed that he had taken a life. Either on the advice of his attorney and PBA leadership or because he really felt it, he never publicly expressed remorse about shooting Eleanor. Nor did he ever offer words of condolence to the Bumpurs family. He was eager to resume his life and regain his anonymity, hoping that the death threats and calls would stop and that local people would not have to "keep an eye on his house."[38] And he was ready to return to the job he loved and to socializing with his brothers in blue. That evening, Sullivan celebrated his legal victory with fellow NYPD officers and Emerald Society members at a Bronx-Yonkers pub. Long into the night, the men toasted Sullivan's win, laughing, singing, and praising Sullivan for his fortitude in withstanding the long legal process.

On the other side of the courtroom, the verdict was met with despair and fury. No surviving families of police violence ever want to hear the words "not guilty." The ruling left the Bumpurs family heartbroken and angry with the legal system. This was an injustice that would never leave them; it was an injustice that would haunt them and their future generations for decades. The verdict brought the family back to October 29, 1984, the day their mother was murdered. It was like their mother was being killed all over again. The lack of legal accountability gave the family the impression that Eleanor's life and death did not matter and that her murder did not warrant institutional retribution.

"Years of fury," borrowing from writer Audre Lorde, "surge[d] upward like a wall" when Mary heard the ruling.[39] The teary-eyed daughter could not contain her sadness and rage. Articulating her feelings to reporters, Mary, standing with sisters Keenie and Terry and her fourteen-year-old son, Kareem, looked into the news cameras, and said the "D.A. presented the facts and the judge overlooked them. The verdict was terrible. Terrible. It was just not right. It shows there is no justice for black people. What this verdict means is that if you are black you have no rights. They took my mother and I'm getting no justice. It was a racist decision." Mary compared the verdict to the long history of white violence against Black Southerners. "The only difference is this is not down South where there are trees and they'll take a rope and hang you." Ignoring historically rooted racial tropes of Black female rage as anti-normative and maddening, Mary leaned into her anger, refusing to project an appearance of respect or forgiveness for the man who killed her mother and the judicial system that denied the Bumpurs family justice. Her words signaled a readiness to confront police violence with street justice and physical aggression. "I won't let that guy get away with it. That man is mine. I'm gonna get him." She even hoped that a disruptive form of divine intervention would punish Sullivan for his deadly actions. "I am praying something bad happens to Officer Stephen Sullivan."[40]

In the wake of judicial disappointment, public memorialization and family loss were on Mary's mind. Just as she had consistently done throughout the long journey toward legal justice, Mary took time to humanize her mother, repudiating public portrayals of Eleanor as an abandoned elderly woman and as a violent person. "My mother was a loving mother. My mother wasn't a criminal. . . . None of her children were criminals. We are a solid family. This was a woman who was loved. She belonged to a family and community. She had 13 grandchildren." Mary also reminded New Yorkers of her loss—a daughter's loss. "I lost my mother. This is not fair. They took the only thing that was mine—my mother. I'll never get that back"[41]

Mary wasn't the only one disappointed with the ruling. ADA Lebowitz and the entire Bronx DA's office took issue with the verdict. Lebowitz and his fellow prosecutors and investigators did everything they could to convict Sullivan. They'd devoted long hours to thoroughly investigating the case, interviewing witnesses, filing legal appeals to

New York's intermediate and high courts, and on numerous occasions met with Mary and her family. "We put forth all the evidence. All the exhibits. The judge chose to interpret it as he did." Lebowitz voiced his disenchantment with Eggert's twenty-three-page decision with Merola, telling him, "Look at what he said—how could he say this?" Merola's answer to a dejected Lebowitz and to local reporters about the verdict was: "Life goes on. We go on to the next case. I didn't agree with Eggert's verdict, but there was nothing I could do about it. We're sorry Eleanor Bumpurs died. We hope she didn't die in vain, and the fact that police procedures have been changed because of this case shows that she hasn't."[42]

The *People of the State of New York v. Stephen Sullivan* was one of several losses for the District Attorney's Office that year. On October 27, 1987, two days shy of the three-year anniversary of Eleanor's killing, sixty-five-year-old Mario Merola suffered a cerebral hemorrhage and heart failure.[43] Around 8 a.m., an unconscious Merola arrived at Woodlawn's Our Lady of Mercy Hospital. Doctors including Harold Osborn, who had tried to preserve Eleanor's life, unsuccessfully tried to revive Merola.[44]

While Bronx prosecutors were stunned with the verdict, Sullivan's acquittal was not surprising to many Black and Latinx New Yorkers. Throughout the legal life of the case—from the 1985 indictment to the multiple court dismissals to the first day of opening statements—political activists and ordinary residents were skeptical about the trial. Many recognized the limits of New York's justice system, especially as it concerned African Americans' claims of urban inequality, racial injustice, and police terror and victimization. And recent history had shown them that securing legal retribution for police violence and abusive power was virtually impossible. In 1985, residents saw how six NYPD transit cops escaped legal conviction for the 1983 beating and death of Brooklyn artist Michael Stewart. Underserved New York communities of color witnessed how the NYPD-controlled Civilian Complaint Review Board (CCRB) dismissed and failed to investigate complaints of police misconduct. "The CCRB is a completely worthless entity. It is a fraud on the public. They never resolve cases in favor of the citizens except in the most extreme cases," noted New York Civil Liberties Union executive director Richard Emery.[45] During the mid-1980s, the CCRB, consisting of civil managers employed by the NYPD, reviewed over 6,600 cases involving force, abuse of authority, discourtesy, and racial slurs. Less than 10 percent of all the cases were found by the CCRB to be substantiated.[46] Many community leaders, like anti-apartheid activist Jeanne M. Woods, had little faith that the judicial system could deliver justice for Eleanor Bumpurs. A close follower of the trial, Woods believed, "There is no way they are going to convict Sullivan."[47]

Woods wasn't alone in her feelings about the trial. Other political organizers were not shy about publicly critiquing Justice Eggert or the defense and prosecution teams. A week after trial testimonies began, the EBJC released a press statement expressing concerns about the trial. "We are compelled and obligated to point out the illusion, no the mockery, of justice that is going on now at the Bronx Supreme Courthouse in the case of police officer Stephen Sullivan for the killing of Eleanor Bumpurs." In a February 1987 protest flyer titled "The Bumpurs Verdict: A Mockery of Justice," the Bronx group argued that "there is no doubt of the outcome, that Sullivan will be acquitted of all charge[s] by the handpicked trial judge Fred Eggert. [The judge] was not impartial and allowed defense attorney Smirti to badger witnesses." The flyer even targeted Lebowitz, alleging that the prosecutor was purposely botching the case and colluding with opposing counsel to help Sullivan:

> The prosecuting attorney Lebowitz has acted as if he is Smirti's law partner. It was his mishandling and bungling before the Bronx grand jury which caused that body to return an indictment of 2nd-degree manslaughter (reckless endangerment) rather than the more serious charge of manslaughter in the first degree. Whether consciously or unconsciously one can only conclude that Eggert, Lebowitz, and Smirti are all acting in concert to see that Sullivan will never go to jail and will be cleared of all charges and will retire with a pension at our expense.[48]

Not pleased with Lebowitz's courtroom performance, EBJC members even made several visits to the Bronx DA's office during the trial. The EBJC made the point that since "the case was important, it warranted the best from his office to try it." They "made a serious suggestion that [Merola] step in and take the case, [believing that] Lebowitz was giving the case away." Merola scoffed at the recommendation, stating, "I haven't tried a case in 15 years." In 1987 Merola had at least three hundred ADAs on his staff. They, not Merola, prosecuted criminal cases on behalf of the District Attorney's Office.[49]

However skeptical they'd been of New York's judicial system, the acquittal was still painful and infuriating to activists. Sullivan's acquittal was a miscarriage of justice for Eleanor, her family, and New York communities of color. The verdict reinforced the belief that the legal system did not care that police officers destroyed Black lives with impunity. "The decision was the court's way of saying to hell with black people," lamented one activist. Immediately after hearing the verdict, trial attendees walked throughout the courthouse, yelling "Guilty," "No justice, no peace," "Today's pig, tomorrow's bacon!" and "Heil Hitler." Those on the courthouse steps screamed and waved placards and banners that said, "PBA, KKK, different name, same game!" "It's not over!" "Educate, Agitate, Organize!" "Stop Killing Black & Latino People," and "Vengeance for Dennis Groce [Grice], Michael Stewart, Eleanor Bumpurs." Talking with journalists, political leader Reverend Herbert Daughtry reminded them of the many police brutality victims who were denied justice. "We have seen today, justice American style. I don't think that any of us are surprised. This is the same thing that happened with Michael Stewart, Randolph Evans and other victims of police murder."[50] Community activist and lawyer Colin Moore agreed with Daughtry. "Eggert's decision was consistent with history. The police are at war with our people. No white officer has ever been convicted of killing a Black person."[51] The lawyer for the Michael Stewart and Michael Griffith families, Alton Maddox, blamed Lebowitz for losing the case. "The case was obviously murder. The District Attorney deliberately threw out the case. I had expected a not guilty verdict. I had indicated if Sullivan were found guilty, I would leave town. It seems now I'll be around for a while."[52]

<hr />

The not guilty verdict did not stop community leaders from pursuing justice for Eleanor. Grassroots organizers saw the acquittal as a renewed call to action. They understood that the struggle against police brutality and other forms of state violence was an ongoing one, requiring them to remain in the trenches for civil and human rights. "We are disappointed with this outcome. But don't mourn, organize," one activist encouraged Bumpurs defenders. "Eleanor Bumpurs needs more than your tears. Don't let the case die, organize."[53] Another community advocate insisted that justice-seeking New Yorkers continue to partner with existing and emerging anti–police brutality and civil rights organizations. "Organize, everyone should join an organization and keep fighting for political and economic power and justice. [The Bumpurs case] proves that blacks in the city have to organize into political and economic power."[54] Amid dwindling legal remedies and media coverage, activists sustained political efforts on behalf of Eleanor, organizing social justice programs throughout 1987.

On March 26, the South Bronx's Christ Church held the Black Survival in the Bronx/NYC event. Neighborhood men, women, and children turned out in droves to hear stirring words from Mary Bumpurs, Bronx Community College president Roscoe Brown, NAACP leader Hazel Dukes, and pastor Wendell Foster. Speakers offered the crowd rousing orations, emphasizing the links between Eleanor's killing and the morbidly growing list of Black people who lost their lives to police brutality and white violence. Foster told attendees, "From the legalized killing of Eleanor Bumpurs to the hit and run of Michael Griffith in Queens, Howard Beach, these attacks are not only against the acts of individuals but the major results of a systematic undeclared war against Black people. We must find ways to empower ourselves to make justice a reality."[55] On the third-year anniversary of Eleanor's killing on October 24, the EBJC and several Bronx organizations co-sponsored the "Eleanor Bumpurs' Fighting Spirit Lives On" program. This event and others thereafter were evidence of activists' commitment to keeping Eleanor's story on New Yorkers' minds, especially as many became involved in legal justice campaigns for Michael Griffith, alleged 1987 sexual assault victim Tawana Brawley, and 1987 police brutality victim and Bronx mother Yvonne Smallwood.[56]

Activists also continued to pursue legal channels. "We still feel the officer used excessive force when he tried to subdue Mrs. Bumpurs and he should be punished," noted Herbert Daughtry. Engaging every available legal option, they appealed to federal officials, requesting that the US attorney for the Southern District of New York (SDNY) and the Department of Justice criminally charge Sullivan and any other police officer involved in Eleanor's eviction. Activists insisted that the NYPD violated Eleanor's civil rights. Federal officials did not issue arrest warrants, but federal prosecutor Rudolph Giuliani did investigate the Bronx shooting case.[57]

Appointed by President Reagan to head the SDNY in 1983, thirty-eight-year-old Giuliani's main priority was organized crime and government corruption cases. Sitting in his lower Manhattan office in Foley Square, Giuliani and his team of over one hundred assistant federal prosecutors and investigators, prepared legal briefs for high-profile prosecutions against the Mafia's High Commission (Genovese, Colombo, Lucchese, Gambino, and Bonnano crime family leaders), low-level drug traffickers, Wall Street executives, and wealthy tax evaders like flamboyant hotel magnate Leona Helmsley.[58] The future 107th mayor of New York City and proponent of zero-tolerance policing in the 1990s was a staunch defender of the NYPD. When it came to allegations of police brutality, Giuliani sided with cops, claiming they were "taking undue heat." Speaking on the subject in a 1985 *Daily News* interview, the federal prosecutor believed that "the recent rash of controversial cases involving cops has fostered a mistaken impression—particularly among minorities—that police brutality is on the rise in the city. I don't think so, having been involved in law enforcement for 15 years, that police brutality is any worse now than it's ever been. The situation is quite a bit better now than it used to be 10, 15, or 20 years ago. Today, cops are more honest and professional."[59]

Giuliani did not openly support Officer Sullivan. Yet given the prosecutor's pro-police stance, he likely opposed Sullivan's indictment and agreed with Justice Eggert's not guilty ruling. Despite personal sensibilities about the NYPD, Giuliani had a job to do. The SDNY's "marching orders" from the Department of Justice under Attorney General Edwin Meese, according to former assistant SDNY attorney Harriet Goldberg, "was to investigate, but once the local authorities [were] taking actions, not to prosecute."[60]

In December 1984, Giuliani requested that the FBI conduct a civil rights inquiry into the fatal shooting of Eleanor Bumpurs, a federal inquest EBJC activists pushed hard for. The investigation was "routine" and "precautionary." Giuliani noted, "It's done in any case where there may be a violation of a person's civil rights. What the F.B.I. generally does is to try to gather whatever they can gather early and then wait to see what the outcome is in the state court or in the district attorney's office."[61] Investigating the October 29 eviction, the FBI collected thousands of documents from the NYPD and other city agencies. Police records and department guidelines on persons with mental illness, medical reports, and trial transcripts were handed to the FBI. Federal agents also requested that Sullivan and other ESU officers who were present in Eleanor's apartment be available for possible interviews. Results from the FBI's investigation would be given to Giuliani for a decision on whether there was a basis for prosecution under civil rights statutes. There was still a chance Sullivan could legally be held accountable for Eleanor's death and face jail time. Violations of an individual's civil rights that resulted in death carried the maximum penalty of life imprisonment.[62]

The FBI and SDNY made their decision in August 1987. After a three-year review of evidence, federal investigators and prosecutors concluded that there was no basis for a federal grand jury investigation into Eleanor's death. "There is nothing indicating that the case was not tried fully, fairly and competently. It would be inappropriate to pursue a further prosecution," said Giuliani.[63] The Department of Justice sided with the SDNY, adding that the NYPD did not violate Eleanor's civil rights. They declined to file civil rights charges against Sullivan. This decision closed the door on further legal actions to hold Sullivan or any other officer accountable for Eleanor's killing.[64]

Lack of federal criminal charges did not end legal proceedings. Going into a new decade, an emotionally drained Mary and her family faced another legal struggle with the City of New York. This battle would put the family in conversation with a new slate of city leaders, resurrect painful family memories, and unmask more secrets.

CHAPTER 11

THE LAWSUIT

T he New York City Gay Men's Chorus belted out "New York, New York." Korean entertainers performed a traditional dance. Cardinal John O'Connor, archbishop of New York, delivered an inspiring benediction. World-renowned artist and longtime civil rights activist Harry Belafonte was the master of ceremonies. It was January 1, 1990, and Washington DC, mayor Marion Barry, civil rights leader Jesse Jackson, actress Cicely Tyson, NAACP leader Hazel Dukes, New York governor Mario Cuomo, former mayor Edward Koch, labor leaders, and New York's "gorgeous mosaic" of inhabitants stood outside Manhattan's decorated city hill. They braved light rain and chilly temperatures to witness history: the 1990 inauguration of the city's first African American mayor. Other New Yorkers like Mary Bumpurs watched the historic event from home. Surrounded by close to twelve thousand dignitaries, friends and supporters, the dapper former Manhattan Borough president David Norman Dinkins, sporting a beige coat and bright-red scarf, placed his left hand on a century-old family Bible held by his wife, Joyce Burrows Dinkins, and took the oath of office. Earning the support of over nine hundred thousand New York City voters, the soft-spoken sixty-two-year-old Democrat became the 106th mayor of the nation's premier city. In a twelve-minute speech, Dinkins swore to "be the mayor of all people," pledging to address crime and drugs, the AIDS crisis, homelessness, the city budget, social services for children, racial tensions, and other issues that had bedeviled past administrations.[1]

Another important order of business for the Dinkins administration would be settling the 1985 civil suit *Mary Bumpurs v. New York City Housing Authority*.

Mary Bumpurs, serving as the executor of the Eleanor Bumpurs estate, and her attorney, George Stone, partner at the Burke & Stone law firm, filed a $10 million wrongful death lawsuit against the nation's largest public housing authority in December 1984. Mary's lawsuit had four elements: the wrongful death of Eleanor; Eleanor's conscious pain and suffering prior to death; the survivors' loss of companionship, comfort, and assistance; and punitive damages. The city and NYCHA denied negligence and affirmatively proceeded against elements of damages. In 1986 the city filed with New York's Appellate Division of the Supreme Court to dismiss the wrongful death claim. The court agreed with the city. In April 1988, they dismissed all but one of the claims. The court did not consider punitive damages or the Bumpurs family's claim of "loss [of] companionship and comfort." The jurists ruled that the economic value of the lawsuit would focus on a single element: the conscious pain and suffering of Eleanor and the time between the gunshot blasts to the hand and chest and when Eleanor lost consciousness. Court records noted that: "There was a short period of conscious pain and suffering, and there was value to the family in this element of damages, but only modest value."[2]

No doubt the appellate court decision to dismiss key elements of the lawsuit disappointed the Bumpurs family. Yet Mary was not concerned about the money. "No amount of money can bring my mother back. I'm not interested in money. I'm interested in justice," Mary frequently told reporters.[3] And no amount of money could take away or ease the family's pain and suffering. Suing for wrongful death and familial loss was the family's last chance at securing some measure of justice for their mother and having city leaders acknowledge the impact of state violence on their family. It was the family's last opportunity to hold the city and NYCHA accountable for the deadly eviction and legally compel them to admit their wrongdoing. But with the wrongful death dismissal, the Bumpurs family would never hear city officials or housing workers admit any wrongdoing—at least not in open court. Like Sullivan's 1987 acquittal, this was another injustice that would dwell in the family's hearts and minds for generations to come.

It was serendipitous that the Dinkins administration brought the Bumpurs lawsuit to a close. Popularly known to New Yorkers as the "gentleman politician," Dinkins was well acquainted with the 1984 police shooting. Like Bronx councilor Wendell Foster, Dinkins was among a handful of city and state politicians who passionately advocated for legal justice for Eleanor and her family. Then city clerk of New York, Dinkins was one of several hundred New Yorkers who attended Eleanor's funeral in 1984. He stood shoulder to shoulder with Herbert Daughtry, Ossie Davis, and Ruby Dee, sadly staring at Eleanor in her casket. His feet hit Bronx streets for night vigils and protest demonstrations. He shared political stages with Mary and other justice-seeking activists. And Dinkins challenged the Koch administration on the Bumpurs case. He called on Koch and Ward to suspend Sullivan from the NYPD. Dinkins demanded that Mayor Koch "take personal responsibility for his [administration's] bureaucracy which was not caring enough or diligent enough or sufficiently competent to act appropriately in preventing" Eleanor's death.[4] And Dinkins did not mince words when talking about the NYPD. He posed several critical questions about police procedures. "Was a shotgun really necessary? Were two shots really necessary? Is it civilized public policy in such a situation to shoot to kill? Are all tenants of New York City housing projects who are behind in their rent now faced with the specter of shotgun carrying police offices coming to forcibly evict them?"[5]

No doubt the new mayor was sympathetic to the Bumpurs family, but Dinkins would not be directly involved in the lawsuit. Settling into his new political role, Dinkins would not have one of his aides invite Mary and her attorney to city hall to discuss the case. He could not guarantee that the Bumpurs family would be satisfied with the civil suit's legal journey. Nor would the mayor determine the case's outcome. Dinkins could only ensure that his administration's Law Department, in conversation with the family, would work toward an amicable course of action—whether that meant going to trial or settling out of court.

Dinkins elicited New York City's Law Department chief corporation counsel Victor Kovner to represent the city and NYCHA in the Bumpurs lawsuit. Appointed to the municipal unit in December 1989, the tall and thin fifty-two-year-old Kovner, one of Dinkins's long-time friends and trusted political advisers, headed a legal staff of over 550 attorneys in sixteen legal divisions across the five boroughs. The Law Department's General Litigation Division handled the Bumpurs suit, considering only one element of the lawsuit: Eleanor's period of conscious pain and suffering. Meeting in the Law Department's Grand Concourse office in the Bronx, city lawyers along with George Stone and the Bumpurs family chose to settle out of court. They engaged in, what legal documents called, a "quiet and steady process of negotiation."[6]

For the city, the motivation for a settlement, according to Leonard Olarsch, chief of the Tort Division of the City Corporation Counsel, was the risk of litigation. A jury could possibly find the city and NYCHA liable for Eleanor's death, awarding the Bumpurs family millions of dollars.[7] The city did not want to take that chance.

It's unclear why the Bumpurs family chose not to pursue a jury trial. Attorney Stone may have advised the family against a trial. Going to court was risky. Juries were unpredictable. The family faced the possibility, like in the criminal trial, of losing the case and never receiving a dime from the city. And perhaps Mary and her family, still emotionally reeling from Sullivan's acquittal, did not possess the mental bandwidth to attend court proceedings again. Daily trial attendance, potentially testifying in court, and having the next few years of their lives play out in court or in the media conceivably did not appeal to the family. Settling out of court would allow the Bumpurs family and the city to conceal negotiation details and the settlement amount. An out-of-court arbitration would also grant a faster legal process for the Bumpurs family, allowing them to collect compensation much sooner.

Negotiating out-of-court settlements was also dicey. Months and even years of private conversations between plaintiffs' and defendants' lawyers about punitive damage award amounts, emotional pain and suffering, familial loss, and mental distress could work against plaintiffs and have unexpected outcomes. Monetary awards could be substantially less than what plaintiffs originally filed for. Many late twentieth-century victims and family survivors of police violence or city abuse received out-of-court settlements that did not reflect their harrowing experiences and loss.

Fifty-seven-year-old Harlem resident Ruby Baker was one of the first persons arrested under New York's Rockefeller drug laws. She sued the city after police officers mistakenly raided her Harlem apartment in September 1973. The new drug statutes became New York and nation's strictest narcotic laws. Merely a few hours after the drug laws' authorization, which carried a mandatory minimum sentence of fifteen years to life for possession of small amounts of narcotics, several plainclothes officers were at Baker's apartment door. They believed she had drugs in her home. Around 1 a.m., police, posing as utility workers, banged on the door, requesting to fix a leak. Thinking the "utility workers" were burglars, a terrified Baker fled her apartment, running onto her fire escape. Losing her balance, Baker fell down the stairs, injuring her arms, hands, and shoulders. Hospitalized at Manhattan's Presbyterian Medical Center, a tearful Baker noted that the entire ordeal was a "nightmare."[8] Determined to hold the police and the city accountable for property damage, physical injuries, and mental stress, Baker sued the city for $2 million. In 1979, she was awarded $95,000.[9]

After the tragic 1973 police killing of her ten-year-old son, Clifford Glover, in South Jamaica, Queens, mother Eloise Glover filed a $17 million suit against the city in 1974. Five years later, the city awarded the Glover family $100,000, "$15,000 of which was paid to Human Resources Administration in settlement of a $70,000 welfare lien against Eloise." Reflecting on the negotiations between the city and the Glovers, Glover family lawyer Harry Lipsig reasoned that "city lawyers make it a practice to delay resolutions of police suits for as long as possible, figuring that after years go by the suing party will take whatever is offered. They drag their feet in every way, completely unconcerned for the delay of justice."[10]

In 1985, Michael Stewart's family filed a $10 million wrongful death lawsuit against the New York Metropolitan Transit Authority. In 1990, the MTA agreed to pay the Stewart family $1.7 million.[11] Veronica Perry, mother of slain Harlem high school student Edmund Perry and one of Mary's political comrades, filed a $145 million wrongful death suit in 1987. Two years later, the Perry family received $75,000.[12]

These families were among countless New Yorkers who were awarded from thousands to millions of dollars in police misconduct civil suits throughout the late twentieth century.[13] In 1971, the city, under mayor John Lindsey's administration, paid out $599,000 to families; that amount rose to an estimated $2.1 million in 1980. Under mayor Edward Koch, the city paid approximately $5.8 million in out-of-court settlements between 1983 and 1984. And between 1987 and 1992, the Koch and Dinkins administrations paid a little over $50 million in damages to plaintiffs.[14]

Notwithstanding lower monetary awards, out-of-court settlements have other drawbacks for plaintiffs. Negotiations between plaintiffs' and defendants' lawyers do not result in criminal charges against abusive cops or an admission of wrongdoing. Nor do settlements reduce incidents of police brutality, address systemic abuse, or ignite policy changes in policing. Cases of police violence persist, and municipalities, with taxpayers often footing the bill, continue to settle claims of misconduct. City payouts to police brutality survivors have increased astronomically in the last couple decades. According to a 2022 *Washington Post* article on police brutality, cities around the nation spent more than $1.5 billion between 2010 and 2020 on civil suits.[15] Payouts to New Yorkers have also increased. In 2022, the City of New York paid $239.1 million in tort claim settlements and judgments, and the next year that number jumped to $266.7 million in settlements.[16] Every dollar municipalities spend on settling police brutality cases is an affront against citizens and their constitutional rights.

———

Negotiations between the city and the Bumpurs estate ceased in early 1990. Mayor Dinkins did not publicly discuss negotiations or the settlement, refusing to comment on the Law Department's work. However, Dinkins may have expressed to city lawyers, or even to the Bumpurs family, what he stated to reporters about the 1990 lawsuit payout to Michael Stewart's family: "No amount of money can compensate a mother, or a father, a sister or a brother for such a loss. I hope this settlement helps members of [the] family to continue rebuilding their lives."[17] Dinkins's chief corporation counsel, Victor

Kovner, did publicly comment on the settlement. According to Kovner, the Bumpurs family and the Dinkins administration agreed to a "fair compromise" for an out-of-court settlement. With the settlement, the city, as stated in legal records, hoped that a "bitter wound in our city's past will begin the process of healing."[18] At the same time, the city made clear that the settlement was not an admission of guilt. Law Department lawyer Leonard Olarsch noted that "the city is absolutely not admitting any wrongdoing."[19]

The settlement amount was nowhere close to the $10 million the family filed for. The out-of-court settlement was $450,000, an amount worth a little over $1 million today and a figure that would radically transform the sisters and their families' everyday economic lives.[20] Half a million dollars would be more money than the family ever had. That kind of money would lessen the burden of navigating the nation's brief recession of 1990. Worrying about affording rent, utility bills, public transportation, food, clothing, and other necessities would dissipate. Longtime working-class dreams of economic stability, decent housing, investing in their financial futures, and living comfortably could be realized.

But the Bumpurs family did not receive $450,000. They received an estimated $200,000, an amount equivalent to over $460,000 today. As the executor of the Bumpurs estate, Mary made no public statements about the settlement amount. In legal documents drawn up by her lawyer, she noted that accepting the city's settlement offer was a collective decision, one made by her sisters and lawyer. "After lengthy discussions with my attorney, as well as with my siblings, I have reached the conclusion that the settlement of this case for the amount of Two Hundred Thousand is fair, compensatory and in the best interest of all beneficiaries."[21]

The City of New York deducted over $250,000 from the $450,000 settlement. A lien had been placed on the settlement for social security benefits to several of Eleanor's daughters. New York State law permitted the city to place liens and assert claims against personal lawsuit settlements of public assistance recipients. City records reveal that: "Three of the five distributees [Mary, Keenie, and Deborah Bumpurs] in intestacy of Eleanor Bumpurs received significant social service benefits over varying periods of time." According to the city, those benefits totaled almost $274,000: "Keenie Bumpurs: $110,140 from 1968; Mary Bumpurs: $101,054 from 1969; and Deborah Bumpurs: $62,641 from 1978." A reduced payout allowed former congressional leader and city comptroller Elizabeth Holtzman to save the city money. Equally importantly, the deduction, although legal, served to penalize the Bumpurs family for initiating a lawsuit against the City of New York. In the end, the Bumpurs estate received $177,500 from the city and $22,500 from NYCHA.[22] Funds were deposited into an interest-bearing escrow account.

Once law firm Burke & Stone collected their legal fees, totaling an estimated $65,000, Eleanor's living daughters, which included Mary Bumpurs, Terry Ann Bumpurs, Deborah Bumpurs, and other surviving descendants each stood to receive between $24,000 and $28,000.[23] Deceased sister Fannie Mae Baker's living adult children were legally entitled to her portion of the settlement, yet they would undergo a lengthy legal battle to receive the money.[24] The three adult children of Keenie Louise Bumpurs, one of Eleanor's youngest daughters, would follow suit. In 1988 twenty-nine-year-old Keenie Louise Bumpurs suddenly died from natural causes, leaving her share of the settlement to her children.[25] Economically, this was a significant amount for the family. But receiving less than $30,000 would not transform anybody's life. Living paycheck to paycheck and navigating the high cost of urban living would still be a frustrating reality, compelling some family members to continue to rely on state and city welfare programs. Financial security would still be a distant dream.

Before any funds could be allocated to Eleanor's heirs, Mary and administrators at the Bronx Surrogate's Court underwent the legal process of settling Eleanor's estate. Settling an estate for a decedent who did not have a will was a complex endeavor. Procedures involved identifying persons who were and were not distributees of the decedent, as well as issuing notices to distributees who are eligible to receive funds. New York law defines a distributee as a "person entitled to take or share in the property of a decedent under the statutes governing descent and distribution."[26] In determining Eleanor's distributees, those entitled to a share of the $200,000 settlement, the

Surrogate's Court unknowingly resurrected painful family memories and raised questions about Eleanor's former lover and Mary's father, John "Sonny-Man," Bumpers, and her two abducted sons, Glenn and James Bumpurs. Legal inquiries centered on whether the boys and John were alive and if they were entitled to any settlement money.

The Bronx Surrogate's Court's search for possible heirs was difficult for the Bumpurs family. This may have been some family members' first time hearing about the 1950s kidnapping and Eleanor's thorny relationship with John. For Mary, these stories were not new. They dredged up a painful past of family loss and secrets. Answering the Surrogate's Court's questions about her father and brothers, she recounted deep hurt and traumatic scenes from her childhood. She relived the nightmare of her brothers' abduction and witnessing her heartbroken mother do everything in her power to locate the boys.

Regarding her missing brothers, Mary, in written statements to the Surrogate's Court, stated that she had not seen her brothers since their abduction:

> I have two brothers but neither I, nor any member of my family, nor anyone I know has contact with either James Edward Bumpurs or Glenn Bumpurs for a period of approximately twenty years. In spite of the extensive media coverage afforded the death of my mother, neither [brothers] appeared at the funeral or in any way contacted myself, family, friends, or the media. Neither I nor any other family member has any information which would serve as a basis for locating either [brother].

After a thorough research process, Bronx Surrogate's Court lawyer Lee Holzman concluded that Glenn and James preceded Eleanor in death. "Therefore, the portion of the net distributable estate that would have been paid to them may be distributed, in equal shares, to the distributees whose status has been established herein."[27]

The Bronx Surrogate's Court then turned its attention to John Bumpers. Mary believed her estranged father was entitled to nothing. In written statements to the court, she stated, "He abandoned us and did not support my mother and [the family] for over twenty years."

Mary was correct. John was not entitled to any money. But being an absentee parent did not prevent John from being considered a distributee. John was not a distributee because he and Eleanor likely never legally married. The Harlem resident and former hospital worker and bus driver died of natural causes at Manhattan's Mount Morris Park Hospital in 1961.[28]

Mary knew about her father's death. In fact, John's death marked an important turning point in her family's life. In legal documents, she revealed that "a time after 1961, the year of my father's death, I and my family changed the spelling of our name." Originally, their surname was spelled "Bumpers," the way John spelled his name. After John's death, the family started using Bumpurs.[29] The Bumpurs family likely did not file name petitions in New York's civil court. In mid-twentieth-century New York, an individual could change their names without filing paperwork. Studying twentieth-century Jewish New Yorkers' lives, scholar Kirsten Fermaglich writes that "all one had to do was use a new name consistently and without any intent to commit fraud, and one's new name was legal."[30] The Bumpurs family's reason for altering their surname is unknown. However, identifying as Bumpurs may have signaled a desire to disconnect from John and to distinguish themselves from John's North Carolina family.

The Surrogate's Court presented Mary with her father's death certificate. The one-page black-and-white Department of Health document confirmed whispers about her father's infidelity and about his wife and children in North Carolina. Reviewing the death certificate, Mary learned that her father was fifty-five when he died, that he was buried in Louisburg, North Carolina, and that he was still married at the time of her death. The 1961 document listed John as widowed; his first wife, Lillie Bell Bumpers, died in 1960. Mary also observed an unrecognizable name listed as the "informant." The individual who provided the personal information about the deceased to city and state administrators was Dazell Bumpers Wright of Louisburg, North Carolina. Wright was John's first-born daughter. She was also Mary's older half-sister. Born in 1923, Wright was twenty-two years older than Mary. This was perhaps Mary's first encounter with her father's North Carolina family and her first time learning of Wright. She later told Surrogate's Court administrators: "The informant [Wright] on the death certificate is someone I do not know and in all likelihood did not know of my mother's existence."[31] Wright's knowledge of her father's affair with Eleanor and his New York family is unclear. It's possible that her North Carolina family wished to conceal complicated family narratives. At the same time, Wright, as a young child and teen, perhaps remembered or heard from family members stories about her father leaving his Louisburg family in the 1940s and migrating to New York with a younger woman.

The Surrogate's Court process did not unite the blood-related strangers. The legal ordeal did grant Mary and her family closure. Eleanor's offspring finally had the chance to close a painful chapter in their lives and take a break from the media whirlwind of the past six years. Or so they thought.

New Yorkers caught wind of the settlement amount one year later, in the spring of 1991. Local newspapers reported on the latest chapter of the Bumpurs story amid front-page news stories about motorist Rodney King's brutal beating by LAPD officers, a faltering city economy and budget crisis, the United States ending its occupation in Iraq, and pleas for Mayor Dinkins to do something about the high volume of crime and the crack cocaine epidemic. Stories about the Bumpurs settlement were characterized as another episode in a tragic tale that sparked "hot and angry debate." City officials claimed that the settlement amount was leaked because of "a family squabble" over how the money should be shared.[32] Claims about Bumpurs family squabbles are unsubstantiated. Yet the city's statement about the family could serve to redirect public attention away from the settlement amount to allegations of family drama.

Around the city, heads shook, eyes rolled, and mouths gasped in disbelief and anger over the paltry settlement. Political activists, journalists, and civil rights lawyers, those who marched down city streets demanding justice for Eleanor were not concerned with "family squabble" claims. They took issue with what they considered to be a "ridiculously low" monetary judgment, citing that a "black life is worth nothing as far as the city is concerned."[33]

Longtime *Daily News* Black journalist Earl Caldwell posed the question "what is a life of a black woman worth? What amount of money ought to be paid for the shotgun killing of Eleanor Bumpurs? That's the subject of what has now become a hot debate." Herbert Daughtry thought no amount of money was sufficient to remunerate the loss of a loved one but acknowledged that financial settlements for victims of state violence were rare. "[I] know of many persons killed by police whose relatives never received a dime of settlement," said Daughtry. Attorney Colin Moore, contending that the Bumpurs lawsuit should have gone before a trial jury, said, "We see that whenever the victims of police brutality are blacks, out-of-court settlements by the city are insultingly low. The award in the case would have been larger had the matter been decided by a jury, rather than out-of-court settlement. I am certain a predominantly Black and Latino jury in the Bronx would have awarded no less than $25 million to the family." Civil rights lawyer C. Vernon Mason, known for his involvement in the 1984 subway vigilante case, the 1986 Howard Beach incident, and the 1987 alleged sexual assault of Tawana Brawley, said that "the violent death of a grandmother is no way comparable to her life. $200,000 only reinforces the concept that [Black] lives are not of any value to the cops who take them."[34]

Amid public critiques, the Bumpurs family remained quiet about the payout and any supposedly family conflicts. Prioritizing their emotional needs, the Bumpurs family retreated from the public eye and the labor of political activism. Mary and her family were exhausted. Political work and building one of New York City's most important anti–police brutality campaigns of the 1980s had afforded few moments to rest, to breathe, and to find peace. Six years of media interviews, crisscrossing the city for protest rallies, and battling the NYPD, PBA, city bureaucracy, and white supremacy had taken its toll. While the Bumpurs family remained in contact with some "fighting family" members, they rarely gave media interviews and occasionally appeared at anti–police brutality demonstrations. The family was no longer front-page news. When New York journalists did mention the Eleanor Bumpurs case, their editorials focused on the legacies of her killing, linking Eleanor's death to inadequate and limited city services and the NYPD killings of Black and Brown citizens during the late 1980s and 1990s.

Not having their faces plastered on city papers was probably a relief for the family. It gave them the much-needed gift of privacy, a luxury compromised by ongoing state surveillance over Black bodies and ripped away the moment Sullivan killed Eleanor.[35] Privacy engendered possibilities for Black women and their families. Without the public gaze and constant scrutiny, Mary and her family could openly articulate thoughts and words and emotions, those expressions purposely withheld from the public and buried in their hearts. They could convey to relatives and close friends masked feelings about how much they had lost throughout the 1980s. Police violence had snatched Eleanor away. Sisters Fannie Mae and Keenie Louise were gone. And another relative, Baxter Baker Jr., one of Fannie Mae's sons, died in a drowning accident in 1989.[36] With the deaths of close family members, the Bumpurs's mourning was continuous. It seemed like every few years or so the family was planning a funeral and saying goodbye to a loved one. Privacy would be welcomed, affording family members the space and time for rest and to reflect on their losses and journeys.

Now in her mid-forties, Mary had much to ponder. The 1980s had been a roller-coaster for the community activist. Highs and lows, sharp twists and curves, and sudden drops and upside-down flips left parts of her life spiraling in various directions. At times, it seemed like the rapid and slow falls and spins would never end. But they did stop. The ride for legal justice for her mother finally ended. And now it was time for Mary, as best she could, to embrace self-care practices that prioritized physical and mental wellness.

As various parts of Mary's life slowed down, she experienced important life changes during the late 1980s and early 1990s. Her long-held dreams of securing employment and a decent apartment, one free of environmental hazards, were realized. After years of unemployment, Mary obtained employment as a mail clerk, receiving a steady income and some financial stability.[37] And years after unsuccessfully appealing to city officials and municipal workers for housing assistance, Mary finally moved from her poorly ventilated University Avenue basement apartment to a spacious two-bedroom apartment in the Morris Heights community.[38] From the comforts of her new home, Mary reflected on the lessons that often emerge from tragic loss.

Leading New York City's first "say her name" campaign taught Mary much about herself. She discovered an inner strength and power, one that wrested purpose from tragedy and grave injustices. Organizing alongside some of the city's most influential activists, politicians, and religious leaders, Mary recognized herself as a thoughtful leader, as someone with a natural ability to connect with everyday folks and mobilize communities for social and political transformation. Her straightforward approach to weighty issues and her unpretentious demeanor were her charms. The slow, long, and uncertain journey toward justice and against police violence engendered another valuable lesson, one that was vital to the longevity of New York City's civil and human rights campaigns. Crisscrossing city neighborhoods with other anti–police brutality activists, Mary learned, as theorized by prominent civil rights leader and Manhattan resident Ella Baker, who died two years after Eleanor in 1986, that ordinary working-class people like herself could be agents of societal transformation. Such people were vital to creating a just world. Ordinary city folks like herself were sources of wisdom and leadership, ideas, and solutions, and, as articulated by Baker, could "see the world for what it is, and move to transform it."[39] They never turned away from societal injustices and stood ready to tackle challenges that impacted their day-to-day lives.

The Bumpurs matriarch reflected on her mother's full life and ways to honor that life. Mary could always visit her mother and place flowers on her gravesite at Frederick Douglass Memorial Cemetery; she could always celebrate her mother's birthday with her sisters; and she could always continue to represent her mother at future anti–police brutality forums and protests. Yet Mary believed (and continues to believe) that one of the best ways to honor her mother was "to tell her story." She wanted her mother's powerful life stories of struggle, resilience, family pain, and love to be known for generations to come.

She wanted the American public to continue to "say her name," and as political activist Angela Davis told Florida State University students in 1985, "to defend the memory of Eleanor Bumpurs."[40] Public testimonials about her mother, according to Mary, would be an important way of "keeping her [Eleanor's] spirit moving."[41]

THE ENDURING LEGACY OF ELEANOR BUMPURS

I spent summer 2017 mustering the courage to contact Mary Bumpurs. Toward the end of that summer, I stood outside Mary's apartment, hoping she would not slam the door in my face or give me a tongue-lashing for showing up unannounced. A seventy-something-year-old silver-haired Mary slightly opened the door, holding a large barking dog by the collar. I was frozen. After several moments of fear, I introduced myself and the reason for my spontaneous visit. Mary graciously listened to me and surprisingly gave me her phone number. Several days later, I was sitting in Mary's apartment, one she shared with her son, two dogs, and two Cockatiel birds named George and Weezy. That one visit turned into many visits with Mary.

"What is the legacy of your mother's case?" During many conversations with Mary, I frequently posed that question to her. She always answered the same way, fiercely saying, "To keep her spirit moving. To let people know what happen to her. No more people killed by police." Mary connected her mother's legacy to public memorialization and to contemporary activists' fights for police reform and abolition.[1]

Mary's hope for public acknowledgment of her mother's death is not lost on today's activists and cultural artists. They remember Eleanor and have introduced her tragic story to new generations of social justice advocates. Thirty years after Eleanor's death, New Yorkers and those beyond the Empire State continue to #SayHerName. Her name and story are mentioned in scholarly conversations, books, newspaper editorials, and in social media posts. Her widely circulated 1980s

New York Daily News photograph is featured on political activists' protest placards and in museum and art exhibitions across the nation. In February 2017, the Bronx Documentary Center debuted the photography show *Whose Streets? Our Streets*, an exhibit that featured the photography of more than thirty-eight photojournalists, including that of September 11 victim Bill Biggart. Photographs show 1980s and 1990s New Yorkers taking to the streets, demonstrating against racial injustices and advocating for legal justice for Eleanor Bumpurs and other victims of police brutality.[2] Renowned visual artist and painter Mickalene Thomas features Eleanor Bumpurs in her 2023 *Resist* series. Thomas is known for her mixed-media paintings and collage installations featuring rhinestones, colorful acrylic, and enamel. Eleanor appears in "Resist #11," a collage, according to Thomas, inspired by a series of police and racial killings from 2014 to 2022.[3]

Mary's vision to see an end to police violence has not been realized. Police brutality continues to be a pressing issue for Black women and girls. They are beaten, placed in chokeholds, sexually violated, and gunned down as they socialize, travel, and work on city streets, as they navigate the nation's carceral institutions, and as they enjoy the comforts of their homes. And those living with mental health illnesses are also vulnerable to police abuse. They are more likely than the general population to be victimized by police.[4] Despite the NYPD's and other local law enforcement agencies' decades-old investments in de-escalation and specialized crisis intervention trainings and their revised use-of-force policies and procedures, individuals living with mental disabilities still face incarceration and militarized police units. They rarely if ever receive assistance from mental health professionals. And some, especially those experiencing mental health crises, continue to die at the hands of police.

Sixty-six-year-old Bronx mental health patient Deborah Danner hoped her disability would not bring her into contact with the NYPD. In a 2012 six-page personal essay, Danner described the mortal dangers Eleanor Bumpurs and others living with mental health issues face when interacting with police. In "Living with Schizophrenia," the former computer specialist wrote: "We are all aware of the all too frequent news stories about the mentally ill who come up against law enforcement instead of mental health professionals and end up dead. Teaching law enforcement how to deal with the mentally ill in crisis so as to prevent another 'Gompers' [Bumpurs] incident. Gompers was killed by police by shotgun because she was perceived as a 'threat to the safety' of several grown white men who were also police officers. They used deadly force to subdue her because they were not trained sufficiently in how to engage the mentally ill in crisis."[5] Danner's fears of experiencing a mental health crisis and encountering police came true on October 18, 2016. That day, NYPD sergeant Hugh Barry fatally shot Danner in her Bronx home.

Hearing of Danner's killing, Mary was reminded of her mother's death. "I have never gotten over the outrage of that day. I relive it every time someone is killed by the police. That's something that I'll never get over."[6] Eleanor Bumpurs's granddaughter Shantel Bumpurs, who was not yet born when Eleanor was killed, spoke to a reporter about the parallels between Danner and her grandmother's killings. Articulating the Bumpurs family's lingering pain and lack of police accountability, she said, "My family went through a lot the same troubles, but nothing has changed. It's shocking after all these years there is no justice."[7]

Unlike the killings of Deborah Danner and Eleanor Bumpurs, many Black women's police murders are barely visible. Their narratives garner little-to-no media attention or political mobilization, and their stories are seldom foregrounded in contemporary conversations about state violence. Erasure from such conversations suggest that women, particularly Black women, are not victims of police violence and that gender protects them from police brutality. This is hardly the case.

Gender and femininity have never shielded Black women and girls from unfettered anti-Blackness or police violence. In a 2015 statement titled "Modern Day Lynching of Black Women in the U.S. Justice System," the Association of Black Women Historians (ABWH) rightfully stated that Black women and girls "have never been afforded a femininity that deemed them innocent." On the contrary, they "are readily blamed and maligned [brutalized] rather than assisted or protected."[8] A failure to produce gender-inclusive narratives on policing and recognize "the terror of the mundane and quotidian" has

broad implications for victims and survivors.[9] Limited visibility of
the varying intersections between race, gender, and policing overlooks
the everyday dangers looming over women's and girls' lives and dis-
regards their collective struggles against what ABWH describes as a
"modern-day Red Record of anti-Black female violence."[10]

Like their foremothers of the 1980s, Black women scholars, cultural producers, and political activists continue to spearhead anti–
police brutality movements. In 2014, one year after organizers Alicia
Garza, Patrisse Cullors, and Opal Tometi created the #BlackLives-
Matter movement, legal scholar Kimberlé Crenshaw's African American Policy Forum and Center for Intersectionality and Social Policy
Studies and surviving families of police brutality launched the #Say-
HerName campaign. #SayHerName "mobilizes around the stories
of Black women who have lost their lives to police violence."[11] The
campaign makes clear that women's violations should not be an af-
terthought. Documentary filmmakers and other artists have lent their
labor to bringing greater visibility to gendered police violence. In 2020
Black filmmaker Yoruba Richens and the *New York Times* premiered
The Killing of Breonna Taylor, a moving film that centers on the
no-knock police raid that led to the twenty-six-year-old emergency
medical technician's death.[12] In October 2020, New York City activist
Tamika Mallory and other members of the social justice group Until Freedom organized the State of Emergency Rally. Held near 2020
Republican presidential candidate Donald Trump's Manhattan hotel
on 62nd Street, the demonstration, while highlighting the importance
of voter participation in the presidential election, brought together
"the mother of #BreonnaTaylor, the family of #EleanorBumpurs &
and many others who have lost their loved ones to police violence."[13]
In a rare public appearance, Mary Bumpurs and her children and
grandchildren participated in the rally.

Standing next to her grandmother Mary, Eleanore Bumpurs, a
working-class mother of two and a public housing resident, spoke
on behalf of the family. She gave an impassioned speech about her
great-grandmother, Eleanor, her namesake and someone she has only
known through family stories and newspaper accounts. Eleanore tearfully articulated her frustrations with ongoing police violence, asking

the crowd, "When does it stop?" and "Where is the justice?" for her grandmother and for Breonna Taylor and other victims. The budding activist wanted attendees not to forget what happened to her great-grandmother. Eleanore's appearance at the State of Emergency Rally is telling. Her testimony reveals intergenerational family pain. "The death of my great-grandmother really messed up my whole family. It's still a sore soul-touching subject for the family. [My family] still get angry about it."[14] It also exposed to rally attendees a different kind of trauma. For Eleanore and other Bumpurs grandchildren and great-grandchildren, Eleanor's death meant mourning the loss of a woman they never got the chance to know. Police violence robbed Eleanor's progeny of experiencing the often special relationship between grandmothers and grandchildren.

A new generation of family activists like Eleanore Bumpurs, political organizers, and scholars are committed to telling Black women's heartbreaking stories of police violence. Those complicated and often hidden stories are important to share with society. They spark global outrage and empathy for victims and their families. They inspire international movements for legal justice and police reform and abolition. Collective stories and testimonies about police violence represent powerful resistance strategies against inequitable policing and racist socioeconomic and political regimes. Yet, as this book has shown, we must go beyond narratives primarily centered on human violation and death.

Stories focused on violence reduces individuals to one-dimensional portrayals. They often ignore people's complex life histories. They advance incomplete narratives and falsehoods, causing victims to lose their identities. Singular stories leave persons frozen in time, limiting their socioeconomic and political possibilities and trapping them in death photographs, video footages, and protest hashtags.

We need histories that render visible victims' full and multifaceted lives. Restoration of personal identities acknowledges rich and sometimes complicated life experiences: the joys, the connections to family and community, and the personal hardships. An account of state violence victims' interior worlds encourages the public to invest in their layered and vibrant lives and compels us to analyze their tragic deaths in more meaningful ways.

ACKNOWLEDGMENTS

T he process of researching and writing a book is an exciting yet arduous endeavor. Fortunately, I had the guidance, wisdom, and encouragement of many individuals.

To my family, I extend profound feelings of appreciation and love. To my New York City family: Estella Cooper, Sherema Fleming, and Ambrose Fleming. Your unwavering love and encouragement made this book possible. Thank you to my Michigan family: Frances and Prospero Dagbovie, Sika and Asilah Dagbovie-Mullins, and Perovi, Kokou, and Agbele Dagbovie. Being accepted into your family has meant the world to me. And many thanks to Pero G. Dagbovie, my partner in life and scholarly mentor and personal copyeditor. I appreciate you for pushing me to embark on unknown territory with this book, and for always being a shining example of excellence and kindness. You're an inspiration.

This book was tremendously improved because of the insightful comments and conversations with a handful of scholars and friends. My writing partners, Kidada Williams, Paula Austin, and Robyn Spencer-Antoine, read various parts of the manuscript. Their scholarly brilliance and keen editorial eye helped me break up long chapters, reorganize sections, and sharpen my analysis. Their scholarly feedback was accompanied with professional advice about the craft of writing and trade press publishing. Thank you, Sharita Jacobs Thompson, Tiffany Gill, Shannon King, Cheryl Hicks, and Terrion Williamson for listening to me discuss various aspects of Eleanor Bumpurs's life. Your astute suggestions pushed the manuscript in new directions. Longtime friend Jeanne Theoharis introduced me to Beacon Press director Gayatri Patnaik. Jeanne insisted that I submit my book proposal to Beacon Press. While working on her own research projects, Jeanne made time to read several of my chapters. I'm grateful for her insight and friendship. My fellow Beacon Press author Cheryl Neely provided valuable feedback on several rough chapters and walked me through Beacon Press's publishing process. Editor extraordinaire Katie Adams was indispensable to this project.

I know a lot of brilliant people. Generous colleagues shared ideas, knowingly or unknowingly, that sharpened ideas in this book. I'm grateful to them for their scholarly guidance and mentorship. Big shout-outs to: Sowande Mustakeem, Keisha Blain, Robert Thompson, Raymond Hylton, Kali Gross, Jarvis Givens, Gerald Horne, Mary Phillips, Blair Kelley, Kellie Carter Jackson, Heather Thompson, Brenda Stevenson, Francille Rusan Wilson, Randal Jelks, Carl Suddler, Max Felker-Kantor, Tama Hamilton-Wray, Jeff Wray, Mason Williams, Gloria Ashaolu, Johanna Fernandez, Kim Phillips-Fein, Glenn Chambers, Terah Chambers, Louis Woods, Sarah Haley, J. T. Roane, Ashley Farmer, Sylvia Cyrus, G. Derek Musgrove, Charisse Burden-Stelly, Ajamu Dillahunt-Holloway, Jada Gannaway, Christen Smith, Tanisha Ford, Stephanie Evans, Keeanga-Yamahtta Taylor, Estela Goncalves, Deidre Cooper Owens, Daina Ramey Berry, Siobhan David-Carter, Billie Dee Tate, Ula Taylor, Marcia Chatelain, and Jeffrey Ogbar. My colleagues in Michigan State University's (MSU) Department of History consistently offered words of encouragement throughout the publication process. Special thanks to Michael Stamm, Nakia Parker, Nwando Achebe, Delia Fernandez-Jones, Walter Hawthorne, Peter Algei, Michelle Moyd, and Elyse Hansen. I am beholden to MSU's Office of the Vice President for Research and Graduate Studies for awarding me the Humanities and Arts Research Program Development grant. This grant allowed me the opportunity to work full-time on the book.

I'm truly thankful to those individuals who talked with me about the Bumpurs case, their lives, and 1980s New York City. Thank you: Dennis Bernstein, Rev. Herbert Daughtry, Dr. Jim Fairbanks, Laurence Lebowitz, Dr. Natalie Byfield, Jim Estrin, Nancy Siebel, Chela Blitt, Victor Kovner, Kim Glover, Antoine Nurse (rest in peace), Crystal

McDowell, Rise Brown, Mary Bumpurs, and the residents of New York City Housing Authority's Sedgwick Houses.

Much of my research was conducted in my home City of New York. I would like to thank the many archivists and librarians at the New York Municipal Archives, New York Public Library, Columbia University, New York University, Schomburg Center for Research in Black Culture, LaGuardia Community College, Bronx Historical Society, Center (Centro) for Puerto Rican Studies at Hunter College, and the Library of Congress for helping me navigate archival and photograph collections and instructing me on how to access some of New York City's richest archival materials. Special thank you to East Lansing, Michigan, artist Jennifer Taggart for drawing beautiful images of Eleanor Bumpurs. Many thanks to the archivists at *New York Daily News* Photograph Archives, Getty Images, and municipal workers at the Franklin County (North Carolina) Register of Deeds.

Thank you, Beacon Press. This book would not be possible without Beacon director Gayatri Patnaik and my editor, Maya Fernandez. Both believed in this project from the beginning. Gayatri introduced me to Maya, who became my advocate at the press. Displaying care and patience, Maya ushered me through the editing and production processes while offering useful tips about writing for a broad audience. She encouraged me at every turn. Thank you to Beacon's excellent marketing and publicity teams from designing the beautiful book cover to promoting Eleanor Bumpurs's story.

And last but certainly not least, thank you Eleanor Gray Bumpurs. Thank you for allowing me, for the past ten years, to excavate and document various aspects of your life. This book is dedicated to you.

NOTES

INTRODUCTION

1. Spike Lee dedicated *Do the Right Thing* to police shooting victims, including Brooklyn businessman Arthur Miller (killed in 1978), graffiti artist Michael Stewart (killed in 1983), Brooklyn resident Michael Griffith (killed in 1986), high school honor student Edmund Perry (killed in 1985), and Bronx mother Yvonne Smallwood (killed in 1987). Elahe Izadi, "What Inspired 'Do the Right Thing' Character Radio Raheem, and Why He's Still Relevant Today," *Washington Post*, Sept. 26, 2016, https://www.washington post.com/news/arts-and-entertainment/wp/2016/09/26/what-inspired-do -the-right-thing-character-radio-raheem-and-why-hes-still-relevant-today/.

2. *Do the Right Thing*, dir. Spike Lee, 1989, 40 Acres and a Mule Filmworks/ Universal Pictures.

3. Robyn Maynard, *Policing Black Lives: State Violence in Canada from Slavery to the Present* (Nova Scotia: Fernwood Publishing, 2017); Joy James, *Resisting State Violence: Radicalism, Gender, and Race in U.S. Culture* (Minneapolis: University of Minnesota Press, 1996).

4. Marisa Fuentes, *Dispossessed Lives: Enslaved Women, Violence, and the Archive* (Philadelphia: University of Pennsylvania Press, 2016), 5–6.

5. Ashley Farmer, "In Search of the Black Women's History Archive," *Modern American History* 1, no. 2 (2018): 289–93.

6. Sarah Haley, *No Mercy Here: Gender, Punishment, and the Making of Jim Crow Modernity* (Chapel Hill: University of North Carolina Press, 2016), 63.

7. Samantha Pinto and Shoniqua Roach, "Black Privacy Against Possession," *Black Scholar: Journal of Black Studies and Research* 51, no. 1 (2021): 1–2.

8. Darlene Clark Hine, "Rape and the Inner Lives of Black Women in the Middle West," *Signs* 14, no. 4 (Summer 1989): 915.

9. Saidiya Hartman, "Venus in Two Acts," *Small Axe* 12, no. 2 (June 2008): 3.

10. Toni Morrison, *Sula* (New York: Knopf Doubleday, 2021), 174.

11. Kidada E. Williams, "Writing Victims' Personhoods and People into the History of Lynching," *Journal of the Gilded Age and Progressive Era* 20, no. 1 (2021): 2.

12. Kidada E. Williams, "Regarding the Aftermaths of Lynching," *Journal of American History* 101, no. 3 (2014): 856.

13. Williams, "Regarding the Aftermaths of Lynching," 856.

14. Rob Nixon, *Slow Violence and the Environmentalism of the Poor* (Cambridge, MA: Harvard University Press, 2011), 2.

CHAPTER 1: SOUTHERN GIRL

1. Several legal documents including census records list Eleanor's last name as Williams and Williamson, "Elna Gray Williams," Delayed Certificate of Birth Registration (#259), May 8, 1943, County of Franklin, State of North Carolina.
2. "Marriages: Colored," *Franklin Times*, Jan. 3, 1901.
3. US Department of Labor, Bureau of Labor Statistics, "Wages and Hours of Labor in the Lumber Industry in the United States: 1930," Mar. 1932, Washington, DC: US Government Printing Office (GPO), 1932.
4. "Zollie Williamson/Williams," *North Carolina, U.S., Marriage, 1741–2011,* Ancestry.com; Fourteenth Census of the United States, Population, vol. 3, Washington, DC: US GPO, 1923; "Elna Gray Williams," Delayed Certificate of Birth Registration; Fifteenth Census of the United States, Population, vol. 3, pt. 2, Washington, DC: US GPO, 1932.
5. Jennifer Rittenhouse, *Growing Up Jim Crow: How Black and White Southern Children Learned Race* (Chapel Hill: University of North Carolina Press, 2006), 5; Stephen A. Berrey, "Resistance Begins at Home: The Black Family and Lessons in Survival and Subversion in Jim Crow Mississippi," *Black Women, Gender and Families* 3, no. 1 (Spring 2009): 65–90.
6. Silas X. Floyd, *Floyd's Flowers or Duty and Beauty for Colored Children* (Boston: Hertel, Jenkins, & Co., 1905); Stephanie Shaw, *What a Woman Ought to Be and to Do: Black Professional Women Workers During the Jim Crow Era* (Chicago: University of Chicago Press, 1996).
7. Rittenhouse, *Growing Up Jim Crow*, 5; Berrey, "Resistance Begins at Home," 65–90; Grace Elizabeth Hale, *Making Whiteness: The Culture of Segregation in the South, 1890–1940* (New York: Knopf Doubleday, 1999).
8. LaKisha Simmons, *Crescent City Girls: The Lives of Young Black Women in Segregated New Orleans* (Chapel Hill: University of North Carolina Press, 2016).
9. Audley (Queen Mother) Moore, interview by Cheryl Townsend Gilkes, June 6, 1978, Black Women's Oral History Project, Schlesinger Library, Radcliffe College.
10. "Huge Spectacle Coming to Louisburg: Birth of a Nation," *Franklin Times*, Nov. 24, 1916; "Unveil Beautiful Monument," *Franklin Times*, Sept. 21, 1923; "Luzianne Coffee," *Franklin Times*, Jan. 18, 1918.
11. David Cunningham, *Klansville, U.S.A.: The Rise and Fall of the Civil Rights-Era Ku Klux Klan* (New York: Oxford University Press, 2013), 25; "Ku Klux Makes Contributions," *Franklin Times*, June 16, 1923; "Resolutions," *Franklin Times*, July, 11, 1924; "The Ku Klux Writes the Times," *Franklin Times*, May 26, 1922; "Resolutions," *Franklin Times*, July 15, 1924; "Ku Klux Handles Negro," *Franklin Times*, May 26, 1922.
12. Ed Pilkington, "Woman Who Faced Jim Crow Takes on North Carolina's Power over Voting Rights," *The Guardian*, Sept. 25, 2014, https://www

.theguardian.com/world/2014/sep/25/north-carolina-voter-id-law-jim-crow
-african-american.

13. "Mary Bumpurs: 'They're Not Going to Get Away with What They Did,'"
    Workers Vanguard, Oct. 4, 1985, 7; Modibo Baker, "Exclusive Interview
    with Mary Bumpurs," *UNITY*, Oct. 25, 1985, 5.

14. Vann R. Newkirk, *Lynching in North Carolina: A History 1865–1941*
    (Jefferson, NC: McFarland, 2014).

15. "Powell Green Lynched," *Franklin Times*, Jan. 2, 1920; "Ugly Lynching,"
    Lincoln County News, Aug. 28, 1919.

16. Chad Williams, *Torchbearers of Democracy: African American Soldiers
    in the World War I Era* (Chapel Hill: University of North Carolina Press,
    2010), 235–36.

17. "Franklin County Mob Reported," *Franklin Times*, Sept. 6, 1935; Homer
    F. Lucas, "Rumors Fly in Franklin," *Raleigh Times*, July 31, 1935; Charles
    J. Parker, "Mob in Franklin County Lynches Negro Who Slew Farmer; In-
    quiry Started," *News and Observer*, July 31, 1935; "NAACP Names N. C.
    Lynchers," *Los Angeles Sentient*, Sept. 5, 1935; "North Carolina Officials
    Are Given Names of Ward Lynchers by N.A.A.C.P.," *Pittsburgh Courier*,
    Sept. 7, 1935; "Negro Lynched Last Night by Franklin Mobs," *Evening
    Telegram*, Aug. 21, 1919; NAACP Branch Files: Raleigh, N.C. (Jan.–Dec.
    1935), Papers of the National Association for the Advancement of Col-
    ored People (NAACP), pt. 12: Selected Branch Files, 1913, Series A: The
    South, ProQuest History Vault; "Lynching: Louisburg, N. C.," Papers of
    the NAACP, pt. 07: The Anti-Lynching Campaign, 1912–1955, Series A:
    Anti-Lynching Investigative Files, 1912–1953, ProQuest History Vault;
    "Nine Lynchers Known," *New Journal and Guide*, Sept. 7, 1935.

18. "Colored Graded School Will Open Tuesday," Sept. 4, *Franklin Times*,
    Aug. 24, 1928; "Two Negro Schools Doing Good Work in the Commu-
    nity," *Franklin Times*, Sept. 17, 1926; "Colored Graded School to Open,"
    Franklin Times, Aug. 28, 1925; John Hadley Cubbage, "The Louisburg
    Rosenwald School: Franklin County Training School," PhD diss., North
    Carolina State University, 2005, https://repository.lib.ncsu.edu/items
    /c862de79-bb93-408a-8a51-816b40f61c82.

19. Karen Clay, Ethan Schmick, and Werner Troesken, "The Rise and Fall of
    Pellagra in the American South," *Journal of Economic History* 79, no. 1
    (Mar. 2019): 32–62; W. Michael Byrd and Linda A. Clayton, *An Ameri-
    can Health Dilemma: Race, Medicine, and Healthcare in the United States,
    1900–2000* (New York: Psychology Press, 2000), 159, 231–32; Karen
    Kruse Thomas, *Deluxe Jim Crow: Civil Rights and American Health
    Policy, 1935–1954* (Athens: University of Georgia Press, 2011), 12–13;
    Richard Mizelle Jr., *Backwater Blues: The Mississippi Flood of 1927 in
    the African American Imagination* (Minneapolis: University of Minne-
    sota Press, 2014); "Fannie Bell Williams," Certificate of Death #162 (Nov.
    1929), North Carolina State Board of Heath, Bureau of Vital Statistics,
    Ancestry.com; "Kitchen Proper Place to Fight Dread Pellagra," *Franklin
    Times*, Jan. 20, 1928.

20. "Fannie Bell Williamson," North Carolina, US Death Certificates, 1909–1976, Ancestry.com.

21. "Low Wages Bring Death, Pellagra in Carolina," *Pittsburgh Courier*, Aug. 30, 1930.

22. Renate Yarborough Sanders, interview by LaShawn Harris, summer 2021.

23. Hope Edelman, *Motherless Daughters: The Legacy of Loss* (Cambridge, MA: Da Capo Press, 2014); Mae C. Henderson, "Pathways to Fracture: African American Mothers and the Complexities of Maternal Absence," *Black Women, Gender & Families* 3, no. 2 (Fall 2009): 29–47; Josephine Bacchus, transcript, Federal Writers Project: Slave Narrative Project, vol. 14, South Carolina, pt. 1, Abrams-Durant, Library of Congress.

24. Richard Wright, *12 Million Black Voices: A Folk History of the Negro in the United States of America* (London: Lindsay Drummond, 1947), 63.

25. Franklin County," *Franklin Times*, Jan. 31, 1930; Fifteenth Census of the United States, 1930, Washington, DC: National Archives and Records Administration.

26. W. E. B. Du Bois, *The Souls of Black Folk: Essays and Sketches* (Auckland: Floating Press, 2010).

27. "Zollie Williamson," North Carolina, US Death Certificates, 1909–1976, Ancestry.com; "Zollie Williams and Laura Belle Alston," North Carolina, US Marriage Records, 1741–2011, Ancestry.com; Mary Bumpurs, interview by LaShawn Harris, July and Aug. 2017.

28. Patricia Hill Collins, *Black Feminist Thought: Knowledge, Consciousness, and the Politics of Empowerment* (New York: Routledge, 1990).

29. Tyrone McKinley Freeman, *Madam C.J. Walker's Gospel of Giving: Black Women's Philanthropy During Jim Crow* (Urbana: University of Illinois Press, 2020).

30. Tera Hunter, *To Joy My Freedom: Southern Black Women's Lives and Labor After the Civil War* (Cambridge: Harvard University Press, 1997), 57.

31. Hunter, *To Joy My Freedom*, 53, 57.

32. Bumpurs, interview.

33. Jennifer Jensen Wallach, *Every Nation Has Its Dish: Black Bodies and Black Food in Twentieth-Century America* (Chapel Hill: University of North Carolina Press, 2018), 5.

34. Rebecca Sharpless, *Cooking in Other Women's Kitchens: Domestic Workers in the South, 1865–1960* (Chapel Hill: University of North Carolina Press, 2013); Jennifer Jensen Wallach, ed., *Dethroning the Deceitful Pork Chop: Rethinking African American Foodways from Slavery to Obama* (Fayetteville: University of Arkansas, 2015); Jessica B. Harris, *High on the Hog: A Culinary Journey from Africa to America* (New York: Bloomsbury, 2011).

35. Bumpurs, interview.

36. Cheryl Townsend Gilkes, "Holding Back the Ocean with a Broom: Black Women and Community Work," in *The Black Woman*, ed. L. Rodgers-Rose (London: Sage, 1980), 217–32.

37. Robert A. Margo, *Race and Schooling in the South, 1880–1950* (Chicago: University of Chicago Press, 1994), 10–11; Nazera Sadiq Wright, *Black*

Girlhood in the Nineteenth Century (Urbana: University of Illinois Press, 2016); Joyce Ladner, *Tomorrow's Tomorrow: The Black Woman* (New York: Doubleday, 1972).

38. Simmons, *Crescent City Girls*, 23.
39. Official documents list several first names for Eleanor: Elna (Elner) Gray Williams, Evelyn Gray Williams, Eleanor Williams, Elenor Gray Williams, and Ella Gray Hayes; "Earnest Hayes," "U.S. WWII Draft Cards Young Men, 1940–1947" Ancestry.com; Fifteenth Census of the United States, 1930.
40. David Medina, "Bumpurs' Kin See Apartment," *New York Daily News (NYDN)*, Nov. 29, 1984.
41. Ernest Hayes's 1978 death record indicates he never married. It's possible he and Eleanor had a common-law marriage. "Ernest Hayes," North Carolina, Death Indexes, 1908–2004, Ancestry.com.
42. "Fannie Gray Hays," North Carolina State Board of Health, Mar. 22, 1939.
43. Federal Writers' Project, *The WPA Guide to North Carolina: The Tar Heel State* (San Antonio: Trinity University Press, 2013), 51–57; Madonna Harrington Meyer, *Care Work: Gender, Labor, and the Welfare State* (New York: Routledge, 2002); Earnest Hayes," "U.S. WWII Draft Cards Young Men, 1940–1947"; Sixteenth Census of the United States, Population, vol. 2, pt. 6, Washington, DC: US GPO, 1943.
44. Federal Works Agency, *Report on Progress of the WPA Program* (Washington, DC: US Projects Administration), June 30, 1939, 11.
45. Sixteenth Census of the United States, Population, vol. 2, pt. 6, Washington, DC: US GPO, 1943; "New Franklin Hotel Opens at Louisburg," *News and Observer*, Oct. 10, 1915; W. F. Shelton, "$250,000 Fire Razes Hotel in Louisburg Business Area," *News and Observer*, Dec. 15, 1949.
46. "Wilborn and Boyd 8 Months," *Franklin Times*, May 8, 1942.
47. North Carolina restricts public access to certain inmate records, https://www.ncleg.net/EnactedLegislation/Statutes/HTML/ByChapter/Chapter_132.html, accessed Aug. 11, 2016.
48. Bumpurs, interview.
49. Gertrude "Ma" Rainey, "Sweet Rough Man," Sept. 1928, Paramount 12926.
50. "Wilborn and Boyd 8 Months."
51. Trina N. Seitz, "The Wounds of Savagery: Negro Primitivism, Gender Parity, and the Execution of Rosanna Lightner Phillips," *Women and Criminal Justice* 16, nos. 1–2 (2005): 29–64; *Biennial Report, 1942–1944* (Raleigh: State Highway and Public Works Commission, Prison Department, 1942).
52. "Mrs. Strickland First Woman to Head Prison in the State," *Herald Sun*, Mar. 22, 1942; Bob Thompson, "Women Prisoners Working Only 30 Hours Per Week," *High Point Enterprise*, Apr. 8, 1942; Bess D. Thompson, "Population of Women's Prison Trebles in Year," *Asheville Citizen-Times*, July 5, 1942; "Women Prisoners Sew Shirts for U.S. Navy," *Franklin Press and the Highlands Maconian*, Dec. 2, 1942; Richard F. Jones Jr., *Prison Labor in the United States, 1940* (Washington, DC: US GPO, 1941).
53. Haley, *No Mercy Here*, 56, 117.

54. Richard Wright, *Black Boy* (New York: World Publishing Company, 1945), 76.
55. Haley, *No Mercy Here*, 220.
56. Joe William Trotter, *The Great Migration in Historical Perspective: New Dimensions of Race, Class, and Gender* (Bloomington: Indiana University Press, 1991); Lisa Krissoff Boehm, *Making a Way Out of No Way: African American Women and the Second Great Migration* (Jackson: University Press of Mississippi, 2010).
57. Wallace Thurman, *Negro Life in New York's Harlem: A Lively Picture of a Popular and Interesting Section* (Girard: Haldeman-Julius Publications, 1927), 1.
58. Carla J. DuBose-Simons, "The 'Silent Arrival': The Second Wave of the Great Migration and Its Effects on Black New York, 1940–1950," PhD diss., City University of New York, 2013, 26, https://academicworks.cuny.edu/gc_etds/2231/.
59. "Mary Bumpurs: 'They're Not Going to Get Away with What They Did,'" 7.
60. "John Bumpass," North Carolina, US Marriage Records, 1741–2011, Ancestry.com; "John Bumpers," Certificate of Death (June 21, 1961) 61-113915, File 788, 1984, Surrogate's Court of the State of New York, County of Bronx (Eleanor Bumpurs); James "Manny" Wright, *Heirs of the Great Migration: How the Past Became the Future* (self-published, 2022), 5.
61. Anastasia C. Curwood, *Stormy Weather: Middle-Class African American Marriages Between the Two World Wars* (Chapel Hill: University of North Carolina Press, 2010); Tera Hunter, *Bound in Wedlock: Slave and Free Black Marriage in the Nineteenth Century* (Cambridge, MA: Harvard University Press, 2017).

CHAPTER 2: NEW YORK, NEW YORK
1. "John Bumpers," Certificate of Death (June 21, 1961) 61-113915, File 788, 1984, Surrogate's Court of the State of New York, County of Bronx (Eleanor Bumpurs).
2. Elmer A. Carter, "Plain Talk: Strangers and Strangers," *New York Amsterdam News* (*NYAN*), Oct. 9, 1943.
3. Gabriel N. Mendes, *Under the Strain of Color: Harlem's Lafargue Clinic and the Promise of an Antiracist Psychiatry* (Ithaca, NY: Cornell University Press, 2015), 164.
4. "City Shopper," *NYAN*, Aug. 14, 1943.
5. James Weldon Johnson, *Black Manhattan* (New York: Atheneum, 1968), 162–63; Ula Taylor, "Archival Thinking and the Wives of Marcus Garvey," in *Contesting Archives: Finding Women in the Sources*, ed. Nupur Chaudhuri, Sherry J. Katz, and Mary Elizabeth Perry (Urbana: University of Illinois Press, 2010), 125–35.
6. Dan Burley, "Backdoor Stuff," *NYAN*, July 27, 1949.
7. Isabel Wilkerson, *The Warmth of Other Suns: The Epic Story of America's Great Migration* (New York: Knopf Doubleday, 2011), 228.
8. Johnson, *Black Manhattan*, 162–63.

9. Roi Ottley, "New World A-Coming," *NYAN*, May 13, 1944.
10. Ottley, "New World A-Coming."
11. Thomas J. Sugrue, *Sweet Land of Liberty: The Forgotten Struggle for Civil Rights in the North* (New York: Random House, 2008), 4, 12; Shannon King, "A Murder in Central Park: Racial Violence and the Crime Wave in New York During the 1930s and 1940s," in *The Strange Careers of the Jim Crow North: Segregation and Struggle Outside of the South*, ed. Brian Purnell, Jeanne Theoharis, and Komozi Woodard (New York: New York University Press, 2019), 43–66.
12. "Worse Than Mississippi," *NYAN*, May 16, 1959.
13. Martha Biondi, *To Stand and Fight: The Struggle for Civil Rights in Post-war New York* (Cambridge, MA: Harvard University Press, 2009); Purnell, Theoharis, and Woodward, *The Strange Careers of the Jim Crow North*, 6.
14. Shannon King, *The Politics of Safety: The Black Struggle for Police Accountability in LaGuardia's New York* (Chapel Hill: University of North Carolina Press, 2024).
15. Melvin Johnson, "False Report That Solider Was Killed Leads to Outburst," *Afro-American*, Aug. 7, 1943; "Riot Starter Sentenced," *New York Times* (*NYT*), Sept. 11, 1943; "Other 9 ('The Ballad of Margie Polite')," *NYAN*, Oct. 2, 1943.
16. Bianca C. Williams, *The Pursuit of Happiness: Black Women, Diasporic Dreams, and the Politics of Emotional Transnationalism* (Durham, NC: Duke University Press, 2018).
17. Robin D. G. Kelley, *Race Rebels: Culture, Politics, and the Black Working Class* (New York: Free Press, 1994), 36.
18. "Mary Bumpers," New York, NY, US Birth Index, 1910–1965, Ancestry.com; "Eleanor Bumpurs," File 788 (1984) Bronx Surrogate's Court Records.
19. "Deborah Bumpurs," New York, NY, US Birth Index, 1910–1965, Ancestry.com; "Keenie Bumpurs," New York, NY, US Birth Index, 1910–1965, Ancestry.com; "Terry Bumpurs," New York, NY, US Birth Index, 1910–1965, Ancestry.com; "Keenie Louise Bumpurs," File 362 (1991), Bronx Surrogate's Court Records; "Eleanor Bumpurs," File 788; "Fannie Mae Baker," File 1789 (1991), Surrogate's Court of the State of New York, County of New York. The author is unable to locate vital statistics for Eleanor Bumpurs's two sons.
20. Emma Azalia Hackley, *The Colored Girl Beautiful* (Kansas City: Burton Publishing, 1916).
21. Mai'a Williams and Loretta Ross, *Revolutionary Mothering: Love on the Front Lines* (Oakland: PM Press, 2016).
22. Baker, "Exclusive Interview with Mary Bumpurs," 5.
23. Cecelie Berry, *Rise Up Singing: Black Women Writers on Motherhood* (New York: Harlem Moon, 2004); Collins, *Black Feminist Thought*; Nella Larsen, *Passing* (New York: Knopf, 1929), 121.
24. Bumpurs, interview; LaShawn Harris, "Beyond the Shooting: Eleanor Gray Bumpurs, Identity Erasure, and Family Activism Against Police Violence," *Souls: A Critical Journal of Black Politics, Culture, and Society* 20,

no. 1 (2018): 86–109; Baker, "Exclusive Interview with Mary Bumpurs,"
5; Evelyn Jaffe Schreiber, *Race, Trauma, and Home in the Novels of Toni
Morrison* (Baton Rouge: Louisiana State University Press, 2010); Badia
Ahad-Legardy, *Afro-Nostalgia: Feeling Good in Contemporary Black Culture* (Urbana: University of Illinois Press, 2021).

25. Psyche Williams-Forson, *Building Houses Out of Chicken Legs: Black
    Women, Food, & Power* (Chapel Hill: University of North Carolina Press,
    2006), 110, 113.
26. Bumpurs, interview; Baker, "Exclusive Interview with Mary Bumpurs," 5.
27. Bumpurs, interview.
28. Arnold Rampersad, *Collected Poems of Langston Hughes* (New York:
    Vintage Classics, 1995), 709.
29. Judith Worrell and Carol D. Goodheart, eds., *Handbook of Girls' and
    Women's Psychological Health* (New York: Oxford University Press,
    2006), 21–22.
30. Premilla Nadasen, *Household Workers Unite: The Untold Story of African
    American Women Who Built a Movement* (Boston: Beacon Press, 2015), 11.
31. Bumpurs, interview.
32. Bumpurs, interview.
33. Baker, "Exclusive Interview with Mary Bumpurs," 5.
34. "Links Lunch at Waldorf Top Easter Social Event," *NYAN*, Apr. 4, 1959;
    "Nkrumah to Be Honored at Waldorf," *NYAN*, June 28, 1958; "Negro
    History Week Breakfast at Waldorf," *NYAN*, Feb. 15, 1958; "Bronx Chap-
    ter of NCNW Has Party at Waldorf," *NYAN*, May 5, 1951; "Delta Sigma
    Theta "Lena Horne Is Honorary Delta Member," *NYAN*, Dec. 13, 1958;
    "Designers Close Convention with National Show: 17 Cities Represented
    at Meeting," *NYAN*, Apr. 28, 1951; David Freeland, *The Waldorf-Astoria
    and the Making of a Century* (New Brunswick, NJ: Rutgers Univer-
    sity Press, 2021), 213; "Up Town Low Down," *NYAN*, May 26, 1956;
    "Dandridge Wins Raves in Waldorf Debut," *Jet*, Apr. 28, 1955; James
    Gavin, *Stormy Weather: The Life of Lena Horne* (New York: Atria Books,
    2009), 259.
35. Herbert R. Tacker, "Household Employment Under OASDHI, 1951–
    1966," *Bulletin* (1970), https://www.ssa.gov/policy/docs/ssb/v33n6/
    v33n6p10.pdf; US Bureau of Labor Statistics, *Occupational Outlook
    Handbook* (Washington, DC: Bureau of Labor Statistics, 1959), 566, 568;
    US Bureau of Labor Statistics, *Occupational Outlook Handbook* (Wash-
    ington, DC: Bureau of Labor Statistics, 1957), 481.
36. *100 Years of U.S. Consumer Spending: Data for the Nation, New York
    City, and Boston*, US Department of Labor, May 2006, https://www.bls
    .gov/opub/100-years-of-u-s-consumer-spending.pdf, 21–23.
37. Rhonda Williams, *The Politics of Public Housing: Black Women's Strug-
    gles Against Urban Inequality* (New York: Oxford University, 2004), 4.
38. The 1968 Supreme Court decision *King v. Smith* held that Aid to Families
    with Dependent Children could not be withheld because of the presence
    of a substitute father. "19 Plead Guilty in $70,000 Tax Fraud," *NYAN*,
    July 25, 1953; "Mother of 3 Says Welfare Pushed Her Around," *NYAN*,

Aug. 30, 1952; Anne M. Valk, *Radical Sisters: Second-Wave Feminism and Black Liberation in Washington, D.C.* (Urbana: University of Illinois Press, 2008), 49.

39. "Magistrate Scores Relief Clients and Declare They Act Worse Than Dogs," *NYAN*, Jan. 18, 1936; "Blacks and Puerto Ricans Protest 'Mistreatment' at Welfare Center," *NYAN*, Feb. 27, 1977.

40. Lisa Levenstein, *A Movement Without Marches: African American Women and the Politics of Poverty in Postwar Philadelphia* (Chapel Hill: University of North Carolina Press, 2008), 37.

41. Bumpurs, interview.

42. Charles Murray, *Losing Ground: American Social Policy 1950–1980* (New York: Basic Books, 1984), 19; Ellen Reese, *Backlash Against Welfare Mothers: Past and Present* (Berkeley: University of California Press, 2005).

43. Bumpurs, interview; "Mary Bumpurs: 'They're Not Going to Get Away with What They Did,'" 7.

44. "Shooting of Eleanor Bumpurs," YouTube, uploaded by Fox5NY, Oct. 20, 2016, https://www.youtube.com/watch?v=GMmU70OB2KI.

45. "Proceeding of Limited Letter of Administration, Estate of Eleanor G. Bumpurs," "Estate of Eleanor G. Bumpurs, Nov. 18, 1992," in "Eleanor Bumpurs," File 788 (1984) Surrogate's County Court, County of the Bronx.

46. When Eleanor Bumpurs's killing made national news, the missing boys, who would have been adults at the time, did not resurface. "Eleanor Bumpurs," File 788.

47. Paula S. Fass, *Kidnapped: Child Abduction in America* (New York: Oxford University Press, 1997).

48. "Eleanor Bumpurs," File 788.

49. Jen Periera, Rich McHugh, and Imaeyen Ibanga, "N.Y. Mom Tracks, Retrieves Missing Son in South Korea," ABC News, Mar. 31, 2008, https://abcnews.go.com/GMA/TurningPoints/story?id=4556584&page=1.

50. "In The Matter of the Accounting of Mary H. Bumpurs," File 788, 1984, Surrogate's Court of the State of New York, County of Bronx (Eleanor Bumpurs).

51. Bumpurs, interview.

52. Jessica Millward, "Black Women's History and the Labor of Mourning," *Souls* 18, no 1, (2016): 161–65.

53. Dana-Ain Davis, "'The Bone Collectors': Comments for Sorrow as Artifact; Black Radical Mothering in Times of Terror," *Transforming Anthropology* 24, no. 1 (2016): 8.

54. "Mary Bumpurs: 'They're Not Going to Get Away with What They Did,'" 7.

55. Bumpurs, interview.

56. Alex S. Vitale, *City of Disorder: How the Quality of Life Campaign Transformed New York Politics* (New York: New York University Press, 2008), 126; Richard J. Meislin, "Fear of Crime Is Now Woven into Fabric of City Lives," *NYT*, Jan. 31, 1982.

57. Kim Phillips-Fein, *Fear City: New York's Fiscal Crisis and the Rise of Austerity Politics* (New York: Metropolitan Books, 2017), 35; Marilyn Johnson, *Street Justice: A History of Police Violence in New York City* (Boston:

Beacon Press, 2003), 245; Robert Snyder, "Crime," in *Encyclopedia of New York City*, ed. Kenneth Jackson (New Haven, CT: Yale University Press, 1995), 297.

58. "True's City Tally of Crime Pushed Rates Up Sharply," *NYT*, Apr. 5, 1966; Martin Gansberg, "Murders Rose 14% in City Last Year," *NYT*, Apr. 18, 1968.

59. Les Matthews, "A Little Girl Is Slain and Grandma Tells an Unbelievable Story," *NYAN*, Mar. 14, 1964; "Teenage Girl Slain By Strange Man," *NYAN*, July 23, 1966; "Raped Tots Buried," *NYAN*, Sept. 10, 1966; George Todd, "Seize Suspect in Nude Girl Slaying," *NYAN*, Jan. 14, 1967.

60. James Baldwin, *The Fire Next Time* (New York: Vintage, 1963), 21, 23.

61. Michael Flamm, *In the Heat of the Summer: The New York Riots of 1964 and the War on Crime* (Philadelphia: University of Pennsylvania Press, 2017); Biondi, *To Stand and Fight*, 1-2.

62. Marsha E. Barrett, *Nelson Rockefeller's Dilemma: The Fight to Save Moderate Republicanism* (New York: Cornel University Press, 2024), 166–68.

63. Carl Suddler, *Presumed Criminal: Black Youth and the Justice System in Postwar New York* (New York: New York University Press, 2020).

64. George Todd, "Girl, 16, Shot by Police, Dies in Her Mom's Arms: Boro Group Links Killing to Racism," *NYAN*, Feb. 3, 1973; Robert D. McFadden, "'Defensive' Police Shots Kill a Girl, 16," *NYT*, Jan. 28, 1973; Elizabeth Hinton, *From the War on Poverty to the War on Crime: The Making of Mass Incarceration in America* (Cambridge, MA: Harvard University Press, 2016), 190.

65. Mary Breasted, "Grand Jury to Get Report on Police Killing of Boy," *NYT*, Sept. 17, 1974; "Many in Brownsville March in Memorial to Slain Boy," *NYT*, Sept. 19, 1974; "500, at City Hall, Protest Reese Slaying," *NYT*, Sept. 26, 1974; McFadden, "'Defensive' Police Shots Kill a Girl, 16."

66. Derrick Jackson, "Report on Slaying Enrages Daughter," *Newsday*, Nov. 21, 1984.

67. "Says Harlemites Arm Themselves Because of Crime Rise in Area," *NYAN*, Oct. 21, 1967.

68. Phillips-Fein, *Fear City*, 131–32; Michael Oreskes, "Fiscal Crisis Still Haunts the Police," *NYT*, July 6, 1985.

69. Themis Chronopoulos, *Spatial Regulation in New York City: From Urban Renewal to Zero Tolerance* (Hoboken, NJ: Taylor & Francis Group, 2011), 119.

70. Subcommittee on Criminal Justice of the Committee on the Judiciary House of Representatives, Ninety-Eighth Congress (pt. 1), *Police Misconduct* (Washington, DC: US GPO, 1984), 472.

71. Eli B. Silverman, *NYPD Battles Crime: Innovative Strategies in Policing* (Lebanon, NH: University Press of New England, 1999); "Eleanor Bumpurs/Arrest Report and Complaint Report," Case 526303 (Nov. 1, 1973), Police Department Legal Bureau, City of New York.

72. Lindsey Devers, "Plea and Charge Bargaining," Bureau of Justice Assistance, US Department of Justice, Jan. 24, 2011, https://bja.ojp.gov/sites/g /files/xyckuh186/files/media/document/pleabargainingresearchsummary.pdf.

73. Peter L. Zimroth, "101,000 Defendants Were Convicted of Misdemeanors Last Year," *NYT*, May 28, 1972.
74. "Racism Is 'American as Apple Pie': Ward," *NYDN*, Nov. 17, 1984.
75. Sam Roberts, "People Fled the Bronx in the 1970s," *NYT*, Sept. 15, 2016, https://www.nytimes.com/2016/09/16/nyregion/as-new-york-city-grows -the-bronx-especially-is-booming.html; "NYC Population Manhattan, Bronx, Brooklyn, 1970–1980," *NYC Open Data*, https://data.cityofnewyork.us /City-Government/NYC-Population-Manhattan-Bronx-Brooklyn-1970 -1980/yddj-a7un.
76. Bench Ansfield, "Born in Flames: Arson, Racial Capitalism, and the Rein- suring of the Bronx in the Late Twentieth Century," *Enterprise & Society* 23, no. 4 (Dec. 2022): 923–27; Evelyn Diaz Gonzalez, *The Bronx* (New York: Columbia University Press, 2004); Phillips-Fein, *Fear City.*
77. Ahmasi Bustani, "A Walk thru the South Bronx," *NYAN*, Nov. 25, 1978.
78. Denis J. Mondesire, "Pits of the Bronx," *NYAN*, Nov. 18, 1978.
79. Peter L'Official, *Urban Legends: The South Bronx in Representation and Ruin* (Cambridge, MA: Harvard University Press, 2020), 2.
80. John Melia and Ruth Landa, "Bumpurs Kin Lied to Hospitalize Her," *NYDN*, Jan. 28, 1987.
81. Randy Young, "The Homeless: The Shame of the City," *New York Mag- azine*, Dec. 21, 1981; Jeffrey Antevil, "Mental Patients Win Big Case," *NYDN*, June 27, 1975.
82. Jonathan Soffer, *Ed Koch and the Rebuilding of New York City* (New York: Columbia University Press, 2010), 280–81, 291, 296.
83. Young, "The Homeless," 27.
84. Robin Herman, "Mental-Patient Release Program Leaves Many to Face Harsh Fate," *NYT*, Nov. 18, 1979; Antonio G. Olivieri, "Mentally Ill, 'Dumped' and Isolated," *NYT*, Mar. 11, 1978.
85. Suzanne Golubski and David Medina, "Bumpurs's Past Was Violent One," *NYDN*, Dec. 1, 1984; Frank J. Prial, "Daughter Cites Bumpurs's Stay in State Hospital," *NYT*, Jan. 28, 1987; "Hosp Aides Face Grilling on Bum- purs," *NYDN*, Dec. 3, 1984, 5; "Anatomy of a Tragedy: A Troubled His- tory," *NYDN*, Dec. 2, 1984.
86. Sharyl J. Nass, Laura A. Levit, and Lawrence O. Gostin, *Beyond the HI- PAA Privacy Rule: Enhancing Privacy, Improving Health Through Re- search* (Washington, DC: National Academies Press, 2009).
87. Robert Clurman, "The Patients Can Walk Out at Any Time at Bronx State Mental Hospital," *NYT*, Apr. 2, 1972; Murray Schumach, "Abuses Charged in Mental Wards," *NYT*, Mar. 13, 1975; Murray Schumach, "Many Mental Patients Simply Walk Out," *NYT*, Aug. 8, 1974; Murray Schumach, "Men- tal Hospitals for Criminal Only Urged by Merola," *NYT*, Apr. 14, 1975.
88. Schumach, "Abuses Charged in Mental Wards."
89. Martin Gottlieb, "System Seems the Culprit in Teen Inmate's Suicide," *NYDN*, Aug. 1, 1976; Edith Evans Asbury, "Mental Patient Killed in Plunge," *NYT*, Sept. 17, 1974.
90. Suzanne Golubski and David Medina, "Bumpurs' Past Was Violent One," *NYAN*, Dec. 1, 1984.

91. Michael Oreskes, "Still a Lot of Walk-Aways at Mental Hospital," *NYDN*, May 31, 1977.

92. Golubski and Medina, "Bumpurs's Past Was Violent One"; Prial, "Daughter Cites Bumpurs's Stay in State Hospital"; Clurman, "The Patients Can Walk Out at Any Time at Bronx State Mental Hospital"; Schumach, "Abuses Charged in Mental Wards"; Schumach, "Many Mental Patients Simply Walk Out."

93. "A Troubled History," *NYDN*, Dec. 2, 1984, 19.

94. *People v. Sullivan*, No. 394-85.

95. Malcolm X, *The Autobiography of Malcolm X* (New York: Random House, 2015), 23.

96. Smoki Harris, "Green Haven," *NYAN*, Feb. 11, 1978.

97. Melia and Landa, "Bumpurs Kin Lied to Hospitalize Her"; *People v. Sullivan*, 394-85.

CHAPTER 3: LIFE AT SEDGWICK HOUSES

1. Marva York, "In This Bronx Building, It's a Hell Frozen Over," *NYDN*, Jan. 6, 1981.

2. Peter McLaughlin and Martin Gottlieb, "Frost Bites Northeast," *NYDN*, Jan. 5, 1981.

3. York, "In This Bronx Building, It's a Hell Frozen Over."

4. John J. Goldman "Residents with No Heart Given Shelter: Bitter Winter Turns N.Y. Apartments into Freezers," *Los Angeles Times*, Jan. 31, 1981.

5. Thomas Raftery and Don Flynn, "2 Are Found Dead in Unheated Flats," *NYDN*, Jan. 21, 1981; Peter McLaughlin and Fred Kerber, "Find 2 Women Frozen to Death in Bronx, B'klyn," *NYDN*, Jan. 21, 1981; "Deaths of 2 Women Attributed to Cold," *Newsday*, Jan. 22, 1981, 32.

6. "The Death of Jessie Smalls," *National Catholic Review*, Feb. 13, 1981, 17.

7. Marva York, "Deal with Lefrak Ends Long Rent Strike," *NYDN*, July 3, 1981.

8. In 1965, the Department of Labor's Office of Policy Planning and Review prepared the historic and controversial "Moynihan Report," which focused on poverty and the Black family during the 1960s; "Dear Senator," Philip Halpen and Doris Bowers to Honorable Daniel Moynihan, Sept. 25, 1977, Box 91/D2, Folder: Chairman Files (J. Christian–Police, July 1977–Dec. 1977), New York City Housing Authority (NYCHA), La Guardia Wagner Archives.

9. "Commissioner Anthony Gliedman to Mayor Edward Koch," Jan. 31, 1981, Box 0000175, Folder 06, Edward I. Koch Papers, LaGuardia and Wagner Archives; "Joseph Jeffries-El to Honorable Edward I. Koch," Jan. 15, 1981, Koch Papers, Box 0000175, Folder 06, Koch Papers; Lee A. Daniels, "Shivering Tenants Continue Complaints as Koch Listens," *NYT*, Jan. 14, 1981; Martin King, "City Swamped by No-Heat Complaints," *NYDN*, Jan. 13, 1981.

10. York, "In this Bronx Building, It's Hell Frozen Over," 125.

11. Bench Ansfield, "Born in Flames: Arson, Racial Capitalism, and the Reinsuring of the Bronx in the Late Twentieth Century," *Enterprise & Society*

23, no. 4 (Dec. 2022): 923–27; Jonathan Soffer, *Ed Koch and the Rebuilding of New York City* (New York: Columbia University Press, 2011), 2; Joseph C. Ewoodzie Jr., *Breaking Beats in the Bronx: Rediscovering Hip-Hop's Early Years* (Chapel Hill: University of North Carolina Press, 2017), 23; Glenn Fowler, "City Fires Down in '79 for a 3rd Year," *NYT*, Jan. 10, 1980; Joe Flood, *The Fires: How Computer Formula, Big Ideas, and the Best of Intentions Burned Down New York City—and Determined the Future of Cities* (New York: Penguin, 2010); Evelyn Gonzalez, *The Bronx* (New York: Columbia University Press, 2004); Marva York, "Bronx Only No. 2 in Fires but Oh, How They Burn," *NYDN*, Jan. 13, 1981.

12. Leslie Maitland, "2 Children Among 6 Killed in a Fire in South Bronx," *NYT*, Nov. 9, 1978; Emanuel Perlmutter, "Two Arrested in Arson at Bronx Club That Killed 25," *NYT*, Jan. 3, 1977; "2 Children and Their Father Killed in Bronx Fire," *NYT*, June 3, 1981; Thomas Hanrahan and Paul La Rosa, "Their Lives in Ashes," *NYDN*, June 3, 1981.

13. Marva York, "2d Fire in a Week Drives 30 Tenants into Subzero Cold," *NYDN*, Jan. 5, 1981; "Committee on Governmental Affairs of the U.S. Senate," *Arson in America* (Washington, DC: US GPO, 1979), 44; Ansfield, "Born in Flames," 923–27.

14. York, "2d Fire in a Week Drives 30 Tenants into Subzero Cold."

15. York, "2d Fire in a Week Drives 30 Tenants into Subzero Cold."

16. Les Matthews, "Rats Invade Home of Harlem Family," *NYAN*, Sept. 4, 1982.

17. Angela Jones, "Tenants Live with Fear, Fleas," *NYAN*, Oct. 12, 1981.

18. Angela Jones, "Nightmare to End for Brooklyn Family," *NYAN*, Sept. 4, 1982.

19. York, "2d Fire in a Week Drives 30 Tenants into Subzero Cold."

20. York, "2d Fire in a Week Drives 30 Tenants into Subzero Cold."

21. Saidiya Hartman, "Venus in Two Acts," *Small Axe* 26, no. 2 (June 2008): 2; Nikki M. Taylor, *Driven Toward Madness: The Fugitive Slave Margaret Garner and Tragedy on the Ohio* (Athens: Ohio University Press, 2016), 78.

22. Saidiya Hartman, *Wayward Lives, Beautiful Experiments: Intimate Histories of Social Upheaval* (New York: W. W. Norton, 2019), 17–18.

23. Simon Anekwe, "Dinkins Accuses Koch of Betraying Workers," *NYAN*, June 7, 1986.

24. Lee Dembart, "Koch, Criticized by Many Blacks, Seeks to Repair Ties with Them," *NYT*, Feb. 27, 1979.

25. Themis Chronopoulos, "The Making of the Orderly City: New York Since the 1980s," *Journal of Urban History* 46, no. 5 (2017): 5.

26. Josh Barbanel, "New York City's Economy Booms, and the Poor Begin to Profit," *NYT*, May 16, 1988.

27. Bayard Rustin, "Three Years Later, the Poor Get Poorer," *New Pittsburgh Courier*, Sept. 15, 1984.

28. Rustin, "Three Years Later, the Poor Get Poorer."

29. Brittany C. Slatton, *Mythologizing Black Women: Unveiling White Men's Racist Deep Frame on Race and Gender* (New York: Routledge, 2016), 20.

30. US Department of Labor Women's Bureau, "Facts on Working Women: Black Women in the Labor Force," no. 90–94, (June 1991), 1; The People of the State of New York Against William Stephens, May 1994, A93–94; Samuel M. Ehrenhalt, "Economic and Demographic Change: The Case of New York City," *Monthly Labor Review* (Feb. 1993): 50; Barbanel, "New York City's Economy Booms, and the Poor Begin to Profit."

31. Rosemary Bray, "Managing as a Black Woman," *NYDN*, Feb. 27, 1987; "City Jobs Off Limits to Blacks, Hispanic," *NYAN*, Apr. 6, 1985; Gerald C. Horne, "Poverty Hits Elderly, Black Women the Hardest," *Afro-American*, Sept. 20, 1980, 5.

32. Elizabeth Kolbert, "Illegal Workers as Domestics: Uneasy Alliance," *NYT*, Oct. 30, 1985.

33. Marisa Chappell, *Family, Poverty, and Politics in Modern America* (Philadelphia: University of Pennsylvania Press, 2012); David Stoesz and Howard Jacob Karger, *Reconstructing the American Welfare State* (Lanham, MD: Rowman & Littlefield, 1992), 29; Clarence Lusane and Dennis Desmond, *Pipe Dream Blues: Racism and the War on Drugs* (Boston: South End Press, 1991), 15–16; Althea T. L. Simmons, "1984: The Most Crucial Vote . . . Civil Rights and Reaganomics," *The Crisis*, Apr. 1984, 166–67; John Ehrman and Michael Flamm, *Debating the Reagan Presidency* (Lanham, MD: Rowman & Littlefield, 2002), 50–51; Daniel S. Lucks, *Reconsidering Reagan: Racism, Republicans, and the Road to Trump* (Boston: Beacon Press, 2020); "Congress Study Finds Reagan Budget Curbs Put 557,000 People in Poverty," *NYT*, July 26,1984.

34. Simon Anekwe, "Poor Folks Are High on President Reagan's Hit List," *NYAN*, Feb. 28, 1981.

35. "Policy Paper: Senior Citizens," Box 12, Folder 8, Policy Papers: Rent Control, Youth, Housing, Disabled, David N. Dinkins Archives and Oral History Project, Columbia University.

36. "'I Want a Chance,' Says Welfare Mother," *NYAN*, Sept. 19, 1981.

37. Bill Price, "Blacks React to Reagan's Proposed Cuts," *NYAN*, Feb. 28, 1981.

38. "Housing Authority Application," Box 0000033, Folder 21 (City Hall Staff, Victor Botnick, Eleanor Bumpurs Case), Koch Papers; York, "2d Fire in a Week Drives 30 Tenants into Subzero Cold."

39. New York City Housing Authority, "Project Data: Jan. 1, 1982," https://www.nyc.gov/assets/nycha/downloads/pdf/pdbjan1982.pdf, 43.

40. Jack Leahy, "Exhibit on Public Housing Set," *NYDN*, Nov. 12, 1987; "Banking Housing Unit to Cost to $5,849,994," *NYT*, Jan. 22, 1947; "Bank Housing Unit to Cost $4,750,000: New Housing Development Proposed for the Bronx," *NYT*, Jan. 10, 1946.

41. "Mary Bumpurs: 'They're Not Going to Get Away with What They Did,'" 7; *People v. Sullivan*, 394-85.

42. "SWAT Cops Blow Away Bronx Grandmother: Her Life for Her Rent," *Workers Vanguard*, Nov. 9, 1984; "The People of the State of New York Against Stephen Sullivan," New York Court of Appeals Records and Brief, 68 NY2d 495, Appellants Appendix, pt. 4; *People v. Sullivan* (Bronx County Indictment No. 394/1985).

43. Hearing Before the Subcommittee on Housing and Community Development of the Committee on Banking, Finance and Urban Affairs, House of Representatives, Ninety-Eighth Congress, Second Session (May 7, 1984) Washington, DC: US GPO, 1984, 86–88, 91; Dan O'Grady, "Housing Woe Aired," *NYDN*, June 18, 1985; Dan O'Grady, "A Near Garden of Eden," *NYDN*, June 19, 1985.

44. Rhonda Y. Williams, *The Politics of Public Housing: Black Women's Struggles Against Urban Inequality* (New York: Oxford University Press, 2004), 12.

45. Bumpurs, interview; Helen Bierra, interview by LaShawn Harris, Aug. 2017; "Housing Urban Development's (HUD) Support of Local Public Housing Authorities," Subcommittee on the Committee on Government Operations Houses of Representatives, Ninety-Seventh Cong., 1st sess., May 19–20, 1981 (Washington, DC: US GPO, 1981).

46. "Barry Carey to Terry Bumpurs," Sept. 28, 1984; "Barry Carey to Mary Bumpurs," Sept. 28, 1984," Box 0000033, Folder 21 (City Hall Staff, Victor Botnick, Eleanor Bumpurs Case), Koch Papers.

47. Bumpurs, interview; *People v. Sullivan*, 394-85.

48. "Mary Bumpurs: 'They're Not Going to Get Away with What They Did,'" 7; *People v. Sullivan*, 394-85.

49. Jimmy Breslin, "Double-Barreled Double-Talk," *NYDN*, Nov. 11, 1984.

50. Jimmy Breslin, "Shot Down Like a Lynx," *NYDN*, Nov. 4, 1984.

51. *People v. Sullivan*, 394-85.

52. Lisa Levenstein, "Myth #11: 'Tenants Did Not Invest in Public Housing,'" in *Public Housing Myths: Perception, Reality, and Social Policy*, ed. Fritz Umbacj and Lawrence J. Vale (Ithaca, NY: Cornell University Press, 2015), 223–34.

53. Elizabeth Alexander, *The Black Interior* (Saint Paul, MN: Graywolf Press, 2004), 9.

54. Leonard Buder, "School Boycott to Be Held Today in Rights Protest," *NYT*, Feb. 3, 1964; "N. Y. Boycott Huge Success!," *Chicago Daily Defender*, Feb. 4, 1963.

55. *People v. Sullivan*, 68 NY2d 495, vol. 3 (pt. 4), A1204–A1212; "Find Bumpurs Finger in Apt.," *NYAN*, Dec. 1, 1984.

56. Jennifer C. Nash, "From Lavender to Purple: Privacy, Black Women, and Feminist Legal Theory," *Cardozo Women's Law Journal* (2005): 326.

57. *People v. Sullivan*, 394-85; "Johnnie Junious Williamston," North Carolina, US Death Certificates, 1909–1976, Ancestry.com; "Spencer Williamson," North Carolina, US Death Certificates, 1909–1976, Ancestry.com.

58. Pat Barile, "Demand Probe of Shooting," *Daily World*, Nov. 3, 1984, 11; Tom Quinn, "A New Kind of Church," *NYDN*, May 13, 1984.

59. "Says Bumpurs 'Could've Been Locked Outside,'" *NYDN*, Dec. 5, 1984.

60. "Cops in Touch in the Bronx," Honorable Robert Garcia, Congressional Record, Mar. 21, 1985, 5991–92.

61. Breslin, "Shot Down Like a Lynx."

62. Breslin, "Shot Down Like a Lynx"; Victor Garcia, "Eyewitness to the Bumpurs Shooting," *City Sun*, Nov. 7–13, 1983.

63. Victor Garcia, "Eyewitness 'It Was Like a War,'" *City Sun*, Nov. 7–13, 1984.

64. "Personal Courage Aids a Community," *New Pittsburgh Courier*, Jan. 5, 1985.

65. Breslin, "Double-Barreled Double-Talk."

66. Nora Bonosky, "Outrage Over Eviction Killing," *Daily World*, Nov. 4, 1984.

67. "Anatomy of a Tragedy."

68. Peter Moses and Kieran Crowley, "Woman Shot to Death in Eviction," *New York Post*, Oct. 29, 1984.

69. Suzanne Golubski and David Medina, "Bumpurs's Past Was Violent One." *NYDN*, Dec. 1, 1984.

70. *People v. Sullivan*, 68 NY2d 495, vol. 1 (pt. 2), A136–A137.

71. Bella English, "A Trust Abused? Scandals Spark Probe of HRA," *NYDN*, Aug. 12, 1984, 3.

72. *People v. Sullivan*, 68 NY2d 495, vol. 1 (pt. 2), A129.

73. *People v. Sullivan*, 68 NY2d 495, vol. 1 (pt. 2), A371.

74. *People v. Sullivan*, 68 NY2d 495, vol. 1 (pt. 2).

75. *People v. Sullivan*, 394-85.

76. *People v. Sullivan*, 68 NY2d 495, vol. 1 (pt. 2), A69.

77. *People v.* Sullivan, 68 NY2d 495, vol. 1 (pt. 2), A6–A7.

78. *People v. Sullivan*, 68 NY2d 495, vol. 1 (pt. 2), A69.

79. Alice Walker, *Horses Make a Landscape Look More Beautiful* (San Diego: Harcourt Brace Jovanovich, 1984), 51.

80. Slatton, *Mythologizing Black Women*, 20; William E. Leuchtenburg, *The American President: From Teddy Roosevelt to Bill Clinton* (New York: Oxford University Press, 2015), 593.

81. *People v.* Sullivan, 68 NY2d 495, vol. 1 (pt. 2), A188.

82. *People v.* Sullivan, 68 NY2d 495, vol. 1 (pt. 2), A1202.

83. Jonathan Mandell, "Knock on Any Door," *NYDN*, Oct. 27, 1985.

84. *People v.* Sullivan, 68 NY2d 495, vol. 1 (pt. 2), A259.

85. *People v. Sullivan*, 68 NY2d 495, vol. 1 (pt. 2), A259.

86. Farah Jasmine Griffin, *Read Until You Understand: The Profound Wisdom of Black Life and Literature* (New York: W. W. Norton, 2021), 8; Deirdre Carmondy, "Study Blames Poverty for Most Homelessness," *NYT*, Nov. 2, 1984; Shelia Rule, "Report Says City Homeless May Double in Two Years," *NYT*, Dec. 24, 1983.

87. "Housing Authority Application," Box 0000033, Folder 21 (City Hall Staff, Victor Botnick, Eleanor Bumpurs Case), Koch Papers; "Dennis de-Leon to Edward I Koch," Nov. 20, 1984, Box 000210, Folder 03 (Eleanor Bumpurs Case), Koch Papers; "Day of Death, Days of Anger," *NYDN*, Dec. 2, 1984; "Anatomy of a Tragedy"; Utrice C. Leid, "An Eviction with Two Purposes," *City Sun*, Dec. 5–11, 1984.

88. *People v. Sullivan*, 394-85.

89. Jack Newfield, "Tales of the Other New York," *City Sun*, Nov. 7–13, 1984; Todd S. Purdum, "Questions Swirl Around a Fatal Shooting by Police," *NYT*, Jan. 5, 1988; Garcia, "Eyewitness: 'It Was Like a War'"; "Short

Term Notes: Deadly Eviction," *City Limits Magazine*, Dec. 1984; Leid, "An Eviction with Two Purposes"; Jonathan Mandell, "Knock on Any Door," *NYDN*, Oct. 27, 1985.

90. *People v. Sullivan*, 394-85.

91. *People v. Sullivan*, 394-85; Frank Lynn, "State Party Completes Delegation for G.O.P. National Convention," *NYT*, June 16, 1984.

92. *People v. Sullivan*, 394-85.

CHAPTER 4: THE EVICTION

1. The People of the State of New York v. Stephen Sullivan, No. 394-85 (New York City, Feb. 2, 1987).

2. David A. McEntire, ed., *Disciplines, Disasters, and Emergency Management: The Convergence and Divergence of Concepts, Issues and Trends from Research Literature* (Springfield: Charles C. Thomas Publisher, 2007), 227–99; David Vidal, "Questions Raised in Death of Man Whom Police Had Shot 16 Times," *NYT*, Aug. 24, 1979; Housing Authority Application," Box 0000033, Folder 21 (City Hall Staff, Victor Botnick, Eleanor Bumpurs Case), Koch Papers; *People v. Sullivan*, 68 NY2d 495, vol. 1 (pt. 2); "Day of Death, Days of Anger," *NYDN*, Dec. 2, 1984; Mario Merola, *Big City D.A.* (New York: Random House, 1988), 12.

3. Selwyn Raab, "Police and Victim's Daughter Clash on Shooting," *NYT*, Nov. 1, 1984.

4. "Victor Botnick to Edward Koch," Nov. 9, 1984, Box 000033, Folder 21 (City Hall Staff, Victor Botnick, Eleanor Bumpurs Case), Koch Papers.

5. Leslie Bennetts, "Report Tells Plight of Elderly Women," *NYT*, June 23, 1982.

6. Matthew Desmond, *Evicted: Poverty and Profit in the American City* (New York: Penguin Random House, 2016).

7. *People v. Sullivan*, 68 NY2d 495, vol. 2 (pt. 3), A428.

8. Wolfgang Saxon, "Using a New Strategy, Police Spray Chemical to Stop Knife-Wielder," *NYT*, Sept. 8, 1979; "No Rights Violation Seen in 21-Shot Police Slaying," *NYT*, July 11, 1980; Robert Lane and Mark Lieberman, "Cop in Killing Guilty in '78 Rights Case," *NYDN*, Sept. 2, 1979; Joseph P. Fried, "Brooklyn Woman, 35, Slain After Slashing an Officer," *NYT*, Aug. 30, 1979; Mark Lieberman, "Tenants Hit Latest Killing by Cop," *NYDN*, Aug. 31, 1979.

9. "The Hero Cops," *NYDN*, Dec. 2, 1984.

10. *People v. Sullivan*, 68 NY2d 495, vol. 3 (pt. 4), A1227.

11. Bob Leuci, "Macho Merola: The Bronx's Fighting DA," *NYDN*, Mar. 31, 1985.

12. "A Mother Died for $447.20," *NYAN*, Nov. 3, 1984.

13. Camille Nelson, "Racializing Disability, Disabling Race: Policing Race and Mental Status," *Berkeley Journal of Criminal Law* 15, no. 1 (2010): 13–17; Andrea J. Ritchie, *Invisible No More: Police Violence Against Black Women and Women of Color* (Boston: Beacon Press, 2017), 91.

14. Anna Mollow "Unvictimizable: Toward a Fat Black Disability Studies," *African American Review* 50, no. 2 (Summer 2017): 105–21.

15. Marc Lamon Hill, *Casualties of America's War on the Vulnerable, from Ferguson to Flint and Beyond* (New York: Atria Books, 2016), xx, xxi, xix.
16. David Medina, "Says Bumpurs Could've Been Locked Outside," *NYDN*, Dec. 5, 1984.
17. "Commissioner Benjamin Ward to Mayor Edward I. Koch," Nov. 16, 1984, Box 0000033, Folder 21 (City Hall Staff, Victor Botnick, Eleanor Bumpurs Case), Koch Papers; "The Hero Cops"; "Florence Peaks" *Chapel of Peace*, Dec. 19, 2022, https://www.thechapelofpeace.com/obituaries/florence-peaks.
18. Victor Garcia, "Eyewitness: 'It Was Like a War,'" *City Sun*, Nov. 7–13, 1984; Derrick Johnson, "Another Look at a Tenant's Fatal Ousting," *Newsday*, Nov. 1984.
19. Jerry Schmetterer, "Crime: Dispelling the Myth . . . Fighting the Reality," *NYDN*, Mar. 20, 1983.
20. "Boros Contaminated as Crime Pox Rages On," *NYAN*, Aug. 21, 1982; "Crime Rate in New York City, *NYT*, Apr. 5, 1986.
21. "Housing Chief of Police to Deputy Mayor Nicholas Scoppetta," Aug. 31, 1977, Box 91/D2, Folder: Chairman Files (J. Christian–Police, July 1977–Dec. 1977), New York City Housing Authority (NYCHA, La Guardia Wagner Archives.
22. Jackson, "Another Look at a Tenant's Fatal Ousting."
23. *People v. Sullivan*, 68 NY2d 495, vol. 1 (pt. 2), A16–A19; *People v. Sullivan*, 394-85, 2406.
24. Jackson, "Another Look at a Tenant's Fatal Ousting."
25. Merola, *Big City D.A.*, 13.
26. *People v. Sullivan*, 68 NY2d 495, (pt. 1) Appellant Brief, 25.
27. Stuart Marques, "Tracking the Tragedy," *NYDN*, Feb. 1, 1985; Ruben Rosario and Stuart Marques, "Cops are Hot as a Pistol," *NYDN*, Feb. 1, 1985; "Memo from Police Commissioner Ward," *City Sun*, Nov. 29–Dec. 4, 1984; Christopher LeBron, *The Making of Black Lives Matters: A Brief History of an Idea* (New York: Oxford University Press, 2017), 67–70; Lewis H. Lapham, "What Killed Mrs. Bumpurs," Dec. 29, 1984; Michael Wilson, "When Mental Illness Meets Police Firepower," *NYT*, Dec. 28, 2003; "The Hero Cops," 67; Merola, *Big City D.A.*, 13–14.
28. *People v. Sullivan*, 68 NY2d 495, vol. 2 (pt. 3), A495.
29. Merola, *Big City D.A.*, 16.
30. Garcia, "Eyewitness: 'It Was Like a War'"; Patrice O'Shaughnessy, Murray Weiss, and Don Gentile, "Cops Kill Woman, 67, During Eviction Attempt," *NYDN*, Oct. 13, 1984; Pat Barile, "Demand Probe of Shooting," *Daily World*, Nov. 3, 1984.
31. Jimmy Breslin, "Bumpurs Witness Justified in Fear," *NYDN*, Jan. 29, 1985; "Civil Rights Journal: Personal Courage Aids a Community," *Pittsburgh Courier*, Jan. 5, 1985; Garcia, "Eyewitness: 'It Was Like a War'"; Patrice O'Shaughnessy, Murray Weiss, and Don Gentile, "Cops Kill Woman, 67, During Eviction Attempt," *NYDN*, Oct. 13, 1984; Medina, "Says Bumpurs Could've Been Locked Outside"; Barile, "Demand Probe of Shooting."

32. Jimmy Breslin, "Worms in the Big Apple," *NYDN*, Nov. 1, 1984; Audre Lorde, *The Collected Poems of Audre Lorde* (Latham, MD: Kitchen Table/Women of Color Press, 1986), 411.

33. Pat Barile, "Demand Probe of Tenant Shooting," *Daily World*, Nov. 3, 1984.

34. James Murphy, "Tenant Leader: It's a Nightmare," *City Sun*, Nov. 7–13, 1984.

35. Jack Newfield, "Tales of the Other New York," *City Sun*, Nov. 7–13, 1984; Todd S. Purdum, "Questions Swirl Around a Fatal Shooting by Police," *NYT*, Jan. 5, 1988; Garcia, "Eyewitness: 'It Was Like a War'"; Derrick Johnson, "Woman, 66, with Knife Killed by Police," *Newsday*, Oct. 30, 1984; Medina, "Says Bumpurs Could've Been Locked Outside."

36. Harold H. Osborn, "The Bumpurs Case: Nagging Problems," *NYT*, Apr. 20, 1985; J. Zamgba Browne, "Public Still Angry Over Cop Killing," *NYAN*, Nov. 10, 1984.

CHAPTER 5: "THEY SHOT A GRANDMOTHER!"

1. The People of the State of New York v. Stephen Sullivan, No. 394-85 (New York City, Feb. 2, 1987).

 2. *People v. Sullivan*, 394-85.

 3. Peter Noel, "Group Decries 'Sham' Bumpurs Murder Trial," *NYAN*, Jan. 31, 1987.

 4. *People v. Sullivan*, 394-85.

 5. *People v. Sullivan*, 394-85.

 6. Police Department City of New York, "Annual Report," 1984, https://www.ojp.gov/pdffiles1/Digitization/121490NCJRS.pdf, 22.

 7. Earl Caldwell, "He Has Police Facts, in Black and White," *NYDN*, Sept. 19, 1983.

 8. Bob Kappstatter, "An Unwelcome No. 1," *NYDN*, Sept. 22, 1984.

 9. Peter Noel, "Bumpurs' Kin Wants Ben Ward to Resign," *NYAN*, Feb. 9, 1985; Richard Esposito and David Ng, "Bumpurs' Kin Wants to Be a Cop," *New York Post*, Nov. 23, 1984.

10. Murray Weiss, Don Gentile, David Medina, and Thomas Hanrahan, "Woman, 67, Killed in Eviction," *NYDN*, Oct. 30, 1984.

11. "Tenants Call It 'Murder,'" *NYAN*, Nov. 3, 1984; Murray Weiss, David Medina, and Thomas Hanrahan, "Eviction Row: Crowd Calls It 'Murder!'" *NYDN*, Oct. 31, 1984.

12. "Tenants Call It 'Murder'"; Weiss, Medina, and Hanrahan, "Eviction Row: Crowd Calls It 'Murder!'"

13. "Tenants Call It 'Murder'"; Weiss, Medina, and Hanrahan, "Eviction Row: Crowd Calls it 'Murder!,'" *NYDN*, Oct. 31, 1984.

14. Correspondence from James Murphy to New York City Housing Authority chairman Joseph J. Christian, Nov. 1, 1984, Box 1, Folder: Constituents, 1982–1986, Reverend Wendell Foster Papers, Bronx County Historical Society; Murphy, "Tenant Leader: It's a Nightmare"; Eric Pace, "Joseph Christian, 84, Head of Housing Agency," *NYT*, Apr. 19, 2000; "Shooting of Eleanor Bumpurs," Fox 5 New York, streamed Oct. 20,

2016, YouTube video, 4:16, https://www.youtube.com/watch?v=GMm
U70OB2KI&list=PLtqRLdlJwhOA6ET0JOKTK3P2A-nCBtc5r&index
=1&t=8s.

15. Patia Braithwaite and Tiffanie Graham, "The Toll of Police Violence on
Black Peoples' Mental Health," *NYT*, May 25, 2023, https://www.nytimes
.com/interactive/2023/05/25/well/mind/black-mental-health-police-violence
.html; Jordan E. DeVylder et al., "Police Violence and Public Health,"
Annual Review of Clinical Psychology 18 (2022): 527–52.
16. "Short Term Notes: Deadly Eviction."
17. Barile, "Demand Probe of Tenant Shooting."
18. "Tenants Call It 'Murder.'"
19. "300 March in Bronx to Protest Shooting," *Reporter Dispatch*, Nov. 20,
1984.
20. Jimmy Breslin, "Double-Barreled Double-Talk," *NYDN*, Nov. 11, 1984.
21. Dennis J. Bernstein, "Remembering the 12-Gauge Police Eviction of a
67-Year-Old Grandmother in the South Bronx," *Reader Supported News*,
July 16, 2018, https://readersupportednews.org/opinion2/277–75/38070
-focus-remembering-the-12-gauge-police-eviction-of-a-67-year-old
-grandmother-in-the-south-bronx.
22. Jeanne Theoharis, *A More Beautiful and Terrible History: The Uses and
Misuses of Civil Rights History* (Boston: Beacon Press, 2018).
23. "Black Film Festival," *NYAN*, Aug. 7, 1993; "Harlem Week '94 Film Festival—Best Ever!" *NYAN*, July 30, 1994; Dennis Bernstein, interview by
LaShawn Harris, Aug. 6, 2019; *Eleanor Bumpurs: 12 Gauge Shotgun*, dir.
Bronx Media Collective, Bronx, NY, 1984.
24. Bernstein, "Remembering the 12-Gauge Police Eviction of a 67-Year-Old
Grandmother"; Bernstein, interview; David Hinckley, "A Month of Mov-
ies at Harlem Week Fest," *NYDN*, Aug. 1, 1994.
25. Bernstein, interview; *Eleanor Bumpurs: 12 Gauge Shotgun*.
26. Bernstein, interview; *Eleanor Bumpurs: 12 Gauge Shotgun*.
27. "Black Film Festival," 26; "Harlem Week '94 Film Festival—Best Ever!";
Bernstein, interview; *Eleanor Bumpurs: 12 Gauge Shotgun*.
28. "Readers Write," *NYAN*, Dec. 29, 1984.
29. "BUF Brutality Unit Outraged at Killing," *Big Red News*, Nov. 3, 1984, 4.
30. Mason B. Williams, "How the Rockefeller Laws Hit the Streets: Drug Policing and the Politics of State Competence in New York City," *Modern
American History* 4, no. 1 (Mar. 2021): 67–90.
31. Alexander, *The Black Interior*, 5.
32. Christen Smith, "Impossible Privacy: Black Women and Police Terror,"
Black Scholar 51, no. 1 (2021): 21.
33. "Gestapo Tactics in USA," *Afro-American*, May 10, 1980; "FBI: Didn't
Overreact in Chesimard Search," *NYDN*, Apr. 22, 1980; Simon Anekwe,
"$92 Million Suit Filed Against the FBI," *NYAN*, Jan. 31, 1981; "Photo
Standalone—No Title," *NYAN*, Apr. 26, 1980; Kathleen Cleaver and
George Katsiaficas, *Liberation, Imagination and the Black Panther Party:
A New Look at the Black Panthers and Their Legacy* (New York: Rout-
ledge, 2014), 16.

34. Ashley Farmer, "Tracking Activists: The FBI's Surveillance of Black Women Activists Then and Now," *American Historian* (Sept. 2020): 24.

35. Farmer, "Tracking Activists"; Stuart Taylor Jr., "Senate Panel Approves 'Preventive Detention' Bill," *NYT*, Dec. 9, 1981; Stuart Taylor, "New Crime Act a Vast Change, Officials Assert," *NYT*, Oct. 15, 1984; Jill Nelson, "The Blacks and the Blues," *Essence*, Sept. 16, 1985, 5.

36. Patrick Clark, Murray Weiss, and Mary Ann Giorando, "9 Arrested as 'Urban Guerillas,'" *NYDN*, Oct. 19, 1984; Andrew Kirtzman, *Rudy Giuliani: Emperor of the City* (New York: Harper Collins, 2019); Jerald Podair, "The Struggle for Equality in Rudolph Giuliani's New York," in *Civil Rights in New York City*, ed. Clarence Taylor (New York: Fordham University Press, 2011), 204–18; Selwyn Rabb, "U.S. Attorney Steering Office in New Directions," *NYT*, Jan. 9, 1984; Irin Carmon, "Dorothy Roberts Tried to Warn Us," *New York Magazine*, Sept. 6, 2022, https://nymag.com/intelligencer/2022/09/dorothy-roberts-tried-to-warn-us.html.

37. This became known as the Sons of Brink's case. In *United States v. Chimurenga*, a federal jury acquitted the New York 8 of conspiracy charges; they were convicted of weapons possessions and sentenced to community service and probation. D. J. Saunders and Marcia Kramer, "7 Beat the Rap in Brink's Case," *NYDN*, Aug. 6, 1985.

38. "Memorial Services for Mrs. Eleanor Bumpurs," *Big Red News*, Nov. 17, 1984, 20.

39. Dennis Duggan, "125th Street Reacts to Shooting by Police," Mar. 3, 1987, 9.

40. "Voice of the People," *NYDN*, Nov. 8, 1984.

41. James Gilbert, "Roving Camera," *NYAN*, Nov. 17, 1984; Wilbert A. Tatum, "So Long, Jimmy . . . It's Post Time," *NYAN*, July 24, 2003.

42. Carolyn Davis, "Readers Write: Where Is the Black Pride?" *NYAN*, July 13, 1985.

43. June Jordan, *Directed by Desire: The Collected Poems of June Jordan* (Port Townsend, WA: Copper Canyon Press, 2012), 272.

44. "How the Rent Gets Paid: The Death of Eleanor Bumpurs," *Village Voice*, Nov. 12, 1984; Jamilah King, "Maxine Waters' Battle Against Powerful White Men Began When Eula Love Was Killed in 1979," mic.com, Apr. 26, 2017, https://www.mic.com/articles/174565/maxine-waters-battle-against-powerful-white-men-began-when-eula-love-was-killed-in-1979; "Bill Lane in Hollywood," *Afro-American*, Sept. 20, 1980.

45. Betty Pleasant, "Shades of Eula Love," *Los Angeles Sentient*, Nov. 29, 1984; "Controversy Brew in Shooting of L.A. Woman," *Jet*, Feb. 1, 1979; L. C. Fortenberry, "Gas Bill Results in Death," *Los Angeles Sentinel*, Jan. 11, 1979.

46. Nora Bonosky, "Slams Police Brutality," *Daily World*, Nov. 21, 1984.

47. "The Reminiscences of Benjamin Ward" (Sept. 1992), Edward I. Koch Administration Oral History Project, Oral History Research Office at Columbia, Rare Books & Manuscript Library, Columbia University, 184–85; *MacNeil/Lehrer NewsHour*, Mar. 3, 1985, NewsHour Production, American Archives of Public Broadcasting (WGBH and the Library of Congress),

Boston, MA, and Washington, DC, Jan. 31, 2021, https://american archive.org/catalog?q=bumpurs&utf8=✓&f[access_types][]=online.

48. Beth Fallon, "Hiding the Homeless in Statistics," *NYDN*, Nov. 5, 1984.

49. "Tenants Call It Murder."

50. Abiola Sinclair, "Media Watch," *NYAN*, May 17, 1986.

51. "Woman, 67, Killed in Eviction: Who Will Be Next?" Metropolitan Council on Housing Records (TAM 173), Box 49, Folder: Eleanor Bumpers, Tamiment Library and Robert F. Wagner Labor Archives, New York University.

52. "Letters: Share the Outrage," *Village Voice*, Nov. 27, 1984.

53. "Voice of the People: The Bumpurs Case," *NYDN*, Feb. 15, 1985.

54. Robert D. McFadden, "Gabe Pressman, 93, Dean of New York News, Dies," *New York Times*, June 24, 2017, D6.

55. Abiola Sinclair, "About Racist Writers and Disappointment with Gabe," *NYAN*, Dec. 8, 1984; "The Hero Cops."

56. Phil Reisman and Marie Cortissoz, "Bumpurs Ruling Brings Relief, Cheers, Chants," *Reporter Dispatch*, Apr. 13, 1985.

57. Dylan Gottlieb, "1-800-BE-ANGRY: Media and White-Ethnic Conservatism in New York," in *New Histories of New York City Since the 1970s*, ed. Kim Phillips-Fein, Mason Williams, and Johanna Fernandez (forthcoming).

58. Joseph Volz, "House Report Cites Racism in Police Dept." *NYDN*, Nov. 15, 1984.

59. John Stapleton, "The Inquiring Photographer," *NYDN*, Dec. 21, 1984.

60. Kali Nicole Gross, "Policing Black Women's and Black Girl's Bodies in the Carceral United States," *Souls: A Critical Journal of Black Politics, Culture, and Society* 20, no. 1 (Dec. 2018): 3.

61. "Defends Cop's Action," *NYDN*, Nov. 28, 1984.

62. "Letters: Thanks for Not Blaming Cops in Bumpurs Tragedy," *New York Post*, Dec. 6, 1984; Gillian Brockell, "She Was Stereotyped as the Welfare Queen," *Washington Post*, May 21, 2019, https://www.washingtonpost .com/history/2019/05/21/she-was-stereotyped-welfare-queen-truth-was -more-disturbing-new-book-says/; "Welfare Queen Becomes Issue in Reagan Campaign," *NYT*, Feb. 15, 1976.

63. "Voice of the People: Bumpurs Eviction," *NYDN*, Dec. 10, 1984.

64. Martin Gilens, *Why Americans Hate Welfare: Race, Media, and the Politics of Antipoverty Policy* (Chicago: University of Chicago Press, 2009); Ange-Marie Hancock, *The Politics of Disgust: The Public Identity of the Welfare Queen* (New York: New York University, 2004); "Welfare: A Burden to Either Give or Receive," *NYDN*, Oct. 25, 1980.

65. "Where's the Family?" *NYDN*, Dec. 10, 1984; "Where Was the Bumpurs Family?" *New York Post*, Nov. 30, 1984; Sinclair, "About Racist Writers and Disappointment with Gabe"; Rhonda Williams, *The Politics of Public Housing: Black Women's Struggles Against Urban Inequality* (New York: Oxford University Press, 2005); Gilens, *Why Americans Hate Welfare.*

66. Judith Butler, *Frames of War: When Is Life Grievable?* (London: Verso, 2009).

67. "Columnist Abiola Sinclair Honored," *NYAN*, June 1, 1991; J. Zamgba Browne, "Abiola Sinclair, 56, Amsterdam News Columnists Dies," *NYAN*, Mar. 22, 2001; Sinclair, "Media Watch"; Sinclair, "About Racist Writers and Disappointment with Gabe."

68. "Pay or Die," *City Sun*, Nov. 7–13, 1984; Wayne Dawkins, *City Son: Andrew W. Cooper's Impact on Modern-Day Brooklyn* (Jackson: University Press of Mississippi, 2012).

69. "A Petition to Stop Police Brutality and Violence Now," *City Sun*, Nov. 7–13, 1984.

70. "A Petition to Stop Police Brutality and Violence Now."

71. H. Brown, "Fire Out-of-Town Cops and Housing Officials," *City Sun*, Dec. 12–18, 1984.

72. Beatrice Gresham Brooklyn, NY, "Letters," *City Sun*, Nov. 14–20, 1984.

73. Baker, "The Law Was Not for Her," *UNITY*, Oct. 28, 1985, 4–5.

CHAPTER 6: SAYING GOODBYE TO ELEANOR

1. "Still Dreaming the Dream," *NYT*, Feb. 15, 2009; "Obituary: Homegoing Celebration for the Honorable Reverend Thomas Wendell Foster," 2019.

2. "Councilman Wendell Foster: Rev.: Not the Lord's Will," *City Sun*, Nov. 7–13, 1984; Correspondence from Mr. King to Council W. Foster, Oct. 29, 1984, Box 1, Folder: Constituents, 1982–1986, Reverend Wendell Foster Papers.

3. "Councilman Wendell Foster: Rev.: Not the Lord's Will."

4. Ruben Rosario, "Peace, at Last," *NYDN*, Nov. 4, 1984; Robert Carroll, "Dog That Fatally Mauled Girl May Be Put to Death," *NYDN*, Oct. 16, 1984.

5. "Around the Bronx," *NYAN*, Dec. 1, 1979; "Housing Clinic," *NYAN*, Jan. 16, 1982; Charles W. Bell, "Churches Mix Faith and Fun," *NYDN*, Aug. 28, 1983.

6. "Correspondence from Mary Bumpurs to Wendell Foster," Feb. 17, 1983, Box 1, Folder: Constituents, 1982–1986, Reverend Wendell Foster Papers; *People v. Sullivan*, 394-85, 1456.

7. "Correspondence from Wendell Foster to Commissioner, NYC Housing Authority," May 23, 1983, Box 1, Folder: Constituents, 1982–1986, Reverend Wendell Foster Papers.

8. Fred Kerner and Neal Hirschfeld, "Family Hits Cop in Teen Slaying," *NYDN*, Apr. 17, 1982.

9. "Councilman Wendell Foster: Rev.: Not the Lord's Will."

10. "Preachers and Black Stars Take to Streets to Crack Down on Crack," *Jet*, Aug. 25, 1986, 12–14; Katherine Bindley, " Still Dreaming the Dream," *NYT*, Feb. 13, 2009; J. Zamgba Browne, "Public Still Angry Over Cop Killing," *NYAN*, Nov. 10, 1984; "Councilman Wendell Foster: Rev.: Not the Lord's Will"; Katherine Bindley, "Still Dreaming the Dream, *New York Times*, Feb. 13, 2009, http://www.nytimes.com/2009/02/15/nyregion/thecity /15fost.html; "Eleanor Bumpurs," File 788 (1984), Bronx Surrogate's Court Records.

11. "On Black Charity," *NYAN*, July 31, 1982; Mary Ann Giordano, "Prayed Together & Died Together," *NYDN*, June 27, 1982.
12. Suzanne Golubski, Murray Weiss, and Mike Santangelo, "Eviction Killing Spurs Review," *NYDN*, Nov. 3, 1984; Derrick Johnson, "300 Participate in Bx. Protest Against Shooting of Bumpurs," *Newsday*, Nov. 19, 1984.
13. "Correspondence from Martin Goodman to Councilman Wendell Foster & The Below Named Inmates Donated Their Funds to Mrs. Eleanor Bumpurs," Nov. 21, 1984, Box 1, Folder: Constituents, 1982–86, Reverend Wendell Foster Papers; Browne, "Public Still Angry Over Cop Killing"; Jackson, "300 Participate in Bx. Protest Against Shooting of Bumpurs."
14. Nancy Siesel, interview by LaShawn Harris, July 11, 2018; "Councilman Wendell Foster: Rev.: Not the Lord's Will"; "Rites for Woman Police Killed," *NYT*, Nov. 4, 1984.
15. "Councilman Wendell Foster: Rev.: Not the Lord's Will"; "Rites for Woman Police Killed," *NYT*, Nov. 4, 1984; Rueben Rosario, "Peace, at Last" *NYDN*, Nov. 4, 1984; Jackson, "300 Participate in Bx. Protest Against Shooting of Bumpurs"; "WCBS News–November 3, 1984 (Incomplete)," from the archives, streamed June 25, 2021, YouTube, 13:17, https://www.youtube.com/watch?v=ZxkdeiFJzLw.
16. Jimmy Breslin, "Shot Down Like a Lynx," *NYDN*, Nov. 4, 1984; Bumpurs, interview; "WCBS News–November 3, 1984 (Incomplete)."
17. "Councilman Wendell Foster: Rev.: Not the Lord's Will"; "Rites for Woman Police Killed," *NYT*, Nov. 4, 1984; Rueben Rosario, "Peace, at Last" *NYDN*, Nov. 4, 1984.
18. "Eleanor Bumpurs," File 788; Judith Weisenfeld, *New World A-Coming: Black Religion and Racial Identity During the Great Migration* (New York: New York University Press, 2018), 156; "Frederick Douglass Memorial Park, a 53-Acre Cemetery in Staten Island to Be Controlled by Negroes," *New York Age*, June 22, 1935.
19. "Mary Bumpurs: 'They're Not Going to Get Away with What They Did,'" 7.
20. Kidada E. Williams, "Regarding the Aftermaths of Lynching," *Journal of American History* 101, no. 3 (2014): 856.
21. Mary Bumpurs, interview by LaShawn Harris, July 22, 2019; "Tenants Call It Murder"; "Bumpurs' Heirs to File Suit," *City Sun*, Nov. 28–Dec. 4, 1984; Weiss, Gentile, Medina, and Hanrahan, "Woman, 67, Killed in Eviction"; Moses and Kieran Crowley, "Woman Shot to Death in Eviction," *New York Post*, Oct. 29, 1984; Eden Wales Freedman, *Testimony, Witnessing Trauma: Confronting Race, Gender, and Violence* (Jackson: University Press of Mississippi, 2020), 4.
22. David Medina, "Bumpurs' Kin at Death Apt.," *NYDN*, Nov. 28, 1984; *People v. Sullivan*, 394-85.
23. Medina, "Bumpurs's Kin at Death Apt."; "Find Bumpurs Finger in Apt."
24. Murray Weiss, Marcia Kramer, and David Medina, "Daughter Calls Eviction Death 'Assassination,'" *NYDN*, Nov. 1, 1984.
25. Bumpurs, interview, July 22, 2019.
26. "Councilman Wendell Foster: Rev.: Not the Lord's Will."

27. Jackson, "Report on Slaying Enrages Daughter"; Mario M. Cuomo, "The Crime Victim in a System of Criminal Justice," *Journal of Civil Rights and Economic Development* 8, no. 1 (Fall 1992): 1–20; "The Victims of Crime Assistance Act of 1984," Hearing Before the Committee on the Judiciary United States Senate, Ninety-Eighth Congress, Second Session, May 1, 1984 (Washington, DC: US GPO, 1985), 105; Valena Beety, "Compensating Victims of Police Violence," *Emory Law Journal* 70 (2021): 48–58, https://scholarlycommons.law.emory.edu/cgi/viewcontent.cgi?article=1038 &context=elj-online.

28. Jackson, "Report on Slaying Enrages Daughter"; Valena Beety, "Compensating Victims of Police Violence," *Emory Law Journal* 70 (2021): 48–58, https://scholarlycommons.law.emory.edu/cgi/viewcontent.cgi?article=1038 &context=elj-online.

29. Bumpurs, interview, Aug. 2017.

30. Bumpurs, interview, Aug. 2017; "Fannie Mae Baker," File 1789.

31. Matt Taibbi, *I Can't Breathe: A Killing on Bay Street* (New York: Random House, 2017), 136.

32. Andrew Hsiao, "Mothers of Invention: The Families of Police-Brutality Victims and the Movement They've Built," in *Zero Tolerance Quality of Life and the New Police Brutality in New York City*, ed. Andrea McArdle and Tanya Erzen (New York: New York University Press, 2001), 182; Tom Hays, "Bronx Shooting Sparks Mother's Crusade Against Cops," Associated Press, Aug. 6, 1995; Ron Howell, "Marches Vow to Keep Stewart Memory Alive," *Newsday*, Apr. 5, 1986; "Supporters Remember Slain Michael Stewart," *NYAN*, Dec. 14, 1985.

33. Chimamanda Ngozi Adichie, *Notes on Grief* (New York: Knopf Doubleday, 2021), 4.

34. Farmer, "Tracking Activists," 24–29.

35. Mike McAlary, "City Sending 'Crack' Troops to Battle New Drug Menace," *Newsday*, May 22, 1986; Thomas Raftery, "Bumpers' Grandson Charged," *New York Post*, May 30, 1985.

36. Taibbi, *I Can't Breathe*, 136.

37. George Todd, "Arthur Miller's Widow Having Faith," *NYAN*, Aug. 5, 1978.

38. "Racist Murder in Up South New York," *Workers Vanguard*, Feb. 20, 1987.

39. "Racist Murder in Up South New York," *Workers Vanguard*, Feb. 20, 1987.

40. Tina Marie Campt, "Black Visuality and the Practice of Refusal," *Women & Performance*, Feb. 25, 2019, https://www.womenandperformance.org/ampersand/29-1/campt.

41. Audre Lorde, *Sister Outsider: Essays and Speeches* (New York: Penguin Books, 1984), 118.

42. Mamie Till-Mobley and Christopher Benson, *Death of Innocence: The Story of the Hate Crime That Changed America* (New York: Random House, 2011), 31.

43. Howell, "Marches Vow to Keep Stewart Memory Alive"; John Hamill, "Mother of Boy Slain by Cop Struggles On and Helps Others, Too," *NYDN*, June 15, 1979; Baker, "Exclusive Interview with Mary Bumpurs,"

5; "Mary Bumpurs: 'They're Not Going to Get Away with What They Did,'" 7.

44. "Mary Bumpurs: 'They're Not Going to Get Away with What They Did,'" 7.

CHAPTER 7: SAY HER NAME

1. WBAI Folio May 1985, 2, 6, 8, 10, Pacifica Radio Archives Digitized Folio Collection, Pacifica Radio Archives.

2. "What Eleanor Bumpers Means to Me," WBAI Folio, Summer 1985, 5, Pacifica Radio Archives Digitized Folio Collection, Pacifica Radio Archives, https://archive.org/details/wbaifoliosumm85wbairich/page/4/mode/2up.

3. "What Eleanor Bumpers Means to Me," 5.

4. Charles E. Cobb, "Police Bullets and Blacks," *Afro-American*, Mar. 23, 1983.

5. Derek Dingle, "Laura Kelly Killing: Was It Necessary?" *New Journal and Guide*, July 2, 1980, 1; Subcommittee on Criminal Justice of the Committee on the Judiciary House of Representatives, Ninety-Eighth Congress (pt. 1), *Police Misconduct* (Washington, DC: US GPO, 1984); Heather Ann Thompson, "Saying Her Name," *New Yorker*, May 16, 2021.

6. Joshua B. Freeman, "City of Workers, City of Struggle: How Labor Movements Changed New York; "Way to Go Is 1 Step at a Time," *NYDN*, Apr. 2, 1980.

7. Roy Rosenzweig and Elizabeth Blackmar, *The Park and the People: A History of Central Park* (Ithaca, NY: Cornell University Press, 1992).

8. Jeff Chang, *Can't Stop Won't Stop: A History of the Hip Hop Generation* (New York: St. Martin's, 2005); Stefan M. Bradley, *Harlem vs. Columbia University: Black Student Power in the Late 1960s* (Urbana: University of Illinois Press, 2009).

9. "Alliance Sets Confab, Maps Anti-Bigotry Fight," *NYAN*, Aug. 7, 1982; Peter Noel, "Black Groups Differ in Gravesend Protest," *NYAN*, July 24, 1982.

10. Nora Bonosky, "Racists Firebomb Black Family's Home," *Daily World*, Nov. 27, 1984; Daniel O'Grady and Thomas Hanrahan, "Black Couple Find New Home Torched," *NYDN*, Nov. 20, 1984.

11. Peter Noel, "Outrage Greets Race Killing," *NYAN*, Dec. 27, 1986.

12. Crystal Nix, "Protesters Express Frustration and Mistrust," *NYT*, Jan. 4, 1987.

13. Baker, "Exclusive Interview with Mary Bumpurs."

14. Barbara Ransby, *Ella Baker and the Black Freedom Movement: A Radical Democratic Vision* (Chapel Hill: University of North Carolina Press, 2003), 310.

15. Baker, "The Law Was Not for Her," 5.

16. Raphael Sugarman, "School Prez Sold Jobs: Lawsuit," *NYDN*, Nov. 23, 1993; "Rally Set for School Elections on April 21," *NYAN*, Apr. 22, 1989; "Road Renamed for King," *NYDN*, Jan. 13, 1989; Crystal Nix, "Protesters Express Frustrations and Mistrust," *NYT*, Jan. 14, 1987; Laura Elizabeth Rocke, "Reinternment at the African Burial Ground: The Material Result of Ideology," University of Nevada, Reno, Aug. 2015, 48; Andrea E. Frohne, *The African Burial Ground in New York City: Memory, Spirituality, and*

Space (Syracuse, NY: Syracuse University, 2015), 375; Crystal Nix, "Protesters Express Frustration and Mistrust," *NYT*, Jan. 4, 1987.

17. J. Zamgba Browne, "Bronx Teacher Seeks Seat on School Board," *NYAN*, Apr. 26, 1986; "Bound for Moscow," *NYAN*, July 27, 1985; "Vote September 11," *NYDN*, Sept. 10, 1984; Les Matthews, "Cutting Remarks Send 2 Women to Jacobi Hospital," *NYAN*, Sept. 1, 1984; "Councilman Wendell Foster: Rev.: Not the Lord's Will"; Loose Jaws, "Tattler: The Crusade Against Smoking," *NYAN*, July 21, 1984.

18. Simon Anekwe, "Around the Bronx: Black Agenda," *NYAN*, Mar. 1, 1980; "10,000 Protestors Denounce Reagan," *NYAN*, Mar. 27, 1982.

19. "Justice for Eleanor Bumpurs," Tamiment Library and Robert F. Wagner Labor Archives, New York University.

20. "Eleanor Bumpurs: Coalition Aborning," *NYAN*, Nov. 24, 1984; "Group 'Angry' Over Cop Killing of Mrs. Bumpurs," *NYAN*, Nov. 17, 1984; Errol Louis, "The Brooklyn Progressive Who Shaped New York," *Intelligencer*, July 24, 2022, https://nymag.com/intelligencer/2022/07/al-vann-the -brooklyn-progressive-who-reshaped-new-york.html.

21. Simone Anekwe, "Ask Gov. Probe Police Brutality, *NYAN*, Apr. 27, 1985; Peter Noel, "Angry Protesters Call on Ward to Quit Post," *NYAN*, Jan. 10, 1987.

22. Sinclair, "Media Watch"; "Bumpurs' Heirs to File Suit."

23. Letitia James, "Prosecutors and Police: The Inherent Conflict in Our Courts," MSNBC, Dec. 5, 2014, https://www.msnbc.com/msnbc/prosecutors -police-inherent-conflict-our-courts-msna473016.

24. Anekwe, "Ask Gov. Probe Police Brutality"; Michael Oreskes, "Man in the News; Criminal Justice Chief," *NYT*, Nov. 24, 1982.

25. "Justice For Eleanor Bumpurs," Metropolitan Council on Housing Records (TAM 173), Box 49, Folder: Eleanor Bumpers, Tamiment Library and Robert F. Wagner Labor Archives, New York University.

26. Baker, "Thanks for Coverage," *NYAN*, July 19, 1986.

27. "Justice for Eleanor Bumpurs," Metropolitan Council on Housing Records.

28. "A Year Since the Bumpurs' Murder," *UNITY*, Oct. 25, 1985, 4.

29. Matthew Scott, "Bumpers Case Ignites Weekend of Activity," *Big Red News*, Nov. 24, 1984, 3.

30. Baker, "The Law Was Not for Her," 4; "Justice for Eleanor Bumpurs," Metropolitan Council on Housing Records.

31. Wendell Foster Papers; Les Matthews, "Beck Memorial Celebrates its 169th Anniversary," *NYAN*, Oct. 29, 1983; Les Matthews, "Rikers Detention Facilities Failing to Correct Inmates," *NYAN*, Dec. 6, 1975.

32. Baker, "The Law Was Not for Her," 4–5; "Justice for Eleanor Bumpurs," Metropolitan Council on Housing Records.

33. Medina, "Bumpurs' Kin See Apartment."

34. Noel, "Bumpurs' Kin Wants Ben Ward to Resign."

35. "Mary Bumpurs: 'They're Not Going to Get Away with What They Did,'" 7.

36. "Bumpur Killing: Group Will March to Protest on Saturday," *NYAN*, Nov. 17, 1984; "Stop Racist Attacks on Black Community/Demonstrate Against the Brutal Murder of Eleanor Bumpurs: November 17," American

Federation of State, County, and Municipal Employees (AFSCME) Local 420 (Hospital Workers), Box 4, Folder: Eleanor Bumpers, Tamiment Library and Robert F. Wagner Labor Archives, New York University.

37. Utrice C. Leid, "Justice for Eleanor Bumpurs Now!," *City Sun*, Nov. 21–27, 1984.

38. Ed Caldwell, "Miami's No Hotter Than N.Y., Rev. Daughtry Reminds," *NYDN*, May 24, 1980; Arthur S. Hayes, "Widow Demands Justice," *NYAN*, Oct. 20, 1979; Les Matthews, "Police Accused in Man's Murder," *NYAN*, June 30, 1979.

39. Jackson, "300 Participate in Bx. Protest Against Shooting of Bumpurs."

40. Leid, "Justice for Eleanor Bumpurs Now!"; Jackson, "300 Participate in Bx. Protest Against Shooting of Bumpurs"; "Down with Koch's Killer Cops!" *Workers Vanguard*, Dec. 7, 1984.

41. Frederick Douglass Opie, *Upsetting the Apple Cart: Black-Latino Coalitions in New York City from Protest to Public Office* (New York: Columbia University Press, 2015); Komozi Woodward, *A Nation Within a Nation: Amiri Baraka (LeRoi Jones) & Black Power Politics* (Chapel Hill: University of North Carolina Press, 1999).

42. Daughtry was born in Savannah, Georgia, in 1931. In the early 1940s, he and his family moved to Brownsville, Brooklyn, where his father established the House of the Lord Pentecostal Church. Daughtry dropped out of school and engaged in criminal activities. By twenty-two, he was imprisoned at Trenton State Prison. Upon release, he became a prominent New York civil rights organizer and leader. Herbert Daughtry, *No Monopoly on Suffering: Blacks and Jews in Crown Heights (and Elsewhere)* (Trenton, NJ: Africa World Press, 1997); Herbert Daughtry, interview by LaShawn Harris, June 29, 2017.

43. Clarence Taylor, *The Black Churches of Brooklyn* (New York: Columbia University Press, 1996), 192; Claire Jean Kim, *Bitter Fruit: The Politics of Black-Korean Conflict in New York City* (New Haven: Yale University Press, 2003); "Black Rage Grows in Brooklyn," *Black Enterprise*, Sept. 1978, 17; Clarence Taylor, "Voices of the Black Religious Community of Brooklyn, New York," in *New York Glory: Religions in the City*, ed. Tony Carnes and Anna Karpathakis (New York: New York University Press, 2001), 368; Herbert Daughtry Sr., *Made to Master: Tapping the Power Within to Live a Victorious Life* (Bloomington: Author House, 2012); Joe Klein, "The Power Next Time: Albert Vann Is the City's Hottest Black Politician," *New York Magazine*, Oct. 10, 1983, 39–45.

44. "Protestors Angry in Bumpurs Slaying," *NYAN*, Nov. 24, 1984, 3.

45. Scott, "Bumpers Case Ignites Weekend of Activity," 3.

46. Noel, "Group Decries 'Sham' Bumpurs Murder Trial"; "Group Will March in Protest on Saturday"; Leid, "Justice for Eleanor Bumpurs Now!"; "Protestors Angry in Bumpurs Slaying," *NYAN*, Nov. 24, 1984; Leid, "Justice for Eleanor Bumpurs Now!"

47. "A Memorial Service for Eleanor Williams Bumpers," AFSCME, Local 420, Box 4, Folder: Eleanor Bumpers, Tamiment Library and Robert F. Wagner Labor Archives, New York University.

48. Taylor, *The Black Churches of Brooklyn*, 199; Daughtry, *Made to Master*; Sherry S. DuPree, *African American Holiness Pentecostal Movement: An Annotated Bibliography* (New York: Routledge, 2013), 310.
49. J. Zamgba Browne, "Miller Protest Sparks Black Solidarity Day," *NYAN*, Nov. 11, 1978; George Todd, "Profile of an Activist," *NYAN*, Apr. 8, 1978.
50. Robert Fleming and Thomas Hanrahan, "Cleric Plans Big March Over Eviction Killing," *NYDN*, Nov. 19, 1984.
51. Fleming and Hanrahan, "Cleric Plans Big March Over Eviction Killing"; Bonosky, "Slams Police Brutality," 3D, 18D; "Owens Issues Program to Fight Police Brutality," *People's Daily Worker*, July 29, 1987, 2-A; Peter Noel, "Did the Police Hang Yonkers Man in Jail?" *NYAN*, Nov. 24, 1984; "Prosecutor Clears Police in Hanging," *NYT*, Dec. 20, 1984; "Car Caravan to Link Deaths of Bumpurs, Parsons," *Big Red News*, Dec. 8, 1984, 3; Golubski, Weiss, and Santangelo, "Eviction Killing Spurs Review."
52. "Coalition for Justice for Eleanor Bumpurs," AFSCME, Local 420, Box 4, Folder: Eleanor Bumpers; "March & Rally," AFSCME, Local 420, Box 4, Folder: Eleanor Bumpers; "News from Wendell Foster," Nov. 15, 1984, Box 1, Folder: Constituents, 1982–1986, Reverend Wendell Foster Papers.
53. "Coalition for Justice For Eleanor Bumpurs," AFSCME; "Wendell Foster, David Dinkins, and Father Flynn Press Conference, Nov. 15, 1984," (Video ID 08.003.DV106), Edward I. Koch Papers; "March & Rally," AFSCME.
54. "Independent Inquiry Is Sought in Eviction Death," *NYT*, Nov. 16, 1984; "Minicam News Unit Producer: Frank Rosa Jr./Wendell Foster Press Conference," Nov. 15, 1984, Koch Collection.
55. Leandra Ruth Zarnow, *Battling Bella: The Protest Politics of Bella Abzug* (Cambridge, MA: Harvard University Press, 2019).
56. Barbara T. Rochman and Geraldine Miller to Editor, Dec. 3, 1984, Wendell Foster Collection, Bronx County Historical Collection.
57. Loie Hayes, "Not in Our World: Lesbians, Feminists Take It to Wall Street," *Gay Community News*, Dec. 8, 1984; Peter McLaughlin and Paula Bernstein, "Arrest 102 Women at Stox Mart," *NYDN*, Nov. 20, 1984; Grace Paley, *A Grace Paley Reader: Stories, Essays, and Poetry* (New York: Farrar, Straus, and Giroux, 2017); Barbara Epstein, *Political Protest & Cultural Revolution: Nonviolent Direct Action in the 1970s and 1980s* (Berkeley: University of California Press, 1991).
58. Patrice O'Shaughnessy, Suzanne Golubski, and Ruth Landa, "Bare Gun Record of Cop in Eviction," *NYDN*, Nov. 20, 1984; Baker, "New York Cops Kill Black Grandmother," *UNITY*, Nov. 16, 1984, 3.
59. Nora Bonosky, "Rally Mon. to Protest Cop Killing of Tenant," *Daily World*, Nov. 17, 1984, 2-D; "News Release: November 19, 1984," AFSCME, Local 420, Box 4, Folder: Eleanor Bumpers, Tamiment Library and Robert F. Wagner Labor Archives, New York University; "Coalition for Justice for Eleanor Bumpurs," AFSCME; "March & Rally," AFSCME.
60. "Cover Up?" *NYDN*, Nov. 28, 1984.
61. Correspondence from Victor Botnick to Edward I. Koch," Nov. 9, 1984, Box 0000033, Folder 21 (City Hall Staff, Victor Botnick, Eleanor

292 NOTES

Bumpurs Case), Koch Collection; Douglas Martin, "Victor Botnick, 47, Youthful Adviser to Koch," *NYT*, Oct. 17, 2002.

62. Suzanne Golubski and Owen Mortiz, "New HRA Captain Has Titanic Task," *NYDN*, Sept. 23, 1984.

63. Michael Goodwin, "Gross Takes Over at H.R.A.," *NYT*, Oct. 10, 1984; Selwyn Raab, "Head of H.R.A. Faults Actions in Eviction Case," *NYT*, Nov. 10, 1984.

64. Suzanne Golubski and David Medina, "HRA Fumbled Rent Payment," *NYDN*, Nov. 9, 1984.

65. Suzanne Golubski, Murray Weiss, and Don Singleton, "Bumpurs Need Not Have Died: City," *NYDN*, Nov. 21, 1984.

66. Correspondence from Eleanor Walton to Bobbie Poussaint Nov. 15, 1984, Box 0000033, Folder 23 (City Hall Staff, Botnick Bumpurs Case: Response to Botnick Report), Koch Collection; Suzanne Golubski, "Report Details Safeguards Put into Place," *NYDN*, Apr. 13, 1985; Mandell, "Knock on Any Door"; "City's Report on the Bumpurs Killing," *City Sun*, Nov. 28–Dec. 4, 1984.

67. "How They Acted Reacted in Bumpurs Crisis," *NYDN*, Dec. 2, 1984.

68. Peter McLaughlin and Ruth Landa, "Hosp Aides Face Grilling on Bumpurs," *NYDN*, Dec. 3, 1984; Mary Ann Giordano, "Doc Defends His Bumpurs Report," *NYDN*, Nov. 21, 1984; "Correspondence from Robert John to Edward I. Koch," Nov. 15, 1984, Box 0000033, Folder 24 (Bumpurs' Psychiatrist Report), Koch Collection.

69. James Harney, "Bumpurs Doc Sues," *NYDN*, Mar. 28, 1985, 77.

70. Mandell, "Knock on Any Door"; Golubski, "Report Details Safeguards Put into Place."

71. "Chronology of Police Actions," Box 0000033, Folder 22 (Police Commissioner's Report), Koch Collection.

72. Michael Goodwin, "Disciplinary Action Being Urged for 2 Workers in Eviction Death," *NYT*, Nov. 18, 1984; Goodwin, "Koch and His Aides: The Bumpurs Case Gives a Glimpse of How the Major Delegates Power," *NYT*, Nov. 26, 1984; Correspondence from Victor Botnick to Edward I. Koch.

73. Selwyn Raab, "Eviction Death Leads the City to Demote Two," *NYT*, Nov. 21, 1984; Volz, "House Report Cites Racism in Police Dept."

74. Raab, "Eviction Death Leads the City to Demote Two"; "Bumpurs: The HRA Report," *NYAN*, Nov. 17, 1984.

75. "Commissioner Benjamin Ward to Mayor Edward I. Koch."

76. "FBI Enters Probe of Ex-Mental Patient Death," *Daily Argus*, Aug. 28, 1979; "McGuire Says He Won't Let Police Be 'Fall Guy' for All the City's Ills," *NYT*, Sept. 1, 1979; Joseph Volz and Hugh Bracken, "Baez Killing Brings Cop-Procedure Review," *NYDN*, Aug. 28, 1979.

77. Correspondence to Police Commissioner Benjamin Ward from Mayor Ed I. Koch, Nov. 8, 1985," Box 0000033, Folder 21 (City Hall Staff, Victor Botnick, Eleanor Bumpurs Case), Koch Collection; "The Reminiscences of Benjamin Ward," 183–85: Correspondence to Benjamin Ward from Edward I. Koch, Nov. 16, 1984, Box 0000033, Folder 22 (City Hall Staff,

Victor Botnick, Bumpurs Case: Police Commissioner's Report), Koch Collection; "The Rules Are Revised," *NYDN*, Dec. 2, 1984.
78. David J. Krajicek, "We'll Teach the Cops Restraint: Ward," *NYDN*, Jan. 6, 1988; Robert D. McFadden, "Man with Lead Pipe Shot Dead on Harlem Street by 3 Policemen," *NYT*, Mar. 2, 1987; Patricia Clark and Mary Ann Giordano, "Grand Jury Clears Cops in Killing," *NYDN*, May 9, 1987.
79. Arnold H. Lubasch, "Koch Endorsed by Police Union for Re-election," *NYT*, Aug. 1, 1989.
80. "Philip Caruso" (1994), Oral History Research Office, Rare Books and Manuscript Library, Columbia University, https://dlc.library.columbia.edu/catalog/cul:r2280gb7fx.
81. Christopher Hayes, *The Harlem Uprising: Segregation and Inequality in Postwar New York City* (New York: Columbia University Press, 2021).
82. "Philip Caruso" (1994), Oral History Research Office, Columbia University.
83. James Baldwin, *The Price of the Ticket: Collected Nonfiction: 1948–1985* (Boston: Beacon Press), 540.
84. David Medina, Suzanne Golubski, and Don Singleton," Union Hits Koch for Blaming HRA," *NYDN*, Nov. 22, 1984.
85. Raab, "Eviction Death Leads the City to Demote Two"; Michael Goodwin, "Koch, in Harlem, Discusses Shooting," *NYT*, Nov. 21, 1984; Simon Anekwe, "Angry Group Clashes with Koch over Bumpurs," *NYAN*, Nov. 24, 1984.
86. Medina, Golubski, and Singleton, "Union Hits Koch for Blaming HRA."
87. Correspondence to Ward from Koch, Nov. 16, 1984.

CHAPTER 8: DAUGHTER-ACTIVIST
1. Jackson, "Report on Slaying Enrages Daughter."
2. Jackson, "Report on Slaying Enrages Daughter."
3. Baker, "Exclusive Interview with Mary Bumpurs," 5.
4. Bumpurs, interview, July 22, 2019.
5. Suzanne Golubski and David Medina, "Koch Visits Kin of Victim in Eviction," *NYDN*, Nov. 23, 1984; Esposito and Ng, "Bumpurs's Kin Wants to Be Cop."
6. Jackson, "300 Participate in Bx. Protest Against Shooting of Bumpurs."
7. "Mary Bumpurs: 'They're Not Going to Get Away with What They Did,'" 7; Golubski and Medina, "Koch Visits Kin of Victim in Eviction"; Stuart Marques, "Carol Hits Kochie Bunker Mentality at City Hall," *NYDN*, Nov. 18, 1984; Esposito and Ng, "Bumpur's Kin Wants to Be Cop."
8. "Mary Bumpurs: 'They're Not Going to Get Away with What They Did," 7; Golubski and Medina, "Koch Visits Kin of Victim in Eviction"; Marques, "Carol Hits Kochie Bunker Mentality at City Hall"; Esposito and Ng, "Bumpur's Kin Wants to Be Cop."
9. Esposito and Ng, "Bumpur's Kin Wants to Be Cop."
10. Golubski and Medina, "Koch Visits Kin of Victim in Eviction."
11. "Mary Bumpurs: 'They're Not Going to Get Away with What They Did,'" 7; Golubski and Medina, "Koch Visits Kin of Victim in Eviction";

Marques, "Carol Hits Kochie Bunker Mentality at City Hall"; Esposito and Ng, "Bumpur's Kin Wants to Be Cop"; "Mayor Ed Koch's All-American Chocolate Chip," *Esquire*, Nov. 1, 1984, https://www.esquire .com/food-drink/food/recipes/a5341/mayor-ed-kochs-recipe-chocolate -chip-cookies-1184/.

12. Don Singleton, "Bumpurs' Kin Sue City for 10M," *NYDN*, Dec. 21, 1984; "Bumpurs' Heirs to File Suit"; Jennifer Preston, "$10 Million Sought in Eviction Slaying," *Newsday*, Dec. 21, 1984; "Mary H. Bumpurs, Administratrix of the Estate of Eleanor G. Bumpurs Against the New York City Housing Authority," File 18482, 1985, Surrogate's Court of the State of New York, County of Bronx (Eleanor Bumpurs).

13. Jim Estrin, interview by LaShawn Harris, Feb. 2023.

14. Esposito and Ng, "Bumpur's Kin Wants to Be Cop."

15. Clarence Taylor, *Fight the Power: African Americans and the Long History of Police Brutality in New York City* (New York: New York University Press, 2019); Johnson, *Street Justice*, 4–7.

16. Johnson, *Street Justice*, 245; Johanna Fernandez, *The Young Lords: A Radical History* (Chapel Hill: University of North Carolina Press, 2020), 74–75; Philip H. Dougherty, "Advertising: Civilian Review Board Fight," *NYT*, Oct. 18, 1966.

17. "A Challenge from the PBA," *NYDN*, May 18, 1983; Jerry Schmetterer, Paul Meskil, and Robert Carroll, "Nudie Cop Gets a Pink Slip," *NYDN*, May 12, 1983; Jimmy Breslin, "The Naked & the Dread," *NYDN*, May 12, 1983; Jimmy Breslin, "PBA Took Her Money and Ran," *NYDN*, May 22, 1983.

18. Johnson, *Street Justice*, 282–83.

19. Leonard Buder, "P.B.A. Head Says It Is the Police Who Are Brutalized in New York," *NYT*, July 28, 1983.

20. Phil Caruso, "Police Brutality Hearings: 'Political Charade'" *NYT*, July 18, 1983; Daniel Hays, "Cops Protest at Liz's Office," *NYDN*, Nov. 8, 1985; Murray Weiss, "Caruso Rips Liz on 'Double Standards,'" *NYDN*, July 17, 1985; William Serrin, "Philip Peter Caruso," *NYT*, July 1, 1982.

21. Vincent Lee and Ruth Landa, "PBA Mounts Ad Drive on Evict Case," *NYDN*, Dec. 12, 1988; Sol Stern, "PBA for the Defense," *The Voice*, Jan. 1, 1985, 15; Phil Caruso, "Why the Police Have Had to Buy Ads," Jan. 9, 1985; "The Bumpurs: A Case for Indictment?" Box Number: 2003-274/124, Folder: Bumpurs Murder by Cops, 1984–1985, Jack Newfield Papers, Briscoe Center for American History, University of Texas at Austin; "Bumpurs Justice Commission," *NYAN*, Dec. 22, 1984; Leonard Buder, "Officers' Union Runs Ads Backing Action of Police in Bumpurs Case," *NYT*, Dec. 13, 1984; Daughtry, interview; "Press Conference at the House of the Lord with Mary Bumpurs and Herbert Daughtry," WNYC, Jan. 31, 1985.

22. Calvin John Smiley and David Fakunle, "From 'Brute' to 'Thug': The Demonization and Criminalization of Unarmed Black Male Victims in America," *Journal of Human Behavior in the Social Environment* 26, nos. 3–4 (2016): 350–66; Kali Gross, *Colored Amazons: Crime, Violence, and*

Black Women in the City of Brotherly Love, 1880–1910 (Durham, NC: Duke University, 2006), 25.

23. Michael Amon-Ra, "Fears Repeat of Stewart Case," *City Sun*, Nov. 7–13, 1984.

24. Ava Purkiss; Sabrina Strings, *Fearing the Black Body: The Racial Origins of Fat Phobia* (New York: New York University Press, 2019); Smith, "Impossible Privacy," 20–29.

25. Nash, "From Lavender to Purple," 320.

26. "Press Conference at the House of the Lord with Mary Bumpurs and Herbert Daughtry."

27. "Editorials: Bumpurs: The Charade Continues," *NYAN*, Dec. 8, 1984; "Bumpurs Justice Commission."

28. "Prejudging the Bumpurs Case," *NYDN*, Dec. 17, 1984, 33.

29. Merola, *Big City D.A.*, 18.

30. Lee and Landa, "PBA Mounts Ad Drove on Evict Case."

31. Lee and Landa, "PBA Mounts Ad Drove on Evict Case."

32. "Anatomy of a Tragedy."

33. Christina Sharpe, *In the Wake: On Blackness and Being* (Durham, NC: Duke University Press, 2016), 26.

34. Lorde, *Sister Outsider*, 40.

35. Bumpurs, interview, July 22, 2019; Baker, "Exclusive Interview with Mary Bumpurs," 5, 33.

36. Bumpurs, interview, July 22, 2019; Baker, "Exclusive Interview with Mary Bumpurs," 5, 33.

37. "Anatomy of a Tragedy."

38. David Medina and James Barney, "Anger and Blame," *NYDN*, Nov. 21, 1984.

39. Baker, "Exclusive Interview with Mary Bumpurs," 5; Jackson, "Report on Slaying Enrages Daughter."

40. Baker, "Exclusive Interview with Mary Bumpurs," 5; Jackson, "Report on Slaying Enrages Daughter."

41. Darlene Clark Hine, *Hine Sight: Black Women and the Re-Construction of American History* (Bloomington: Indiana University Press, 1994), 41.

42. Daughtry, interview.

43. Daughtry, interview.

44. bell hooks, *All about Love: New Visions* (London: Women's Press, 1999), 215; "Families of People Killed by Violence," *USA Today*, Sept. 7, 2021, https://www.usatoday.com/story/opinion/policing/2021/09/07/floyd-taylor -jefferson-monterrosa-police-violence-families/5652653001/.

45. Karen Heller, "Black America's Attorney General Is on a Mission for Justice," *Washington Post*, June 22, 2020.

46. Charles Baillou, "Blacks Told to Unite Against Cop Brutality," *NYAN*, May 17, 1986; Charles Baillou "Relatives Remember Police Slay Victims," *NYAN*, Oct. 4, 1986; "Police Brutality," *NYAN*, Apr. 26, 1986; "News Brief: Remembering Bumpurs," *NYAN*, Oct. 24, 1987; "Bumpurs Program," *NYAN*, Oct. 26, 1985; Jon Sarlin, "A Father Was Choked to Death

by the NYPD 42 Years Ago," CNN.com, June 21, 2020, https://www.cnn
.com/2020/06/21/us/arthur-miller-death-nypd/index.html.

47. Gwen Carr and Dave Smitherman, *This Stops Today: Eric Garner's
Mother Seeks Justice After Losing Her Son* (New York: Rowman & Littlefield, 2018), 80.

48. Daughtry, interview.

49. Christen A. Smith, "Facing the Dragon: Black Mothering, Sequelae, and
Gendered Necropolitics in America," *Transforming Anthropology* 24, no.
1 (Apr. 2016): 33.

50. "5 Scottsboro Mothers Cheered," *Afro-American*, May 5, 1934; "Scottsboro Mothers and Rudy Bates in D.C.," *Afro-American*, May 19, 1934;
"Scottsboro Mothers Guests of Stevedore," *NYAN*, May 19, 1934; "President Refuses to See Mothers of Scottsboro Boys," *Chicago Defender*,
May 26, 1934; "5 Scottsboro Mothers Lead New York May Day Parade,"
Chicago Defender, May 5, 1934; Emerald Garner, *Finding My Voice* (Chicago: Haymarket Books, 2022).

51. Joy Damousi, "Private Loss, Public Mourning: Motherhood, Memory and
Grief in Australia During the Interwar," *Women's History Review* 8, no. 2
(1999): 365–66.

52. Carr and Smitherman, *This Stops Today*, 80, 93.

53. The Spartacist Forum was founded in 1966. Harvey Klehr, *Far Left of
Center: The American Radical Left Today* (New Brunswick, NJ: Transac-
tion Publishers, 1988), 71–72.

54. Taylor, *Fight the Power*, 35.

55. "Jail the Killer Cop! Point-Blank Racist Murder in NYC," *Workers Vanguard*, Nov. 1976, 12.

56. "Cops Gun Down Bronx Mother in Her Home," *Workers Vanguard*, Nov.
16, 1990, 14; Ralph Blumenthal, "Accounts Differ in Killing of Bronx
Woman by Officer," *NYT*, Nov. 6, 1990.

57. Robert Sam Anson, *Best Intentions: The Education and Killing of Edmund Perry* (New York: Knopf Doubleday, 2011).

58. "Vote Spartacist!" *Workers Vanguard*, Nov. 1, 1985, 11.

59. "Veronica Perry, Teacher 44," *NYT*, Oct. 22, 1991; "The Death of Edmund Perry," *NYT*, June 23, 1985; "Mary Bumpurs: 'They're Not Going
to Get Away with What They Did,'" 7; "Veronica Perry: We Will Not
Stand for KKK in Blue Uniforms," *Workers Vanguard*, Oct. 4, 1985, 7.

60. "Mary Bumpurs: 'They're Not Going to Get Away with What They
Did,'" 7.

61. James Baldwin, *Notes of a Native Son* (Boston: Beacon Press, 2012), 115.

62. Keisha Blain, "We Will Overcome Whatever [It] Is the System Has Become
Today: Black Women's Organizing Against Police Violence in New York
City in the 1980s," *Souls: A Critical Journal of Black, Culture, and Society*
20, no. 1 (Jan.–Mar. 2018): 111.

63. "Mary Bumpurs: 'They're Not Going to Get Away with What They
Did,'" 7; "Veronica Perry: We Will Not Stand for KKK in Blue Uniforms," 7.

64. "Mary Bumpurs: 'They're Not Going to Get Away with What They
Did,'" 7.

CHAPTER 9: THE INDICTMENT

1. Patrice O'Shaughnessy and Frank Lombardi, "Grand Jury Rips City Over Bumpurs," *NYDN*, Feb. 5, 1985; Mario Merola, *Big City D.A.* (New York: Random House, 1988), 19–20; Andy Logan, "Around City Hall: States of Confusion," *New Yorker*, Feb. 25, 1985, 74; Bernice Kanner, "Rough Justice," *New York Magazine*, May 10, 1993, 48.

2. Mario Merola, *Big City D.A.* (New York: Random House, 1988), 20.

3. Merola, *Big City D.A.*, 20.

4. Patrice O'Shaughnessy and Frank Lombardi, "Grand Jury Rips City Over Bumpurs," *NYDN*, Feb. 5, 1985.

5. Murray Weiss, "New Rules Limit the Use of Shotgun," *NYDN*, Feb. 2, 1985.

6. Don Singleton, "Ward's Taser Decision May Spark Controversy," *NYDN*, Feb. 3, 1985.

7. O'Shaughnessy and Lombardi, "Grand Jury Rips City Over Bumpurs"; "Koch Press Conference, Roll 4," Nov. 9, 1984, Koch Collection.

8. "After Bumpurs: New Police Rules May Hinder, Not Help," *New York Magazine*, Dec. 17, 1984, 13.

9. "Cops Remove Woman from Apartment," *NYDN*, Nov. 24, 1984.

10. Clint Rosewell, Patrice O'Shaughnessy, and Don Gentile, "Bronx Mom Kills Son and Nephew," *NYDN*, Dec. 1, 1984; "Crazed Mom Kills Two Children," *NYDN*, Nov. 30, 1984; "After Bumpurs: New Police Rules May Hinder, Not Help"; Murray Weiss, "Evict Cop Sent to Harbor Unit," *NYDN*, Nov. 28, 1984, 3; William R. Greer, "Woman Kills Two Children," *NYT*, Nov. 30, 1984; "Statement on Behalf of Mrs. Rosella Davis, Mother of Renee Green and Grandmother of the Victimized Children," Nov. 1984, Box 1, Folder: Constituents, 1982–1986, Reverend Wendell Foster Papers.

11. Thomas Hanrahan, Don Gentile, Jared McCallister, Murray Weiss, and Alex Michelini, "Cops Tag It Politics," *NYDN*, Feb. 1, 1985; Frances A. McMorris, "Element of Surprise," *New York Post*, Feb. 1, 1985; "St. John's University School of Law Announces Endowment of Bruce A. Smirti Memorial Scholarship," *Italian Voice*, Nov. 24, 2005.

12. "Cops in Touch in the Bronx," 5991–92.

13. Hanrahan, Gentile, McCallister, Weiss, and Michelini, "Cops Tag It Politics"; McMorris, "Element of Surprise."

14. D. H. Russell, "What Blacks Really Fear Is Injustice," *NYAN*, Feb. 27, 1988.

15. Robyn Maynard, "No, Canada Isn't the Beacon of Racial Tolerance," *THIS: Progressive Politics, Ideas & Culture*, Nov. 22, 2017, https://this.org/2017/11/22/no-canada-isnt-the-beacon-of-racial-tolerance-that-its-made-out-to-be/.

16. Isabel Wilkerson, "Jury Acquits All Transit Officers in 1983 Death of Michael Stewart," *NYT*, Nov. 25, 1985.

17. Alex Vitale, *The End of Policing* (New York: Verso Books, 2017).

18. Peter L. Davis, "Rodney King and the Decriminalization of Police Brutality in America," *Maryland Law Review* 53, no. 2 (1994): 271–357.

19. David Medina, Patrice O'Shaughnessy, and Don Singleton, "Indict Cop in Bumpurs Killing," *NYDN*, Feb. 1, 1985.

20. "Fannie Mae Baker," File 1789.
21. Christen A. Smith, "Slow Death: Is the Trauma of Police Violence Killing Black Women?" *The Conversation*, July 11, 2016, https://theconversation .com/slow-death-is-the-trauma-of-police-violence-killing-black-women -62264?utm_medium=amptwitter&utm_source=twitter; Smith, "Facing the Dragon," 31–48; Christen Smith, "Lingering Trauma in Brazil: Police Violence Against Black Women," *NACLA Report on the Americas* 50, no. 4 (2018): 374.
22. Utrice C. Leid, "15 Years Is Not Enough," *City Sun*, Feb. 6–12, 1985; "Press Conference at the House of the Lord with Mary Bumpurs and Herbert Daughtry."
23. Leid, "15 Years Is Not Enough"; "Press Conference at the House of the Lord with Mary Bumpurs and Herbert Daughtry."
24. Ronald L. Kuby and William M. Kunstler, "Homicide by Another Name," *NYAN*, Mar. 30, 1985.
25. Charles Seaton, Alex Michelini, and Mary Ann Giordano, "Ed Tells of 'Right' & 'Wrong,'" *NYDN*, Feb. 8, 1985.
26. "Vigilante: New York's Subway Hero," *Time*, Jan. 7, 1985, https://content .time.com/time/subscriber/article/0,33009,956260,00.html.
27. For details on Goetz's legal fate, see Soffer, *Ed Koch and the Rebuilding of New York City*, 343–45; Dave Walker, "Bumpurs, Goetz Cases Are Being Mishandled," *Big Red News*, Feb. 9, 1985, 5; Selwyn Raab, "Mayor Backs Jury Goetz; Questions Action on Office," *NYT*, Feb. 9, 1985; Seaton, Michelini, and Giordano, "Ed Tells of 'Right' & 'Wrong'"; "The Goetz Case by Edward I. Koch," Mar. 8, 1985, Box 0000074, Folder 18 (City Hall Staff, Goetz Case), Koch Collection; "Stephen Sullivan Indicted (Eleanor Bumpurs)," Jan. 31, 1985, Koch Collection.
28. Murray Weiss and Don Singleton, "Prey Turns Predator," *NYDN*, Dec. 30, 1984; Barry Sussman, "Poll Shows Americans Split Over Goetz Case," *Washington Post*, Jan. 19, 1985.
29. John Randazzo and Paul Meskil, "Ward: If Sullivan Was Indicted, How About Me?," *NYDN*, Feb. 14, 1985; "The Reminiscences of Benjamin Ward," 185.
30. "Officer Sullivan Back on Full Duty," Associated Press, Apr. 18, 1985; "Statement of Police Commissioner Benjamin Ward, Feb. 1, 1985," Box 0000033, Folder 9 (Police Department), Koch Collection.
31. Leonard Buder, "Officer Indicted in Bronx Slaying Back on Payroll," *NYT*, Feb. 2, 1985; O'Shaughnessy and Frank Lombardi, "Grand Jury Rips City Over Bumpurs"; Murray Weiss and Stuart Marques, "Reverses Bumpurs Case Ruling," *NYDN*, Feb. 2, 1985.
32. "2 Officers Acquitted in Fatal '81 Shooting," *NYT*, Feb. 2, 1983; "Five Percenters," *NYAN*, Apr. 11, 1981; Selwyn Raab, "Officer Accused of Shooting Fleeing Man Fatally in Back," *NYT*, June 19, 1981; James Duddy and Don Gentile, "Probe Suspect's Death in Bronx Shootout," *NYDN*, Apr. 1, 1981; Keith Moore and Bob Herbert, "PBA Blasts Indictment of 2 Cops," *NYDN*, June 19, 1981; Thomas Raftery and Brian Kates, "Off-Duty Cop Confronts 3, Kills 1," *NYDN*, Mar. 29, 1981.

33. Murray Weiss and Don Singleton, "Ever On-Ward," *NYDN*, Jan. 29, 1985; Murray Weiss, "Police Commish Ward Says He Has Been Humbled but Feels That His Position Is Secure," *NYDN*, Nov. 3, 1984.
34. Michael Goodwin, "Ward Is Under Fire over Conduct," *NYT*, Oct. 19, 1984; "Why I Stand by My Man: Top Cop's Wife," *New York Post*, Nov. 6, 1984.
35. Soffer, *Ed Koch and the Rebuilding of New York* City, 335.
36. Stuart Marques, "Bumpurs Kin: Ward's a Fool," *NYDN*, Feb. 3, 1985; Frank Lynn, "Bellamy Enters Race for Mayor," Feb. 9, 1985; Noel, "Bumpurs' Kin Wants Ben Ward to Resign"; George Arzt, Pat Wilks, and Jack Peritz, "He's Back on the Job," *New York Post*, Feb. 2, 1985.
37. Earl Caldwell "Downhill at the Medical Examiner's Officer," *NYDN*, Nov. 9, 1983.
38. Alex Michelini, Ruth Landa, and Marcia Kramer, "City, State to Probe Gross," *NYDN*, Jan. 25, 1985.
39. Philip Shenon, "Chief Medical Examiner's Reports in Police-Custody Cases Disputed," *NYT*, Jan. 27, 1985.
40. Patrick Clark and Stuart Marques, "Feds Join the Gross Probers," *NYDN*, Feb. 1, 1985.
41. "Don't Let Koch Probe Gross," *NYAN*, Feb. 2, 1985.
42. Clark and Marques, "Feds Join the Gross Probers."
43. Soffer, *Ed Koch and the Rebuilding of New York City*, 341–42; Lindsey Gruson, "Injuries of a Police Prisoner Did Not Kill, Autopsy Finds," *NYT*, Sept. 30, 1983; Peter Noel, "Docs: Where Are Victim's Eyes?" *NYAN*, Oct. 15, 1983; Sydney H. Schanberg, "The Stewart Case," *NYT*, Jan. 14, 1984; Peter Noel, "Questions Arise About Gross's Actions," *NYAN*, Feb. 4, 1984.
44. Selwyn Raab, "Officer Indicted in Bumpurs Case," *NYT*, Feb. 1, 1985; "Caruso: We're Life-Savers, Not Life-Takers," *NYDN*, Feb. 17, 1985.
45. Alexander Reid, "Thousands of Officers Protest Indictment of Colleague in Bumpurs Shooting," *NYT*, Feb. 8, 1985; Selwyn Raab, "Indictment Stirs 250 in Police to Seek Transfer," *NYT*, Feb. 5, 1985; "10,000 NYC Cops Rally for Racist Murder," *Workers Vanguard*, Feb. 22, 1985.
46. Merola, *Big City D.A.*, 8; Robert D. McFadden, "Convicted Killer, Ex-Policeman, Turns Himself In," *NYT*, Mar. 24, 1981.
47. Rosario and Marques, "Cops Are Hot as a Pistol."
48. "Voice of the People," *NYDN*, Feb. 6, 1985.
49. Michael Hanrahan, "Support Cops on Streets, PBA Warns," *NYDN*, Feb. 13, 1985; Wayne McMorrow, "An Open Letter to the Citizens of New York City," *NYDN*, Feb. 13, 1985.
50. "Back Indicted Cop," *NYDN*, Feb. 27, 1985.
51. Don Gentile, "Bumpurs Cop Draws Honor," *NYDN*, Feb. 15, 1985; Mark Sherman, "Jubilant March Up Fifth Avenue Salutes the Irish," *NYT*, Mar. 17, 1985; Linda Dowling Almeida, *Irish Immigrants in New York City, 1945–1995* (Bloomington: Indiana University Press, 2001); Murray Kempton, "Spirit of Columbus Proves Less Feisty Than St. Patrick's," *Newsday*, Oct. 5, 1985.

52. "100% Behind Cop," *NYDN*, Feb. 8, 1985.
53. "Cop Is Denied the Right to Save Another's Life," *New York Post*, Feb. 15, 1985.
54. "Sympathy Vote," *NYDN*, Feb. 15, 1985.
55. Phil Reisman, "Tragic Day," *Reporter Dispatch*, Feb. 14, 1985.
56. James Peters, Ruth Landa, and Murray Weiss, "252 Special Cops Want Out," Feb. 5, 1985.
57. "Elite Cops Ask Out," *NYDN*, Feb. 5, 1985.
58. Merola, *Big City D.A.*, 7.
59. Merola, *Big City D.A.*, 8
60. Reid, "Thousands of Officers Protest Indictment of Colleague in Bumpurs Shooting."
61. Ruben Rosario, Patrice O'Shaughnessy, and Stuart Marques, "Demonstration of Anger," *NYDN*, Feb. 8, 1985.
62. Rosario, O'Shaughnessy, and Marques, "Demonstration of Anger."
63. Ruben Rosario, Patrice O'Shaughnessy, and Stuart Marques, "Fury of the Finest," *NYDN*, Feb. 8, 1985; Nina Mjagkij, *Organizing Black America: An Encyclopedia of African American Associations* (New York: Garland Publishing, 2001), 221.
64. Medina and Harney, "Anger and Blame"; Derrick Jackson, "Cop Indicted in Slaying of Bronx Grandmother," *New York Post*, Feb. 1, 1985.
65. Neal Hirschfeld, "Blacks Urged to Quit PBA Over Bail Posted for Cop in Shooting," *NYDN*, Dec. 2, 1976; Michael Patterson, "Black Cops Leave PBA Exit a Question," *NYDN*, Dec. 9, 1976; Ezra Bookstein, *The Smith Tapes: Lost Interviews with Rock Stars & Icons, 1969–1972* (New York: Princeton Architectural Press, 2015), 251–58.
66. Andrew T. Darien, *Becoming New York's Finest: Race, Gender, and the Integration of the NYPD, 1935–1980* (New York: Palgrave Macmillan, 2013).
67. Founded in the 1970s, the organization (also called the Armed Resistance Unit, Red Guerrilla Resistance, and May 19th) was linked to at least sixteen other bombings in New York and Washington, DC, including the US Capitol, the New York offices of the Israeli Aircraft Industries, and the South African consulate. "New York Bombing May Be Linked to Other Explosions," *Herald-Journal*, Feb. 24, 1985; "Police Union's Officers in Manhattan Bombed," *NYT*, Feb. 23, 1985; Chang, *Can't Stop Won't Stop*, 197; "2 Women Seen at Site of Blast," *NYT*, Feb. 24, 1985; Adolfo Perez Esquivel, *Let Freedom Ring: A Collection of Documents from the Movement to Free U.S. Political Prisoners* (Oakland: PM Press, 2008), 29, 387–88; Douglas C. Lovelace Jr., *Terrorism Documents of International and Local Control* (New York: Oxford University Press, 2008), 604; Ruben Rosario and Stuart Marques, "Cops Hunt 2 Fems in PBA Blast," *NYDN*, Feb. 24, 1985.
68. Dan Berger and Emily Hobson, *Remaking Radicalism: A Grassroots Documentary Reader of the United States, 1973–2001* (Athens: University of Georgia Press, 2020), 150–52; Safiya Bukhari and Laura Whitehorn, *The War Before: The True Life Story of Becoming a Black Panther; Keeping*

the Faith in Prison & Fighting for Those Left Behind (New York: Feminist
Press, 2010), xxxii–xxxiii; William Rosenau, *Tonight We Bombed the U.S.
Capitol: The Explosive Story of M19, America's First Female Terrorist
Group* (New York: Atria Books, 2019), 216–17; Laura Whitehorn, "Letter
to a Young Activist: Left to Learn from the '60s," *On the Issues*, Fall 2011,
https://ontheissuesmagazine.com/feminism/letter-to-a-young-activist-left
-to-learn-from-the-60s-2/.

69. Kali Gross, "African American Women, Mass Incarceration, and the Politics of Protection," *Journal of American History* 102, no. 1 (June 2015): 25–33.
70. Patrice O'Shaughnessy and Frank Lombardi, "Bumpurs Indictment Is KOd," *NYDN*, Apr. 13, 1985.
71. O'Shaughnessy and Lombardi, "Bumpurs Indictment Is KOd"; David Medina and Stuart Marques, "I'd Do It Again," *NYDN*, Apr. 13, 1985; Reisman and Cortissoz, "Bumpurs Ruling Brings Relief, Cheers, Chants."
72. Clint Roswell, David Medina, and Stuart Marques, "Lightning Rod," *NYDN*, Apr. 13, 1985.
73. David Medina and Robert Carroll, "Mayor's Panel Clears Dr. Gross," *NYDN*, Apr. 24, 1985.
74. Koch fired Gross in 1987. D. J. Saunders and Stuart Marques, "Gross Cleared in Fed Probe," *NYDN*, Sept. 13, 1985; Marcia Kramer, "Pressure Mounts on Gross to Quit," *NYDN*, Dec. 13, 1985; Clark and Marques, "Feds Join the Gross Probers"; Marcia Kramer and Ruth Landa, "Koch Fires Gross," *NYDN*, Oct. 30, 1987; Saunders and Marques, "Gross Cleared in Fed Probe"; Wilbert A. Tatum, "Koch Must Resign," *NYAN*, Nov. 7, 1987.
75. Phil Reisman and Marie Cortissoz, "Officer Says He Wants to Unwind," *Tarrytown Daily News*, Apr. 13, 1985.
76. Osborn, "The Bumpurs Case: Nagging Problems."
77. "1 Year since NY Police Murder," *UNITY*, Nov. 8, 1985, 1.
78. O'Shaughnessy and Lombardi, "Bumpurs Indictment Is KOd"; Medina and Marques, "I'd Do It Again"; Selwyn Raab, "State Judge Dismisses Indictment of Officer in the Bumpurs Killing," *NYT*, Apr. 13, 1985; Janice Tudy Jackson, "Miscarriage of Justice," *NYAN*, July 6, 1985.
79. O'Shaughnessy and Lombardi, "Bumpurs Indictment Is KOd."
80. *People v. Sullivan*, 68 NY2D 495, Appellants Appendix, pt. 2; *People v. Sullivan*, 394/1985, A1.
81. "Bumpurs-Case Cop Back on Full Duty," *NYDN*, Apr. 15, 1985; Murray Weiss, "Officer Sullivan Back," *NYDN*, Apr. 18, 1985.
82. "Services Set for Bumpurs," *NYAN*, May 18, 1985.
83. "Services Set for Bumpurs"; Sonia Song-Ha Lee, *Building a Latino Civil Rights: Puerto Ricans, African Americans, and the Pursuit of Racial Justice in New York City* (Chapel Hill: University of North Carolina Press, 2014).
84. "1 Year since NY Police Murder," 1, 4.
85. "Ujamaa Black Theater Produces Anti-Apartheid Recording," *NYAN*, Jan. 26, 1985.

86. Serious Bizness, "Old Glory's Story," track 1, *How Many More?*, Folkways, 1985.

87. Jaribu Hill, interview by LaShawn Harris, Mar. 2020; Shana L. Redmond, *Anthem: Social Movements and the Sound of Solidarity in the African Diaspora* (New York: New York University Press, 2013), 1; "Ujamaa Black Theater Produces Anti-Apartheid Recording."

88. "1 Year since NY Police Murder," 1, 4; Samuel A. Hay, *African American Theatre: An Historical and Critical Analysis* (New York: Cambridge University Press, 1994), 51; Stephon Johnson, "Playwright, Director, Activist Titus Walker, 54, Passes," *NYAN*, Mar. 4, 2011, http://amsterdamnews.com/news/2011/apr/12/playwright-director-activist-titus-walker-54/; Harrison, "Committed to Song," *Washington Post*, Mar. 27, 1983; "Serious Bizness Lights 10 Birthday Candles Dec. 3," *NYAN*, Dec. 3, 1988; "Eleanor Bumpurs: One Year Later," Metropolitan Council on Housing Records (TAM 173), Box 49, Folder: Eleanor Bumpers, Tamiment Library and Robert F. Wagner Labor Archives, New York University.

89. Baker, "The Eleanor Bumpurs Case," *NYAN*, Sept. 20, 1986; "No More Eleanor Bumpurs—Never Again!!," AFSCME, Local 420, Box 4, Folder: Eleanor Bumpers, Tamiment Library and Robert F. Wagner Labor Archives, New York University.

90. "Court Upholds Clearing of Bumpurs Cop," *NYDN*, Apr. 2, 1986; *People v. Sullivan*, 68 NY2d 495, Appellants Appendix, pt. 2; *People v. Sullivan* 394/1985), A30–38; Ernst H. Rosenberger, "Remembering the Freedom Riders: An Interview with the Honorable Ernest H. Rosenberger," *New York Law School Law Review* 59 (2014–15).

91. "Court Upholds Clearing of Bumpurs Cop"; Court of Appeals vol. 1; Rosenberger, "Remembering the Freedom Riders."

92. Merola, *Big City D.A.*, 25.

93. Phil Makotsi, "Seek Re-Indictment of Killer Cop," *City Sun*, Apr. 9–15, 1986.

94. Baillou, "Relatives Remember Police Slay Victims."

95. Dennis Hevesi, "Manslaughter Charge Against Officer Revived," *NYT*, Nov. 26, 1986; *People v. Sullivan*, Nov. 25, 1986 503 NE2d (NY, 1986), https://casetext.com/case/people-v-sullivan-162.

96. Dennis Hevesi, "Court Allows Bumpurs Case to Be Tried," *NYT*, Nov. 26, 1986.

97. Leonard Levitt, "Court Orders Trial for Cop in Bumpurs Case," *Newsday*, Nov. 26, 1986; Mary Ann Giordano and Don Singleton, "Trial Ordered on Bumpurs," *NYDN*, Nov. 26, 1986; Kathy Moore, "Cop Charged in Bumpurs Shooting," *Standard-Star*, Nov. 26, 1986.

98. Mae Ngai, "Over Two Years Later, Cop Shot Bumpurs Goes on Trial," *UNITY*, Jan. 19, 1987, 6.

99. Ngai, "Over Two Years Later, Cop Shot Bumpurs Goes on Trial," 6.

100. Alex Michelini, "Bumpurs' Kin Pleased," *NYDN*, Nov. 26, 1986, Bx. 1.

101. Ngai, "Over Two Years Later, Cop Shot Bumpurs Goes on Trial," 6; Peter Noel, "Group Moves to Ensure Trial of Bumpurs Killer," *NYAN*, Dec. 20, 1986; Michelini, "Bumpurs' Kin Pleased."

102. Giordano and Singleton, "Trial Ordered on Bumpurs"; Nagi, "Over Two Years Later, Cop Who Shot Bumpurs Goes on Trial," 2, 6; Baker, "The Eleanor Bumpurs Case"; Michelini, "Bumpurs' Kin Pleased."
103. "Eric Garner: No Charges Against White Police Officer over Chokehold Death," *The Guardian*, July 16, 2019, https://www.theguardian.com/us -news/2019/jul/16/eric-garner-death-new-york-no-charges.

CHAPTER 10: THE TRIAL

1. Charles Montgomery, "Readers Write: Stewart Ruling Is No Surprise," *NYAN*, Dec. 7, 1985; Charles Montgomery, "Surprised at Support for Goetz," *NYAN*, Feb. 23, 1985; Charles Montgomery, "Why Glorify Nick Barnes?" *NYAN*, Nov. 12, 1983; Noel, "Group Decries 'Sham' Bumpurs Murder Trial"; William Barlow, *Voice Over: The Making of Black Radio* (Philadelphia: Temple University 1999), 233–34; Heather Thompson, *Blood in the Water: The Attica Prison Uprising of 1971 and Its Legacy* (New York: Vintage Books).
2. Basil Wilson, *David Dinkins and the Goliaths of New York City: The 1989 Mayoral Campaign* (Albany: New York African Institute, 1991); Kim, *Bitter Fruit*, 243; "WLIB," *NYAN*, Mar. 7, 1981; Steven Kurutz, "Urban Tactics: For the Heartbeat of Harlem, a New Amen Chorus," *NYAN*, Sept. 10, 2006; Abiola Sinclair, "Media Watch . . . But for Us, No Apology," *NYAN*, Aug. 8, 1987; E. R. Shipp, "WLIB: Radio 'Heartbeat' of Black Life," *NYT*, Jan. 22, 1988.
3. Montgomery, "Readers Write: Stewart Ruling Is No Surprise"; Montgomery, "Surprised at Support for Goetz"; Montgomery, "Why Glorify Nick Barnes?"; Noel, "Group Decries 'Sham' Bumpurs Murder Trial"; Barlow, *Voice Over*, 233–34; Thompson, *Blood in the Water*; Karu F. Daniels, "Radio Vet Thompson, 83," *NYDN*, June 26, 2019.
4. Mike Santangelo, "Toughest, Judge Says," *NYDN*, Feb. 27, 1987; Raab, "Trial of Officer in Bumpurs Case with Request for No Jury."
5. Laurence Lebowitz, interview by LaShawn Harris, Oct. 1, 2020.
6. Raab, "Trial of Officer in Bumpurs Case Starting with Request for No Jury."
7. Michael Amon, "Defense Took Gamble," *Newsday*, Apr. 26, 2008; Andrea McArdle, "No Justice, No Peace," in *Zero Tolerance: Quality of Life and the New Police Brutality in New York City*, ed. Andrea McArdle and Tanya Erzen (New York: New York University Press, 2001), 147–78.
8. Ruth Padawer, "Howard Beach Calm But Racist," *NYAN*, Nov. 7, 1987.
9. Benjamin Hooks, "Howard Beach Verdict," *NYAN*, Jan. 9, 1988; Ronald Smothers, "1,200 Protesters of Racial Attack March in Queens," *NYT*, Dec. 28, 1986; Noel, "Angry Protesters Call on Ward to Quit Post"; Joseph P. Fried, "Black Witness Describes Beating in Howard Beach," *NYT*, Nov. 17, 1987; Joseph P. Fried, "Man Struck in Howard Beach Recalls Start of Confrontation," *NYT*, Oct. 16, 1987.
10. Raab, "Trial of Officer in Bumpurs Case with Request for No Jury"; Josh Barbanel, "Officer Plans to Ask for a Nonjury Trial in Bumpurs Killing," *NYT*, Feb. 11, 1985.

11. Baldwin, "A Report from Occupied Territory," 40; Sam Roberts, "On Bronx Juries, Minority Groups Find Their Peers," *NYT*, May 19, 1988.
12. Ngai, "Over Two Years Later, Cop Shot Bumpurs Goes on Trial," 6.
13. Raab, "Trial of Officer in Bumpurs Case with Request for No Jury."
14. Moore, "Cop Charged in Bumpurs Shooting."
15. Denis Hamill, "Hamill on Eleanor Bumpurs," *Newsday*, Apr. 15, 1987.
16. Frank J. Prial, "Amid Protest, Bumpurs Case Nears Its End: Summations Interrupted by a Demonstration," *NYT*, Feb. 18, 1987.
17. Selwyn Raab, "Angry Outburst by Spectators Disrupts Start of Bumpurs Trial," *NYT*, Jan. 13, 1987.
18. Raab, "Angry Outburst by Spectators Disrupts Start of Bumpurs Trial."
19. Raab, "Angry Outburst by Spectators Disrupts Start of Bumpurs Trial."
20. Raab, "Angry Outburst by Spectators Disrupts Start of Bumpurs Trial"; John Melia and Mike Santangelo, "Disorder in the Court," *NYDN* Feb. 18, 1987.
21. Raab, "Trial of Officer in Bumpurs Case with Request for No Jury."
22. Lebowitz, interview.
23. *People v. Sullivan*, 394-85.
24. *People v. Sullivan*, 394-85.
25. Prial, "Daughter Cites Bumpurs's Stay in State Hospital"; Melia and Landa, "Bumpurs Kin Lied to Hospitalize Her"; *People v. Sullivan*, 68 NY2D 495, Appellants Appendix, pt. 2; *People v. Sullivan*, 394/1985, 142.
26. "Sullivan Takes Stand," *Daily Challenge*, Feb. 6, 1987; Frank J. Prial, "Officer Tells of Two Shots at Bumpurs," *NYT*, Feb. 6, 1987; *People v. Sullivan*, 68 NY2D 495, Appellants Appendix, pt. 4; *People v. Sullivan*, 394/1985, A1155–A1156.
27. "Sullivan Takes Stand."
28. Jeffrey K. Parker, "Acquittal of White Sparks Cries of Injustice," *Daily Challenger*, Feb. 27, 1987; *People v. Sullivan*, 394-85.
29. Barbara Goldberg, "Demand Justice in Bumpurs Case," *Daily Challenger*, Feb. 18, 1987.
30. Prial, "Amid Protest, Bumpurs Case Nears Its End"; Selwyn Raab, "Civilian Describe Struggle Before Shooting of Bumpurs," *NYT*, Jan. 14, 1987; Frank J. Prial, "A Doctor Denies He Exaggerated Bumpurs Injury," *NYT*, Feb. 3, 1987; Melia and Santangelo, "Disorder in the Court"; "Sullivan Takes Stand."
31. Prial, "Amid Protest, Bumpurs Case Nears Its End"; Raab, "Civilian Describe Struggle Before Shooting of Bumpurs"; Prial, "A Doctor Denies He Exaggerated Bumpurs Injury"; Melia and Santangelo, "Disorder in the Court"; "Sullivan Takes Stand"; John Melia and Mike Santangelo, "Defense Sets Off Bumpurs Protest," *NYDN*, Feb. 18, 1987.
32. Prial, "Amid Protest, Bumpurs Case Nears Its End"; Raab, "Civilian Describe Struggle Before Shooting of Bumpurs"; Prial, "A Doctor Denies He Exaggerated Bumpurs Injury"; Melia and Santangelo, "Disorder in the Court"; "Sullivan Takes Stand."
33. Frank J. Prial, "Judge Acquits Sullivan in Shotgun Slaying of Bumpurs," *NYT*, Feb. 27, 1987.

34. John Melia and Brian Kates, "'Guilty,' They Say," *NYDN*, Feb. 27, 1987.
35. Melia and Kates, "'Guilty,' They Say"; John Melia and Ruth Landa, "Bumpurs Case Cop Found Innocent," *NYDN*, Feb. 27, 1987; "Full Duty to Be Restored," *NYT*, Feb. 27, 1987; Mae Ngai, "Bumpurs' Killer Freed," *Unity*, Mar. 2, 1987, 1.
36. Melia and Kates, "'Guilty,' They Say"; Melia and Landa, "Bumpurs Case Cop Found Innocent"; "Full Duty to Be Restored."
37. "Bumpurs Trial Ends in Acquittal and Anger," *NYT*, Mar. 1, 1987; Larry Celona and Mary Ann Giordano, "Verdict Brings Sighs of Relief & Grief," *NYDN*, Feb. 27, 1987; Jennifer Preston, "Cop Cleared in Slaying of Bumpurs Is Promoted," *Newsday*, May 23, 1987; Nicole Hemmer, *Messengers of the Right: Conservative Media and the Transformation of American Politics* (Philadelphia: University of Pennsylvania Press, 2016), 260.
38. Kathy Moore, "Exonerated Office Eager to Regain Anonymity," *Citizen Register*, Feb. 28, 1987.
39. Audre Lorde, "A Poem for Women in Rage," *Iowa Review* 12, no. 2 (1981): 220–22.
40. Clint Roswell and Brian Kates, "Daughter Calls Verdict Racist," *NYDN*, Feb. 27, 1987; Melia and Landa, "Bumpurs Case Cop Found Innocent"; Leonard Levitt, "For the Family, a Search for Justice," *Newsday*, Feb. 27, 1987; Jeffrey K. Parker, "Acquittal of White Cop Sparks Cries of Injustice," *Daily Challenger*, Feb. 27, 1987.
41. Roswell and Kates, "Daughter Calls Verdict Racist."
42. "Bumpurs Trial Ends in Acquittal and Anger"; Paul D. Colford, "Soapbox on the Air, WABC's Conservative Talk-Host," *Newsday*, Mar. 11, 1987; "Celebrating the Victory," *NYDN*, Feb. 28, 1987; Merola, *Big City D.A.*, 26; Kiley Armstrong, "N.Y. Policeman Is Innocent in Killing of Evicted Woman," *Arizona Daily Star*, Feb. 27, 1987.
43. John Melia and Frank Lombardi, "DA Merola Dead at 65," *NYDN*, Oct. 28, 1987; Melia and Lombardia, "Tribute to Merola," *NYDN*, Oct. 29, 1987.
44. Jimmy Breslin, "Take Heart, City, You Had Merola," Oct. 29, 1987; John Melia, "DA's Staff Carries On," *NYDN*, Oct. 29, 1987, Bx. 1.
45. Arthur Browne, "Cop Brutality Probed Here," *NYDN*, July 17, 1983.
46. "Review Board Has Had Critics Since Its Start," *NYT*, Apr. 28, 1985.
47. Christopher Atwell, "Bumpurs Trial: Merola Spurns Watchdog Group," *City Sun*, Feb. 4–10, 1987.
48. "The Bumpurs Verdict: A Mockery of Justice!," AFSCME, Local 420, Box 4, Folder: Eleanor Bumpers, Tamiment Library and Robert F. Wagner Labor Archives, New York University.
49. Atwell, "Bumpurs Trial: Merola Spurns Watchdog Group"; "Eleanor Bumpurs Justice Committee," Jan. 20, 1987, Ritchie Perez Papers/CENTRO/Lehman College (CUNY); Christopher Atwell, "Bumpurs Trial: Prosecutor's Competence Comes Under Question," *City Sun*, Jan. 1987; Merola, *Big City D.A.*, 30.
50. Mae Ngai "Bumpurs Killer Freed," *UNITY*, Mar. 2, 1987, 1, 7; Grover Ryder and Paul Meskil, "Stickup Suspect, 15, Slain in Scuffle with Cop," *NYDN*, Feb. 11, 1980; David Hardy, "Tragic Career of 11-Year-Old

Killed by Cop," *NYDN*, Sept. 4, 1972; Zamgba Browne, "Feds May Probe Bumpurs Killing," *NYAN*, Mar. 7, 1987.

51. Christopher Atwell, "Sullivan's Acquittal Serves as Call to Action," *City Sun*, Mar. 4–10, 1987.

52. Browne, "Feds May Probe Bumpurs Killing."

53. Atwell, "Sullivan's Acquittal Serves as Call to Action."

54. Ngai, "Bumpurs Killer Freed," 1, 7.

55. "Rev. Foster to Sponsor a Rally on Black Survival in New York," *NYAN*, Mar. 28, 1987.

56. "Eleanor Bumpurs' Fighting Spirit Lives On: October 29, 1987," Metropolitan Council on Housing Records (TAM 173), Box 49, Folder: Eleanor Bumpers, Tamiment Library and Robert F. Wagner Labor Archives, New York University; "Remembering Bumpurs"; Harrison, "Committed to Song."

57. "Bumpurs Civil Rights Also Violated," Metropolitan Council on Housing Records (TAM 173), Box 49, Folder: Eleanor Bumpers, Tamiment Library and Robert F. Wagner Labor Archives, New York University.

58. Kirtzman, *Rudy Giuliani: Emperor of the City*, 4; Michael Winerip, "High-Profile Prosecutor," *NYT*, June 9, 1985; Podair, "The Struggle for Equality in Rudolph Giuliani's New York," 204–18; Rabb, "U.S. Attorney Steering Office in New Directions"; Richard Goldstein, "Race, Gender & Rudy Giuliani," *Village Voice*, Apr. 25, 1989, https://www.villagevoice.com/race-gender-rudy-giuliani/.

59. D. J. Saunders and Frank Lombardi, "Rudy Defends Cops," *NYDN*, June 23, 1985.

60. Goldstein, "Race, Gender & Rudy Giuliani."

61. Leonard Buder, "F.B.I. Investigating Killing by Police in Eviction," *New York Times*, Nov. 30, 1984.

62. Thomas Hanrahan, "FBI Probing Bumpurs Case," *NYDN*, Dec. 1, 1984.

63. T. J. Collins, "Giuliani Won't Reopen Bumpurs Case," *Newsday*, Aug. 5, 1987.

64. Alex Michelini, "Fed Probe of Bumpurs Is Called Unwarranted," *NYDN*, Aug. 5, 1987.

CHAPTER 11: THE LAWSUIT

1. Paul LaRosa and Marcia Kramer, "Dinkins Is Sworn In as 1st Black Mayor," *NYDN*, Jan. 1, 1990; "Voters' Turnout," *NYDN*, Nov. 8, 1989; Lyle V. Harris, "On 11th Floor, Pride & Joy," *NYDN*, Jan. 1, 1990; Wilbur C. Rich, *David Dinkins and New York City Politics* (New York: State University of New York Press, 2012).

2. Don Singleton, "Bumpurs' Kin Sue City for 10M," *NYDN*, Dec. 21, 1984; "Bumpurs' Heirs to File Suit," *City Sun*, Nov. 28–Dec. 4, 1984; Jennifer Preston, "$10 Million Sought in Eviction Slaying," *Newsday*, Dec. 21, 1984; "Mary H. Bumpurs, Administratrix of the Estate of Eleanor G. Bumpurs Against The New York City Housing Authority," File No. 18482, Year: 1985, Surrogate's Court of the State of New York, County of Bronx (Eleanor Bumpurs).

3. Leonard Levitt, "For the Family, a Search for Justice," *Newsday*, Feb. 27, 1987.

4. David Medina, Suzanne Golubski, and Don Singleton, "Union Hits Koch for Blaming HRA," *NYDN*, Nov. 22, 1984.

5. David N. Dinkins, "Death Sentence for Being Poor," *City Sun*, Nov. 7–13, 1984.

6. *Bumpurs v. New York City Housing Authority*; Tom Robbins and Jack Newfield, "Dinkins to Tap Pal as Counsel," *NYDN*, Oct. 28, 1989; Arnold H. Lubasch, "Victor A. Kovner: Corporation Counsel," *NYT*, Dec. 9, 1989; Felicia R. Lee, "Kovner Quits Lawyer's Post for New York," *NYT*, Aug. 3, 1991.

7. Rose Marie Arce, "City Settles Bumpurs Suit," *Newsday*, Mar. 28, 1991.

8. "First Casualty of Drug Law Recuperating," *NYAN*, Sept. 8, 1973; "No-Knock Raid Bungles, Woman Cuts Hands Fleeing," *Afro-American*, Sept. 15, 1973; "Wrong Door Crashed," Sept. 4, 1973, 21.

9. "First Casualty of Drug Law Recuperating"; Frank Lombardi, "Cops on Trial," *NYDN Magazine*, Mar. 28, 1982.

10. "Boy's Mother Bitter Over Shea Verdict," *NYAN*, June 15, 1974; Les Matthews and Wayne Dawkins, "$115,000 Bounty for Boy's Life," *NYAN*, July 14, 1979.

11. Marshall Miller, "Police Brutality," *Yale Law & Policy* Review 17, no. 1 (1998): 156; Selwyn Raab, "City Now Suing Some Who File Brutality Cases: New Tactic in Brutality Cases," *NYT*, Feb. 20, 1985; William G. Blair, "Family Gets $1.7 Million For Stewart's Death," *NYT*, Aug. 29, 1990; "Boy's Mother Bitter Over Shea Verdict," *NYAN*, June 15, 1974; Les Matthews and Wayne Dawkins, "$115,000 Bounty for Boy's Life," *NYAN*, July 14, 1979; Alex Michelini, "Stewart's Family Settles for 1.7M," *NYDN*, Aug. 29, 1990; Robert D. McFadden, "Settlement Reached in Perry Wrongful-Death Suit," *NYT*, May 13, 1989; Thomas Hauser, *The Trial of Patrolman Thomas Shea* (New York, NY: First Seven Stories Press, 2017); Lombardi, "Cops on Trial, " 6–7, 10–11, 15.

12. Miller, "Police Brutality," 156; Raab, "City Now Suing Some Who File Brutality Cases"; Blair, "Family Gets $1.7 Million For Stewart's Death"; "Boy's Mother Bitter Over Shea Verdict"; Matthews and Dawkins, "$115,000 Bounty for Boy's Life"; Michelini, "Stewart's Family Settles for 1.7M"; McFadden, "Settlement Reached in Perry Wrongful-Death Suit"; Lombardi, "Cops on Trial, " 6–7, 10–11, 15.

13. Marilynn S. Johnson, *Street Justice: A History of Police Violence in New York City* (Boston: Beacon Press, 2004), 222; Themis Chronopoulos, "The Making of the Orderly City: New York Since the 1980s," *Journal of Urban History*, 46, no. 5 (2020): 1–32.

14. Miller, "Police Brutality"; Raab, "City Now Suing Some Who File Brutality Cases; Lombardi, "Cops on Trial."

15. Keith L. Alexander, Steven Rich, and Hannah Thacker, "The Hidden Billion Dollar Cost of Repeated Police Misconduct," *Washington Post*, Mar. 9, 2022.

16. Jake Pearson, "As New York Pays Out Millions in Police Misconduct Settlements, Lawmakers Ask Why They Keep Happening," *Propublica*, Mar. 21, 2023, https://www.propublica.org/article/nyc-nypd-police-misconduct-settlements-protests; Samar Khurshid, "City Law Department Defends Approach to Lawsuits Over NYPD Misconduct," *Gotham Gazette*, Mar. 24, 2023, https://www.gothamgazette.com/city/11898-nyc-law-department-nypd-misconduct-lawsuits; Brad Lander, "Annual Claims Report, Fiscal Year 2023," Apr. 13, 2024, https://comptroller.nyc.gov/reports/annual-claims-report/.
17. Blair, "Family Gets $1.7 Million for Stewart's Death."
18. *Bumpurs v. New York City Housing Authority*.
19. Arce, "City Settles Bumpurs Suit."
20. J. Zambba Browne, "Outcry over $200,000 Court Settlement in Bumpurs Case," *NYAN*, Apr. 6, 1991; *Bumpurs v. New York City Housing Authority*.
21. Browne, "Outcry over $200,000 Court Settlement in Bumpurs Case"; *Bumpurs v. New York City Housing Authority*.
22. *Bumpurs v. New York City Housing Authority*.
23. *Bumpurs v. New York City Housing Authority*.
24. "Fannie Mae Baker," File 1789.
25. "Keenie Louise Bumpurs," File 362; J. Zamgba Browne, "Eleanor Bumpurs's Case Drags Heir into Court," *NYAN*, Aug. 3, 1996.
26. New York State Legislative Bill Drafting Commission, *Laws of the State of New York*, vol. 2, 1980, 1520.
27. *Bumpurs v. New York City Housing Authority*.
28. *Bumpurs v. New York City Housing Authority*; Wright, *Heirs to the Great Migration*, 2022.
29. "Eleanor Bumpurs," File 788 (1984), Bronx Surrogate's Court Records.
30. Kirsten Fermaglich, *A Rosenberg by Any Other Name: A History of Jewish Name Changing in America* (New York: New York University Press, 2018), 27.
31. "Eleanor Bumpurs," File 788.
32. Browne, "Outcry over $200,000 Court Settlement in Bumpurs Case."
33. Robert D. McFadden, "Violent Crimes Rise Sharply in New York," *NYT*, Sept. 15, 1990; George James, "New York Killings Set a Record, While Other Crimes Fell in 1990," *NYT*, Apr. 23, 1991; Arce, "City Settles Bumpurs Suit"; Browne, "Outcry over $200,000 Court Settlement in Bumpurs Case"; Ed Caldwell, "Bumpers Case Refuses to Die Gracefully," *NYDN*, Apr. 8, 1991.
34. Arce, "City Settles Bumpurs Suit"; Browne, "Outcry over $200,000 Court Settlement in Bumpurs Case"; Caldwell, "Bumpers Case Refuses to Die Gracefully"; *Bumpurs v. New York City Housing Authority*.
35. Samantha Pinto and Shoniqua Roach, "Black Privacy against Possession," *Black Scholar: Journal of Black Studies and Research* 51, no. 1 (2021): 1–2.
36. "Keenie Louise Bumpurs," File 362.
37. Douglas Montero, "Lessons of 1984 Unlearned," *New York Post*, Sept. 1, 1999, https://nypost.com/1999/09/01/lessons-of-1984-unlearned/.

38. Bumpurs, interview, Aug. 2017.
39. Ransby, *Ella Baker & The Black Freedom Movement*, 7.
40. Angela Y. Davis, *Violence Against Women and the Ongoing Challenge to Racism* (Latham, MD: Kitchen Table/Women of Color Press, 1985), 12.
41. Bumpurs, interview, Aug. 2017.

CONCLUSION: THE ENDURING LEGACY OF ELEANOR BUMPURS
1. Bumpurs, interview, June 2018.
2. "'Whose Streets? Our Streets!' New York City: 1980–2000," Bronx Documentary Center, https://www.bronxdoc.org/exhibits/whose-streets-our -streets-new-york-city-1980-2000/detail.
3. Mickalene Thomas (@mickalenethomas), photo of "Resist #11, Instagram, July 23, 2023, https://www.instagram.com/mickalenethomas/p/ CupPxznLbuO/.
4. Hyun-Jin Jun, Jordan E. DeVylder, and Lisa Fedina, "Police Violence Among Adults Diagnosed with Mental Disorders," *Health and Social Work* 45, no. 2 (2020): 81.
5. Andrea J. Ritchie, *Invisible No More: Police Violence Against Black Women and Women of Color* (Boston: Beacon Press, 2017); Deborah Danner, "Living with Schizophrenia," *NYT*, Oct. 19, 2016, https://www .nytimes.com/interactive/2016/10/19/nyregion/document-Living-With -Schizophrenia-by-Deborah-Danner.html.
6. Stephanie Pagones, "NYPD Shooting of Mentally Ill Woman Invokes Memory of Eleanor Bumpurs," *New York Post*, Oct. 20, 2016, http:// nypost.com/2016/10/20/nypd-shooting-of-mentally-ill-woman-invokes -memory-of-eleanor-bumpurs/; Graham Rayman and John Annese, "Cop Sued for Past Assaults," *NYDN*, Oct. 20, 2016; Danner, "Living with Schizophrenia"; "Bumpurs Kin: No Justice for Slaying in 1984," *NYDN*, Oct. 21, 2016.
7. Pagones, "NYPD Shooting of Mentally Ill Woman Invokes Memory of Eleanor Bumpurs."
8. "ABWH Statement on the Modern-Day Lynching of Black Women in the U.S. Justice System," Association of Black Women Historians, July 28, 2015, http://abwh.org/2015/07/28/abwh-statement-on-the-modern-day -lynching-of-Black-women-in-the-u-s-justice-system/.
9. Saidiya Hartman, *Scenes of Subjection: Terror, Slavery, and Self-Making in Nineteenth-Century America* (New York: Oxford University Press, 1997), 4.
10. "ABWH Statement on the Modern-Day Lynching of Black Women in the U.S. Justice System."
11. African American Policy Forum, *Say Her Name: Resisting Police Brutality Against Black Women* (New York: Center for Intersectionality and Social Policy Studies, 2015), 2.
12. Matthew Carey, "FX's 'The Killing of Breonna Taylor' Investigate Police Shooting That Shook America," Deadline.com, May 1, 2021, https:// deadline.com/2021/05/the-killing-of-breonna-taylor-filmmakers-interview -yoruba-richen-lora-moftah-contenders-tv-1234748258/.

13. Phylicia Ashley, "Breonna Taylor Family Takes Calls for Change to New York City," wave.com, Oct. 16, 2020, https://www.wave3.com/2020/10/16/breonna-taylor-family-takes-calls-change-new-york-city-thousands-expected-rally/.

14. Greg B. Smith, "Eleanor Bumpurs' Namesake Kin Inherits Legacy of NYCHA Neglect and Disrepair," *The City*, Jan. 24, 2021, https://www.thecity.nyc/2021/1/24/22247526/eleanor-bumpurs-nycha-disrepair-bronx-nypd.

PHOTO INSERT CREDITS

Page 1, Thomas Monaster/New York Daily News Archive via Getty Images

Page 1, Yvonne Hemsey/Getty Images

Page 2, Karjean Levine/Getty Images

Page 2, Dan Cronin/New York Daily News via Getty Images

Page 3, Misha Erwitt/New York Daily News via Getty Images

Page 3, Bill Turnbull/New York Daily News via Getty Images

Page 4, Pat Carroll/New York Daily News via Getty Images

Page 4, Tom Monaster/New York Daily News via Getty Images

Page 5, Gene Kappock/New York Daily News via Getty Images

Page 5, Dan Cronin/New York Daily News via Getty Images

Page 6, Robert Rosamilio/New York Daily News via Getty Images

Page 6, Anthony Casale/New York Daily News via Getty Images

Page 7, Pat Carroll/New York Daily News via Getty Images

Page 7, Library of Congress, Prints & Photographs Division, photograph by Bernard Gotfryd

Page 8, Jennifer Taggart Wilson

INDEX

pellagra, 8–9
people of color, portrayal by police as dangerous and mentally disturbed, 150
People of the State of New York v. Stephen Sullivan (1986), 217–36; attendance at, 220–21, 229; bench *vs.* jury, 217–20; closing arguments, 226–28; courtroom disruptions, 221–22, 228–29; judge, prosecutor, and defense, 217–18; opening statements, 221–23; as racial case, 219; renewed call to action after, 236–39; response of community to verdict, 233–36; response of DA's office to verdict, 232–33; response of family to verdict, 231–32; response of Sullivan to verdict, 230–31; testimony at, 223–26; verdict to acquit, 228–36. *See* trial
People v. Benjamin (1980), 192
Perry, Edmund, 178, 180–81, 212, 214, 217, 263n1
Perry, Sallie, 3
Perry, Veronica, 179, 180–81, 212, 214
petitions, 142
"A Petition to Stop Police Brutality and Violence Now," 112–13
Petrie, Daniel, 39
Petrocelli, Lucille, 84
phone campaigns, 145
physical search, 101
pinback buttons, protest, 144–45, 146–47
Pinkett, Mary, 151
Pinn, Samuel, 147
plea bargaining, 37–38
Pleasant, Betty, 104
pleasure politics, 25
Plummer, Viola, 101
police home invasions, 100–102
police violence: against Black women and girls, xi, 257–58; bringing visibility to, xi, xii;

communal trauma due to, 95–96; community of survivors of, 177–82; congressional hearings on, 168–69; continuation of, 256–59; in *Do The Right Thing*, x; impact on family, xviii, 122, 193; legal justice for Black victims and survivors of, 191–92; mental health issues and, 256–57; mental health services for victims and families of, 125–27; in New York City, 23–24, 136–37; by NYPD, 99–102; rap artists on, vii; services to address exposure to, 125–27; and standards for deadly use of force, 192, 256; victim-centered perspective on, xvii–xviii; victims' compensation program for, 126–27; white citizens' view of, 109–10
Polite, Marjorie, 24
political activist(s): Mary Bumpurs as, 127–32; raids of homes of, 101
Pollard, George, 8
Popieluszko, Jerzy, 121
"Post-Mother's Day Memorial Service," 208–9
Poussaint, Bobbie, 156
Powell, Adam Clayton, Jr., 22
Powell, James, 34–35
Presbyterian Medical Center, 244
Pressman, Gabe, 107–8, 111
Professor Griff, x
protests, 89–113, xvii; in *City Sun*, 112–13; citywide, xvi, 92, 99–103, 134–37; first wave of, 145–53; in international community, 104–5; in media, 96–99; nationwide, 103–4; in neighborhood, ix; November 17 march, 146–49; November 19 march, 150–53; planned by Eleanor Bumpurs Justice Committee, 144, 145; police presence at, 147; by Sedgwick Houses tenants, 93–96; in support of Stephen Sullivan,

Bumpurs of, 150; defense of Stephen Sullivan by, 104–5; and *The Eleanor Bumpurs Case* (report), 154, 158–59, 161, 163; and Eleanor Bumpurs Justice Committee, 140; and Eleanor's funeral, 119; on eviction process, 75; on indictment of Sullivan, 195–96; investigation and report on, 197; and new guidelines for shotguns and nonlethal methods, 189; on NYPD, 162; on overturning indictment of Sullivan, 206; and policy for handling mental health breakdowns, 158–59; public criticism of, 125; suspension and reinstatement of Sullivan by, 196–97
Ward, Govan "Sweat," 7
Ward, Olivia, 197
Washington Post (newspaper), 245
WBAI, 99, 133–34, 142
Weinberger, Peter, 32
Welfare Action Coalition, 140
"Welfare Queens," 53
welfare recipients, disdain for, 110–11
welfare rights movement, 140
welfare system, 30–31; war on, 53–55
welfare workers: blaming of, at trial of, 226; blaming of, by *The Eleanor Bumpurs Case* (report), 155, 161; and demands for social justice, 141
Weusi, Jitu, 147
White, Joyce, 54
white supremacy, 4
white terrorism, in New York City, 136–37
Whose Streets? Our Streets (photography exhibition), 256

Williams, Charlie, 4
Williams, Elna (Eleanor) Gray. *See* Bumpurs, Eleanor Gray
Williams, Enoch, 151
Williams, Fannie Belle Egerton, 3–4, 8–9, 27, 68
Williams, James Edward, 4, 10
Williams, John Hilliard, 3–4, 10
Williams, Johnnie, 60
Williams, Kidada, xviii, 122
Williams, Laura Silver Belle Alston, 11–12, 16, 27
Williams, Ralph, 93
Williams, Raymond, 4, 10, 13
Williams, Spencer, 60
Williams, Zollie, 4, 11, 60
Wilner, Noah, 180
Winters, Mary, 34
WLIB, 142, 216–17
"Woman's Trouble Blues" (song), 17
Women's Prison (North Carolina), 16
women's rights groups, 151, 152
Wonder, Stevie, 103
Woods, Jeanne M., 234
Workers Vanguard (newspaper), 179–80
Works Progress Administration (WPA), 10, 15
Wright, Dazell Bumpers, 249–50
Wright, Richard, 10, 17
wrongful death lawsuit. *See People of the State of New York v. Stephen Sullivan* (1986)

X-Clan, x

Young Lords, 138

Zuckerman, Julius, 45